'Great history combines warm-heartedness and cool appraisal. Peter Woodley brings both to this superb history of the place of his own origins, the farmlands of the Dubbo district—a place that he has come to know even better through a truly formidable research effort. Dr Woodley tells a story that transforms our understanding of the evolving relationship of 'the country' to colony, state and nation. This model local history sets a new standard for the field.'

Frank Bongiorno AM, Professor of History
at The Australian National University

'... local history ... that speaks to much larger themes of community, place, identity and even nation'.

Anna Clark, Professor of Social and Political Sciences
at the University of Technology Sydney

'A wonderfully evocative kaleidoscope of a farming district in its formative years. It explores class and community, place and heritage, nation and identity through rich and wide-ranging prisms. A model history, detailed and creative, it sees meaning in the commonplace and consequences in what people thought and did. A story for all Australia.'

Bill Gammage AM, Adjunct Professor at
The Australian National University

'Bit by bit, the lost worlds of the Dubbo farmlands are recreated and explored with an eye that is empathetic but also critical.

'... an impressive and meticulous piece of work, shot through with flashes of deep insight into social and community formation in rural Australia.

'... a significant and engaging regional history which might serve as a model for the many people interested and active in local, regional and family history, but would also contribute to the larger and very moving stories of what rural people experienced in Australian environments, the great rhythms and cycles of human lives, and how they made their places and communities.'

Grace Karskens, Emeritus Professor at the
University of New South Wales

'We are a farming class'

DUBBO'S HINTERLAND,
1870–1950

'We are a farming class'

DUBBO'S HINTERLAND, 1870–1950

PETER WOODLEY

Australian
National
University

ANU PRESS

Australian
National
University

ANU PRESS

Published by ANU Press
The Australian National University
Canberra ACT 2600, Australia
Email: anupress@anu.edu.au

Available to download for free at press.anu.edu.au

ISBN (print): 9781760466756
ISBN (online): 9781760466763

WorldCat (print): 1479779599
WorldCat (online): 1479779579

DOI: 10.22459/WAFC.2025

Cover design and layout by ANU Press. Cover photograph: Gathering at the Westella tennis courts, 1920s. Woodley family collection.

This book is published under the aegis of the Social Sciences editorial board of ANU Press.

Contents

Acknowledgements

Much of the support I have received to produce this book stems from the preceding journey to produce the PhD thesis on which it is based. I am fortunate and grateful to have had the professional, deeply knowledgeable, decisive, but also gentle supervision of Professor Frank Bongiorno AM. Professor Nicholas Brown provided invaluable insights on several draft chapters during the thesis phase. Colleagues in the School of History at The Australian National University have provided useful feedback and encouragement throughout. The book has benefited from the constructive and encouraging feedback provided by the thesis examiners: Professor Anna Clark (University of Technology Sydney), Professor Clare Griffiths (Cardiff University) and Emeritus Professor Grace Karskens (University of New South Wales).

In the Dubbo district, many people provided generous support. In no particular order: Maurice Campbell provided advice on freemasonry and access to Lodge Allan Stuart, Geurie. The staff of Holy Trinity Anglican Church, Dubbo, opened their records to me. Simone Taylor of the Dubbo Regional Council's Western Plains Cultural Centre provided access to the centre's archival collection. Norma Meadley threw open the wonderful Narromine local history collection at the Narromine Library for my use. Phil Purcell of the New South Wales Office of Environment and Heritage, Dubbo, contributed his expertise on local archaeology. At the Dubbo and District Family History Society, Linda Barnes, Kathy Furney and others made me feel welcome among their collection and provided valuable leads. Frank Rowe showed me his grandfather's minute book of the Gollan branch of the Farmers and Settlers Association, and the Wongarbon branch of the Country Women's Association shared records maintained impeccably since 1927. 'Riverbank' Frank Doolan and Paul Roe shared lunch and perspectives on local race relations, Shirley Trethowan contributed insights on the Mawbey and Trethowan families, and Colleen Braithwaite generously allowed me to use images and reminiscences she collected in the

1980s from older Wongarbon residents. Faye Wheeler, then of the *Daily Liberal*, helped to publicise the project; David Martin talked to me about his family's history at Dulla Dulla; Penny Stevens and Rob Ingram passed on a copy of Nancy Nott's recollections of the Cobbora hall, and Nancy's daughter Lynne Burke also shared her reminiscences of Cobbora.

I recorded interviews with Don Graham, Robert Woodley and Nora Mines, who also showed me records of the Ballimore branch of the Red Cross. Their insights have enhanced the project. Many hours of recorded and casual conversations with my father, Harold Woodley, have contributed far more than the references accompanying the text would indicate.

Elsewhere, the following people provided generous advice: Paul Davey on New South Wales Progressive/Country Party records, David Clune and Eamonn Clifford on New South Wales electoral maps, Ben Raue on federal electorate maps, and Patrick Burke on farming women in the Wellington-Dubbo district. Narelle Heiniger, Dale Ramm, Robert Cotterell, and Lois Jones shared valuable images.

The project would not have been possible without the patience and guidance of many archivists and librarians at the following institutions: the National Archives of Australia's Chester Hill repository; the State Library of New South Wales; State Archives and Records NSW; the Westpac Archive (particularly Kim Eberhard); the National Library of Australia; the Noel Butlin Archives Centre (Sarah Lethbridge); the Page Library of Charles Sturt University, Wagga Wagga (Wayne Doubleday); the Office of the New South Wales Nationals (Olivia Kerr); the National Film and Sound Archive of Australia (Stephanie Carter); and the Australian War Memorial.

John Frith of Flat Earth Mapping crafted the maps, and Dr Rani Kerin provided professional copyediting and indexing assistance. At the ANU Press Dr Nathan Hollier, Gabrielė Gaižutytė and Elouise Ball were a source of helpful encouragement and advice, as was Dr Emily Gallagher, secretary of the Social Sciences Editorial Board.

Finally, I thank my wife Pauline for her support, patience, forbearance and good humour over the course of the marathon.

List of figures

Abbreviations

ABC	Australian Broadcasting Commission
AIF	Australian Imperial Force
ALP	Australian Labor Party
APB	Aborigines Protection Board (NSW)
ATCJ	*Australian Town and Country Journal*
AWU	Australian Workers Union
CWA	Country Women's Association of New South Wales
DD	*Dubbo Dispatch and Wellington Independent*
DL	*Dubbo Liberal and Macquarie Advocate*
FSA	Farmers and Settlers Association of New South Wales
GA	Graziers Association of New South Wales
HRA	*Historical Records of Australia*
MLA	Member of the Legislative Assembly
MLC	Member of the Legislative Council
MPRC	Macquarie Picnic Race Club
MUIOOF	Manchester Unity International Order of Oddfellows
NAA	National Archives of Australia
NLA	National Library of Australia
NSW	New South Wales
PA&HA	Pastoral, Agricultural and Horticultural Association
PLL	Political Labor League
RWU	Rural Workers Union
SARNSW	State Archives and Records Authority of New South Wales
SLNSW	State Library of New South Wales

SMH	*Sydney Morning Herald*
UCP	United Country Party of New South Wales
WMDA	Sydney Working Men's Defence Association
WT	*Wellington Times*
WVP	*Wellington Valley Project*

Conversions and conventions

1 acre = 0.405 hectares

1 mile = 1.609 kilometres

Imperial currency is expressed as £ (pounds) s (shillings) d (pence). One pound is equivalent to 20 shillings, and 1 shilling to 12 pence.

For the period from 1906, prices are generally expressed as a proportion of the prevailing minimum wage as determined by the Australian Arbitration Court, taken from the Australian Fair Work Commission's website.

Punctuation

In the formal names of associations (e.g. the Australian Workers Union and the Farmers and Settlers Association), possessive plural apostrophes are omitted unless they appear within direct quotations.

Placenames

The spelling of several places in the Dubbo district varies in the written record. Other than any variations in direct quotations, the following spellings are adopted for consistency:

- Coalbaggie (rather than Coolbaggie)
- Coboco (rather than Cobocco)
- Cobbora (rather than Cobborah)
- Willandra (rather than Wylandra)
- Windora (rather than Windorah).

Several locales changed their official names. Local vernacular usage might have lagged behind official changes, but, in general, places are referred to in the text by the name that applied officially during the period to which the text refers, with explicit clarification as necessary. These places are:

- Murrumbidgerie (village) became Wongarbon from 1908
- Belarbigal became Rawsonville in 1903
- Goonoo became Mogriguy in 1909
- the railway station that was first known as Ponto became Geurie in 1888, though the official name of the village surrounding the station was not changed until 1922
- the locality of Glenara became known as Westella in 1921.

Prologue

When I go back to the place where I spent my early years, I notice the lingering traces that settler Australians have left in that distinctive landscape: gates and fences, windmills, gullies, treeless vistas, sheds and abandoned rusting machinery. The settlers, oblivious to the meaning that the Wiradjuri people had already given to country, also claimed those places with names— Westella, Windora, Coalbaggie, Mogriguy—and the very sounds evoke an exclusive familiarity for those who knew them and the places they stood for. Imported along with machinery, animals, seeds and ideas, they defined the centres and limits of places. My curiosity is born of a tension between being connected to the place through ancestry and childhood, and returning to see it afresh, detached, as though a stranger. I want to understand why this landscape was transformed in just these ways. What environmental, economic and social forces caused people here to respond in just such a manner, to build from those materials, in those locations, in those forms? I sought to read the landscape as an archive, or a cultural tableau. Like the British historian W. G. Hoskins:

> I felt like everything I was looking at was saying something to me if only I could recognise the language. It was a landscape written in a kind of code.[1]

I notice the halls, and one in particular, long since defunct: it was once a venue for dances, school 'Christmas trees', occasional church services, and a site for serving refreshments during tennis tournaments on adjoining clay courts. What did *they* signify, these rare public spaces, locally conceived and

---

1   W. G. Hoskins, *English Landscapes* (London: British Broadcasting Corporation, 1973), 5, quoted in D. W. Meinig, 'Reading the Landscape: An Appreciation of W. G. Hoskins and J. B. Jackson', in *The Interpretation of Ordinary Landscapes: Geographical Essays*, ed. D. W. Meinig (Oxford: Oxford University Press, 1979), 198. See also Tim Bonyhady and Tom Griffiths, 'Landscape and Language', in *Words for Country: Landscape and Language in Australia*, ed. Tim Bonyhady and Tom Griffiths (Sydney: University of New South Wales Press, 2002), 1–13; George Seddon, 'Prelude: Dual Allegiances', in *Landprints: Reflections on Place and Landscape* (Cambridge: Cambridge University Press, 1997), xv.

sustained in otherwise highly privatised landscapes? Don Watson interprets rural halls as cultural artefacts—evidence that cooperation, along with work and religion, were the 'eternal verities and the condition of success'.[2] But I want to understand *this* landscape and through it the people of *these* places. Though their lived experiences here might have been consistent with or subject to the influence of broader structures and relationships, were they also different by virtue of occurring in *this* setting? Why were halls located in some places and not others? Who built them, and when? What motivated people to devote land, time and resources to construct and maintain them? Who was involved, and who—through explicit or tacit exclusion, or even a plain lack of interest on one side or both—was not? What did these institutions, with no commercial purpose, signify about the social lives and sense of place among the sorts of people reputed to be dully, single-mindedly fixated on making their time and land pay?

This is the country surrounding the town of Dubbo in the Central West region of New South Wales, within a radius of about 50 kilometres. Dubbo lies on the Country of the Tubba-Gah people of the Wiradjuri nation, abutting Wongaibon Country west of the Macquarie River (or Wambool) towards Cobar, and Wailwan Country encompassing the lower Macquarie and the Castlereagh.[3] The Aboriginal presence there has never ceased. Its long legacy is evident in places like the sharpening stones by the river at Terramungamine, and the few remaining carved trees marking burial sites. It is there, too, in the names Europeans gave to places, including Dubbo itself, corruptions of local sounds and meaning, but legacies nonetheless of the first cross-cultural encounters (see Figure 0.1).

The district lies in a transitional zone, between the cooler, wetter and hillier terrain of the central slopes to the east, and on the verge of the hotter, drier and flatter western plains. The land is most fertile on the eastern edge towards Wellington and in places by the Macquarie River. The country is also cut by the Talbragar (or Dhalburagaa) and some lesser rivers, and with creeks that flow only after heavy upstream rain. This is mainly flat or gently

---

2   Don Watson, 'Once a Jolly Lifestyle', in *Watsonia: A Writing Life* (Carlton: Black Inc., 2020), 108.
3   Peter Rimas Kabaila, *Wiradjuri Places: The Macquarie River Basin and Some Places Revisited* (Jamison: Black Mountain Projects, 1998); Michael Davis, '"I Live Somewhere Else but I've Never Left Here": Indigenous Knowledge, History, and Place', *Counterpoints: Indigenous Philosophies and Critical Education: A Reader* 379 (2011): 113–26. Edward Garnsey, who grew up in Dubbo, refers to 'Dubba-Ga' people. See Edward Josiah Garnsey, 'A Treatise on the Aborigines of Dubbo and District', unpublished manuscript, 1942, B 1056, SLNSW. Areas associated with broad language groups are taken from the Australian Institute of Aboriginal and Torres Strait Islander Studies' 'Map of Indigenous Australia' (David R. Horton, creator).

undulating country, studded with box and other eucalyptus timber, and patches of kurrajong. A discontinuous band of ironbark and white cypress pine forests running north towards the Warrumbungle Range marks less fertile land, which was nevertheless for settlers an important source of timber for railway sleepers and fencing.[4] These places are what I call the Dubbo 'farmlands', to emphasise the dominant culture and economic activity over most of the land in this period. These places and people are the subjects of this quest.

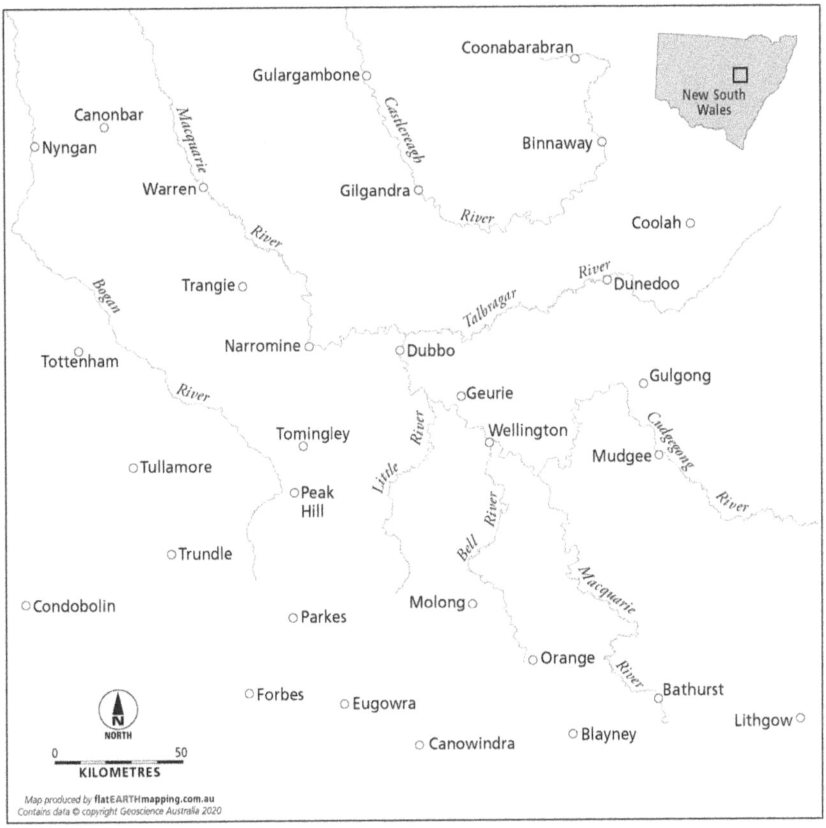

Figure 0.1: Dubbo in the context of rivers and current towns.
Source: Flat Earth Mapping.

---

4   New South Wales, Division of Reconstruction and Development, *The Macquarie Region: A Preliminary Survey of Resources* (Sydney: Government Printer, 1950), 7–13, 16; Iris Clayton and Alex Barlow, *Wiradjuri of the Rivers and Plains* (Port Melbourne: Heinemann Library, 1997), 27.

Introduction

The Sydney Royal Easter Show was as big as ever in 2022. For several years the coronavirus pandemic had disrupted not just the show but also social and economic life on a scale few could recall. But the show was a symbol— a familiar sign that things were returning to normal and that some age-old verities still applied. A 'staggering' 900,000 people streamed through the gates to participate in what the publicity described as a 'celebration of Australian culture'.[1] At its centre, this iconic event created by the Royal Agricultural Society of New South Wales was, as ever, the latest performance of an imagined country life deeply embedded in many Australians' concepts of a collective past and identity. The recently appointed minister for agriculture and western New South Wales, and member for Dubbo in the state's Central West, Dugald Saunders, was amazed to see 'so many people celebrate our regional communities and agricultural achievements'.[2] His comments marking the show's conclusion emphasised its royal patronage (it was opened by Princess Anne that year), the prodigious productivity of the Country Women's Association (they baked no less than 34,204 scones for show-goers) and the enormous volume of farm animals and produce on display, leading to two essential points: the event demonstrated both the 'extraordinary resilience of our primary producers' and 'the important role people in regional NSW play in the prosperity of NSW as a whole'. The language has changed over time—primary producers used to be farmers or settlers, and regional New South Wales was once 'the country'—but the sentiments could have been delivered by any number of country politicians, and many other advocates for rural interests, since the show began in 1873. It was just the latest instalment of a very old story.

---

1   Sydney Royal Easter Show, 'About Us', accessed 4 April 2023, www.eastershow.com.au/about-us/.
2   '900,000 Attend 2022 Sydney Royal Easter Show', [media release by Department of Primary Industries], 21 April 2022, dugaldsaunders.com.au/900000-attend-2022-sydney-royal-easter-show/.

Despite Australia being a substantially urbanised place, its rural regions continue to exert a firm hold on what settler society—the waves of people and their descendants who have been here since 1788—regards as essential to its character, and what sets it apart. It is, in some measure, an imagined place, sustained through advertising, or politicians seeking to associate themselves with people who, by virtue of living 'on the land', are represented as courageous and enterprising: harder-working, harder done by, more stoic and more morally worthy than their city counterparts. The historian John Hirst gave it a name—the 'pioneer legend'.[3] Finding it harnessed for conservative political ends and, borrowing a term current in the 1920s, the political scientist Don Aitkin called it 'countrymindedness'.[4] Hirst surmised that the qualities constituting this 'national myth' did not necessarily 'strain too much at the truth'. But do we really know? To what extent, if any, did the legend have roots in the lived experience of the people it purported to represent? How did they relate to these representations of their own lives? Who were they? And who was excluded from being considered among the 'pioneers', as constituting this 'backbone of the nation'?

The historiography

The Central West of New South Wales, and the Dubbo district in particular, have largely eluded historians' scholarly attention.[5] More generally, the lives of rural, settler Australians have, for some time, ceased to be a favoured subject of historical inquiry. The social history turn of the 1970s and 1980s, in the hands of historians including John Merritt, Patricia Grimshaw, Charles Fahey, Marilyn Lake, John McQuilton and Gerald Walsh, contributed to a fuller understanding of farming communities, as it applied new methods to bring fresh attention to the operation of class and gender, using surveys, diaries and land records to argue that women and labourers, previously overlooked, were integral to farm production. Lake, and more recently Bruce Scates and Melanie Oppenheimer, extend the analysis of

---

3   J. B. Hirst, 'The Pioneer Legend', *Historical Studies* 18, no. 71 (1978): 316–37.
4   Don Aitkin, '"Countrymindedness"—The Spread of an Idea', *Australian Cultural History* 4 (1985): 34–41.
5   Cameron Muir's environmental history is an exception, covering the Dubbo-Narromine-Trangie region. See Cameron Muir, *The Broken Promise of Agricultural Progress: An Environmental History* (Oxford: Routledge, 2014). Local publications have dealt mainly with the town of Dubbo rather than its surrounds, notably Marion Dormer, *Volume I, Dubbo to the Turn of the Century. An Illustrated History of Dubbo and Districts, 1818–1900* (Dubbo: Macquarie Publications, 1981); Marion Dormer, *Volume II, Dubbo: City of the Plains, 1901–1980* (Dubbo: Macquarie Publications, 1988).

rural Australia into the twentieth century, examining the social dimensions of the post–World War I soldier settlement schemes.[6] More recently, and not without good reason, historians have sought to bring into the foreground other, previously neglected, aspects of Australia's rural past, such as the dispossession and continuing injustices experienced by Aboriginal people, and the damage wrought by settlers and their introduced animals and seeds on a fragile environment.[7] These are important correctives to our understanding of settler Australians and their impact on this place and its First Peoples. But, in the meantime, some historians have noticed a void— a lack of attention directed to understanding the lives of rural dwellers. In 2005, Jill Roe, when commenting on these newer emphases, observed that 'from an historiographical point of view they [Australian rural settlers] have been largely left behind', and that the field of study had become 'more or less stagnant'. That year, Graeme Davison and Marc Brodie went so far as to assert that there was relatively little history written about twentieth-century rural Australia, describing 'the country' as 'probably the neglected theme in Australian history'.[8] Little has changed since.

Community, class and place

This book seeks to address that gap by examining how communities among farming people evolved around Dubbo—what I call the farmlands. More specifically, it argues that class and place shaped ideas about what constituted communities. Because these terms are central to the arguments that follow, I need to explain the sense in which they are used. The word 'place' stands where others might prefer 'locality'. By place, I mean

6   Marilyn Lake, *The Limits of Hope: Soldier Settlement in Victoria, 1915–38* (Melbourne: Oxford University Press, 1987); Bruce Scates and Melanie Oppenheimer, *The Last Battle: Soldier Settlement in Australia, 1916–1939* (Cambridge: Cambridge University Press, 2016).
7   Relevant texts include Jane Lydon and Lyndall Ryan, eds, *Remembering the Myall Creek Massacre* (Sydney: NewSouth Publishing, 2018); Peter Read, *A Hundred Years War: The Wiradjuri People and the State* (Canberra: Australian National University Press, 1988); Heather Goodall, *Invasion to Embassy: Land in Aboriginal Politics in New South Wales, 1770–1972* (St Leonards: Allen & Unwin in association with Black Books, 1996); Henry Reynolds, *The Other Side of the Frontier: An Interpretation of the Aboriginal Response to the Invasion and Settlement of Australia* (Townsville: History Department of James Cook University, 1981). See also many of Reynolds's subsequent works. On environmental history, see Geoffrey Bolton, *Spoils and Spoilers: A History of Australians Shaping Their Environment*, 2nd ed. (Sydney: Allen & Unwin, 1992), 135–46; Muir, *The Broken Promise*; Rebecca Jones, *Slow Catastrophes: Living with Drought in Australia* (Clayton: Monash University Publishing, 2017).
8   Jill Roe, 'Women and the Land', *History Australia* 2, no. 1 (2005): 3-1-3-2; Graeme Davison and Marc Brodie, 'Introduction', in *Struggle Country: The Rural Ideal in Twentieth Century Australia*, ed. Graeme Davison and Marc Brodie (Melbourne: Monash University ePress, 2005), ix–xvi.

more than a geographical space. It means a space having meaning for its inhabitants, arising from their day-to-day experiences of its physical, biological, social and cultural dimensions. The idea of place often has at its centre a subjective sense of attachment and belonging—often to a physical and sometimes to a social space. I draw on Doreen Massey's idea that the essence of place consists in the everyday exchanges and negotiations among people, each having arrived with their own trajectories—their 'stories-so-far'. This 'throwntogetherness' gives each place its distinctiveness. In the country I am examining, its inhabitants' sense of place might have been especially significant because of a particular intensity of experience: it was not only where people dwelt, but also often where they socialised and where they worked—not just *on* the land, but also, in the process, deliberately or incidentally changing it.

Massey also emphasises that the subjective meanings of places change through time, modified by connections within, and with other places. This book explores the idea of 'localism' or 'the determinism of place'. To put this another way, places might not just be where people feel they belong, or where they are subject to the shifting effects of external economic and cultural influences. Places might also, through people's quotidian engagements with others sharing that space, actively and uniquely modify their experiences of, and responses to, those broader influences, as well as their behaviours, self-perceptions and allegiances.[9]

The other idea that is central to the book is that people's shared experience as a class of farmers affected their behaviours and their identification with a broader, imagined community. Robert Patten provides a fitting example. In April 1901 this 42-year-old farmer occupying 465 acres at Comobella near Wellington wrote to the local member, John Hayes, on behalf of the Mitchells Creek Farmers and Settlers Association (FSA) branch. Two tiny schools nearby were sharing a teacher, so each was open for only two or three days each week. Patten's branch considered that inadequate:

---

9   Doreen Massey, *For Space* (London: Sage Publications, 2005), 24–32, 265–6, 282–5; Doreen Massey, 'Places and Their Pasts', *History Workshop Journal*, no. 39 (Spring 1995): 188; Peter Read, *Returning to Nothing: The Meaning of Lost Places* (Cambridge: Cambridge University Press, 1996), 2–4; Greg Patmore, 'Working Lives in Regional Australia: Labour History and Local History', *Labour History*, no. 78 (May 2000): 1–6; Tom Griffiths, 'Introduction', in *George Seddon: Selected Writings*, ed. Andrea Gaynor (Carlton: La Trobe University Press in conjunction with Black Inc., 2019), 7. See also Donald W. Meinig, 'Spokane and the Inland Empire: Historical Geographic Systems and the Sense of Place', in *Spokane and the Inland Empire: An Interior Pacific Northwest Anthology*, ed. David H Stratton (Pullman: Washington State University Press, 1991), 1–2.

You know *we are farming class*[,] very busy as a rule & very desirous of affording our children during the short time they can attend school every advantage they are entitled to.[10]

Patten was claiming to represent more than the interests of a handful of like-minded locals. He had not been a farmer for long, and was a tenant on his father-in-law's land, but would soon go on to play a part in rural, state and federal politics on behalf of what he considered his 'class'. His invocation of the idea of class in 1901 located him in a history dating from the late eighteenth century, as people sought to understand and explicate the disruptions arising from Britain's industrial revolution. But Patten's most immediate influence is likely to have been the increasing prominence and language of a *working* class and its political face in the emerging Labor Party, which had gained 16 lower house seats in the new Commonwealth Parliament at the election just two weeks earlier. At that time, the 'working class' was more commonly contrasted with the 'middle class' or 'capitalist class'.[11] His letter implied that there was another class in the field, a community sharing a coherence of experience and outlook defined by its members' common calling and relationship to the land.

However, as Gareth Stedman Jones cautions, historians have made eclectic use of the term 'class': 'a congested point of intersection between many competing, overlapping, or simply differing forms of discourse—political, economic, religious and cultural'.[12] I take as a starting point the groundbreaking work of E. P. Thompson in *The Making of the English Working Class* (1963). In response to narrow Marxist definitions in which classes consisted of those who occupied the same position in relation to the productive process, Thompson emphasised people's common, subjective experiences of those relationships and their cultural expression in customs, work practices and traditions. For Thompson, workers were active and conscious participants in class formation. Class did not exist other than

---

10   Robert Patten to John Hayes MLA, 16 April 1901, Criefton School Administrative File, 5/15566.3, NRS 3829, SARNSW (emphasis added).

11   Asa Briggs, 'The Language of "Class" in Early Nineteenth-Century England', in *History and Class: Essential Readings in Theory and Interpretation*, ed. R. S. Neale (Oxford: Basil Blackwell, 1983), 2–29; John Rickard, *Class and Politics: New South Wales, Victoria and the Early Commonwealth, 1890–1910* (Canberra: Australian National University Press, 1976), 287–311.

12   Gareth Stedman Jones, *Languages of Class: Studies in English Working Class History, 1832–1982* (Cambridge: Cambridge University Press, 1983), 2; Gareth Stedman Jones, 'From Historical Sociology to Theoretical History', in *History and Class: Essential Readings in Theory and Interpretation*, ed. R. S. Neale (Oxford: Basil Blackwell, 1983), 73–85.

in their feeling and expression of a common interest, arising from their experience of work and culture. William H. Sewell summarised Thompson's position thus: 'No consciousness, no class.'[13]

I adopt a modified version of Thompson's conception of class. Class is experiential—a relationship and a process rather than a thing. It derives from people's common experience of productive relations in which they recognise 'an identity of interests as between themselves', as distinct from others with different relationships to production.[14] In this context, class is not merely a sense of common purpose or interest, but arises from struggle or contention through productive processes, either to resist exploitation or to retain or strengthen power. That is, classes do not so much form and then vie with other classes for control over production and its rewards as come into being only through that contest. People's expression of their class consciousness will vary according to social contexts and political opportunity but can manifest in institutions and cultural forms, inflecting language, dress, recreation and norms of social behaviour.

I would argue that this definition of class is compatible with Patten's use of the term. That is, we can read into his (and others') language the idea that farmers had a unique relationship with land as a form of capital and factor of production, which influenced relationships with capital more broadly, and with labour, fundamentally shaping their politics and their shared life experience. This book examines both how farming people used the term as a rhetorical device when arguing their case in relation to labour, capital and government, and how class shaped people's sense of community.

But class here is one of a range of interacting identities, each capable of influencing consciousness and identification with one community or another. As Sewell puts it, 'rival discourses may coexist not only in the same

---

13   E. P. Thompson, *The Making of the English Working Class* (Harmondsworth: Penguin Books, 1980). William H. Sewell Jr, 'How Classes Are Made: Critical Reflections on E. P. Thompson's Theory of Working-Class Formation', in *E. P. Thompson: Critical Perspectives*, ed. Harvey J. Kaye and Keith McClelland (Cambridge: Polity Press, in association with Basil Blackwell, 1990), 54; Stuart Macintyre, 'The Making of the Australian Working Class: An Historiographical Survey', *Historical Studies* 18, no. 71 (October 1978): 233, 248. Thompson's work was criticised in some quarters. Notably, Joan Wallach Scott observed that Thompson gave relatively little attention to women's encounters with productive processes, and interpreted his major work as implicitly defining class as a male experience. Sewell argued that, notwithstanding Thompson's emphases on individuals' experiences and agency, he still reduced all systems (kinship, customs, faith and so on) to class experience, such that no other factor had ultimate causal effect in its own right.

14   Thompson, *The Making of the English Working Class*, 11.

class, but in the same mind'.[15] Akin to the concept of intersectionality, this understanding allows that multiple structures or influences can inform experience, not just additively but with each transforming the other.[16]

Finally, the term 'community' carries some weight in what follows. Some sociologists regard the term suspiciously, as being vague, value-laden and having so many definitions as to possess doubtful explanatory value.[17] And yet, it is used so commonly as to suggest that people need a way to express a sense of belonging to a social group, one that is broader than kinship but narrower than an abstraction such as 'society', with which they share experience, interests and values.[18] The best response, then, is not to abandon the concept but to define more precisely how it will be used. 'Community' here is taken to refer to individuals' sense that they share certain affinities— common values and norms—with like people and as distinct from others. It can arise in any number of ways: from where people live, the nature of their work, their common experiences of gender, their interests or their shared sense of historical associations. Community is also as much about what its members are not as what or who they perceive themselves to be. It is likely to be most starkly evident and rigorously asserted at its boundaries, where it is contrasted with, and perhaps challenged by, the 'other'. Individuals might associate with multiple communities, their identification emerging or receding according to immediate pressures, or depending on with whom they are engaging and for what purpose. Finally, communities are neither static nor closed systems. Rather, they are contingent and dynamic, forming and transmuting in response to changing pressures and individuals' choices. Though the concept is agnostic concerning the factors determining the nature of a community, I will argue that two of those affecting community formation, especially relevant to the farmlands of the Central West, are class and place.

---

15   Sewell, 'How Classes Are Made', 72.

16   Kimberle Crenshaw, 'Demarginalizing the Intersection of Race and Sex: A Black Feminist Critique of Antdiscrimination Doctrine, Feminist Theory and Antiracist Politics', *University of Chicago Legal Forum* (1989): 139–68.

17   For example, Colin Bell and Howard Newby, *Community Studies: An Introduction to the Sociology of the Local Community* (London: George Allen & Unwin, 1971).

18   A. P. Cohen, *The Symbolic Construction of Community* (Oxford: Routledge, 2015), 15. See also Grace Karskens, *The Rocks: Life in Early Sydney* (Carlton South: Melbourne University Press, 1997), 50–1; Lucy Taksa, 'Like a Bicycle, Forever Teetering between Individualism and Collectivism: Considering Community in Relation to Labour History', *Labour History*, no. 78 (2000): 7–32; Stuart Macintyre, *Little Moscows: Communism and Working-Class Militancy in Inter-War Britain* (London: Croom Helm, 1980), 176.

The timeframe

This book is not about the whole European occupation of the Central West but starts substantially when settler colonists had been there, in one way or another, for about 50 years. And, of course, it is about an infinitesimally small part of the period over which people have occupied this place.

So, why 1870–1950? As the book is about community formation, it begins at a time when farming people barely had any sense of themselves, locally or as a class, as an identifiable and self-aware whole. In the 1870s, people then known as 'free selectors' began to arrive in the Dubbo district in significant numbers to create farms on country where pastoralists had leased large tracts of Crown land to produce wool. In the course of the decade, they went from being a straggling and sparse scattering of disconnected individuals and households to gathering as farming smallholders to assert political influence—even if irregularly and ineffectually—on matters of mutual interest. The book ends in 1950 when some quite precise moments affected economic and social life as well as people's ideas about what constituted farmland communities. Petrol rationing ended finally on 8 February 1950 as people were becoming more mobile, and the United States of America announced its support for South Korea in its conflict with the North on 27 June, which would contribute to soaring wool prices presaging a period of expanding rural wealth. But in truth, the year was just one moment at the intersection of several unfolding transformations, some of which had commenced much earlier, and others that would continue into the next decade and beyond. Mobility was aided not just by access to fuel, but also by an immense increase in private motor vehicle ownership, with registrations doubling in New South Wales between 1946 and 1954. Farm productivity, profitability and reliance on wage labour were affected by rapid mechanisation, there being twice as many tractors on the state's farms in 1959 compared with 1949.[19] The decline of small centres of the rural population was evident in the 20 per cent drop in the number of schools functioning in Dubbo's hinterland for all or part of the 1950s as compared with the 1940s, though both decades were part of a longer-term, waning trend. And an increasing emphasis on a farming sector based on science and efficiency, encouraged by the Rural Reconstruction Commission particularly, was challenging the ideology and rhetoric of agrarianism and

---

19 Commonwealth Bureau of Census and Statistics, *Official Year Book of New South Wales, No. 57, 1961* (Sydney: Government Printer, 1964), 410, 799.

smallholding that had supported farmers' sense of community and class.[20] The confluence of these several influences, and others, brought a new potential to disrupt people's local and distant relationships, making the early 1950s a compelling point at which to conclude this story.

Thematic and local

The book approaches its central questions thematically and through the lens of local history. The method enriches our understanding of concepts such as gender, class, community and belonging, and their complex intersecting influences, using the granular detail and nuance of individuals' and small communities' connections to elucidate such wider themes. In Alan Atkinson's words, the value lies in 'looking inward in a more concentrated way … finding something of absolute importance in small places and in the everyday'.[21] Historians have frequently appealed for more of this type of investigation, none more enthusiastically than R. M. Crawford who asserted in 1965 that 'we cannot write our national history adequately without first writing our local history'.[22] Richard Waterhouse developed this theme in 2009 by arguing that 'we can never comprehend the complexity and contradictions of Australian history without further local studies', while Alan Mayne made much the same point in 2011, but in relation to rural and regional history:

> By acknowledging the small scale and the everyday … and by multiplying those experiences across time and place, historical analysis can tease out the complex human dynamics of making and remaking the social landscape of inland Australia.[23]

---

20   Stuart Macintyre, *Australia's Boldest Experiment: War and Reconstruction in the 1940s* (Sydney: NewSouth Publishing, 2015), 168–75; Bolton, *Spoils and Spoilers*, 154.

21   Alan Atkinson, 'Local History: The Next Step', *Locality* 11, no. 3 (2000): 4. See also Janet McCalman, 'The Originality of Ordinary Lives', in *Creating Australia: Changing Australian History*, ed. Wayne Hudson and Geoffrey Bolton (St Leonards: Allen & Unwin, 1997), 93.

22   Crawford, 'Foreword', in *Echuca: A Centenary History*, by Susan Priestley (Brisbane: Jacaranda Press, 1965), vi.

23   Richard Waterhouse, 'Locating the New Social History: Transnational Historiography and Australian Local History', *Journal of the Royal Australian Historical Society* 95, part 1 (2009): 13; Alan Mayne, 'Outside Country', in *Outside Country: Histories of Inland Australia*, ed. Alan Mayne and Stephen Atkinson (Kent Town: Wakefield Press, 2011), 3–4. See also Bill Gammage, 'A Dynamic of Local History', in *Peripheral Visions: Essays on Australian Regional and Local History*, ed. B. J. Dalton ([Townsville]: Department of History and Politics, James Cook University, 1991), 1–7.

The method complements one of the book's central ideas—that people's constructions of and identification with the community are evident in their commonplace exchanges.

Local history need not—should not—be inward-looking. The Dubbo farmlands were not a closed economic and social system. Their vital enmeshment with wider worlds is a central theme of this book. Other questions of wider significance to which this book contributes fresh insights include education history and practice in the late nineteenth and early twentieth centuries; the evolution of colonial, state and municipal politics; the emergence of a dominant country party from a more ambiguous, contested political landscape in the early years of the twentieth century; and the ways communities' conceptions of themselves draw on their constructions of a local past.

Through a thematic structure, this book examines in turn various aspects of how farming people engaged with others and among themselves or, in some cases, did not engage. Each chapter looks at a different angle, as though through a series of windows, for traces of community—of the values and qualities people attached to themselves and those they considered to be their peers, and sometimes in contrast to the values and qualities they projected onto others. It finds community in the spaces between people: between squatters and selectors, teachers and locals, landowners and labourers, citizens and political candidates, and debtors and creditors; between neighbours; and between rural settler people and their projections of what they took Aboriginal people to represent. As settler Australians—farmers mainly—are the subject of this book, the work makes only a very limited contribution to a deeper understanding of First Nations peoples' subjective experiences in these times and places. But some aspects of their experience do figure, and there is plenty of scope for further historical inquiry.

Like the train tracks that radiated from Dubbo at the peak of the railway age, this project lies at a crossroad—at the intersection of a range of contrasts or tensions: of landscapes and documents as complementary archives; of class and place as alternative and sometimes complementary loci of community; of the interplay between broad social, cultural, political and economic forces, and day-to-day experience in small places; of the seemingly impenetrable divide settler society conceived between itself and First Australians as the ultimate 'other'; and of land, labour and capital on 'family farms' that were simultaneously households and units of production: both ways of living, and ways of making a living.

Albert Mawbey: A note

Albert Mawbey's name and his words appear more than most others' in this book. There was no intention that this should be the case, and it is not because he was especially representative or a leader of the people making up the communities in this story. He is prominent for two reasons. First, he was a very articulate letter writer. Many of his words are preserved in government files at State Archives and Records NSW, and I borrow them to enliven and illuminate arguments. At times, his frustration and heartfelt insights into the condition of the small-scale soldier settler jump off the page. Second, Mawbey got involved—he showed up—whether as an office holder with his local branch of the Farmers and Settlers Association, as secretary of the hall committee or, typically dressed in a dinner suit, as master of ceremonies at almost any event that was staged in that hall until he was too ill in old age to do so. Many of these occasions are also recorded in newspapers and committee minutes. Therefore, his words and deeds are scattered across the chapters. It is not essential to the narrative, but nevertheless worthy of note, that Mawbey and three of his brothers who settled in the Dubbo farmlands, as boys, survived the tragic events at Breelong in July 1900, which became a national story revived and sustained in novel and film in the 1970s, forming part of settler society's local vernacular history-making as discussed here in Chapter 8.

1

'Poor struggling men': The slow emergence of a farming class to 1880

January 1877 was a dry time around Dubbo as two horse-drawn buggies made their way over rich river flats from Wellington towards the town. By then it was a middling-sized inland town, with municipal government since 1871 and a population of around 3,000, smaller than older, established towns such as Bathurst and Goulburn, but outstripping south-eastern neighbours Wellington, Mudgee and Orange. For the last 5 miles from the Eschol Hotel, an enthusiastic procession of locals in buggies and on horseback stretching for a quarter of a mile stirred up dust as they escorted the party into town through an 'arch of flags' proclaiming 'Welcome'. The honoured guests were the New South Wales secretary for public works, John Lackey, and the premier, John Robertson.[1]

Sixty-year-old Robertson, with a thinning mane of white hair and a full beard, was one of the most recognisable men in the colony. He was serving the third of what would become five terms as head of government. Though he owned and leased from the Crown large tracts of land himself, Robertson was a renowned advocate for land and electoral reform. No individual had done more to shape settler society in that district, or indeed across the

---

1   New South Wales, *Census of 1881,* in *Votes and Proceedings of the Legislative Assembly, 1883–84,* vol. VIII (Sydney: Government Printer, 1884), vi–vii; *SMH,* 3 January 1877, 3.

colony's rural regions generally.[2] The land laws he had introduced in 1861—already his most enduring legacy—were transforming the landscape, the population and the politics of the place.[3]

The laws invited aspiring smallholders to compete for title to land that, until then, had been monopolised by pastoralists holding Crown leases over large swathes of country. For much of the twentieth century, debate over the laws' purposes and effects was one of the most prominent strands in the historiography of rural New South Wales. Some historians have argued that the laws failed to deliver the type of change the legislators sought; others have reasoned that, in some places at least, they did. But none have suggested that the laws were not in some way transformative. In 1975, Michael Williams observed that 'more words have been written about [rural land legislation and settlement] ... than about any other aspect of Australian history'. Allan Martin claimed that the effort to settle people on the land was 'the great national question' of the period between the 1870s and the 1890s, and it clearly had an enduring influence on the nature of rural settlement across New South Wales.[4] But how, from day to day, did these laws influence the emergence of a class of small-scale farmers (known throughout this period as 'selectors') in the Dubbo district by the end of the 1870s? After all, they had arrived with little prior connection or common experience, and their circumstances even after they settled were diverse, so on face value they had little basis for a coherent sense of class or community. First, before we

---

2   Bede Nairn, 'Robertson, Sir John (1816–1891)', *Australian Dictionary of Biography*, National Centre of Biography, The Australian National University. Published first in hardcopy 1976. adb.anu.edu.au/biography/robertson-sir-john-4490/text7337.

3   New South Wales, *An Act for Regulating the Alienation of Crown Lands*, no. 26a, 1861; New South Wales, *An Act for Regulating the Occupation of Crown Lands*, no. 27a, 1861; C. J. King, *An Outline of Closer Settlement in New South Wales, Part I: The Sequence of the Land Laws 1788–1956* ([Sydney]: Division of Marketing and Agricultural Economics, Department of Agriculture, [1957]), 82–7.

4   M. Williams, 'More and Smaller Is Better: Australian Rural Settlement 1788–1914', in *Australian Space, Australian Time: Geographical Perspectives*, ed. J. M. Powell and M. Williams (Melbourne: Oxford University Press, 1975), 61; A. W. Martin, 'Pastoralists in the Legislative Assembly of New South Wales, 1870–1890', in *The Simple Fleece: Studies in the Australian Wool Industry*, ed. Alan Barnard (Parkville: Melbourne University Press in association with The Australian National University, 1962), 588. The historiography includes G. L. Buxton, *The Riverina 1861–1891: An Australian Regional Study* (Carlton: Melbourne University Press, 1967); W. K. Hancock, *Discovering Monaro: A Study of Man's Impact on His Environment* (Cambridge: Cambridge University Press, 1972); John Ferry, *Colonial Armidale* (St Lucia: University of Queensland Press, 1999); Bill Gammage, 'Historical Reconsiderations VIII: Who Gained, and Who Was Meant to Gain, from Land Selection in New South Wales?' *Australian Historical Studies* 24, no. 94 (1990): 118; D. W. A. Baker, 'The Origins of Robertson's Land Acts', *Historical Studies Australia and New Zealand* 8, no. 30 (1958): 166–82.

investigate that question, it is necessary to understand the pastoral society and economy that selectors encountered when they first took up land from the early to mid-1870s.

The town

Europeans with their livestock appropriated Wiradjuri Country in this district from the 1820s; however, because this chapter mainly concerns the selectors and the environment they encountered, the narrative begins with the establishment of the village of Dubbo in 1849.[5] Before then, the absence of any substantial local market meant that agriculture and smaller-scale settlement were unviable. The settlement in the Wellington Valley, 50 kilometres up the Macquarie River from Dubbo, where convicts had produced crops from 1824, had been abandoned by 1831.[6] Even with the aid of impressed labour and expropriated land, the settlement could not dispose of the produce efficiently, being so far removed from markets on the coast where most other Europeans lived.[7] Captain Charles Sturt, who passed down the Macquarie in 1828, had understood the possibilities and constraints of the colony when he observed:

> The greatest disadvantage under which New South Wales labours, is the want of means for conveying inland produce to the market, or to the coast ... To an agriculturalist, a residence to the westward of the Blue Mountains is decidedly objectionable ... Although some beautiful locations both as to extent and richness, are to be found to the westward of Bathurst ... it is not probable they will be taken up for many years, or will only be occupied as distant stock stations.[8]

5   *Sydney Gazette and New South Wales Advertiser*, 6 January 1825, 3; Charles Sturt, *Two Expeditions into the Interior of Southern Australia, during the Years 1828, 1829, 1830, and 1831: With Observations on the Soil, Climate, and General Resources of the Colony of New South Wales*, Vol. I (London: Smith, Elder and Co., 1833): 6–12.
6   Surveyor G. B. White noted that Aboriginal people called the river 'Wameerawa'. See George Boyle White, 5 January 1847 – 20 December 1854, item 2/1591B, NRS 13736, SARNSW.
7   *Sydney Gazette and New South Wales Advertiser*, 29 March 1826, 2; Darling to Bathurst, 24 July 1826, *HRA*, series I, vol. XII, 434; P. Cunningham, *Two Years in New South Wales; A Series of Letters, Comprising Sketches of the Actual State of Society in That Colony; Of Its Peculiar Advantages to Emigrants; Of Its Topography, Natural History &c &c, in Two Volumes*, vol. I (London: Henry Colburn, 1827), 167; Darling to Murray, 4 May 1830, *HRA*, series I, vol. XV, 465; Darling to Goderich, 22 December 1827, *HRA*, series I, vol. XIII, 661; Darling to Twiss, 1 October 1829, 186, and Murray to Darling, 21 April 1830, *HRA*, series I, vol. XV, 432–3.
8   Sturt, *Two Expeditions into the Interior of Southern Australia*, xlviii–l.

The establishment of Dubbo as a centre of commerce and public administration was both the product of pastoralists' influence and the imperial government's plan to introduce order to the colony's unruly sprawl. In December 1846, 'Dubbo'—then the name of Robert Dulhunty's pastoral run—was announced as the most westerly of 21 locations in the colony for holding courts of petty sessions.[9] As the place was little more than a day's travel further on from the established court at Wellington, it is likely that the local stock owners and employers had strongly influenced its location as a centre for enforcing law and order on recalcitrant labourers. Local pastoralists (known throughout this period as 'squatters') served as magistrates. The site for a courthouse was selected downstream from Dulhunty's head station, where French émigré Jean Emile Serisier, sensing the potential to sell goods to the surrounding and downriver runs, opened a store on behalf of Sydney merchant Michel Despointes. A chief constable was appointed in February 1847, and by February 1848 a post office there was receiving weekly mail from Wellington. To ensure security of tenure for anyone setting up a business, that year local residents pressed the colonial government to survey a town and offer lots for sale 'to enable the tradespeople in that neighbourhood to establish themselves in a home'.[10]

By then, new regulations governing the occupation of Crown lands—the 1847 Orders in Council—had reached New South Wales. Governor FitzRoy and his Executive Council deliberated on the challenge of replacing annual licences with 14-year leases over surveyed runs in the pastoral districts and determined that spaces should be reserved for villages and townships along the routes into this more closely managed landscape.[11] More such settlements were gazetted in 1849 than in the previous five years combined, and, along with Dubbo, included Wagga Wagga, Armidale, Molong and Cowra.[12] Beside the Macquarie River, surveyor George Boyle White pegged out the spot surrounding the police station; by November 1849, a site had been fixed on ground Wiradjuri people had used as a burial site.[13] White's pessimism about the proposed town's location reinforced the view that local

---

9   *Australian*, 26 December 1846, 3; *SMH*, 24 September 1847, 2; Edward Josiah Garnsey, 'An Early History of Dubbo and District, 1828–90', 1946, unpublished manuscript, B 1055, SLNSW.
10   *SMH*, 10 February, 2, 16 August 1847, 2, 5 February 1848, 5; *Maitland Mercury and Hunter River General Advertiser*, 2 February 1848, 4; *DL*, 15 January 1924, 2; James Jervis, 'History of Dubbo 1818–1949', unpublished manuscript, [1949], 11, Macquarie Regional Library, Dubbo, quoting a letter directing the surveyor W. R. Davidson to report on the suitability of the proposed site.
11   Fitzroy to Grey, 6 December 1847, *HRA*, series I, vol. XXVI, 65.
12   *NSW Government Gazette*, various, 1845–49.
13   *NSW Government Gazette*, no. 157, 23 November 1849, 1742; Garnsey, 'An Early History of Dubbo and District, 1828–90', 9–10.

squatters had influenced the instructions from Sydney and that the site related to, but sat on the periphery of, a vast pastoral region stretching to the north-west:

> The number of allotments I have laid out will be sufficient for the demand of many years—the position of the village being so near to Wellington, is not likely to make it a place of importance, and as a Police station, it is no doubt of service to the immediate neighbourhood, but for the general benefit of the Bligh district, Wellington is as convenient; both of them however are too far from the centre to be of service to the district generally.[14]

Nevertheless, others followed Serisier's lead. By 1851, the Bathurst entrepreneur Henry Rotton was advertising for carriers to take 3 tons of goods to Dubbo with a guarantee of a backloading to either Bathurst or Sydney. In that year, Dubbo recorded a European population of 28 men and 19 women, sufficient to become the westernmost polling place in the united Pastoral Districts of Wellington and Bligh. Once the site for a town had been marked out, allotments offered for sale, and commerce and public administration had settled there, alternative locations nearby faded. As though to dispel any doubt that this was part of a broader project to absorb the so-called wastelands within an orderly colony and empire, the streets running parallel to the river were named for the five governors from Macquarie to Gipps (Fitzroy Street further out would follow later).[15]

Dubbo's prosperity and its potential as a market for agricultural produce were aided by its strategic location on several trade routes, as one commentator observed in the 1870s:

> Standing directly on the overland line between Queensland and Victoria, and fed by those two main arteries from the heart of the squatting country, the Macquarie and the Bogan, the trade of the town should not languish.[16]

---

14   G. B. White to Surveyor General Thomas Mitchell, Dubbo, Macquarie River, 14 May 1849, item 2/1591B, NRS 13736, SARNSW. See also *SMH*, 26 November 1849, 2.

15   G. B. White to Surveyor General Thomas Mitchell, Dubbo, Terramungamine, 24 January 1849, and G. B. White to Surveyor General Thomas Mitchell, Dubbo, Macquarie River, 14 May 1849, and map [undated], item 2/1591B, NRS 13736, SARNSW; *Bathurst Advocate*, 3 March 1849, 3, 10 March 1849, 2; *Bathurst Free Press and Mining Journal*, 29 October 1851, 4; *Maitland Mercury and Hunter River General Advertiser*, 15 November, 4, 11 June 1851, 2; Beryl Dulhunty, *The Dulhunty Papers: Chronicle of a Family* (Sydney: The Wentworth Press, 1959), 56.

16   *Sydney Mail and New South Wales Advertiser*, 10 May 1873, 599.

Figure 1.1: Wool wagons near Serisier's Store, Dubbo, 1873.
Source: Local Studies Collection, Dubbo Regional Council.

On a roughly east–west axis it was a point for the distribution of goods obtained from Sydney and Maitland and sent to the stations on the rivers further out. In turn, wool from the outback stations was transported along the most convenient route over the Macquarie at Dubbo, and further on to the coast (see Figure 1.1).[17] Topography also placed the town at the confluence of north–south trade routes once gold discoveries resulted in a massive influx of people to the Port Phillip District from 1851. Sheep and cattle from the New England and Moreton Bay districts that previously had been driven to Maitland for the Sydney market were now sent up to 1,800 kilometres south to the goldfields. Drovers followed three unofficial routes south, guided by convenient river crossings and access to water, that converged at Dubbo on the Macquarie River where the best places to ford were adjacent to the town. From there, routes diverged again, taking drovers towards either Deniliquin or Wagga Wagga.[18]

---

17   *DL*, 6 April 1904, 2, 13 April 1904, 2.
18   *SMH*, 28 December 1857, 3; *Maitland Mercury and Hunter River General Advertiser*, 26 November 1859, 2; *Empire*, 7 January 1870, 3.

In its unique location, Dubbo could supply droving teams and become a point of exchange of stock heading south. In time, agents who had previously travelled from Victoria to southern New South Wales to buy stock instead continued north to the point where they were assured of encountering southbound stock. Half a century later an old resident recalled that at Dubbo:

> the Victorian buyers with drovers and outfit, would meet sellers from distant parts, buy and take delivery. So there was a constant flow of sellers and buyers, one lot of drovers paid off (wages high), another lot put on; consequently, as that class of men are proverbial for being liberal-minded and handed, business at the old pub (for cash was plentiful) did a roaring trade, and it could not adequately supply the wants of the public.[19]

Local agricultural smallholders would have shared in some of the commercial opportunities arising from Dubbo's position, but they would need access to broader markets and land if they were to expand much beyond the town's fringe. This was overwhelmingly a pastoral, not yet an agricultural, district.

The country

In the 1870s the selectors encountered a society dominated by leaseholders with large swathes of land where they bred merino sheep to produce fine wool for international markets. Properties of between 16,000 and 24,000 acres (6,475 and 9,712 hectares) were common in the Dubbo district and further out towards the western plains, and some were larger.[20] Terramungamine, of 16,000 acres, was typical. It was advertised for sale with 10,000 sheep and 800 head of cattle in 1866:

> On the head station there is a good family cottage lately built, with kitchen, stores, hay-house, sheds etc ... A good stock-yard and tailing-yard, woolshed and excellent drafting yards, garden and hay paddock, two grass paddocks ... with horse yard and box. The out-stations, seven in number, have each a hut and two sheep yards with requisite utensils.[21]

---

19   *DL*, 13 April 1904, 2. See also *Empire*, 11 January 1856, 5; *SMH*, 20 March 1857, 1, 11 December 1857, 3, 28 December 1857, 3; *Maitland Mercury and Hunter River General Advertiser*, 6 August 1857, 1.
20   New South Wales, *Crown Lands under Lease or License beyond the Settled Districts, 1859*, in *Votes and Proceedings of the Legislative Assembly*, vol. III, 1859–60 (Sydney: Government Printer, 1860), 15.
21   *SMH*, 13 April 1864, 6; New South Wales, *Crown Lands (Held under Pastoral Occupation), 1865–66*, in *Votes and Proceedings of the Legislative Assembly*, vol. III, 1865–66 (Sydney: Government Printer, 1866), 30.

Pastoralists in this period were more likely to live on their properties than their predecessors in the days before more secure leasehold tenure was introduced in 1847; however, with a few exceptions, they seemed almost as transient as the workers they employed. They traded properties readily, some lived elsewhere and many moved on before they reached old age. Proprietors were often people of wealth and political influence, and frequently owned other pastoral runs in New South Wales and Queensland. Most of them were men. Exceptions included Eliza Dulhunty, who ran Dubbo station after her husband's death in late 1853 until it was sold in 1866, and Mrs Cruikshank, who was running Murrumbidgerie station in 1857, Mr Cruikshank being 'now absent from the colony'.[22]

Murrumbidgerie's procession of owners illustrates the nature of pastoralists and their business in the district. The property of 24,000 acres had been occupied by 1828, then passed through several hands before being taken up by Joshua Frey Josephson in 1866. Josephson, the son of a convict, rose to become the mayor of Sydney, a barrister, a member of the Legislative Assembly for the electorate of Braidwood from 1864, and Robertson's solicitor general in 1868–69. Later he became a district court judge. Josephson was well-connected with the colonial elite: Robertson married Josephson's wife's sister, and Josephson became a business associate of prominent wool broker and rural entrepreneur Thomas Mort. Murrumbidgerie was just one of his pastoral assets in the Bligh, Wellington and Warrego districts.[23] It is unlikely that he spent much time at his property on the Macquarie. Murrumbidgerie then passed to William Forlonge, who had owned properties in Victoria and been a member of the Victorian Legislative Assembly where he advocated for squatters' interests, before acquiring more property on the Lachlan and Darling rivers. He represented Orange in the New South Wales Legislative Assembly between 1864 and 1867. Twice bankrupt but not deterred, Forlonge acquired Murrumbidgerie in the early 1870s. He lost the property to his creditors, the Australian Joint Stock Bank, who sold it in 1889 to James Rutherford of Bathurst, a wealthy businessman who owned the Cobb

---

22 Dulhunty, *The Dulhunty Papers*, 57–8; *SMH*, 10 September 1857, 15.
23 H. T. E. Holt, 'Josephson, Joshua Frey (1815–1892)', *Australian Dictionary of Biography*, National Centre of Biography, The Australian National University, published first in hardcopy 1972, adb.anu.edu. au/biography/josephson-joshua-frey-3873/text6167. Murrumbidgerie was estimated at around 24,000 acres at various times between 1848 and 1880, but then 178,000 acres in 1885, the latter probably including adjoining leases, of different names, but all owned by the one proprietor. See 'Claims to Leases of Crown Lands', *NSW Government Gazette*, 21 September (no. 104, supplement), 1256; 'Second Annual Report upon the Occupation of Crown Lands ... for the Year 1880', *Votes and Proceedings of the NSW Legislative Assembly, 1881*, vol. III (Sydney: Government Printer, 1881), 21; New South Wales, *Report of the Chief Inspector of Stock, for the Year Ending 31st December 1884*, in *Votes and Proceedings of the Legislative Assembly*, vol. III (Sydney: Government Printer, 1885), 135.

& Co coaching business along with other enterprises and properties in New South Wales and Queensland.[24] Through a series of excisions arising from successive laws to open up land for closer settlement, Murrumbidgerie had ceased to be a substantial property by the early twentieth century.[25]

Labour was the pastoralists' main continuing expense. To an extent that has not been widely acknowledged by historians of rural New South Wales, from the beginning of European occupation, much of the labour had been supplied by First Nations people. Indeed, the continuing negotiation of roles, rights and access to land and other resources in hundreds of different settings in the Wellington Valley and down the Macquarie River was integral to economic, and even social, life in the 1830s and 1840s. Between 1832 and 1844, the Church Missionary Society occupied the site of the former convict settlement at Wellington and set out to convert local Wiradjuri people to Christianity. The missionaries failed, but in the meantime had tried to persuade the prospective converts to work at the mission, the women as domestic servants and the men at growing crops and tending sheep.[26] The relationships between squatters and Wiradjuri might have been no less fraught, but Aboriginal people's labour was essential to pastoral expansion. The commissioner of Crown lands for the district of Bligh reported in 1846 that they were 'in many places found most useful to the Squatter, and at most stations you will find them employed'. The Wellington district's commissioner reported that Aboriginal people were:

> pretty constantly at some of the Stations, acting as assistants to Stockmen and Bullock drivers, occasionally shepherding, herding the Milch Cows, bringing up the horses from the bush when wanted, and fetching wood and Water for use of the huts.[27]

---

24   Nancy Adams, 'Forlonge, William (1811–1890)', *Australian Dictionary of Biography*, National Centre of Biography, The Australian National University, published first in hardcopy 1966, adb.anu.edu. au/biography/forlonge-william-2054/text2549; J. E. L. Rutherford, 'Rutherford, James (1827–1911)', *Australian Dictionary of Biography*, National Centre of Biography, The Australian National University, published first in hardcopy 1976, adb.anu.edu.au/biography/rutherford-james-886/text7415.
25   Dalgety & Company, *Murrumbidgerie Estate* [sales brochure] (Sydney: S. T. Leigh and Co. Printers, 1901).
26   Hilary M. Carey and David A. Roberts, eds, 'Preamble', *The Wellington Valley Project. Letters and Journals Relating to the Church Missionary Society Mission to Wellington Valley, NSW, 1830–45* (A Critical Electronic Edition, 2002), downloads.newcastle.edu.au/library/cultural%20collections/the-wellington-valley-project/ (hereafter *WVP*); Peter Read, *A Hundred Years War: The Wiradjuri People and the State* (Canberra: Australian National University Press, 1988), 12–28.
27   Report on the Aborigines by Graham D. Hunter, commissioner of Crown lands, District of Bligh, for the year 1846, *HRA*, series I, vol. XXV, 563; Report on the Aborigines by Graham D. Hunter, commissioner of Crown lands, District of Bligh, for the year 1847, *HRA*, series I, vol. XXVI, 398; Mr W. C. Mayne to Colonial Secretary Thomson, Wellington, 1 January 1848, *HRA*, series I, vol. XXVI, 400.

Around Wellington, Wiradjuri people with some connection to the former mission were employed on properties in the 1850s. Indigenous people filled all of the 'outdoor servants' positions on one property, and on another were engaged as a laundress, a 'groom and handyman' and a child's nurse.[28] Women were also in demand as sexual partners. The missionaries maintained that this was an almost universal practice. One of them, William Watson, wrote in 1837:

> On some establishments [stations], where there are from 30 to 40 servants, scarcely a hut can be found, where there is not a native female living in adulterous connexion with the European inmates … Honorable exceptions indeed are found as it regards Masters and Overseers, but all we know of amounts to no higher a number than four.[29]

Wiradjuri people's value to the pastoral economy is demonstrated by the fact that the mission and the squatters were obliged, effectively, to bid for their labour. The missionaries tried to persuade them to plough, shear or perform domestic tasks in return for rations. They were regularly frustrated, though, when the Wiradjuri people went off to the stations to work, suggesting that their labour was in demand there, in exchange for more than the Wellington mission offered. William Porter of the mission noted in his journal in 1838:

> Began shearing our last Flock of Sheep to day; nearly all the young [Aboriginal] men went away to assist a neighbouring settler: he having promised to give them rum, and money.[30]

Local women were no doubt exploited by white men, but evidence of cross-cultural intimacy and playfulness can be read into a disapproving missionary's account of a church service in 1839:

> We had rather a better attendance of Europeans, at both Services, than usual; but we were shocked at the conduct of some Gentlemen (as they would be considered) … endeavouring to draw the attention of our Native girls upon them & laughing with them.[31]

---

28 'Lyth' [K. Lambert], *The Golden South: Memories of Australian Home Life 1843–1888* (London: Ward and Downey, 1890), 56, 62.

29 Watson to Jowett, 17 January 1837, *WVP*. See also *Sydney Gazette and New South Wales Advertiser*, 24 June 1834, 2, and 18 July 1837, 2; *Colonist*, 7 July 1836, 3; Rev Taylor to Rev Cowper, 6 February 1839 (enclosure to correspondence from Gipps to Russell, 7 May 1840), *HRA*, series I, vol. XX, 622.

30 William Porter's journal, 30 October 1838, *WVP*. See also Annual Report of the Aboriginal Mission Station, Wellington Valley, 1838, enclosure in Gipps to Russell, 7 May 1840, *HRA*, series 1, vol. XX, 619.

31 James Gunther's journal, 21 April 1839, *WVP*. The question mark is contained in the *WVP* transcription.

Wiradjuri people made use of the mission and the sheep stations in these ways, negotiating access to food and cash in exchange for labour, coming and going as other imperatives arose, to which the Europeans were probably most often oblivious. They gathered for their own cultural purposes, near Dundullimal station for example, and on the Bell River at Wellington where missionary James Gunther estimated 150 people congregated on one occasion in 1838.[32]

That is not to say that this was a benign environment for First Nations people. There were instances of extreme violence. In 1824, a correspondent noted the contrast between the imposition of martial law at Bathurst with the 'perfect amity' that prevailed in the Wellington Valley, but, nonetheless, observed that Aboriginal people 'often' visited the settlement in the valley to have gunshot wounds dressed.[33] In 1834, Governor Bourke noted the 'acts of violence which the [Wellington Valley] Missionaries represent to be perpetrated against them by the stockmen and others residing on the remote frontiers of the Colony'.[34] Watson forcibly took children from their mothers. His colleague James Gunther was distressed to find, when he travelled along the river below Wellington in 1840, that mothers hid their children or claimed that they were dead rather than risk having them taken.[35] And in Gunther's 1842 annual report, he alleged that Aboriginal people were being 'exterminated by violence, which I fear more frequently occurs in the Interior than is publicly known'.[36]

Stations around Dubbo and to the north-west were part of a huge increase in pastoral investment in the 1870s and 1880s, which took the form of buildings, water conservation and plant, but mainly fencing. The *Australian Town and Country Journal*'s Dubbo correspondent reported in 1873 that local pastoralists were:

> fully alive to the benefits to be obtained from improvements ... There is now a tremendous lot of fencing ... in these parts, and, in a few years, an unfenced run will be a rarity in the north-west.[37]

32   William Watson's journal, 26 December 1834, *WVP*; William Watson's diary, 18 July 1835, *WVP*; James Gunther's journal, 25 February 1838, 18 January 1840, *WVP*; Louisa Anne ('Mrs Charles') Meredith, *Notes and Sketches of New South Wales, during a Residence in that Colony from 1839 to 1844* (London: John Murray, 1844; facsimile edition 1973), 91.
33   *Sydney Gazette and New South Wales Advertiser*, 14 October 1824, 2.
34   *Australian*, 3 June 1834, 2.
35   James Gunther's journal, 18 January 1840, *WVP*.
36   Annual Report of the Mission to the Aborigines at Wellington Valley, New Holland, for the year 1841, 7 January 1842, enclosure in Gipps to Stanley, 11 March 1942, *HRA*, series 1, vol. XXI, 737.
37   *ATCJ*, 5 July 1873, 17; N. G. Butlin, *Investment in Australian Economic Development* (Canberra: Department of Economic History, Research School of Social Sciences, The Australian National University, 1972), 59–110.

This investment changed the demand for labour. Fencing reduced the need for resident workers, as each boundary rider replaced tens of shepherds and hutkeepers. One reporter observed in 1870 that 'stations of yore used to be small townships; but now they are only occupied by single men and black gins'.[38] Shearing, however, still required a large itinerant workforce. Each year men walked down the rivers to the stations further out in search of work, and then back up the rivers at the end of the season. The *Maitland Mercury* reported in 1869:

> A great many shearers, or men travelling for work, have gone down the Macquarie, where shearing will commence in two or three weeks. Some have gone to the Castlereagh, while large numbers are travelling on the Bogan.[39]

The town of Dubbo was more a port of call for workers on the way out and on return than a major source of pastoral labour. Returning shearers could also get seasonal agricultural work once farms began to appear close to the town. The *Empire*'s correspondent reported in 1869:

> The town is now well filled with shearers who, having finished nearly all the sheds before them, have come in to get rigged out in clothing, and to have 'a little bit of a messmate spree' before starting with the harvest.[40]

Though the demand for labour declined, Aboriginal people were still part of the workforce on western stations. An 1869 report revealed that two large properties on the Bogan employed only Aboriginal labour; another noted that one in four white pastoralists in the north-west were each living with up to four Aboriginal women.[41] Into the 1890s, the Aboriginal Protection Board was reporting that in the Dubbo district (extending to Peak Hill, Dandaloo and Gilgandra) able-bodied Aboriginal men were 'generally employed on the various stations ... shearing, boundary-riding, kangaroo-shooting, &c'. In the more closely settled district of Wellington, the main occupations for Aboriginal workers were 'farming, shepherding, droving, and ... general station-work'.[42] Even on small farms where the household

---

38 *ATCJ*, 2 July 1870, 7. See also *ATCJ*, 17 January 1874, 15, 30 May 1874, 15, 22 August 1874, 16.

39 *Maitland Mercury and Hunter River General Advertiser*, 20 July 1869, 4–5. See also *ATCJ*, 23 August 1873, 21.

40 *Empire*, 1 November 1869, 3. See also *ATCJ*, 29 October 1870, 7; *Sydney Mail and New South Wales Advertiser*, 22 September 1877, 363.

41 *Empire*, 3 August 1869, 2, 24 September 1869, 3.

42 New South Wales, Aborigines Protection Board, *Protection of the Aborigines (Report of the Board for 1891)*, in *Votes and Proceedings of the Legislative Assembly*, vol. VII, 1892–93 (Sydney: Government Printer, 1893), 30.

supplied most of its own labour, there is evidence that Aboriginal people found employment. An insolvent farmer with a block on the left bank of the Macquarie just above Dubbo listed among the costs he had incurred in the summer of 1871–72, a payment to 'Blacks' for reaping his crop. The contrast between that impersonal appellation and the individual names he recorded for other labourers to whom he paid wages hints at a fundamental disconnection in European minds, between themselves and the first inhabitants of that place.[43] Into the early twentieth century, though, Aboriginal workers were a part of the rural labour force. They included Michael Mickey, one of a number of Aboriginal men who lived and worked at The Meadows, a substantial property towards Obley (see Figure 1.2).[44]

Figure 1.2: Harry Wheeler, Tom Edwards, Michael Mickey and Bob Wilson at 'The Meadows', 1909.
Source: Local Studies Collection, Dubbo Regional Council.

---

43 Insolvent's Supplementary Schedule Part 'B', file no. 10910 (Hawke), NRS 13654, SARNSW.
44 *DL*, 31 October 1906, 4.

The society that the selectors were to encounter below the Wellington Valley from the late 1860s had its roots in an era shaped by rivers, distance to markets, engagements between Indigenous peoples and intruders, and the supply of labour and capital. It was part of a broader pattern of invasion and settlement as squatters established runs with sheep and cattle in the Port Phillip and the Darling Downs, Monaro, Liverpool Plains and New England districts, and along the Lachlan and Murrumbidgee rivers.[45] Fifty years after Europeans first occupied this country, the selectors would come up against wealthy and influential people who were determined to secure their pastoral assets. The selectors would contest the right to occupy that same land and frequently find themselves a part of that workforce.

On their selections

In the period to 1880, there were more barriers to the coalescence of a farming class around Dubbo than there were reasons for one to form. The first impediment to class formation was that, without a more substantial market for agricultural produce, the district could not support an extensive settler population. By 1880, there was more local demand than in the 1820s, but the costs of transport to the far larger markets on the coast were still prohibitive. The district was more likely to import agricultural produce than to sell its surplus. In 1869, pastoralist John Ryrie claimed that flour could be purchased more cheaply from distant markets than it could be produced locally.[46] Local demand for grain, and therefore the prospects of gainful agriculture, improved when a steam flour mill opened in Dubbo in the late 1860s. In July 1869, it was obtaining only two-thirds of its wheat locally; however, by the next summer the mill was operating from 6 am until 10 pm to process grain grown around the town, and surplus wheat was going to Orange and Mudgee.[47] With only one purchaser producing flour for the local market, prices for farmers were constrained and wheat growing remained a marginal proposition.

45   D. N. Jeans, *An Historical Geography of New South Wales* (Sydney: Reed Education, 1972), 139–40; Duncan Waterson, *Squatter, Selector and Storekeeper: A History of the Darling Downs 1859–93* (Sydney: Sydney University Press, 1968), 9–49; Bill Gammage, *Narrandera Shire* (Narrandera: Bill Gammage for the Narrandera Shire Council, 1986), 38–61; Ferry, *Colonial Armidale*, 50–7; Hancock, *Discovering Monaro*, 31–53; Eric Rolls, *A Million Wild Acres: 20 Years of Man and an Australian Forest* (McMahons Point: Hale and Iremonger, 2011), 65–184.
46   Copy of a petition for a road from Dubbo to Mudgee, from Inhabitants of the Town and District of Mudgee to the secretary for lands, 22 August 1861, in ML MSS 301, SLNSW; *SMH*, 18 May 1869, 3.
47   *Empire*, 20 July 1869, 3, 7 January 1870, 3.

The selectors' cohesion was also impeded by their heterogeneity—in their origins, their former occupations, the timing of their arrival and the nature of their enterprises once they settled. The era of free selection extended over several decades. The timing of settlers' arrival was influenced by the expiration of pastoral leases and the revocation of land previously set aside for reserves, as well as the terms of land selection in adjoining colonies and prospects in other ventures such as goldmining. It could also be interrupted by the creation of new reserves, for example, for travelling stock, water, timber or minerals. People of Dubbo, keen to see their town and district grow, sent a petition to the Legislative Assembly in 1866:

> on Thursday ... many persons arrived in ... Dubbo, having travelled, in some instances, nearly two hundred miles, whose only object was to make free selection of certain lands ... and to their utter astonishment they found that their applications had been refused, on the grounds that such lands had been reserved from conditional purchase.[48]

Despite such frustrations, by the early 1870s selectors found that, in some seasons at least, the local climate was compatible with agriculture. A report from 1870 stated that 'upwards of 200 free selectors in the district of Dubbo' were preparing for a good harvest, and another in 1871 claimed:

> Wheat was grown in this district long before Dubbo was proclaimed as a township, and wheat is cultivated now on a much larger scale.... The crops now being put in are wheat, oats, barley, rye, lucerne and ... maize.[49]

But selection did not gain momentum until the mid-1870s. In part, evidence for this comes from the 1883 Report of Inquiry into the State of the Public Lands, and the Operation of the Land Laws, commonly known as the Morris and Ranken report after its conservative pastoralist authors. Historians have rightly regarded the report as deeply flawed and preordained to provide a springboard for the Stuart government's 1884 land reforms. Read closely though, and with due regard for its political context, the sections based on a rapid appraisal of rural districts across the colony provide valuable insights

---

48   *Empire*, 14 March 1866, 5. See also *Empire*, 10 January 1866, 5, 12 January 1866, 5.
49   *Empire*, 26 August 1870, 2; *ATCJ*, 27 May 1871, 7.

into the state of free selection in the Central West.[50] Commenting on the timing of selection in that region, the authors were presumably drawing on the testimony of people with local experience (transcripts of evidence were never published) when they found that:

> Ten years ago [in around 1873] settlement by conditional purchase was as a rule of a limited nature and confined chiefly to the rivers and principal watercourses adjacent to the townships within the agricultural area. The holdings were small and were the result of demand for produce for local consumption; and in some cases agriculture was united in a small degree with grazing.[51]

A report in 1875 claimed that whereas Wellington benefited from the arrival of '"New Blood"—farmers from well-known agricultural districts', Dubbo was still supported by 'some of the wealthiest of our squatters, aided by a few agriculturalists'.[52] From the mid-1870s, though, settlement accelerated. A report, also from 1875, claimed that the lower Talbragar was 'thickly populated' by selectors, and one the following year indicated that selection was proceeding apace:

> Free selection is going on here actively. During the past fortnight 2000 acres have been taken up ... all the selectors are *bona fide*— taken up really for the purposes of settlement ... For fourteen miles around Dubbo settlers are thickly scattered; and they are men of the right sort. Their homesteads are well and comfortably built, and their lands are enclosed.[53]

But it was a fitful, drawn-out process, as the landscape slowly filled with small farms. Cohesion and a shared experience among settlers might have been harder to achieve than elsewhere because many arrived as individuals or as families, sometimes as extended families, but not as ready-made communities. There were no American-style wagon trains, no coordinated treks in the manner of the Dutch-descended colonists in southern Africa,

50 Stephen H. Roberts, *History of Australian Land Settlement, 1788–1920* (Melbourne: Macmillan & Co. in association with Melbourne University Press, 1924), 222–32; New South Wales, *Report of Inquiry into the State of the Public Lands, and the Operation of the Land Laws*, in *Votes and Proceedings of the Legislative Assembly*, vol. II, 1883 (Sydney: Government Printer, 1883). The district they labelled 'Dubbo' extended well to the west and north-west, taking in country watered by the Castlereagh, Macquarie and Bogan rivers and their tributaries. For a summary of the debate among historians, see Gammage, 'Who Gained', 104–22.
51 New South Wales, *Report of Inquiry into the State of the Public Lands*, 54.
52 *Sydney Mail and New South Wales Advertiser*, 1 May 1875, 548. On Wellington, see *SMH*, 17 June 1875, 7.
53 *ATCJ*, 9 October 1875, 19; *Sydney Mail and New South Wales Advertiser*, 12 February 1876, 203.

and, with the small exception of the community of Beni settled mainly by people of Irish Catholic descent, no religious or ethnic migrations akin to the German Lutherans who moved together from South Australia to the Riverina in the late 1860s.[54]

As well as arriving mainly as individual households, selectors were coming from different places, though often from more closely settled districts where land was scarcer. An aspiring selector from Bathurst claimed in 1866 that people from his district, as well as 'scores of struggling farmers and carriers from the Hartley district', were waiting for opportunities to 'push up' towards Dubbo. A local report from 1871 suggested that Dubbo was the destination of a significant wave of selectors from Bathurst, Hartley and Maitland, with land being taken up:

> not by mere penniless adventurers, but by substantial yeomen, for the most part who, owning sheep and cattle, find their present holdings in other parts of the colony becoming yearly too much circumscribed to admit of sufficient pasturage for their increasing stock.

A report from 1875 claimed that selectors around Dubbo were generally farmers and carriers from Bathurst and Maitland, but another that year observed that genuine selectors downriver from Dubbo (that is not acting as agents or 'dummies' for others) were mainly stockmen, presumably off surrounding pastoral stations.[55]

The *Australian Men of Mark* series published in 1889–90 contains further evidence of selectors' backgrounds. These collections of biographical sketches of prominent men in Australian politics and business also include appendices in several editions containing short, one- or two-sentence entries about men (not one woman) of no particular note who nonetheless could be said to have been modestly successful in their chosen field, at least according to their own testimony. Though the publications contain only a small and possibly unrepresentative sample of potentially embellished portraits, they affirm the impression of Dubbo district selectors' diverse origins. Of the 66 profiled men who were both living in the Dubbo district and engaged, at least in part, in farming, about two in five were Australian-born, over half were born in Britain or Ireland, and the balance from elsewhere in Europe. Of the 25 Australian-born, Dubbo district farmers recorded, most

54 Betty Hickey, *A Village that Disappeared: Beni Via Dubbo* (Dubbo: Orana Education Centre, 1987).
55 *Empire*, 12 January 1866, 5; *ATCJ*, 7 October 1871, 7; *SMH*, 11 March 1875, 3; *ATCJ*, 9 September 1875, 7.

were from elsewhere in New South Wales. Of those, approximately half were from east of the mountains (Sydney, St Marys, Penrith, Windsor, Colo River, Hunter River, East Maitland), and half from west of the mountains along a broad corridor between Sydney and Dubbo (Wallerawang, Bathurst, Carcoar, Blayney, Orange).[56]

The most striking aspect of these people's lives, before they became Dubbo selectors, was the varied nature of their previous occupations. Only a handful identified their one vocation as having been 'farmer'. Most had worked at two, three or four occupations on their way to becoming selectors. More than half had been labourers or contractors, one in four had been (or continued to be) carriers and a quarter had also been miners. They included former hoteliers, storekeepers, blacksmiths and cordial makers. These profiles show the selectors to have had very limited experience of farming, and none in the environment they would encounter. Amid their disparate circumstances, they were at least bound by a common aspiration to make a living on land of their own.

The selectors' heterogeneity included their resources and methods. Many of them in the 1870s had very little capital, relying principally on the household's labour. The surveyor William Butler Simpson recorded his impressions as he marked out proposed selections, reserves and roads in the County of Lincoln, north and west of Wellington in the 1860s and 1870s.[57] At the time of his surveys, the most established applicants had built a hut, yards or a dam, and cleared and cultivated some land, with an average value of around £30. Others, though, provided no more evidence of their occupation than what Simpson, evoking in European eyes the epitome of crude impermanence, described as an Aboriginal 'gunyah', usually valued at £1 or £2. Many selected extra blocks in their children's names. In 1876, the surveyor reported one such case:

> App[licant] who is an infant 2 yrs of age resides with his parents on the adjacent selection. There was no-one occupying the ground at time of survey. Some few days afterwards I saw that someone had taken possession of the hut. Improv[emen]ts consist of a small iron roofed hut. Value about £12.[58]

56   Charles F. Maxwell, *Australian Men of Mark*, vol. 2 (Sydney: Charles F Maxwell, [1889–90]), Appendix, 1–35.
57   W. B. Simpson surveyed selections mostly in the Parish of Micketymulga, but also further north as far as the Talbragar River through the parishes of Bodangora, Geurie, Woorooboomi, Tenandra, Bald Hill, Murrumgundie and Narran. See B 899–B 917, SLNSW.
58   Entry of 31 May 1876, B 899–B 917, SLNSW.

The selectors around Dubbo were often both impoverished and inexpert. In 1876, a correspondent to a school inspector reported that most of the 'farmers' north of Wellington (where Simpson had been surveying) were 'poor struggling men'.[59] They learnt what the soil, the climate and the local markets could support by trial and error, experimenting with wheat, corn, potatoes, some with a few sheep and pigs, often with poor results. One relative newcomer living on Mogriguy Creek in 1880 revealed:

> I have been farming here for about four years, and during that time the first two years' crops were failures, owing to the very dry weather … I'm of opinion that farming … in [the] Dubbo district won't pay, owing to there being so many dry seasons. You may get a good crop one year, and most likely the next two years will bring forth nothing in shape of crops to pay for the labour of harvesting.[60]

Even if Morris and Ranken were predisposed towards discrediting Robertson's land settlement project, their assessment of Dubbo district settlers' methods was compatible with other sources, and suggests that many people had started with minimal capital and experience:

> Selectors, with few exceptions, do not improve their lands in a permanent way. Their homesteads and fences are generally of such a temporary character that in a few years, without repair, they would become useless. The cultivated land is generally badly fenced and full of stumps, and their dams and tanks are too small to be of use in time of drought … Farming is carried on in a slovenly and haphazard manner.[61]

The emergence of any common experience and consciousness as a class of farming people was also compromised by the fact that, for many, farming was, of necessity, only a part of their livelihood. Few on blocks of up to 640 acres are likely to have survived just by working the land they had acquired. Morris and Ranken characterised the Dubbo district selectors as men of 'small means' who were 'contented with small holdings' and who 'used them as homes in connection with contract work on the adjacent stations, carrying, trades, &c'.[62] Mark Mathews, a blacksmith by trade, arrived in Dubbo in 1863, then used earnings from the Gulgong gold rush

---

59 C. P. Richards to the inspector of schools, 14 June 1876, Lincoln School Administrative File pre-1939, 5/16609.1, NRS 3829, SARNSW.

60 *ATCJ*, 16 October 1880, 19. See also *ATCJ*, 23 October 1880, 20, 30 October 1880, 20.

61 New South Wales, *Report of Inquiry into the State of the Public Lands*, 55.

62 New South Wales, *Report of Inquiry into the State of the Public Lands*, 54.

of the 1870s to establish a carrying business between Dubbo and Bourke, and select land at Troy Gully north of Dubbo. But, rather than grow cash crops, his household produced fodder and bred horses to support their main business. Thomas Morris grew wheat on a selection on the Macquarie River flats south of Dubbo at Warrie but also ran a butchery and a line of coaches to Obley and Peak Hill.[63] The Swedish immigrant Charles Bagge's entry is typical of many recorded in *Australian Men of Mark*:

> in 1879 [he] came to New South Wales, where, after twelve months, he purchased land at Dubbo. He grows wheat and hay, and grazes 20 head of cattle, and he is also engaged in the carrying trade.

Another selector, from Newbridge near Blayney, had been a carrier for seven years before he and his family took up 600 acres at Warrie in 1874: 'His principal business is butchering and dairying'.[64] A school inspector observed that at Eschol in 1877, other than the publican, all residents 'combine carrying on the roads with farming on a small scale'.[65] Farming was just one part of people's diverse working experience.

Selectors also sold their labour when they could not produce enough wealth from their own blocks to survive. A number of selectors in the Mogriguy area in the early 1880s relied on work with local squatters to get by. One farmer on 200 acres confessed that 'were it not for his sons getting employment from squatters the family would be starved out of farming', and another on 640 acres admitted that 'were it not for himself and daughters being employed by squatters the poor man never could make ends meet by farming'.[66] Others went shearing. The *Dubbo Dispatch* reported in 1872: 'The small selectors are now the principal occupants of the sheds.'[67] On balance, selectors needed income from beyond the farm, at least while they were building, fencing, clearing and cultivating to make it fully productive.

Years after the arrival of the first selectors, much of the country around Dubbo was still dominated by large sheep stations. A journalist with Robertson's party in 1877 observed that, while 'the free selector has put in an appearance

63 Garnsey, 'An Early History of Dubbo and District, 1828–90', 146–8.
64 Maxwell, *Australian Men of Mark*, vol. 2, appendix, 20, 21.
65 Response to an application to establish a school, 10 December 1877, Eschol School Administrative File, pre-1939, 5/15838.1, NRS 3829, SARNSW.
66 *ATCJ*, 30 October 1880, 21.
67 *ATCJ*, 7 September 1872, 10; John Merritt, *The Making of the AWU* (Melbourne: Oxford University Press, 1986), 42–3; New South Wales, Royal Commission on Strikes, *Report of the Royal Commission on Strikes, Minutes of Evidence* (Sydney: Government Printer, 1891), 109–10.

here and there', 'pretty extensive' pastoral runs were still predominant.[68] In 1885, 10 per cent of property holders in the district occupied at least 15,001 acres and accounted for 85 per cent of the occupied country. Further north and north-west of Dubbo, in areas including Warren, Gilgandra and Collie, 32 per cent of landholders occupied those bigger properties, which accounted for over 95 per cent of occupied territory.[69] Of the 162 property holders with at least 10 acres who listed Dubbo as their postal town, 113, or 70 per cent, occupied no more than 640 acres. Together, these smallest properties represented less than 5 per cent of the occupied land.

On the face of it, with the term 'selector' obscuring such a diverse range of people and circumstances, it would be unsurprising if there were no coherent sense of collective interest and purpose among them in this period. Yet, despite a lack of experience, often inadequate acreage and limited access to markets, selectors nonetheless became embedded in many locations by 1880. Over time, enclaves formed at places along the creeks and rivers that squatters had not managed to close off with reserves or their own purchases.[70] At the confluence of the Talbragar and Macquarie, a school inspector in 1877 reported: 'Nearly all the people are free-selectors. There are two publicans. All have a permanent interest in the place and every year is likely to bring new settlers.'[71] Even if they were isolated from other groups of selectors, clusters of small, contiguous blocks allowed for the possibility that some people would develop a sense of themselves as a community based on a shared experience of local climate, topography, markets and, not least of all, relationships with neighbouring pastoralists.

The land contest

The contest with pastoralists might not have consistently dominated selectors' daily lives, but it provided a catalyst for the early stirrings of political organisation among smallholders. From the pastoralists' perspective, selectors were not so much carving out land of their own, as occupying country that other colonisers had laid claim to for 50 years. Tangled perceptions

68 *SMH*, 9 January 1877, 3.
69 New South Wales, *Report of the Chief Inspector of Stock*, 133–7.
70 *ATCJ*, 11 January 1873, 10. See also: District inspector to the chief inspector, October 1880, Eschol School Administrative File, pre-1939, 5/15838.1, NRS 3829, SARNSW; *ATCJ*, 13 January, 13, 14 September 1872, 7, 8 January 1870, 7; *SMH*, 1 December 1875, 7.
71 Inspector's report on an application for a school, 27 March 1877, Brocklehurst School Administrative File, pre-1939, 5/15094, NRS 3829, SARNSW.

of occupancy and title are evident in a local postmaster's 1875 report on country west of Wellington, on a part of a run formerly leased by the squatter William Forlonge: 'There is ... a good road through Mr Furlonge's [sic] paddock in constant use, both by the residents of Arthursville (Gundy) and by the free selectors residing inside the paddock.'[72]

Squatters actively resisted the selectors with strategies that were common across the colony. They purchased what they could in their own names, hemmed in encroaching selectors to prevent them from accumulating viably sized blocks, bought portions of their properties on the basis of strategically placed improvements, lobbied for the creation of water reserves and engaged 'dummies' to select blocks with a view to taking them over once the minimum conditions of occupation had been met.[73] Simpson sometimes suspected that putative selectors were acting as dummies on behalf of larger station owners, especially in situations in which he knew the selector to be an employee of the station or when the proposed selection contained substantial improvements that a station owner might seek to protect. He remarked that family members applying for 320 acres between Wellington and Murrumbidgerie in 1875 were employed as shepherds by the local squatter Joseph Aarons. Owners of the Geurie run, Burns and McKenzie, made arrangements with compliant selectors, as Simpson recorded that same year:

> The imp's [improvements] consist of Hut & portion of a sheep drafting yard. The value of the imp's about £20—I believe the imp's have been erected at the order of Burns & McKenzie—the present owners of Geurie Run and for their use alone.[74]

He also suspected a 'dummy' of applying for 80 acres in Murrungundy parish:

> The imps on this land are old & I believe they are the property of Mr George Davidson, present owner of the Murrungundy Run whom I believe has placed the selector there for the purpose of securing a portion of his run.

---

72   Robert Stace to the postmaster general, 24 February 1875, Ponto Post Office File, part 1, 1872–1900, SP32/1, NAA.

73   *Empire*, 10 January, 5, 14 March 1866, 5. See also Gammage, *Narrandera Shire*, 64–6; Buxton, *The Riverina 1861–1891*, 156–76; Barbara Dawson, *The Bibbenluke Estate and the Robertson Land Acts, 1861–1884: 'One of the Finest Properties in New South Wales (If Not the Best)'* (Weetangera: Barbara Dawson in conjunction with Bombala and District Historical Society, 2016), 114–26.

74   Entry of 15 October 1875, B 899–B 917, SLNSW.

On the Murrumbidgerie station further down the Macquarie towards Dubbo, Simpson suspected Forlonge of using a dummy selector to secure improvements:

> The dam shown was partly in existence before Williams selected. There are traces of a dam having been there. The present dam has been built up and in fact made by Mr Forlong [sic] after Phillip Williams had selected. The imp by Mr Forlong consists of Dam about £80 remains of old station & Hut valued about £4.[75]

Morris and Ranken's findings from the Dubbo district confirmed that, though some selectors had gained a foothold by the early 1880s, in many instances the land laws had reinforced leaseholders' security at genuine selectors' expense. Two of their case studies examined areas bordered very roughly by the Macquarie River on the south and west, and Coalbaggie Creek on the east. In the first case, a station of nearly 155,000 acres was retained mostly intact with a combination of dummy purchases (6 per cent of the area), associated pre-leases (3 per cent), reserves (20 per cent) and areas measured for sale by auction (unspecified). 'Bona fide' selectors secured 7 per cent of the station by purchase and another 10 per cent with associated pre-leases. In the second case, a station of 38,000 acres was secured with a combination of strategically located purchases, reserves and pre-leases covering 46 per cent of its area. There were no bona fide selections on the station.[76] So, despite their disparate circumstances selectors at least shared one experience in common: that their access to more and better land, and even their security over whatever land they had obtained, was impeded by the squatters who preceded them.

Pastoralists organising

From the late 1860s pastoralists were no less aggrieved than the selectors over the land laws, but they were more established, wealthy and politically connected. In their public statements, the squatters were careful to specify that they opposed the land laws rather than the selectors themselves. Seeking to represent their interests as being closely aligned, the prominent pastoralist John Ryrie said in 1869 that 'the free selector is really a squatter on a smaller scale', though they should be confined to the country where

---

75 Entry of 20 November 1875, B 899–B 917, SLNSW.
76 New South Wales, *Report of Inquiry into the State of the Public Lands,* Cases 'Bligh No. 2 and No. 3'.

the squatters considered agriculture was viable.[77] But the sharp distinction between squatters and free selectors was not merely a construct that later historians used to frame rural politics of that era: it infused virtually all contemporary rhetoric about land laws, and tangibly affected the selectors who clustered around Dubbo. Here was a class struggle in the Australian bush, long before the strikes of the 1890s.

The squatters were the first to organise. In May 1869, station owners gathered at the Royal Hotel in Dubbo, being distressed by the prevailing drought that was exacerbated by the lower wool prices brought on by the end of the American Civil War and emerging competition from South American graziers. Under the guidance of the chair Joseph Penzer—the owner of Cumboogle station, magistrate, and future Free Trade member for The Bogan—the pastoralists produced the 'Dubbo petition': a claim that the colony's pastoral potential was being thwarted by short (five year) leases and the threat of free selection. The petition urged that pastoral leases be extended to 21 years, and conditional purchases confined to areas where agriculture would pay. Recognising that they were part of a broader class of landholders in like circumstances, the Dubbo group circulated the petition to other pastoralists' associations. Though the petition does not appear to have had any immediate or direct effect, it inserted Dubbo and its pastoral hinterland into the continuing debate over 'the land question' that would persist through the 1870s.[78]

Pastoralists rallied again in 1878, spurred once more by protracted drought and still convinced that they were a class apart, with not just common interests but also an entitlement built on two generations of endeavour. In January they gathered once more at Dubbo's Royal Hotel to protest the government's proposals to cease the sale of Crown lands by auction and to revoke all reserves. They favoured auction sales to secure their runs because they were better able than selectors to pay the full cost upfront, which such sales required. Squatters also encouraged the gazettal of water reserves to prevent river frontages from being selected. Thomas Baird of Dundullimal station chaired the hastily convened meeting at which prominent graziers asserted their claims—with no reference to the original inhabitants—as 'the pioneers of the colony', standing in the shoes of those who 'purchased their rights' by opening up country that otherwise would have remained

77 *SMH*, 18 May 1869, 3.
78 *SMH*, 18 May 1869, 3; *Wagga Wagga Advertiser and Riverine Reporter*, 2 June 1869, 3, 12 February 1870, 2; *Empire*, 26 January 1870, 3. See P. Loveday and A. W. Martin, *Parliament Factions and Parties: The First Thirty Years of Responsible Government in New South Wales, 1856–1889* (Carlton: Melbourne University Press, 1966), 101–5.

a 'wilderness' and that was only suitable for pastoral purposes anyway. A subsequent meeting drew more squatters to town from up to 150 miles away and resolved to form the North-Western Land League.[79]

The pastoralists asserted their interest not only through their collective advocacy but also via the district's elected representatives who were themselves investors in the pastoral industry. In the era before responsible government, the district was represented from 1851 in an expanded but still only partially elected Legislative Council by James Brindley Bettington (1851–53), a merchant and pastoralist with 90,000 acres of leasehold land in western New South Wales, and Charles Wray Finch (1853–56) whose assets included several thousands of acres in the County of Wellington.[80] Both took their seat unopposed. Of the latter, a Bathurst newspaper noted: 'we have no reason to doubt … that the interests of the squatter will be faithfully represented in his votes'.[81] For the first 24 years of responsible government, the district's squatters put their faith in George William Lord (see Figure 1.3). Born in Sydney in 1818, the son of emancipist, merchant and landowner Simeon Lord and his wife Mary, he was educated in Sydney and took up land at Wellington in 1837. Lord was thoroughly embedded within the colony's landed elite, and typical of the wealthy, absentee members of rural electorates during this period, before better transport and (from 1889) payment for members made representation by locally based men possible. He was living in Sydney in 1856 when he became a member of the combined Pastoral Districts of Wellington and Bligh, which took in Molong, Wellington and Dubbo and stretched over a huge arc from the Lachlan in the south to the Warrego in the north, and out to Fort Bourke on the Darling. From 1858, he represented the new electorate of The Bogan, which also extended over much of the Wellington and Bligh pastoral districts, with Dubbo as the principal town, tucked close to the electorate's eastern fringe.[82] Lord was neither an active parliamentarian nor prone to

---

79   *SMH*, 15 January 1878, 5, 9 February 1878, 6; *ATCJ*, 16 February 1878, 14.

80   Nancy Gray, 'Bettington, James Brindley (1796–1857)', *Australian Dictionary of Biography*, National Centre of Biography, The Australian National University, published first in hardcopy 1969, adb.anu.edu.au/biography/bettington-james-brindley-2989/text4367; Parliament of New South Wales, 'Mr Charles Wray FINCH (1809–1873)', www.parliament.nsw.gov.au/members/formermembers/Pages/former-member-details.aspx?pk=338; *Empire*, 11 May 1853, 2; Enclosure, Gipps to Russell, 7 May 1840, *HRA*, Series I, vol. XX, 610.

81   *Bathurst Free Press and Mining Journal*, 26 March 185, 2.

82   David Henry, 'Lord, George William (1818–1880)', *Australian Dictionary of Biography*, National Centre of Biography, The Australian National University, published first in hardcopy 1974, adb.anu.edu.au/biography/lord-george-william-4037/text6417; Maxwell, *Australian Men of Mark*, vol. 2, 349–52; *NSW Government Gazette*, 23 November 1858, no. 197, 2088.

express strong ideological views. An 1875 audit of members' activity in the previous parliamentary session found that he had missed 210 of around 250 divisions.[83] Very early in his political career, one commentator observed:

> As a member of the Assembly, Mr Lord has never expressed an opinion on any subject whatever, nor would his votes afford any intelligible evidence that the honourable gentleman has adopted any definite political principles.[84]

Figure 1.3: George William Lord (1818–1880).
Source: State Library of New South Wales.

---

83   *Wagga Wagga Advertiser*, 1 September 1875, 4.
84   *Empire*, 29 December 1856, 4. See also *SMH*, 12 May 1880, 3; *Sydney Mail and New South Wales Advertiser*, 15 May 1880, 923.

But then, Lord was preoccupied with other matters, as he continued to run his considerable commercial and pastoral interests, including a directorship with the Commercial Banking Company. Notwithstanding his seemingly nonchalant approach to politics, Lord was consistently the squatters' preferred candidate, winning consecutive elections over 21 years, including four in which he was unopposed, before taking up a life membership of the Legislative Council in 1877. On the hustings in Dubbo before the 1860 election, at which Robertson's proposals for land reform were a central concern, Lord 'stated most emphatically that he was opposed to free selection'. However, as Loveday and Martin observe, once the land laws had been enacted in 1861, all politicians claimed to be liberals, and Lord was no exception.[85] By 1864, with land in the district about to become available for selection as pastoral leases expired, he assumed a neutral public position, claiming to regard squatters' and selectors' interests to be equally important.[86] Nevertheless, Lord's most conspicuous supporters were his fellow pastoralists, including John Ryrie and William Forlonge. He was of their ilk and a safer bet than more consistently liberal candidates.

Lord's rival candidates painted him as the absentee plutocrat and the pastoralists' ally. His rival in 1860, another Sydney man, auctioneer John Godfrey Cohen—a 'gentleman possessing liberal principles'—declared himself 'the poor man's friend' and advocated 'as far as practicable free selection'. By the late 1860s, the town of Dubbo was starting to assert some political strength against the pastoral elite.[87] In 1869, Lord was opposed by a local resident and the proprietor of the *Dubbo Dispatch*, Thomas Manning, who claimed that his newspaper rather than Lord's influence had prompted government spending on the region's infrastructure.[88] In 1872, Serisier challenged him. Since his years as a merchant in the town, he had bought a 4,000-acre property—'Eumalga'—south-east of Dubbo, where he ran cattle and established a vineyard and winery employing between 20 and 30 people. As a former police magistrate, postmaster, electoral returning officer and chair of the Dubbo Mechanics Institute, he was widely known and well-versed in public administration, but hardly a typical selector. Nevertheless, Serisier contested the election as 'a local man who had all his stake in the district' and, placing the contest over land at the centre of his campaign, favoured absentee, income and property taxes, and

85 Loveday and Martin, *Parliament Factions and Parties*, 25; *Empire*, 11 December 1860, 8.
86 *Empire*, 5 July 1859, 6; *SMH*, 27 December 1864, 2.
87 *Empire*, 11 December 1860, 8.
88 *Empire*, 15 December 1869, 3.

claimed to stand against 'the mammoth squatters'. As usual, Lord won with overwhelming support in the pastoral districts' booths. However, as a sign of the electorate's changing demographics and balance of interests, Serisier gathered around a quarter of the vote, and two of every five votes in the town.[89]

The selectors' response

Squatters responded to the threat of free selection in the 1870s not only through political influence and organisation as a class but also with plain intimidation. They are alleged to have poisoned selectors' animals and set fire to grass so as to endanger fences, crops, haystacks and buildings, as well as sponsoring dummying by 'overseers, shepherds, or others for the depasturing of their employers' flocks'.[90] Potential selectors claimed that they were dissuaded from taking up selections on the Warrie Flat because of Murrumbidgerie station owner William Forlonge's 'scheme of fencing in strategically, and using as a sheep-walk a large tract of country (for which he pays nothing), thereby intimidating parties from settling thereon'. Some selectors responded with direct action. Forlonge offered a £25 reward for a conviction when a mile of his fencing was destroyed and some of his sheep killed in 1873.[91]

In this context, and that same year, Serisier and others formed a Warrie and Dubbo Free Selectors Protection Association: the first clear acknowledgement among selectors of one part of the district that they shared the common experience of struggling to remain on the land in the face of pastoralists' hostility. As an employer and the owner of a substantial property, Serisier was unlike other members of the association, except that they bore a strong antipathy towards neighbouring squatters. The selectors' association appears to have lapsed, and there are few signs of overt, continuing conflict, suggesting that tensions escalated in testing economic times. A new Dubbo Freeholders and Free Selectors Association was formed in another drought

89   SMH, 5 March 1872, 3; Evening News, 13 March 1872, 2, 15 March 1872, 2; ATCJ, 9 October 1875, 19; Sydney Mail and New South Wales Advertiser, 9 March 1872, 303; D. I. McDonald, 'Serisier, Jean Emile (1824–1880)', Australian Dictionary of Biography, National Centre of Biography, The Australian National University, published first in hardcopy 1976, adb.anu.edu.au/biography/serisier-jean-emile-4559/text7479.
90   SMH, 17 December 1873, 7; Wagga Wagga Express and Murrumbidgee District Advertiser, 24 December 1873, 2.
91   ATCJ, 27 December 1873, 23; Empire, 10 November 1873, 3.

year, and again on Serisier's initiative, in September 1877, nine months after John Robertson's ceremonial visit.[92] This group's membership hints at the impediments to the emergence of a sustained class consciousness among local selectors. Serisier aside, they were a tiny gathering of small-scale farmers living within a few kilometres of the town on its eastern fringe, so probably familiar to one another but less connected with the hundreds of others in like circumstances who were scattered in other locations. The organisation included George Payne, a farmer with around 800 acres, who was also a builder and would be bankrupt by 1886; William Garnsey, who owned 482 acres on the Talbragar; George Oliver, with 82 acres, also on the Talbragar; and Mark Mathews, the blacksmith and carrier with a selection at Troy Gully.[93]

Tensions between established leaseholders and aspiring freeholders appear to have escalated as the drought wore on, despite one commentator suggesting that 'relations between Crown tenants and conditional purchasers in this district are very amicable, and I scarcely think the [new] association will be a success or a benefit'.[94] In a sign that the association was extending its remit beyond Dubbo's immediate surrounds to encompass a broader community of selectors, Serisier presented a petition to the premier in July 1878 pleading the case of a farmer further up the river, whose meagre 102 acres were hemmed in by water reserves created, it would seem, through an arrangement between surveyors and the owner of an adjoining Crown lease. The Dubbo association also considered the case of a selector even further afield, on the Haddon Rigg run near Warren, whose selections had been rendered unviable by reserves (most likely for water or travelling stock) created through subsequent surveys. That same year, the association drew up a petition urging that land along the railway line that was expected within a few years to be extended through Wellington to Dubbo not be offered for sale by auction. Garnsey, proposing the resolution, argued that around towns where large landowners held sway, such as Bathurst and Wellington, tenant farmers were forced to look for land elsewhere.[95]

92   *SMH*, 6 September 1877, 3, 27 September 1877, 5.
93   Land Registry Services (NSW), 'Historical Land Records Viewer', see parish and historical maps for the parishes of Dubbo, Beni and Warrie, 1884, accessed 22 March 2024, hlrv.nswlrs.com.au; George Goodman Payne, file no. 20395, NRS 13654, SARNSW; *DL*, 19 May 1914.
94   *SMH*, 6 September 1877, 3.
95   *ATCJ*, 6 July 1878, 16; *Sydney Mail and New South Wales Advertiser*, 13 July 1878, 54.

The language supporting the selectors' claims was telling also. In an early portent of farmers' appeal to one version of an agrarian vision as a uniting and distinguishing ideology, Garnsey argued that this land near Dubbo was best placed in the hands of agriculturalists who would:

> send their thousands of bushels of wheat and other produce to market, in the place of a couple of hundred or so bales of wool. Moreover, in the place of a solitary boundary rider … in a few years good homesteads, luxuriant gardens and fine crops would gladden the eye of the traveller.[96]

He was invoking an idea with deep roots in Western culture that was vigorously expressed in settler societies. In the United States, Thomas Jefferson's late eighteenth-century faith in the 'cultivators of the earth' as 'the most vigorous, the most independent, the most virtuous' was sustained through to Theodore Roosevelt's 1911 Commission on Rural Life, which arose from anxiety that this national ideal was unfulfilled: 'Not only in the natural wealth that they produce, but in the supply of independent and strong citizenship, the agricultural people constitute the very foundation of our national efficiency.'[97] Its Australian expression recalled a mythical, pre-industrial time in England, when land was in the hands of independent, virtuous and physically able cultivators in harmony with the earth. Even though 'the farmer' was so often represented as a lone and self-sufficient male, at the centre of the vision, as the essential source of propriety, productivity and *re*-productivity, was the family—man, woman and children. Therefore, according to the vision, the environment was at once testing and sufficiently benign to accommodate idealised qualities of masculinity and femininity, which stood in contrast to the corrupted and debilitating city. A national anxiety over the declining birth rate at the turn of the twentieth century, particularly in the cities, only strengthened the imperative to promote rural settlement in ways that nurtured fruitful and healthy families. Moderation was a part of the idyll too, with each household possessing just enough land for a family to abide without wasteful excess (what would be labelled a 'home maintenance area' under reforms to promote closer settlement from the 1890s). It was also a classless vision, a world without exploitation from a time before industrialisation set labour against capital. The rural idyll contained not just worthy people, but also selfless citizens,

---

96 *ATCJ*, 16 March 1878, 38.
97 Thomas Jefferson to John Jay, Paris, 23 August 1785, in Merrill D. Peterson, ed., *Jefferson: Writings* (New York: Library of America, 1984), 818; Commission on Country Life, *Report of the Commission on Country Life*, with an introduction by Theodore Roosevelt (New York: Sturgis and Walton, 1917), 17.

the ultimate source of wealth, strength and vigour for the nation, empire and race. Among its antitheses in Australia were the squatters, anathema to an orderly and civilised society, denying the land to industrious cultivators while squandering its potential by grazing sheep sparsely and improvidently across the landscape.[98] But the agrarian vision was more than theory and literary fantasy—it was also a powerful rhetorical tool that proponents of agricultural settlement had used to argue their case in parliaments across several colonies.[99] Then, in turn, farmers like Garnsey, alive to the imagery's political potential, weaponised it in their arguments for access to land laws and government amenities in the bush.

The Dubbo selectors' associations were not isolated phenomena; rather, they were part of a rising tide of agitation across rural New South Wales. In the space of a few years, selectors had formed associations in places as diverse as Wagga Wagga, Muswellbrook, Cooma, Grenfell and Yass.[100] Just as the Dubbo pastoralists had strengthened their hand by joining forces with similar associations across the colony, so too this small accretion of selectors in Dubbo's immediate hinterland added their modest weight to this patchy but growing movement. Just weeks after the Dubbo association reformed in 1877, Serisier joined a group of men from around rural New South Wales, gathered at the Imperial Hotel in Sydney for the first attempt to find a common, colony-wide voice for selectors. The impetus came from the south of the colony, the meeting chaired by George Adams, newspaper proprietor and land agent from Albury.[101] It was a rudimentary beginning. The group had no secretariat or continuing administrative presence, and no uniform regional structure; instead, delegates self-identified as representatives of whatever local association had formed. It was determinedly fixated on one basic issue: selectors' secure access to more land. But it was a beginning and, at the 1877 conference and a further gathering the following year, something like a class-based organisation emerged. The Sydney Working Men's Defence Association (WMDA) gave the selectors their first opportunity to define who they were and, as importantly, who they were not. The WMDA had only just formed to represent the interests of 'the labouring orders and struggling denizens' of the colony, with a program of opposing publicly

---

98   Kate Murphy, *Fears and Fantasies: Modernity, Gender, and the Rural-Urban Divide* (New York: Peter Lang, 2010), 35–43.
99   Williams, 'More and Smaller Is Better', 74–6; Martin, 'Pastoralists in the Legislative Assembly', 586.
100   *ATCJ*, 20 June 1874, 33, 20 March 1875, 19, 30 September 1876, 10, 26 May 1877, 15, 28 July 1877, 10.
101   *SMH*, 16 October 1877, 5; *Albury Banner and Wodonga Express*, 22 November 1918, 28; Martin, 'Pastoralists in the Legislative Assembly', 579.

funded immigration and supporting local manufacturing through tariff protection, payment of members of parliament and representation on the basis of population. They also supported reform of the land laws, and so approached the selectors to propose that the two groups amalgamate to form a National Reform League.[102] The selectors took little time to decline the overture on the grounds that they favoured immigration and free trade, but principally because they had just one objective in mind—to reform the colony's land laws. Their manifesto reflected these very specific objectives, listing the many ways they considered the laws favoured established leaseholders and impeded selectors. They resolved also to support at the forthcoming election only candidates who pledged to carry out the entire program of reform.[103]

Although no political party would emerge from these developments, the selectors' actions suggest a group with an incipient view of its class position, based on their common experience of owning and working the land (or aspiring to do so) as agriculturalists. Their refusal of an alliance with the workers of Sydney, even though it might have amplified their political voice, asserted a distinction from urban and working-class interests and identification. The group was determinedly rural. But they also asserted a moral distinction between themselves and those in the established pastoral sector who hindered their ambitions. In accordance with the agrarian idyll, they claimed to be acting in the interests of the whole country as 'men who improved the land', and as distinct from those who 'locked up' the land in sheep walks.[104] While pleading that they were the victims of unjust laws and practices, the leadership was nonetheless assertive and connected. At the end of a subsequent conference in October 1878, they presented their reaffirmed grievances to the minister for lands in person.[105]

Conclusion

The selectors had arrived over several decades as a fitful and miscellaneous cavalcade from various places, with different endowments of experience and capital, which they mostly applied to farming. Usually, by necessity, they

---

102 *Maitland Mercury and Hunter River General Advertiser*, 1 September 1877, 7; *Sydney Mail and New South Wales Advertiser*, 20 October 1877, 490.
103 *ATCJ*, 20 October 1877, 16, 27 October 1877, 24.
104 *SMH*, 17 October 1877, 5.
105 *Sydney Mail and New South Wales Advertiser*, 5 October 1878, 532; *SMH*, 15 October 1878, 6; *ATCJ*, 28 September 1878, 25.

complemented these by selling their labour or combining farming with other enterprises. The contest for land with established pastoralists affected them directly, dictating where they could settle and, in some cases, causing fractious relationships with their bigger neighbours. But many of them also relied on the pastoralists for employment, just as they relied on the town as a small local market for produce. Their circumstances were a product of a range of influences: legislative, environmental, economic and cultural.

Fifteen years after the passage of Robertson's land acts, Serisier was representing, at best, a small proportion of a loose, inchoate collective, huddled mostly on small blocks a short distance from the town, and occupying a space on a social and economic spectrum between the Indigenous, itinerant and marginalised on the one hand, and pastoral and mercantile interests on the other. That such an atypical freeholder—a relatively wealthy French former merchant—represented the Dubbo district indicates that Serisier was a remarkably energetic, perhaps charismatic, character able to draw together people in very different circumstances to his own. But it also proved that in the midst of a predominantly pastoral economy in the 1870s, the free selectors were a fragile, fragmented group, still struggling to turn their common experiences of acquiring and maintaining land in the face of powerful competing interests into political expression. Serisier died on a trip back to France in 1880 and, in his absence, the selectors would take some time to muster the cohesion and collective will to be heard again.

2

'And we are shunned and out in the cold': Schools and the making of community and class

In January 1895, James Gibbs, who farmed 640 acres at Comobella, wrote to an official of the Department of Public Instruction to make the case that he and his neighbours were entitled to a school in their vicinity. '*We are Farmers*', he emphasised:

> that have opened up this place & now find that if our children is to be educated we must sell out & go into some town to get it which is one of the chief reasons that causes many farms to become sheep walks which every Government is trying to avoid.[1]

Once more, a smallholder was harnessing an agrarian idyll to support a case on behalf of people who worked the land. Increasingly, they represented themselves not as *selectors*—emphasising the method by which they acquired the land—but as *farmers*, giving weight to their common occupation and relationship to the land. And their plea was to the government as the ultimate underwriter of the vision of a colony populated by productive and contented smallholders. That schools were so prominent in the evolving dialogue between farmers and government emphasised, too, that the vision was not just of an agricultural society, but also of families, consisting of

---

1   James Gibbs to Mr Garrard, 28 January 1895, Criefton School Administrative File, pre-1939, 5/15566.3, NRS 3829, SARNSW (emphasis added).

women and children as much as men, as its essential foundation. From the 1890s, settlers around Dubbo would often use these arguments as they sought government support for local schools, and in the process defined local communities of place, as well as locating themselves within a broader farming class.

New South Wales schooling to 1880

The first nine rural schools in the Dubbo farmlands were established under the 1866 *Public Schools Act* as the farmlands population grew denser between 1868 and 1879.[2] Designed to cultivate the virtues of regularity, cleanliness and orderly behaviour, the Act was the means by which the state sought to insert itself more methodically and assertively into colonial life—through a more unified, predominantly public, system of school education.[3] With small but growing rural communities in mind, the government supported several types of schools, varying according to the volume of attendance. Public schools required 25 children to attend regularly and had trained teachers. From 1875, the government met the whole cost of building the school. By contrast, provisional schools catered for an average attendance of between 12 and 20, and the teachers were mainly untrained (see Figure 2.1). These were supposed to be 'pioneer' schools that would gain pupils and convert to public schools once their catchments became more densely populated. In practice, though, many rural areas did not conform to a pattern of steady growth, and could never sustain more than a provisional school. For smaller communities still, half-time schools required an average attendance of from 9 to 12. A teacher would spend half their days at each of two locations, and the government met the costs of the salary and basic materials.[4] Between 1867 and 1879, the number of public schools across the colony increased from 159 to 671. There were also 300 provisional schools and 102 half-time schools.[5] In the Dubbo farmlands, the shifting population complicated planning, as the local inspector noted in 1880:

---

2   The schools were Ballarah, Brocklehurst, Buddenbelar, Buninyong, Maryvale, Minore, Mitchell's Creek Mine, Rawsonville (Belarbigal) and Spicers Creek. Though the qualitative evidence is clear, there are no meaningful statistics on the actual population in Dubbo's surrounds before 1891.

3   Alan Barcan, *A History of Australian Education* (Melbourne: Oxford University Press, 1980), 137–40.

4   New South Wales, *An Act to Make Better Provision for Public Education (Public Schools Act)*, no. 33a, 1866, sections 12 and 13.

5   Sir Henry Parkes, Public Instruction Bill, second reading speech, 20 November 1879, in New South Wales, Legislative Assembly, *Hansard* (Sydney: Government Printer, 1879), 264.

it is generally very difficult to decide on the best mode of dealing with applications for schools in rural localities, owing to the frequent and unforeseen changes of the population, with regard to number and position.[6]

Figure 2.1: Windora Provisional School, 1906.
Source: Wellington Historical Society.

The 1880 *Public Instruction Act* further advanced the liberal ideal of a 'free, compulsory and secular' education to remoter parts of the colony. Fees were reduced, and religious instruction was corralled more tightly. The minimum regular attendance needed to sustain a public school reduced from 25 to 20, but that still remained beyond the reach of many isolated communities. Cost impeded schooling in some parts of rural New South Wales, so by 1882 the government had agreed to meet two-thirds of the expense of building a provisional school, whereas previously local residents had to meet the whole cost. The following year, the requirement for locals to pay anything was removed entirely, though a limit on the government's contribution remained. Even still, some communities struggled to support such schools. The minister that year noted that the relevant schools were:

---

6   New South Wales, Department of Public Instruction, *Report of the Minister of Public Instruction for the Year 1880*, in *Votes and Proceedings of the Legislative Assembly*, vol. II, 1880–81 (Sydney: Government Printer, 1881), 53.

situated in the most sparsely populated and therefore the poorest districts; and the burden of defraying the necessary outlay has proved too heavy for the zealous, and a plausible excuse for those who were indifferent to the education of their children.[7]

Children between the ages of 6 and 14 were required to attend school for at least 140 days each year (around 70 per cent of the school year), though they could be exempt on several grounds, including: 'That there is no school maintained under the Act within 2 miles [3.2 kilometres] by the nearest road of the residence of the child.'[8] This would affect community formation in the farmlands.

Beyond the towns and villages, schools sprang up where there was a concentration of settlement on small, contiguous blocks, sometimes each of only 40 acres, typically near waterways in places such as Beni (on the Talbragar), Windora and Comobella (Mitchells Creek), Coalbaggie (Coalbaggie Creek), and Eschol and Belarbigal/Rawsonville (the Macquarie). In these sorts of places, people usually built the school themselves from local materials, roughly to specifications set out in regulations. The school at Comobella in 1882 was typical:

> The floor is in its natural state and consequently is very rough; the sides are made of split slabs, and the roof is covered with old box bark, through which the rains of winter will have no difficulty in finding numerous passages.[9]

The farmlands population was growing but it was also somewhat volatile, such that schools sometimes opened but then closed or were moved. A further 18 rural schools were established in the district between 1880 and 1888.[10] In 1887, in the broader Wellington schools district (encompassing Mudgee and Dubbo subdistricts), some new schools were established, but

---

7   New South Wales, Department of Public Instruction, *Report of the Minister of Public Instruction upon the Condition of Public Schools Established and Maintained under the Public Instruction Act of 1880, for 1882, New South Wales*, in *Votes and Proceedings of the Legislative Assembly*, vol. VII, 1883–84 (Sydney: Government Printer, 1884), 591.
8   New South Wales, *An Act to Make More Adequate Provision for Public Education*, no. 23, 1880, section 20 (iii).
9   Thomas Bond to the district inspector, 16 February 1882, Comobella School Administrative File, pre-1939, 5/15459.2, NRS 3829, SARNSW.
10   Ballimore, Ballimore Lower, Beni, Boothenba, Coalbaggie, Comobella, Dapper, Dulmane, Eschol, Eulomogo, Geurie, Gollan, Lincoln, Medway, Murrumbidgerie, Plain Creek, Willandra and Windora.

10 small schools closed due to low attendance.[11] With provisional and part-time schools sustained by such low numbers, just one household moving on could jeopardise a school's future. Notwithstanding the closures or intermittent functioning of some small schools, another six opened in the district for the first time between 1892 and 1899.[12] Schools were usually the only public buildings in the landscape (see Figure 2.2).[13]

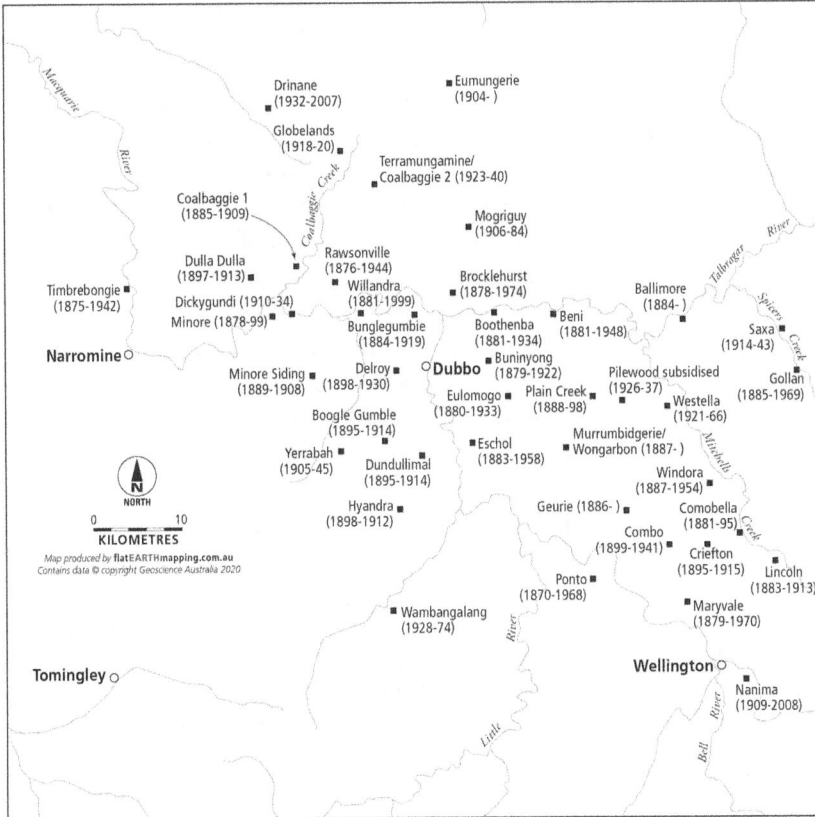

Figure 2.2: Dubbo district schools.
Source: Flat Earth Mapping.

---

11   New South Wales, Department of Public Instruction, *Report of the Minister of Public Instruction for the Year 1887*, in *Votes and Proceedings of the Legislative Assembly*, vol. IV, 1887–88 (Sydney: Government Printer, 1888), 137.

12   Bodangora, Combo, Criefton, Darralume, Dundullimal and Tucklan.

13   Dates represent the first year of opening as a half-time, provisional or public school, and the final closing date. Many of these schools changed status, or were closed for periods of time, between their dates of opening and final closing.

Schools and the creation of place

In places where selectors were taking up land, applying for a school was one of the first common, public purposes to emerge in an environment where most households were immersed in their own private objectives. Don Aitkin argues that farming people had a 'natural community of interest without the suspicion induced by competition', in that they sold homogenous products (wheat and wool) at prices set by distant markets so that one person's success need not be at the cost of another's.[14] While there might have been few grounds for antagonism among farmers, neither were there strong reasons for them to come together to regularly negotiate the terms of their co-location. Settlers had a rational self-interest in single-mindedly making their selections productive and complying with the conditions of their occupation. Balancing Aitkin's view is that of B. D. Graham, who argues that 'each settler's homestead was an island, apart and vulnerable, dependent almost entirely on the economic resources of the land and the human resources of the people who worked it'.[15] Under the terms of the 1861 and 1884 land acts, officials made annual inspections to verify that the selector resided on the land and had improved the property, such as by building fences and clearing land for cropping. Some men also spent time away as carriers and shearers to generate extra income. Thus, there were strong incentives for farming households either to devote their whole attention to their block or to seek income elsewhere until the farm became productive.

Communities of place emerged from the process of applying for government funding for schools in three ways: it provided a common purpose around which a community could coalesce; forced the definition of spatial boundaries; and caused settlers to create, adapt or affirm a name for a place. Three or four residents had to apply on behalf of the district. Several men generally formed a bespoke committee and worked with interested residents to complete a standard form. Applicants had to list the number, ages and denominations of eligible children from committed households. The 1880 report of the chief inspector for the district encompassing Dubbo suggests that residents did not always embrace the opportunity, and that cost could be a barrier:

---

14   Don Aitkin, '"Countrymindedness"—The Spread of an Idea', *Australian Cultural History* 4 (1985): 37.
15   B. D. Graham, *The Formation of the Australian Country Parties* (Canberra: Australian National University Press, 1966), 13.

> In some instances great difficulty has been experienced in getting the prescribed forms filled in and signed; and in only two cases have the applicants for the establishment of Public Schools been willing to erect temporary school rooms, so that the work of instruction could be commenced at once.[16]

But if some were reluctant, many others put their names to applications and pressed officials, local members and ministers to grant them a school and a teacher.

Everyone with children had a stake in establishing a school, which became a common interest based on location and aspiration. Committees had to enlist as many households with as many eligible children as possible to maximise the potential for government support—part of what Lucy Taksa describes as the 'integrative force' of place.[17] In 1879 the applicants for a school at Eulomogo appointed as their secretary a former carrier who had not long been in the district: he had just acquired a selection and moved with his new family from Newbridge near Blayney. Francis and Elizabeth Woodley had only one child, well below school age. Perhaps their new neighbours valued Francis's competence in writing and the forms of formal communication.[18] At Plain Creek in March 1887 Francis's brother Henry and Henry's wife Elizabeth, also just arrived from Newbridge, took up a selection. No available Crown land was suitable for a school site, and though the family would have no school-aged children until 1891, by November they had agreed to lease 2 acres back to the government at a peppercorn rent so that a provisional school could be built, their new property being the most central location for families then with eligible children in the district.[19]

This common purpose brought potential for cooperation, but also for conflict. Some residents complained directly to officials that the proposed locations for schools suited some more than others. In 1895, residents were negotiating to move the Comobella half-time school to a more central location, but one resident wanted it closer still to his house and protested to the department. The inspector reported: 'He hitherto has refused to join

16   See District Inspector Bridges's general report for 1880, in New South Wales, Department of Public Instruction, *Report of the Minister of Public Instruction for the Year 1880*, 57.
17   Lucy Taksa, 'Like a Bicycle, Forever Teetering between Individualism and Collectivism: Considering Community in Relation to Labour History', *Labour History*, no. 78 (2000): 28.
18   Francis Woodley to the Council of Education, 31 October 1879, Eulomogo School Administrative File, 5/15848.1, NRS 3829, SARNSW.
19   Inspector to the chief inspector, 7 December 1887, Eulomogo School Administrative File, 5/15848.1, NRS 3829, SARNSW (papers concerning the Plain Creek school are contained in the Eulomogo school file).

with other residents in establishing a school unless it were placed about a quarter of a mile north of his house.'[20] In a recently settled area on Mitchells Creek in 1906, just three families with a total of 12 children could benefit from a new school, but two of the households took their misgivings to the department:

> In reference to the proposed school at Westella on the property of F Anderson, having viewed [the] proposed site I may here state that the present site only suits the Anderson family being quite adjacent to their home while our children have fully 1½ miles to walk and we consider the proposed site of no use to us.

Differences must have been resolved, however, as only a few weeks later all three households put their names to the application for a school on Anderson's land. [21] In this way, the prospect of securing a government school introduced a new reason (sometimes the first) for people to negotiate towards a single, common objective that, if it were successful, would require a delineation of who was included and who was not.

Enlisting contiguous households to a common cause also defined spatial boundaries, part of what the rural sociologist Frank Vanclay describes as 'place-making'.[22] Applications were often accompanied by hand-drawn maps of a catchment area, with a 2-mile radius drawn around a proposed central site, and the locations of households with school-aged children plotted within the circle. People closest to a proposed site sought the cooperation of those who were more distant. Discord could arise where some families supported an alternative site for the school or a proposed site encroached on the territory claimed by an established school. If a school was under threat because of declining enrolments, people would readily assert their claims over those of adjacent schools.[23] Neighbours sharing a boundary fence could find themselves aligned with different schools and therefore different communities of at least one interest.

---

20   Inspector to the chief inspector, 18 February 1895, Criefton School Administrative File, pre-1939, 5/15566.3, NRS 3829, SARNSW.

21   A. S. Crothers to the under secretary, Department of Public Instruction, 30 July 1906, and application for the establishment of half-time schools, Westella, 8 August 1906, Ballimore School Administrative File, pre-1920, 5/14764.1, NRS 3829, SARNSW.

22   Frank Vanclay, 'Place Matters', in *Making Sense of Place: Exploring Concepts and Expressions of Place through Different Senses and Lenses*, ed. Frank Vanclay, Matthew Higgins and Adam Blackshaw (Canberra: National Museum of Australia, 2008), 4.

23   A Buninyong resident made a case to reopen the school rather than the one at neighbouring Eulomogo in 1926. See A. W. Druitt to the minister for education, 1 January 1926, Buninyong School Administrative File, pre-1939, 5/15171.2, NRS 3829, SARNSW.

Schools' influence on perceptions of spatial boundaries is borne out in an 1883 case where the local inspector recommended that the Comobella school be moved to a location between the residents who were using the school, and another group of around 15 settlers living 4 miles (6.4 kilometres) further north whose children were not attending a school at all. A correspondent living near the established school pointedly distinguished those who, like himself, opposed the move—the 'residents of Comobella'—from the settlers to the north for whom he styled a separate name:

> 1st[:] It is against the wishes of the residents of Comobella to remove it, 2nd[:] If there are sufficient children at the lower Mitchells Creek to form a school why do not the parents apply for one instead of wishing for a removal to the proposed site. [I]t will be too far for the greater part of the children now attending to walk.[24]

For the purposes of making his case, the correspondent was certain who was a part of Comobella and who was not. By attaching a name ('lower Mitchells Creek') to those who he asserted were not from Comobella, he insinuated a difference where perhaps in other circumstances it would not have been considered to exist. But access to the school distinguished his rationale.

The application process also contributed to a sense of place by creating, adapting or reinforcing a name. Naming attaches significance to a space and conflates space with the people who occupy it.[25] Irrespective of the name itself, the very act of naming and the subsequent embedding of the name in general discourse through maps, addresses, conversation and text distinguishes that place and the people who associate with it from others. People's identity, then, became bound up in the idea of a place. Though a school's name needed only to signify the building and its grounds, in practice it extended to a broader space equating to its catchment area and the people living within it. In 1877, residents at a place on the Talbragar River they called 'Erskin' claimed that theirs was a better location for a school than nearby Brocklehurst. Brocklehurst got the school, and the name Erskin never passed into common usage.[26]

---

24   [Name obscured] to the Department of Public Instruction, 8 August 1883, Comobella School Administrative File, pre-1939, 5/15459.2, NRS 3829, SARNSW.

25   Derek H. Alderman, 'Place, Naming and the Interpretation of Cultural Landscapes', in *The Ashgate Research Companion to Heritage and Identity*, ed. Brian Graham and Peter Howard (London: Routledge, 2008), 196. See also D. W. Meinig, 'Introduction', in *The Interpretation of Ordinary Landscapes: Geographical Essays*, ed. D. W. Meinig (Oxford: Oxford University Press, 1979), 3; Paul Carter, *The Road to Botany Bay: An Exploration of Landscape and History* (London: Faber and Faber, 1987), 67, 137–8.

26   W. Garnsey to the Council of Education, 7 September 1877, Brocklehurst School Administrative File, pre-1939, 5/15094, NRS 3829, SARNSW.

With a name and a notional physical boundary encompassing a school's catchment, people could start to think and talk of themselves as a community, but the building itself also contributed to this sense. Schools were valued as a rare public space in an increasingly privatised landscape. They did not need a public space in order to come together for social or political reasons, but they clearly preferred it. The Department of Public Instruction (later Education) received requests to use schools for social functions such as dances and farewells, and for meetings of local associations, such as the Rawsonville Farmers and Settlers Association branch (1912), the Ballimore Progress Association (1914), the Rawsonville Literary and Debating Society (1914), the Mogriguy Political Labour League (1915) and the Terramungamine branch of the Country Women's Association (CWA) in 1926.[27] Residents continued to maintain and use schools that had closed but remained the property of the department. The Windora branch of the CWA had to remind the department of the old school building's history in 1935:

> the Windora Branch has been using the old school building since 1931 … It is the only central & suitable meeting place in a widely spread locality & is also used by the Windora CWA Younger Set & Agricultural Bureau for meetings & social functions.[28]

In short, the process of applying for and maintaining a school introduced a common interest in space with a radius of 2 miles, and therefore a reason for people to talk, negotiate, define spatial and social boundaries, and create or affirm a name.

---

27   Hon. secretary of the Rawsonville FSA to the 'Department of Instruction', 27 March 1912, and Hon. secretary of the Rawsonville Literary and Debating Society to the secretary [Department of Education], 4 June 1914, Rawsonville School Administrative File, pre-1939, 5/17444.4, NRS 3829, SARNSW; Hon. secretary of the Ballimore Progress Association to the district inspector, 27 June 1914, Ballimore School Administrative File, 1884–1920, 5/14763.2, NRS 3829, SARNSW; Hon. secretary of the Mogriguy Political Labour League to the minister for education, [June 1915], Mogriguy School Administrative File, pre-1939, 5/16886.2, NRS 3829, SARNSW; Hon. secretary of the Terramungamine CWA to the inspector, 9 June 1926, Terramungamine School Administrative File, pre-1939, 5/17818.2, NRS 3829, SARNSW.
28   Hon. secretary of the Windora-Comobella CWA to the Department of Education, 26 October 1935, Windora School Administrative File, pre-1939, 5/18139.2, NRS 3829, SARNSW.

Schools and the 'farming class'

By the late 1890s, the processes of establishing and maintaining schools provoked the consistent claims of a 'farming class'. In their engagements with local members, ministers and public officials, communities represented themselves not as passive recipients of government largesse, but as equal parties to a contractual relationship whereby they provided their families' labour and constancy to cultivate and populate the country—to embody the agrarian vision—and, in turn, expected government, as the sponsors of that project, to contribute. In this period the state was asserting a role in more actively ameliorating the harsher aspects of economic and social life, including through enormous investment in public education, to create what Craig Campbell and Helen Proctor describe as 'a more orderly, loyal, better trained and educated, and altogether improved population'.[29] If the country was to be populated by stable and productive families, then schooling had to be extended to the whole of the colony. Country people negotiated to be a part of that project, their claims most often expressed as a demand to be treated equally with city dwellers. People expressed their arguments not just as generic citizens, or in terms of their specific community's or their children's needs, but also as either country dwellers or farmers.

The imagined farming community that emerged through these processes was persistently evoked over several decades and pitched to all sides of politics. In 1895, a Comobella resident, John Toynton, framed his case for government funding of a water tank for the local school in terms of rural disadvantage as compared with the city:

> we are all poor strugglers & it comes hard for us to build our own school simply because we are located a long ways apart for I think if it is looked into the Agriculturalist pay[s] more tax than any other individual.[30]

In complaining to his local member about the state of facilities at the local school in 1904–05, a farmer of Eschol also invoked the claim of rural disadvantage, but added that farmers held a special place as the ultimate source of a country's wealth:

---

29   Craig Campbell and Helen Proctor, *A History of Australian Schooling* (Crows Nest: Allen & Unwin, 2014), 140.
30   John W. Toynton to the under secretary, Department of Public Instruction, 12 September 1895, Criefton School Administrative File, pre-1939, 5/15566.3, NRS 3829, SARNSW.

Are not the people that tills the land as much entitled to justice and comfort as the city man[?]

Who does the city and town men get their bread from only him that toils on the land. Every crumb we get comes out of the land.[31]

Farmer Reggie Forlonge on Mitchells Creek also framed his case in terms of equity and rural disadvantage, contrasting his children's prospects with town dwellers' when he urged his local member to support the Westella half-time school's reopening in 1908:

It grieves me, Sir, to see my boys who will soon be able to go out into the world and do for themselves neglected in the way of Education, while children in townships have every care taken in them so that when they leave school they are able to face their occupations with zeal.[32]

And at Ballimore in 1919, Ellen Booth, on behalf of the local Parents and Citizens Committee, reprised these same arguments:

As the country people and the farmer generally are the backbone of the country we feel justified in claiming recognition, as we see so much comfort for town and city schools when ours have no advantage at all.[33]

These correspondents, along with Robert Patten (quoted in the Introduction), James Gibbs (at the beginning of this chapter) and others, cast themselves not just as representatives of a discrete local community, but also as country dwellers, and, more particularly, as farmers. The very term 'farmer' was invoked to stand not just for a group of people sharing an occupation or relationship with the means of production, but also as a calling, implying worthiness and self-sacrifice by those who worked the land and were the ultimate source of all wealth. They tapped into the longstanding conceptual divide between the city and the country that had particular currency in Australia from the 1890s as governments and others became increasingly concerned about the disproportionate growth in urban populations. And they were deploying the agrarian idyll (described in Chapter 1), attributing

---

31   C. J. Salter to T. H. Thrower [MLA], 9 December 1904, 19 January 1905, Eschol School Administrative File, pre-1939, 5/15838.1, NRS 3829, SARNSW.
32   Forlonge to C. H. Barton MLA, 27 November 1908, Ballimore School Administrative File, 1884–1920, 5/14763.2, NRS 3829, SARNSW.
33   Ellen Booth to the minister for education, 27 December 1919, Ballimore School Administrative File (1920–39), 5/14764.1, NRS 3829, SARNSW.

to farmers an intrinsic moral worth as productive, stable citizens engaged in the most wholesome means of earning a living. In the political sphere, these ideas would coalesce by the 1930s into the values and perspectives that Aitkin has labelled 'countrymindedness'.[34] The relationship between governments and communities over schools did not alone create the rhetoric of a 'farming class', but it did legitimise and amplify its expression at the intersection of the local and the colonial spheres by providing countless opportunities for its articulation.

Teachers, teaching and the bounds of community

Farming communities revealed their priorities and values in the ways they engaged with teachers and the regimes governing children's behaviour and learning during the prescribed hours of school. As Anthony P. Cohen argues, people become most acutely aware of their culture at its boundaries, for this is where they encounter others' cultures, bringing the differences that define their own into sharper relief. In farming places, a teacher could serve to define or emphasise those cultural boundaries and differences.[35] Teachers' presence highlighted who was considered to belong and who was not. Their sometimes-unique position in these increasingly homogeneous farming communities is evident in a correspondent's request for an extra mail delivery at Drill Creek in 1906, when he describes the population as 'thirty-one (31) families served by this mail, all of whom with an exception "a Public School teacher" are settled on the land (farmers)'.[36]

School buildings and timetables provided time, space and authority for teachers, but teachers still continually had to negotiate their place in the broader community. They were usually from somewhere else, though that did not, in itself, make them exceptional. Many people were. Once a teacher had been at the one school for a few years, they also saw people come and go. The longer-serving teachers could even be points of relative continuity.[37]

---

34   Aitkin, 'Countrymindedness', 34–41.
35   Anthony P. Cohen, 'Belonging: The Experience of Culture', in *Belonging: Identity and Social Organisation in British Rural Cultures*, ed. Anthony P. Cohen (Manchester: Manchester University Press, 1982), 2–3.
36   [Illegible] to the deputy postmaster general, 19 March 1906, Drill Creek Post Office File, part 1, 1904–11, box 227, SP32/1, NAA.
37   Teacher to the senior inspector of schools, 13 March 1905, Murrumbidgerie School Administrative File, pre-1939, 5/17017.1, NRS 3829, SARNSW.

Nonetheless, government-appointed teachers stood apart. They brought different knowledge and ways of working—with their intellect and book-learning rather than their hands—and they answered to distant officials who regulated and scrutinised their conduct, and dictated the timing of their arrival and departure.

New teachers' status as outsiders was emphasised when they had to negotiate accommodation. On pastoral stations there had been accommodation for both permanent employees and passing travellers, but with closer settlement, spaces set aside for non-residents largely disappeared. The school building was unquestionably the teacher's space during school hours, but for the remainder of the time, there was usually no alternative but to board in small private houses. In 1902, the minister's report noted this common problem:

> In isolated bush places ... the hardships that teachers have to endure in the way of food and lodging are such that in many cases they are compelled to relinquish charge by either resigning or seeking removal.[38]

The minister's 1909 report asserted that small schools could not continuously operate because of 'the unwillingness of the residents to provide reasonably comfortable accommodation for the teacher'.[39] In many cases, though, modest houses just had no suitable space for a boarder. A teacher at Minore had to sleep in the room used as a school in 1879, and a Comobella resident advised the department in 1892:

> If a teacher is coming you might recommend them to Mrs McLean for Board as she says she could manage it for the most of us our places are to[o] small.[40]

Where there *was* capacity, landlords had ultimate authority, so local residents had a powerful sanction if they were dissatisfied with the teacher. Teachers were present on locals' terms. A teacher at Cannonbar north-west of Dubbo resigned after a falling-out with local families:

38   New South Wales, Department of Public Instruction, *Report of the Minister for Public Instruction for the Year 1902*, in *Votes and Proceedings of the Legislative Assembly*, vol. III, 1903 (Sydney: Government Printer, 1903). See also New South Wales, Department of Public Instruction, *Report of the Minister for Public Instruction for the Year 1909*, in *Joint Volumes of Papers Presented to the Legislative Council and Legislative Assembly*, vol. I (Sydney: Government Printer, 1910), 25.

39   New South Wales, Department of Public Instruction, *Report of the Minister for Public Instruction for the Year 1909*, 25.

40   Inspector to chief inspector, 21 November 1879, Cannonbar School Administrative File, 5/15272.1, NRS 3829, SARNSW; John W. Toynton to the chief inspector, 17 May 1892, Criefton School Administrative File, pre-1939, 5/15566.3, NRS 3829, SARNSW.

> The few pupils in [the] locality enables parents to starve the teacher out at any time he should incur their displeasure. Knowing this the teacher is left entirely at their mercy.[41]

In 1914, the Ballimore teacher was 'ordered' to leave her landlord's house 'as speedily as possible' because she had administered what she described as a 'mild punishment' to the landlord's son. With no alternative accommodation in the area, she moved to Dubbo where she was assigned a position at the public school, and the school at Ballimore was closed.[42]

Outside of the school environment teachers were valued according to their capacity or willingness to 'fit in', but female teachers' experiences were strongly influenced by residents' notions of appropriate gender roles. Kay Whitehead has argued that the category of the female teacher was constructed variously during the first hundred years of compulsory education, but consistently in ways that 'troubled the gender order'. Though there was no formal marriage bar before 1932, until the 1940s female teachers were mainly young and single. With their relative autonomy over the daily life of the school, their economic independence and mobility, their presence challenged conservative norms concerning women's place in the family and the broader community.[43] Until tennis became a regular pastime in these districts from the early years of the twentieth century there were few, if any, public roles for young, single women, other than teaching Sunday school or piano. In 1899, a family at Coalbaggie Creek offered to provide board if the department would appoint a female teacher who could give piano lessons to their daughters.[44] Female teachers were treated paternalistically and assumed to be incompetent in matters beyond their teaching qualifications. They were expected to have a local man attest to the quality of any repairs made around the school. When the department asked Miss Johnson to explain

---

41   Teacher to the under secretary, Department of Public Instruction, 10 November 1882. This letter is located on a different school's file: Dapper School Administrative File, 5/15644.3, NRS 3829, SARNSW.

42   Teacher to the inspector of schools, 27 February 1914, Ballimore School Administrative File, 1884–1920, 5/14763.2, NRS 3829, SARNSW.

43   Kay Whitehead, 'The Spinster Teacher in Australia from the 1870s to the 1960s', *History of Education Review* 36, no. 1 (2007): 1–7.

44   Inspector to the chief inspector, 18 April 1899, Coalbaggie School Administrative File, pre-1939, 5/15418.1, NRS 3829, SARNSW.

her absence from school at Windora in 1909, she responded that the man of the house at which she boarded had 'prevented' her from walking to school on a very wet day.[45]

Teachers were frequently distressed by their isolation, exacerbated perhaps because they could more readily imagine being in other places. The teacher at Buninyong in 1896 was one of many across the farmlands who sought a transfer to the coast or Sydney because of the climate: 'I have been six years in this district and the hot weather has affected my health greatly so that I would like to get to a cooler climate.' In 1899, the teacher at Eschol asked for a transfer to Sydney: 'I have always been teaching in the country, and have had a fair share of "roughing it" and do not wish to spend another twelve months in the bush.'[46]

Social isolation could be equally distressing. There is no indication in the evidence that follows that communities actively excluded teachers from social events, but teachers often felt intensely alienated. In 1892, a female teacher was so overwhelmed that she just left, reporting to the inspector:

> As I cannot be content among the residents of Timbrebungie, I have closed the school today and am going home to Tomingley ... I can't live among some of the residents.[47]

Helena Gleeson, a teacher at Gollan in 1926, asked for a day's leave to coincide with the Ballimore carnival 12 miles away because all families in her district would be attending. She wrote her application on the day of the Geurie carnival when local people were also away:

> I have been here since 9A.M. 'Alone, alone, all, all alone'. There is not a soul within a radius of miles, & the few houses that are in sight are uninhabited today. It is dreadfully lonely in a small school in the Country on one's own.[48]

---

45   Teacher to the inspector of schools, 28 April 1903, Ballimore School Administrative File, 1884–1920, 5/14763.2, NRS 3829, SARNSW; Teacher to the acting chief inspector, [April 1909], Windora School Administrative File, pre-1939, 5/18139.2, NRS 3829, SARNSW.
46   Agnes MacDermott to the chief inspector, 17 November 1899, Eschol School Administrative File, pre-1939, 5/15838.1, NRS 3829, SARNSW.
47   Teacher to the inspector, 29 April 1892, Timbrebungie School Administrative File, pre-1939, 5/17848.3, NRS 3829, SARNSW.
48   Teacher to the inspector of schools, 22 September 1926, Gollan School Administrative File, pre-1939, 5/16063.1, NRS 3829, SARNSW.

In 1927, a young Westella teacher was anxious about the prospect of a forthcoming sports carnival and dance in a nearby village that everyone was likely to attend, meaning no children would be at school. Her letter to the department seeking leave for that day expresses her isolation:

> The residents all assist in the night's entertainment which means that I am alone on the farm during the night with the result that my nerves are properly unstrung next day. This was the case last week on the occasion of the Geurie Carnival & now I feel that I cannot spend another such night.[49]

Alienation did not affect only women. Francis Louis Kendall, the oldest son of the late renowned poet Henry Kendall, was appointed to the Coalbaggie school in September 1900. He was a highly educated, 29-year-old man with a bachelor of arts degree from the University of Sydney, including honours in classics, mathematics, logic and mental philosophy. He was overqualified and temperamentally unsuited to his position. By February 1901 he was asking the department to appoint him to a different school, due to the standard of the students at Coalbaggie and the company of the adults. Without naming the family with whom he boarded (the Kilbys), he wrote: 'Their social circle of ideas does not touch mine.'[50] Dan Kilby conveyed to the department that local parents were also keen for the teacher to find a new position, observing that he 'takes no delight in his school' and 'goes a bit melancholy at times'.[51] The local inspector confirmed to head office that the teacher spent too much time in 'private study, including learning German'. In time, Kilby's patience ran out, and on 24 March 1902, he wrote again to the department:

> we consider him peculiar in [h]is ways I think he is a bit touched in the upper storey I have taken my children away from the school I don't intend to send them any more while he is teaching at the school.

Finally, in July 1902, on the verge of being terminated, Kendall resigned.[52] The unspoken bounds of community were experienced most acutely by those beyond.

---

49 Teacher to the chief inspector of schools, 14 October 1927, Westella School Administrative File, pre-1939, 5/18090.3, NRS 3829, SARNSW. The application was denied.
50 F. L. Kendall to the inspector, 15 February 1901, Coalbaggie School Administrative File, pre-1939, 5/15418.1, NRS 3829, SARNSW.
51 Daniel Kilby to the inspector, 29 May 1901, Coalbaggie School Administrative File, pre-1939, 5/15418.1, NRS 3829, SARNSW.
52 Daniel Kilby to the inspector, 24 March 1902, Coalbaggie School Administrative File, pre-1939, 5/15418.1, NRS 3829, SARNSW; Francis Kendall to the under secretary for public instruction, 7 July 1902, Coalbaggie School Administrative File, pre-1939, 5/15418.1, NRS 3829, SARNSW.

If teachers did come to identify with the local community to the point of taking up local causes with departments and ministers, then inspectors firmly reminded them of where their allegiances as public servants should lie. When, in 1890, teacher Frederick Lovett wrote as honorary secretary of the Murrumbidgerie Progress Association to the minister for public instruction to complain about the quality of the school's accommodation, his inspector considered that Lovett had displayed 'censurable ignorance of his obligations to the service in which he is employed'. Once institutions such as local progress committees, branches of the Farmers and Settlers Association and sports clubs were formed, male teachers were often active in, and even catalysts of, communal activity. For women, on the other hand, the only way to become fully absorbed into a community was to marry a local man, which usually meant ceasing to be a teacher. Three female teachers at Windora married locally between 1907 and 1948.[53] On the whole, though, in the nineteenth century particularly, teachers were essentially outsiders, distinguished from the local population by their roles, those to whom they answered, often by their superior education, and by the fact that they either had the choice to be elsewhere or could be directed to leave. While they remained teachers, they might fulfil extracurricular roles, and could be respected and valued, but they could not be completely of that place.

Residents' responses to teachers' influence over children's behaviour, time and learning also revealed what they valued. In these places, education was regarded as a civilising force—a portal to the highly regarded qualities of orderliness and discipline. One of Kilby's complaints about Kendall was that he 'has no control over his children they just do what they like'.[54] In 1912, farmer Joseph Raines wrote to the minister:

> Just a few lines asking if you could see your way clear to open the provisional school at Ballimore as the children are running about in a wild state & speaking for my own they are in a neglected state as regards education.[55]

---

53 'Teachers at Windora School', 1887–1954, manuscript, Oxley Museum, Wellington NSW.
54 Daniel Kilby to the inspector, 24 March 1902, Coalbaggie School Administrative File, pre-1939, 5/15418.1, NRS 3829, SARNSW.
55 Joseph Raines to the minister for public instruction, 8 December 1912, Ballimore School Administrative File, 1884–1920, 5/14763.2, NRS 3829, SARNSW.

Parents insisted that their children be treated fairly, both as compared with other children and according to standards of proportionate punishment. They were willing to cede control of their children's behaviour during school hours, but only on terms they considered just. Inspectors would interview all parties and adjudicate on a teacher's behaviour when disputes arose. James Gibbs complained when his daughter was sent home from Criefton school in 1895 for refusing a direction from the teacher:

> He sent my girl home therefore I think it my duty to keep all my children at home wile [sic] he has charge of the school. I take it as a mean insult to take such a step.[56]

Teachers also brought different rhythms to farming districts, shaped by rules rather than season, by bureaucracy and not nature. Whereas most farm events were governed by hours of daylight or seasons of cultivation, harvesting, lambing and shearing, school days and terms were prescribed in regulations that also required that teachers 'conduct the operations of their Schools with punctuality and regularity'.[57] Moreover, the seasonal call on children's labour routinely negated school timetables. Older children stayed away if they were needed for farm work, particularly for shearing and harvest.[58] At the same time, people also valued regular, predictable school hours. In 1909, parents complained that the head teacher at Brocklehurst sometimes opened the school late, and that 'unpunctuality teaches the children bad habits'.[59]

People also worked around prescribed school timetables to avoid hot weather and accommodate local events. Individual school communities negotiated earlier starts and closures of the school day in summer to avoid the hottest hours. In 1900, the Eschol school community held a picnic (only the teacher was at school that day), and by the 1930s annual picnics or sports days were commonplace across the region.[60] Sometimes the organisers asked the department to excuse children from school for the day. Most often, though, the teacher would inform the department after the event that,

---

56 James Gibbs to the Hon J. Garrard, 27 November 1885, Criefton School Administrative File, pre-1939, 5/15566.3, NRS 3829, SARNSW.
57 New South Wales, Department of Public Instruction, *Report of the Minister of Public Instruction for the Year 1880*, 20, appendix C [Regulations for Carrying Out the Provisions of the Public Instruction Act of 1880], regulations 66 and 57.
58 For further analysis of children as a source of farm labour, see Chapter 4, this volume.
59 Inspector to the chief inspector, 26 February 1909, Brocklehurst School Administrative File, pre-1939, 5/15094, NRS 3829, SARNSW.
60 Teacher to the inspector, 4 April 1900, Eschol School Administrative File, pre-1939, 5/15838.1, NRS 3829, SARNSW.

though she or he had attended school, *none* of the children had. There were typically foot races for children and adults, novelty events such as stepping 50 yards, three-legged races and sheaf tossing. The day's activities were often followed by a dance in the evening.[61] It was an annual, non-negotiable and all-inclusive part of local culture.

Though people asserted ultimate control over the regulation of their children's behaviour and time, they supported the idea of a period of formal, structured education according to a common, state-sanctioned curriculum. Campbell and Proctor have contended that 'many parents resisted the new public schooling', while Pavla Cook and others maintain that working-class South Australians railed against the incursion of these values identified with middle-class urban society through public schooling.[62] In Dubbo's farmlands, however, schools' records are noticeably silent on residents' views about the content of their children's education. If there was a hegemonic purpose behind schooling, bringing urban bourgeois values to all parts of the colony, then farming people did not particularly object and, in fact, appeared to embrace it. What seems to have mattered most was that their children could participate in the project of nation-building through education on the same terms as town and city dwellers. In this respect, people's conceptual boundaries were broad. As we have seen, depending on the circumstance, they might have identified with a community defined by the school's catchment area, with farming or with country people. In this case, though, they aligned with a broader aspiring middle class that regarded education as a prerequisite to a better life and respectability for their children.

In summary, teachers and schools were agents and reminders of a world beyond in these small farming communities. In the ways they dealt with teachers and the rhythms they brought with them, local people revealed something of themselves and what they valued. They welcomed the teacher who participated in community life beyond the school; however, at least until the early twentieth century, there were few structures around which a teacher could shape a contribution. In their dealings with female teachers,

---

61   These occasions were often reported in the Dubbo and Wellington newspapers. Examples include *DD*, 16 October 1901, 2 (Beni), 31 May 1911, 1 (Rawsonville), 2 October 1925, 2 (Coalbaggie). Schools also routinely closed for one day for either the Dubbo or Wellington annual show (see Chapter 8, this volume).

62   Campbell and Proctor, *A History of Australian Schooling*, 83; Pavla Cook, Ian Davey and Malcolm Vick, 'Capitalism and Working Class Schooling in Late Nineteenth Century South Australia', *ANZHES Journal* 8, no. 2 (1979): 36–48.

people showed that they held to as stringent a set of views about gendered roles as most in colonial and British society at the time. People sought out schooling for their children but seemed more concerned that they had the same privileges of access to schooling as children from the town and the city than with the content of the education. Seasonal demand for children's labour took precedence, as did annual social events and shows. People valued the teacher who conducted an orderly and disciplined school but could be quick to assert parental authority if they considered that their children were being unfairly treated. Whether education was an egalitarian and democratic vehicle for disseminating universal standards of education or an instrument of hegemony, rural communities generally managed the relationship with teachers and the regimes they introduced on their own terms.

Schools and the limits of community

The extent of community—of boundaries and otherness—could be expressed in who was included in or excluded from schools. The regulations linking entitlements to government funding to potential enrolments encouraged communities to include all potential households. But what of racial differences? At least in some instances, the schooling experience of Aboriginal children and families revealed deep divisions, though the archival evidence is sparse and to some extent ambiguous. With the land increasingly privatised and enclosed, and the family farm being the predominant model of production, many Wiradjuri people had little opportunity, incentive or encouragement to reside outside of either the Talbragar Reserve north of Dubbo (from 1899) or the Nanima Reserve east of Wellington (from 1910).

From 1902, the longstanding but ad hoc practice of excluding Aboriginal children from many rural schools was supported by a general, but often muddled and probably illegal, government policy that was justified on the flimsiest grounds—namely, that other residents complained.[63] In 1908, 12 of the 36 school-aged children who lived on the Nanima Reserve attended the public school in Wellington. The local inspector reported: 'A few of the children attend the Wellington School, but not very regularly, and many of the white inhabitants of the town object strongly to their presence.'

---

63   J. J. Fletcher, *Clean, Clad and Courteous: A History of Aboriginal Education in New South Wales* (Carlton: J Fletcher, 1989); Campbell and Proctor, *A History of Australian Schooling*, 127–30; Heather Goodall, *Invasion to Embassy: Land in Aboriginal Politics in New South Wales, 1770–1972* (Sydney: Sydney University Press, 2008 (first published 1996)), 130–2, 175–6, 252–3.

Evidently feeling no necessity to explain or justify such objections, he simply recommended: 'It is, I consider, advisable to educate these children in a school of their own, and so to keep them from the white children', thus reinforcing the local Aboriginal population's segregation. The Aborigines Protection Board built a school on the reserve and the Department of Public Instruction supplied a teacher. A year later the reserve, with the school, was moved 2 miles further from the town.[64]

The bounds defining some people's ideas of community played out in similar scenarios near Dubbo decades later. Children from the Talbragar Reserve had been attending Brocklehurst Public School for around 40 years (see Figure 2.3) when, in 1933, two white parents agitated to have their children taught by correspondence rather than attend the same school as Indigenous students. The department's chief inspector responded to the complainants' advocate George Wilson, a grazier and the local state Country Party member: 'There does not appear to be any strong local objection to the attendance of the dark pupils.'[65] The chief inspector's main concern was that the school would close for want of sufficient pupils if either the 10 Aboriginal or the 15 non-Aboriginal children withdrew. Nevertheless, in 1935 the Aboriginal children were excluded from the school because one parent complained. As at Wellington in 1908, the complainants generally gave no explicit reason, which suggests a construction of a community encompassing a racial divide so embedded that it did not require explication, even though the position was contested, most vocally by the local Presbyterian Church. A newspaper reported that the teacher and all other parents presented a petition to allow the children to return, but David Drummond, the education minister in the United Australia Party – Country Party government, upheld the decision.[66] A grazier on the Talbragar Shire Council expressed himself plainly:

> I quite agree with the objection … It seems to me that only one woman has had the 'inside' to object to them. It is not right to allow them to go to the same school as white children.[67]

64 'Nanima: Summary Report on Application for the Establishment of a Public School for Aborigines and Recommendation, and Queries to be Answered by Inspectors When Reporting upon Applications for the Establishment of Schools', 22 February 1908, Nanima School Administrative File, pre-1939, 5/17051.1, NRS 3829, SARNSW.
65 Chief inspector to G. A. L. Wilson, 12 April 1933, Brocklehurst School Administrative File, pre-1939, 5/15094, NRS 3829, SARNSW.
66 *DL*, 9 July 1935, 2, 20 August 1935, 5; *SMH*, 10 July 1935, 10; *Newcastle Sun*, 4 July 1935, 16.
67 *DL*, 13 July 1935, 3. See also Jack Horner, *Vote Ferguson for Aboriginal Freedom* (Sydney: Australian and New Zealand Book Company, 1974), 45.

Figure 2.3: Brocklehurst Public School, 1912.
Source: Local Studies Collection, Dubbo Regional Council.

The Dubbo branch of the Australian Labor Party urged that either the children be allowed to return to the school, or a separate school be built on the reserve. The council recommended the latter approach, which was adopted and framed in self-congratulatory tones as the solution to extending education to children living on the reserve, rather than a way to exclude them from a 'public' school that would now be exclusively white.[68]

Brocklehurst parents' voices—both Indigenous and non-Indigenous—are muted in the surviving record. At face value, most residents had regarded Aboriginal children as part of the community for decades; however, it is possible that this position had been influenced by the need to maintain enrolments. The schooling experience could highlight a boundary—though sometimes blurred and not universally recognised—separating Aboriginal from non-Aboriginal people. Those who sought to mark it more clearly were, at least in the cases examined here, supported by people in authority, though not invariably by other parents.

---

68   *SMH*, 15 July 1935, 12; *Daily Examiner*, 17 July 1935, 4; *National Advocate*, 23 July 1935, 3; *DL*, 27 August 1935, 6.

Apex and decline

The pattern of communities forming around advocacy for a school continued well into the twentieth century, repeated whenever populations thickened as land opened up for closer settlement schemes or new railways were completed. As former pupils became the next generation of parents, the shared experience of schooling, and a collective memory, embedded a sense of communities of place. As the director of education reported in 1909: 'Some are averse [to school closures] on sentimental grounds. They like the idea of their children attending the little school where they themselves were taught.'[69]

But by the 1920s, other demographic, technological and policy changes had the potential to disrupt the communities of place constructed around local schools. As average property sizes increased (notwithstanding closer settlement schemes) and birth rates declined, there was not enough population density to support more schools. In the combined Talbragar and Cobbora shires, the population of children under 15 years of age fell from 3,202 in 1921 to 2,405 in 1947.[70] The number of schools in Dubbo's hinterland reached its zenith during the period 1911–20 when around 37 schools operated for at least some of those years. However, in each decade from the 1920s to the 1950s there were more closures than openings.

Governments also tried to contain the expense of country schools, estimated in 1902 to cost £10 per pupil per year, as compared with £3 in cities and towns.[71] The notional radius of a school's catchment area remained 2 miles but became less relevant to schools' futures. Revised legislation in 1916 required that, with the aid of a 'conveyance', children were expected to attend school, in the words of the minister, even if the distance was 'much greater'.[72] Within a few years, people were also becoming more mobile. Children still travelled to school on horseback or by horse and sulky into the 1940s and 1950s, but cars and trucks were increasingly common in rural

69   'Report of the Director for Education', in New South Wales, Department of Public Instruction, *Report of the Minister for Public Instruction for the Year 1909*, 36.
70   Commonwealth Bureau of Census and Statistics, *Census of the Commonwealth of Australia Taken for the Night between the 3rd and 4th April, 1921* (Melbourne: Government Printer, [1921]); Commonwealth Bureau of Census and Statistics, *Census of the Commonwealth of Australia, 30th June 1947* (Canberra: Government Printer, [1948]).
71   New South Wales, Department of Public Instruction, *Report of the Minister for Public Instruction for the Year 1902*, 13.
72   New South Wales, *Parliamentary Debates*, second series, session 1915–16, vol. LX and vol. LXIII (Sydney: Government Printer, 1916); New South Wales, *Public Instruction (Amendment) Act*, no. 51, 1916.

areas from the 1920s (see Chapter 6). Amid these changes, schools continued to exert a centripetal force over surrounding areas, even if the impetus came increasingly from efforts to keep a school open rather than to establish a new one, and other facilities—halls, tennis courts, churches—that followed in more established communities also served to define communities of place (see Chapter 7).

Conclusion

A school, or the prospect of a school, was a tangible continuing stimulus or provocation: a reason to engage with distant authority, to negotiate and organise locally, to define who was local and who was not, to name a place and define its boundaries, and to contrast customary behaviours and priorities to others. The nature and extent of a community—its social and spatial boundaries—varied according to the question, stress or encounter to which people were responding at any one time. This is not to say that such expressions were inconsistent but rather multidimensional. People did construct and identify with a place but could just as readily align themselves with an imagined community of country dwellers, a class of farmers, or implicitly with a broader middle class, depending on the circumstance. Schools and schooling were not the only factors in these processes of community and class formation, but they contributed. These processes did not so much reflect the existence of communities as actively aid in their construction.

Community and class formation were contingent on government policies and programs. Farmers deployed to their advantage the rhetoric of an agrarian idyll that underpinned the grand project to populate rural New South Wales with families of smaller-scale agriculturalists. As the ultimate source of land and infrastructure, the government became the new 'other' against which farmers increasingly asserted their grievances as a class, and the standard of provision in cities became the benchmark for what should be offered in the bush. They built their identities in the process of interacting with the state and in the course of articulating their values and interests.

3

'Making a poor man poorer': Credit and debt

In 1913, 22-year-old Albert Mawbey took up a 430-acre block on an area set aside for closer settlement, about 20 kilometres from Wongarbon on what was once part of Murrumbidgerie station. In 1916, he put his farming on hold to enlist in the Australian Imperial Force (see Figure 3.1). He served as an infantryman in France, was wounded and, in 1919, returned to Australia and his block. He applied to have waived the interest that his debt on the purchase of land had accrued while he was on active service (it was partially agreed) and used his returned serviceman's war gratuity bond of £75 11s 6d to reduce his outstanding commitments.[1]

Debt, however, pervaded Mawbey's life from then on. He often sought forbearance from his main creditor, the Department of Lands, received visits from its local inspector who advised the department about his competence and prospects, and negotiated with the local store the terms on which he could continue to obtain basic supplies between wheat cheques. In 1927, Mawbey virtually dared the department to foreclose, challenging the officials to find someone more energetic than himself to work the block. In 15 years his return was less than the interest he would have earned with the money he had started with:

> If the Dept thinks I'm not trying to get along why not just put me out of it and put some[one] else in[.] I feel I can get a living at something else while I am only getting an existence here.[2]

---

1   *NSW Government Gazette*, 8 January 1913, no. 2, 128; 'Mawbey Albert', Service File, item 8215845, B2455, NAA.
2   Mawbey to the under secretary, Department of Lands, 22 October 1927, Soldier Settlement Loan File, 11139 (A. Mawbey), NRS 8058, SARNSW.

Figure 3.1: Albert Mawbey (1890–1963).
Source: Lois Jones.

While no two farmers' circumstances were identical, Mawbey's experience of seemingly chronic indebtedness was common during the period between the wars. The district surveyor had observed in relation to one of Mawbey's neighbours in 1923: 'from my general knowledge of the District I should say that this Settler like the vast majority of other settlers in the West, is not financially strong'.[3] For smaller-scale mixed farmers, including those participating in closer settlement schemes, credit was fundamental to remaining on the land. Some farmers started with capital obtained via inheritance or accumulated through their own labour, but rural debt rose far more rapidly in the early 1930s than in the economy as a whole, and it is reasonable to assume that, over time, almost every landholder in the Dubbo district would have incurred debt in one form or another.[4]

Transactions involving credit and debt might be considered procedural or incidental aspects of business, but they can be intensely social. In response to the notion that 'Economic Man's' decision-making is completely separate from his social context, some writers contend that the production, distribution and exchange of goods and services is, in fact, an integral aspect of human interaction. It is embedded in, and can only be fully understood with reference to, the social.[5] The American sociologist Mark Granovetter argues that economic activity is neither completely independent of social contexts nor entirely subsumed within them. Rather, people's social context is influenced by their economic decision-making and, in turn, is shaped and iteratively refined by those decisions.[6] Moreover, credit can be a source of power that extends beyond the economic sphere—the disparity of status between creditor and debtor is only resolved when the debt has been repaid. Pierre Bourdieu described it as the 'exercise of gentle violence'.[7] So, what *were* the experiences of indebted households of the Dubbo farmlands? How did debt operate as one of the multiple, changing, reinforcing or contradictory influences on the formation and character of communities?

---

3   District surveyor to the under secretary for lands, 15 May 1923, Soldier Settlement Loan File, 5684 (W. Pile), NRS 8058, SARNSW. The settler was W. J. Callaghan who occupied the block before Pile obtained it.

4   C. B. Schedvin, *Australia and the Great Depression: A Study of Economic Development and Policy in the 1920s and 1930s* (Sydney: Sydney University Press, 1970), 292–3.

5   David Graeber, *Debt: The First 5,000 Years* (Brooklyn: Melville House, 2014), 33; Margot C. Finn, *The Character of Credit: Personal Debt in English Culture, 1740–1914* (Cambridge: Cambridge University Press, 2003), 5–6; Karl Polanyi, *The Great Transformation: The Political and Economic Origins of Our Times* (Boston: Beacon Press, 2001); E. P. Thompson, 'The Moral Economy of the English Crowd in the Eighteenth Century', *Past and Present* 50, no. 1 (1971): 76–136.

6   Mark Granovetter, 'Economic Action and Social Structure: The Problem of Embeddedness', *American Journal of Sociology* 19, no. 3 (1985): 486, 493; Thomas L. Haskell and Richard F. Teichgraeber III, 'Introduction: The Culture of the Market', in *The Culture of the Market: Historical Essays*, ed. Thomas L. Haskell and Richard F. Teichgraeber III (Cambridge: Cambridge University Press, 1993), 2–3.

7   Graeber, *Debt*, 302; Pierre Bourdieu, *Outline of a Theory of Practice*, trans. Richard Nice (Cambridge: Cambridge University Press, 1977), 193, quoted in Finn, *The Character of Credit*, 9–10.

The extent of rural debt

Debt had pervaded Australian farmers' experience from the 1860s. In New South Wales, free selection involved settlers receiving 'land credit', in that they needed only to pay to the government a quarter of the cost of the land up front to make immediate use of a block. The selector rendered the remaining instalments over three years or paid interest on the outstanding balance after that time. In theory, this arrangement meant people of lesser means could gain a foothold, retaining more capital with which to make their selection productive. In effect though, few had any significant resources behind them, and they had limited prospects of turning a block into a productive enterprise within a few years. This scenario was reprised in the closer and soldier settlement schemes of the early twentieth century.[8]

Land credit aside, in this predominantly developmental phase of farming, households generated whatever capital they could through their own labour, but otherwise relied for equipment and working capital on an untidy mix of credit through storekeepers and produce merchants, family and others. Even in the 1920s, storekeepers' credit was an essential part of many people's lives, not just farmers'. Bankrupt Murrumbidgerie fettler John McNamara well understood the importance to rural dwellers of transactional or 'carry on' credit. In 1895, he described the relationship between labourers and storekeepers:

> In the bush circumstances compel labourers to get credit and storekeepers to give it. If a workman had always to have sufficient property to pay his debts as they became due all trade would be paralysed and both labourer and storekeeper would have to starve and go naked.[9]

Storekeepers were among several supplementary sources of credit to the nineteenth-century pastoral industry, but to smaller agricultural and mixed farming concerns they were integral, tied to their customers by bonds of mutual dependence expressed through long accounts of goods supplied but still to be paid for. Farmers also borrowed from local people who lent spare capital as an incidental aspect of their business. Lending was probably more

---

8   Evidence of early settlers' lack of capital comes from several sources. See B 899–B 917, SLNSW; MLMSS 301, SLNSW; NRS 13654, SARNSW; NRS 13655, SARNSW; New South Wales, *Report of Inquiry into the State of the Public Lands, and the Operation of the Land Laws*, in *Votes and Proceedings of the Legislative Assembly*, vol. II, 1883 (Sydney: Government Printer, 1883), 54–5.
9   File no. 10324 (McNamara), NRS 13655, SARNSW.

opportunistic than routine, but solicitors particularly knew how to secure their advances. In the mid-1890s, Josiah Cantrill received a loan from a Dubbo solicitor in exchange for a mortgage over what appeared to be all his assets: 'wagon, dray, 18 D[raft] horses, 18 sets of harness, 2 binders, 3 ploughs, buggy and harness, all furniture, 24 cattle'. Larger, more established farmers or graziers, typically with roots in the older squatting class, also lent money to smaller farmers and, like the Dubbo businesses, secured these advances with mortgages or other instruments over the debtor's assets.[10] Farmers sold seed wheat and fodder to other farmers, sometimes on credit, and, finally, it is unremarkable that a farmer's own family was often a source of unsecured credit.[11]

From the late nineteenth century, local sources of credit played a diminishing role. Stores tightened credit in the early years of the Federation drought (1897–1904).[12] As agriculture became more mechanised, machinery manufacturers and their agents supplied the new combine harvesters on credit, generally secured with promissory notes attached to regular instalments. Settlers who produced wool could also obtain 'carry on' credit from buyers pending the sale of their annual clip, with the firms supplying competitively priced finance as an adjunct to their main business.[13] By the mid-1930s, debts owed to storekeepers represented just 1.5 per cent of wheat growers' total debt, unsecured private lending a further 3.1 per cent, while state and commercial banks and government agencies provided more than half of wheat growers' credit.[14]

10 File nos 11611 (Harris), 10837 (Cantrill), 15460 (Reakes), 17923 (Hennessy), 11699 (Birch), NRS 13655, SARNSW.
11 For example, C. P. Inspector, Inspection of Returned Soldiers' Holdings, 2 September 1924, Soldier Settlement Loan File, 10365 (Lingard), NRS 8058, SARNSW; W. Gorrie, Application for Postponement of – or Extension of Time to Pay – Interest on Instalments, 21 May 1932, Soldier Settlement Loan File, 10142 (W. Gorrie), NRS 8058, SARNSW.
12 New South Wales, *Twentieth Annual Report of the Department of Lands Being for the Year 1899*, in *Votes and Proceedings of the Legislative Assembly*, vol. III, 1900 (Sydney: Government Printer, 1901), 9.
13 Simon Ville, *The Rural Entrepreneurs: A History of the Stock and Station Agent Industry in Australia and New Zealand* (Cambridge: Cambridge University Press, 2000), 80–6.
14 Commonwealth of Australia, *Royal Commission on the Wheat, Flour and Bread Industries, Supplement to the First Report of the Commission*, in *Papers Presented to Parliament*, vol. 4 (Canberra: Government Printer, 1934), 99–100, 103.

The expansion of government and private banking credit coincided with a substantial escalation of wheat growers' debt, which increased in New South Wales by about 90 per cent between 1915 and 1920, fell the following year, then increased seven-fold between 1921 and 1934. This coincided with a period of falling wheat prices. As the Great Depression hit in 1930–31, wheat growers' returns per bushel fell to less than a quarter of their peak in 1919–20.[15] Farmers' circumstances were not improved when they sowed more wheat in the 1930 season in response to the Commonwealth government's promise of a guaranteed price per bushel—the ill-fated 'Grow More Wheat' campaign—only for the Senate to block the necessary legislation. By 1934, only about 6 per cent of New South Wales farmers carried debts of less than £100 (about 30 times the minimum weekly wage). Forty per cent of Australian wheat farmers could meet their interest commitments only so long as they maintained themselves on an 'austere standard'. Another 26 per cent could continue only if interest commitments were adjusted, and 34 per cent incurred costs of production and interest such that an interest adjustment alone could not save them. Without more drastic remediation, they were destined to become insolvent.[16]

As capital arrived in larger quantities from institutional lenders, no farmer could escape the fact that they and their peers were tied into vast flows of credit both as part of a broader economy and of a national project to sustain a class of smallholders. Governments' and banks' roles in supplying credit introduced different relationships for farmers to negotiate. As a part of those networks, farmers were not only producers or suppliers but also more entrenched as debtors, with all of the moral weight and judgement attached to that status.

15   Commonwealth Bureau of Census and Statistics, *Official Year Book of New South Wales, No. 53, 1950–51* (Sydney: Government Printer, 1955), 749.
16   Edgars Dunsdorfs, *The Australian Wheat-Growing Industry, 1788–1948* (Carlton: Melbourne University Press, 1956), 425; Commonwealth of Australia, *Royal Commission on the Wheat, Flour and Bread Industries*, 104, 108.

The banks

The wool industry had drawn banks to the west since they secured the right to lend against leased Crown land in the 1850s, with credit also secured through liens on wool, mortgages on stock and station assets, and as overdrafts attached to pastoralists' current accounts.[17] Banks and other lenders operated over all rural regions of the colony, but they concentrated on the pastoral sector.[18] Dubbo attracted banks' attention early in this period. The Commercial Bank opened a branch there in 1865 and in 1867 moved into a substantial two-storey sandstone building in a town still largely fabricated from wood (see Figure 3.2). The Bank of New South Wales transferred its Wellington branch to Dubbo in 1868, a sign of the shifting locus of pastoral wealth towards the country further out.[19]

Figure 3.2: Commercial Bank, Dubbo, c. 1873.
Source: Local Studies Collection, Dubbo Regional Council.

17   This paragraph draws on N. G. Butlin, *Investment in Australian Economic Development* (Canberra: Department of Economic History, Research School of Social Sciences, The Australian National University, 1972), 57–147; N. G. Butlin and A. Barnard, 'Pastoral Finance and Capital Requirements, 1860–1960', in *The Simple Fleece: Studies in the Australian Wool Industry*, ed. Alan Barnard (Parkville: Melbourne University Press in association with The Australian National University, 1962), 383–400.
18   Ville, *The Rural Entrepreneurs*, 74–101.
19   *SMH*, 14 February 1865, 4, 26 January 1867, 5, 29 October 1868, 2.

The agricultural sector was less attractive, being dispersed, its markets constrained (until the advent of railways), and banks uncertain about the security that small farmers could offer.[20] Standard banking products did not always meet farmers' needs, and private banks were content to leave to the government the responsibility for lending to primary industry.[21] Banks were not entirely uninterested though. By the 1880s lending through Bank of New South Wales country branches was based largely on the security of conditionally purchased land, and by 1912 advances for agriculture represented 28 per cent of the bank's 'productive lending'.[22] Further afield, the National Bank was lending extensively to small farmers in Victoria, at high rates of interest to cover uncertain security, but on more favourable terms than storekeepers and other lenders offered.[23] Pastoralism might have been more attractive to the banks; however, by the mid-1930s state and private banks provided 15.0 per cent and 24.4 per cent of wheat growers' secured credit, respectively.[24] Around Dubbo, in the country between Eulomogo and Wongarbon south-east of the town, the proportion of privately owned land that was mortgaged rose from negligible levels before the 1890s, to a quarter or more by the early 1900s, and over 30 per cent by the early 1930s.[25]

A farmer's relationship with their bank manager influenced their prospects and their local standing. It also reinforced qualities considered fundamental to being a good farmer. Local managers understood farming practices and markets, and acquired a thorough knowledge of their clients' assets, prospects and foibles based on the previous managers' advice, local intelligence and their own personal engagement. They kept notes of every

20   R. F. Holder, *Bank of New South Wales: A History*, vol. 1 (Sydney: Angus & Robertson, 1970), 376; Ville, *The Rural Entrepreneurs*, 78.

21   New South Wales, Legislative Council, *Fourth Interim Report from the Select Committee on the Conditions and Prospects of the Agricultural Industry and Methods of Improving the Same, Dealing with Rural Credit and Finance; Together with the Appendices and Minutes of Evidence* (Sydney: Government Printer, 1920), iii. See also Duncan Waterson, *Squatter, Selector and Storekeeper: A History of the Darling Downs 1859–93* (Sydney: Sydney University Press, 1968), 171; S. J. Butlin, *Australia and New Zealand Bank: The Bank of Australasia and the Union Bank of Australia Limited, 1828–1951* (Croydon: Longmans, 1961), 322.

22   Holder, *Bank of New South Wales*, vol. 1, 376, vol. 2, 547.

23   Geoffrey Blainey, *Gold and Paper: A History of the National Bank of Australasia Limited* (Melbourne: Georgian House, 1958), 94–5. Waterson notes that by the 1890s the Bank of New South Wales and the Australian Joint Stock Bank were open to doing business with smaller farmers in Queensland. See Waterson, *Squatter, Selector and Storekeeper*, 173.

24   Commonwealth of Australia, *Royal Commission on the Wheat, Flour and Bread Industries*, 99–100.

25   Peter Woodley, 'Financial Institutions and Land Ownership in the Dubbo District: a Sample Survey, 1884–1931', unpublished paper, 2021.

meeting, and wrote brief portraits of each client, describing their risk profile and value to the bank. Managers personally inspected properties proffered as security for an advance. Occasionally, banks presumed to provide direct advice to clients on their business. In November 1923, the manager of the Bank of New South Wales met with a soldier settler, recently arrived from Forbes, who 'hinted that he might require £20 to take his crop off but I told him it was too early to say whether there would be any crop this year'.[26]

Banks required people seeking advances (or 'accommodation') to provide summaries of assets, liabilities and anticipated future income, as well as quite specific and prosaic details about their immediate challenges and intentions. In November 1933, the Bank of New South Wales noted, concerning one of its farming clients, that:

> He burnt out a big end of his lorry engine & it will cost him £20. Is stripping wheat and will sell some as soon as he can but it may be January before a sale is made if weather is bad.[27]

Bankers also exchanged information with other creditors around the town and beyond. For example, the local branch of the Bank of Australasia sought information from the Department of Lands in 1929 concerning James Falconer, a struggling soldier settler on a farm near Wongarbon. The department held a lien over Falconer's crop to protect a forthcoming instalment on its loan:

> I would be pleased to know what your Department's attitude is on this matter: i.e. how much of the possible Crop proceeds you intend taking; for until this is estimated and known, it is certain that a man in his position can look to no assistance from his Banker or Storekeeper, and I would like to have the facts cleared up, and his position clarified.[28]

The precise details of the arrangement between a farmer and the bank might have been confidential, but accepting credit involved having one's financial position shared with other creditors.

---

26   Series S01-0051, item 80-13-193, folio 22, Westpac Group Archives.
27   Series S01-0051, item 80-13-188, folio 21, Westpac Group Archives.
28   Dubbo branch manager of the Bank of Australasia to the under secretary for lands, 26 February 1929, Soldier Settlement Loan File, 10717 (Falconer), NRS 8058, SARNSW.

Yet just as important as the crude arithmetic of material assets and liabilities was a client's standing and character—what the historian Margot Finn describes as 'a metonym for the fluid constellation of attributes recognised as signifiers of personal credit'.[29] The Bank of New South Wales' standard issue notebook for managers included space for recording 'particulars of *character, standing and means*'.[30] In 1921, the New South Wales Board of Trade argued that character played a more prominent role in determining a farmer's access to credit than for those involved in secondary industry:

> He is a great borrower, but he wants loans for long periods, and not on short call, and the security that he offers is so related to the element of his personal character that it differs from other commercial pursuits.[31]

A narrow range of qualities defined clients the banks considered worthy. Above all, bank managers wanted to avoid surprises—to be confident that they knew who they were dealing with—so common epithets attached to valued clients included 'honest', 'steady', 'reliable', 'careful' and 'straightforward'. Banks valued sobriety, predictability and self-awareness more often than business acumen or flair. A Eulomogo farmer on a modest 360 acres is described as 'a good safe man'.[32] Worthy customers were also commonly described as 'hardworking', the bank valuing the assurance that a farming household's labour was fully supplementing the land and capital. The bank's summation of farmer and widow Sarah Kilfoyle is that 'she is a hard working woman', as well as 'very straightforward and reliable'.[33]

The managers' rare censorious judgements are just as revealing. The bank concluded that a pair of brothers:

> did not appear to be able to curtail their expenditure to meet the times. Their chief aim seems to [be to] enjoy life, think they know a lot and will not acknowledge the seriousness of their position.[34]

29   Finn, *The Character of Credit*, 18–19.
30   Series S01-0051, item 80-13-193, Westpac Group Archives (emphasis added).
31   New South Wales Board of Trade, 'Declaration', *NSW Government Gazette*, 28 October 1921, no. 159, 6121.
32   Series S01-0051, item 80-13-193, folio 176, Westpac Group Archives.
33   Series S01-0051, item 80-13-192, folios 26, 72, Westpac Group Archives.
34   Series S01-0051, item 80-13-191, folio 101, Westpac Group Archives.

One entry cautioned that a client 'makes promises he cannot keep'.[35] Another client was denied unsecured credit, the manager observing that he 'is a reliable young man when sober but drinks at times & loses his head & squanders money at racing meetings'.[36]

In other cases, farming clients were simply portrayed as being worthy 'types', implying qualities of breeding or inheritance. One client was described as 'a particularly fine type, hardworking and capable', and another thus: 'he is Sec[retary] for Farmers and Settlers Mogriguy and seems the right type of man to be assisted'.[37] Managers were also expected to assess 'standing', perhaps a proxy for affirmation of the client's wealth and character, but also the prospect that the client's investment in their local reputation was in itself a form of security for the bank. As Simon Ville suggests, 'standing' also implied that the client could depend on networks of other farmers to provide advice and support, and direct other potential customers to the lender.[38] Such social capital could accumulate (or dissipate) over several generations. A name could carry weight in bankers' assessments of risk. One client was described in 1926 as being of 'good character and [a] member of a well-known district family', and another in 1927 as the 'son of … our valued client … Fine stamp of farmer'.[39] Families contributed not just standing but also material security. Many farmers were able to secure credit because their parents acted as guarantors, such that one generation was leveraging the assets of another.[40]

Many farmers engaged with banks in ways that indicate they understood and accepted constructions of the hierarchical relationship between creditor and debtor, and the deep cultural meaning attached to indebtedness or the dishonouring of debt. Richard Hillier, a Ballimore farmer, sounded, if not obsequious, then at least highly deferential when he sought a temporary increase in his overdraft limit in 1929 to cover shearing costs until the clip sold:

> I hope to pay some back as soon as we get money for clip back. I may not want that much. I will be as light as possible. Hoping I am not asking to[o] much of [a] favour from you.[41]

---

35   Series S01-0051, item 80-13-193, folio 36, Westpac Group Archives.
36   Series S01-0051, item 80-13-193, folio 104, Westpac Group Archives.
37   Series S01-0051, item 80-13-193, folios 80, 182, Westpac Group Archives.
38   Ville, *The Rural Entrepreneurs*, 92.
39   Series S01-0051, item 80-13-193, folios 82, 126, Westpac Group Archives.
40   There are many instances of which just a sample can be seen at series S01-0051, item 80-13-193, folios, 80, 86, 120, 140, 190, 197, Westpac Group Archives.
41   Series S01-0051, item 80-13-193, folio 140, Westpac Group Archives.

In October 1938, after a protracted drought, a farmer with a longstanding loan faced the prospect of not being able to meet an interest instalment unless rain within a few weeks was to revive his struggling crops. The manager noted the farmer's distress: 'Told him to let us know how he gets on with crop & not to worry too much, was much affected during interview about his inability to meet interest.'[42]

This fundamental understanding of the banks' ultimate power did not prevent farmers from engaging closely with their local manager, readily volunteering information in frequent and familiar exchanges of intelligence, and negotiations of minor adjustments to overdraft limits as the season, markets, illness and other exigencies required. Managers recorded serendipitous meetings with client farmers on the street, a reminder of the local and personal nature of these institutional transactions.[43]

Farmers and graziers could also push back if they considered banks to be too intrusive. Customers had a putative choice: if they felt denied or insulted they could take their business to another bank, though wealthier clients might have had more options than others in these circumstances. The Bank of New South Wales took on a well-off client in 1929 after he had left the Bank of Australasia 'over some trifling disagreement about the securities they asked him to sign' for an advance to buy a property.[44]

As the 1930s unfolded and the Depression's effects abated with slowly improving returns on wheat, many farmers, both wealthy and of relatively modest means, worked with overdraft limits from the commercial banks to increase their productive capacity or to meet immediate costs in anticipation of imminent income. They had to prove to their creditors that they possessed the steadiness, sobriety, honesty and penchant for hard work that the image of the yeoman farmer demanded—thereby demonstrating the illusory nature of independence. The agrarian project was hardwired into broader flows of both produce and capital. There were others, though, with insufficient assets to interest the banks. They had different relationships with creditors. It was this cohort that governments stepped in to support from the late nineteenth century.

---

42 Series S01-0051, item 80-13-191, folios 79–80, Westpac Group Archives.
43 For example, series S01-0051, item 80-13-188, folios 22, 55, 64; item 80-13-191, folio 99, Westpac Group Archives.
44 Series S01-0051, item 80-13-193, folio 142, Westpac Group Archives.

Government as creditor

Governments provided credit to smallholders when the private sector would not take on the risk. Credit in this context came with a different culture. Whereas a high proportion of banks' business was in the form of 'investment credit' to enable borrowers to expand assets and productivity from an established base, governments often provided 'transaction credit' to allow a borrower to make essential early investments while they sought to make their farm productive, and just to survive.

The New South Wales government's first foray into rural financing targeted farmers needing 'carry on' loans during the Federation drought. It established the Advance to Settlers Board in 1899 to manage loans of up to £200 to 'settlers in necessitous circumstances who were financially embarrassed owing to recent and existing droughts', with terms of up to 10 years.[45] Some city members of parliament asserted that the legislation discriminated against other, particularly urban, classes. Francis Cotton, journalist, early member of the Labor Electoral League, follower of Henry George's Single Tax and member for Newtown-Camperdown, claimed that 'there is no more right to advance money at a low rate of interest to people farming than to advance money to a Redfern boot factory or a jam factory in Newtown'.[46] Others were concerned that the government's insistence that it hold the first mortgage over a grantee's assets would exclude any farmer already receiving credit from a private lender, or that the government was improperly taking on a role in rural financing for the longer term. The bill's proponents insisted that it was an emergency measure prompted by the worst consecutive years of drought since European occupation. And, tellingly, they argued on the basis of farmers' contributions to the agrarian project, which governments had sought to create, and therefore were obliged to sustain. In the heat of debate, Andrew Ross, medical doctor, Protectionist and member of Molong, considered it relevant to note that:

> Go where you will—in America, on the Continent of Europe, and in Australia—you will always find that the farmer, the yeoman, is in reality the bulwark of the prosperity of the nation.[47]

45 New South Wales, *Twentieth Annual Report of the Department of Lands Being for the Year 1899*, 9; Commonwealth Bureau of Census and Statistics, *Official Year Book of New South Wales 1904–05* (Sydney: Government Printer, 1906), 323.
46 New South Wales, *Parliamentary Debates*, first session 1899, second session of the Eighteenth Parliament (Sydney: Government Printer, 1899), 523.
47 New South Wales, *Parliamentary Debates*, first session 1899, 516.

In time the experiment did become entrenched, with the function's transfer to the Advance Department of the Government Savings Bank in 1906, and in 1920 its scope was extended with the establishment of the Rural Bank Department.[48]

Despite these initiatives, a scarcity of credit continued to impede rural settlement. The 1920 Inquiry into the Conditions and Prospects of the Agricultural Industry in New South Wales concluded that banks were ill-equipped to provide the longer-term accommodations the rural sector needed:

> there exists only a most unsatisfactory and haphazard method of financing the farmers in a period of difficulty when he needs an advance to enable him to carry on ... Unless something much better can be devised there may be a breakdown in the work of settling people on the lands as farmers and producers.[49]

Schemes providing government-sponsored credit for farmers continued to emerge from time to time, as either temporary solutions to economic downturns or attempts at systemic reform. In 1919, the state government offered advances of up to £100,

> with a view to relieving the deep distress being suffered by farmers and settlers in districts where continued losses in past seasons and drought and bush fires in the present season... [coincided with] the inability of storekeepers, &c., to any longer supply on credit.[50]

The Rural Industries Branch of the Department of Lands was established late in 1919 to consolidate the administration of lending to farmers. Throughout the 1920s the branch provided loans for seed wheat, fodder, tractor fuel, stores and superphosphate on the advice of local boards.[51]

---

48 Commonwealth of Australia, *Report of the Royal Commission Appointed to Inquire into the Monetary and Banking Systems*, in *Parliamentary Papers*, vol. 5 (Canberra: Government Printer, 1937), 33. See also Commonwealth Bureau of Census, *Official Year Book of New South Wales, 1934–35* (Sydney: Government Printer, 1937), 581–4.
49 New South Wales, Legislative Council, *Fourth Interim Report from the Select Committee on the Conditions and Prospects of the Agricultural Industry*, v.
50 New South Wales, *Fortieth Report of the Department of Lands Being for the Year Ended 30 June 1919*, in *Joint Volumes of Papers Presented to the Legislative Council and Legislative Assembly* (Sydney: Government Printer, 1920), 3.
51 For example, Soldier Settlement Loan files: 11139 (A. Mawbey), 10717 (Falconer), 10406 (Barling), 9885 (Bransgrove), 7434 (C. Penfold), NRS 8058, SARNSW; New South Wales, Legislative Council, *Fourth Interim Report from the Select Committee on the Conditions and Prospects of the Agricultural Industry*, v.

Government financing of rural settlement was further consolidated with soldier settlement. Building on closer settlement schemes that immediately preceded the war, the *Returned Soldiers Settlement Act* 1916 (NSW) enabled repatriated soldiers to apply for blocks purchased by the government and to pay for them in instalments. Returned soldiers could also borrow up to £625 from the Returned Soldiers Settlement Branch to purchase essential items such as machinery, clearing, water conservation, working stock and seed wheat. The government secured its various advances with mortgages over settlers' machinery and stock, and annual liens over crops and wool.

The most widely held view of the post–World War I soldier settlement schemes is that they failed. Marilyn Lake estimates that at least half the people who took up land under the Victorian scheme were no longer on their blocks by 1938.[52] The 1927 Commonwealth Royal Commission on soldier settlement excoriated the states' schemes, concluding that they 'failed' because of unsuitable settlers (due to disabilities arising from war service and want of training), falling prices, blocks that were too small and, most of all, unrelenting debt. Most settlers started out paying interest on the total value of the land and on advances used to acquire materials and labour at inflated postwar prices, so their debt exceeded the value of their mortgaged assets from the beginning. The commissioner, Justice Pike, concluded:

> The position to my mind became an impossible one … [A]lthough the men were industrious and hardworking and would under ordinary circumstances succeed as farmers, the load of debt was so heavy that it was impossible for them to carry on.[53]

Other than the few who took on these obligations with existing capital or family support, soldier settlers and others involved in closer settlement schemes in the Dubbo district were consistently encumbered until well into the 1930s, if they survived on their blocks that long. Through consecutive poor seasons in 1921, 1922 and 1923, crops produced little more than fodder and seed wheat for the next season. After another poor harvest in 1928, Albert Mawbey's brother and neighbour, Garnet, expressed to his creditor the frustrations of many in his circumstances:

---

52 Marilyn Lake, *The Limits of Hope: Soldier Settlement in Victoria, 1915–38* (Melbourne: Oxford University Press, 1987), 137. See also, Richard Waterhouse, *The Vision Splendid: A Social and Cultural History of Rural Australia* (Fremantle: Curtin University Books, Fremantle Arts Centre Press in partnership with Curtin University of Technology, 2005), 198–203; Ken Fry, 'Soldier Settlement and the Australian Agrarian Myth after the First World War', *Labour History*, no. 48 (1985): 29–43.

53 Justice Pike, *Report on the Losses Due to Soldier Settlement*, in *Papers Presented to Parliament*, vol. II (Canberra: Government Printer, 1929).

> We cannot produce wheat in dry seasons and we are entitle[d] to
> live, so your penal interest won't make us pay because we can't, and
> it is making a poor man poorer.[54]

The point in this context, though, is not so much whether the scheme
succeeded or failed. Our main concern is to assess how the experience of
indebtedness and soldier settlers' relationships with government officials
and fellow farmers affected their sense of being a part of a community of
farmers—of a class. As debtors, soldier settlers were enmeshed in a series of
relationships either with people they would otherwise not have encountered,
or on terms that would not have applied in other circumstances. They
engaged with both the distant sources of decision-making in Sydney and
the local delegates of that authority: repatriation committees, surveyors
and inspectors whose advice informed those remote decisions. Their
experiences were different to those with sufficient assets to obtain credit
from commercial banks.

Soldier settlers' chronic indebtedness diminished their independence of
judgement and decision-making. Until the ledger was balanced, the farmer
not only had to repay principal and interest but also had to cede some
control of their farms. Local inspectors visited settlers' properties at least
annually and reported on the farmer's efforts over the preceding year,
and their prospects. Sydney officials decided the terms of access to credit,
including adjustments or accommodations in response to seasonal and other
unforeseen circumstances. Informed by the inspectors' advice, the Returned
Soldiers Settlement Branch often allowed repayment to be postponed, but
the terms were issued more in the nature of instructions than as the result
of a negotiation. Concessions concerning repayments required the farmer
to grant a lien over crops and wool, and to commit to sowing and leaving
fallow minimum acreages. Most official communication also appears to
have been in writing, between settlers and Sydney officials, as compared
with commercial bank procedures whereby most clients communicated in
person with the local manager.

In their correspondence, both internally and with soldier settlers, Sydney-
based officials used similar markers of character to those deployed by banks
to assess farmers' worth. However, they also judged debtors in terms of
their 'deservedness'. The term implied that the extension of credit or debt

---

54 G. L. Mawbey to the Department of Lands, 10 May 1928, Soldier Settlement Loan File, 5757
(G. L. Mawbey), NRS 8058, SARNSW.

relief was in the nature of an indulgence, an act of charity or of largesse rather than a settlement between equals. The local inspector considered the Mawbeys' neighbour Charles Penfold to be 'an industrious and deserving settler'; however, after a particularly poor harvest in 1928, his creditors still felt entitled to supplement their concessions on his repayments with a gratuitous direction: that he 'should make a special effort during the coming season to retrieve his position'.[55]

Nevertheless, the Dubbo district soldier settlers retained some control within their relationships with creditors. Lake, drawing on Victorian evidence, argues that the state's surveillance resulted in 'a complete loss of autonomy' for soldier settlers. The Dubbo records, though, are more consistent with Bruce Scates and Melanie Oppenheimer's findings that the exercise of authority was qualified: surveillance was 'imperfect and haphazard'.[56] Faced with the state's aim to control settlers' affairs as a trade-off for preferential access to land and credit (however inadequate it might have been), many responded assertively and articulately to these challenges to their autonomy, local standing and character.

Some were irritated by distant officials' lack of understanding of local farming rhythms and practices. In 1922, 35-year-old Nelson Booth, a former driver with a machine-gun company in France, was farming on a block near Narromine. He resented the standard demand for repayments at specific intervals that did not necessarily align with the times of year when farmers could expect a return on their crop or wool clip. He pointed out to the department that 'the end of the harvest is the only time we receive any money, & that is the time most farmers meet their big debts'.[57] Booth owed a quarterly instalment in April 1922, but referred the branch to the established local practice of exchanging promissory notes as standard instruments of exchange:

---

55 Returned Soldier Branch memo, 18 January 1929, Soldier Settlement Loan Files, 7434 (C. Penfold), NRS 8058, SARNSW.

56 Bruce Scates and Melanie Oppenheimer, '"I Intend To Get Justice": The Moral Economy of Soldier Settlement', *Labour History and the Great War, Labour History*, no. 106 (2014): 229–53; Bruce Scates and Melanie Oppenheimer, *The Last Battle: Soldier Settlement in Australia, 1916–1939* (Cambridge: Cambridge University Press, 2016), 24–34; Lake, *The Limits of Hope*, 75.

57 'Booth, Horatio Nelson', Service File, item 3099094, B2455, NAA; Booth to the Returned Soldiers Settlement Branch, 29 April 1922, Soldier Settlement Loan File, 3644 (N. H. Booth), NRS 8058, SARNSW.

> It is impossible for me to meet this amount now … I can't see why the dept cannot accept my P[romissory] N[ote] as all other business firms are doing it to Farmers, as they know that is the only time we get payments.[58]

English-born Joseph Thompson of Maryvale was just as forthright, pointing out to officials that seasons did not align with arbitrary payment cycles:

> As soon as I sell my wheat this little matter will be attended to, about the middle of May … I have earmarked £120 for your department & you'll get it, so don't worry me with these quarterly notices[,] they are no good to me[.] I get my money once a year & you'll get yours when I get mine see.[59]

In 1924, Booth sought the department's authority to sell a piece of machinery over which the Crown held a mortgage, so he could buy a better drill to sow his next crop. The paperwork took too long, so he later wrote to withdraw the request: 'as I have had my crop in 7 weeks, & and it is up & looking well, the exchange is useless to me now'.[60] Such experiences can only have strengthened soldier settlers' consciousness of their common interests. Each communication founded on misaligned language or misunderstandings of farming practices stiffened a belief in the alterity of the city, and the superior practical and moral foundations of rural life.

Place and personal engagement influenced the ways people related to the government as creditor. Whereas customers regarded their obligations to banks as at least equivalent to those of other creditors, some soldier settlers preferred to repay local lenders rather than remote agencies and resisted government demands that might interfere with those more immediate relationships. Charles Penfold asked for leniency from his government creditors in 1924 after his crop was frost affected, 'as the stores will be up against me for the first payment'. Albert Mawbey urged the department to take a lesser amount in return for a lien it held over his crop in 1932 so that he could pay off a 'large private debt' to local businesses: 'it would assist me in reducing those amounts considerably to my creditors who have assisted

58   Booth to the Returned Soldiers Settlement Branch, 26 April 1922, Soldier Settlement Loan File, 3644 (N. H. Booth), NRS 8058, SARNSW.
59   Thompson to the Returned Soldiers Settlement Branch, 5 December 1921, Soldier Settlement Loan File, 3957 (J. Thompson), NRS 8058, SARNSW.
60   Booth to the Returned Soldiers Settlement Branch, 7 July 1924, undated 1922, Soldier Settlement Loan File, 3644 (N. H. Booth), NRS 8058, SARNSW. See also May to the Soldier Settlement Board, 7 June 1921, Soldier Settlement Loan File, 6475 (E. C. N. May), NRS 8058, SARNSW.

me to carry on through adverse seasons and low prices'.[61] Thus, even when local stores were likely to require formal security over their advances, farmers often prioritised creditors with whom they had frequent, personal contact over more distant and abstract institutions, particularly the government, which they regarded as having an obligation to settlers as the architects of the grand aspiration to establish smallholders on the land.[62]

In their dealings with government creditors, soldier settlers around Dubbo could assert principles of fairness and entitlement, but they also understood and accepted that creditworthiness hinged fundamentally on evidence of good character, and the qualities necessary to play their part in the agrarian project. Though he was frustrated by officials' seeming ignorance of local arrangements for managing credit, Nelson Booth nevertheless assured them in 1922 that he was doing his 'best to make good & pay the dept back for the help received', and again later that year: 'I am trying hard to pay my way and make a success of it'.[63] Narromine farmer Robert Kenny sought to have a scheduled repayment postponed in 1922:

> I faithfully promise to meet my obligations … & have work ahead of me that will ensure my having the money by then … Hoping you will see fit to grant me this indulgence.[64]

For some, part of their argument concerning their contribution to the project was that the government was getting not just the soldier settler, but also a family. English-born William Pile, on a farm at Plain Creek, wrote to the Department of Lands in 1929:

> Kindly do your best to help a man that is trying to help himself & Country. I might also mention that I am an incapacitated returned Soldier & have a wife and four children to support.[65]

---

61 Penfold to the Department of Lands, 10 January 1924, Soldier Settlement Loan File, 7434 (C. Penfold), NRS 8058, SARNSW; Mawbey to the under secretary for lands, 14 February 1932, Soldier Settlement Loan File, 11139 (Mawbey), 8058, SARNSW.

62 W. K. Hancock recognised this tendency: 'And the settlers, remembering that the Government has put them there [on the land], not infrequently imagine that it has in some way or other accepted an obligation to keep them there'. See W. K. Hancock, *Australia* (New York: Charles Scriber's Sons, [1930]), 71.

63 Booth to the Returned Soldiers Settlement Branch, 29 March 1922, 15 October 1922, Soldier Settlement Loan Files, 3644 (N. H. Booth), NRS 8058, SARNSW.

64 Kenny to the director of soldiers settlements, 14 March 1922, Soldier Settlement Loan File, 00072 (R. J. Kenny), NRS 8058, SARNSW. See also Mawbey, quoted at the beginning of this chapter.

65 William Pile to the Lands Department, 4 January 1929, Soldier Settlement Loan File, 5684 (W. Pile), NRS 8058, SARNSW.

As further evidence of his commitment to the civilising power of closer settlement, he added that, despite his precarious finances, he had contributed to the cost of erecting a subsidised school on his block.

Settlers' interactions with city officials might have led them to feel part of a broader community of farming people. But then they were also subject to the judgement of the local farmers who were called on, virtually as the creditor's agents, to advise on each debtor's capability. Like the banks, government agencies understood the value of a local presence, but they achieved it differently. The Department of Lands engaged surveyors and inspectors as the first point of contact with settlers, and to provide advice to Sydney on the settlers' performance and prospects. Importantly, though, city-based officials also relied on the advice of local land boards and repatriation committees, consisting largely of established farmers who were thus gatekeepers to the settler's continuing access to credit. They deliberated on how a settler should utilise the branch's advances.[66] The Land Board assessed the applicants' 'qualifications to satisfactorily occupy and develop the land', having regard for their 'experience in farming or pastoral pursuits, physical fitness, capacity to obtain money to supplement his capital, and other similar qualifications', though the boards could not exclude an applicant on the basis of a lack of capital.[67] Robert Kenny had to excavate a tank smaller than he had planned on his block near Narromine in 1917 because of the local Land Board's advice.[68] Cyril Anderson, a salesman in Sydney before he enlisted in 1915, received the Narromine Repatriation Committee's support to receive a loan, but only so long as he acted on the instructions of the committee's executive whose secretary wrote:

> the necessary plant for working his farm can be purchased cheaply, under the supervision and with the advice of my Executive, at the various clearing sales in the district, payment being made for the purchase on the recommendation of my Executive.[69]

66   New South Wales, *Fortieth Report of the Department of Lands Being for the Year Ended 30 June 1919*, 47.
67   'Regulations under the "Returned Soldiers Settlement Act, 1916"—Preliminary', *NSW Government Gazette*, 7 July 1916, no. 123; *DL*, 27 May 1919, 3.
68   Internal memo, Returned Soldiers Settlement Branch, 13 April 1917, Soldier Settlement Loan File, 00072 (R. J. Kenny), NRS 8058, SARNSW.
69   Secretary, Narromine Repatriation Committee, to the director, Soldier Settlements, Sydney, 15 December 1919, Soldier Settlement Loan File, 2794 (C. Anderson), NRS 8058, SARNSW; 'Anderson, Cyril', Service File, item 1975595, B2455, NAA.

By recruiting neighbouring farmers to the creditor's cause, government agencies introduced, or perhaps just reinforced, a ranking among landholders, distinguishing those who were indebted to the government from those who were not. Debtors were subordinate parties to the most basic decisions about running a farm, bearing out David Graeber's observation that 'during the time that the debt remains unpaid, the logic of hierarchy takes hold'.[70] Such surveillance challenged any idea or ideal of the independent family farmer.

This regime also meant that settlers' indebtedness was virtually a public matter. If their status among their peers was not diminished, it was at least altered. Improvements that settlers undertook with the help of Returned Soldiers Settlement Branch advances had to be scrutinised by neighbours. In 1918, the branch would not pay Kenny for fencing until he had arranged 'to have the work inspected, valued and passed by two reliable men in the locality (residents)'.[71] In 1925, the district surveyor at Dubbo asked a farmer who leased land to Nelson Booth whether Booth should receive leniency in repaying an advance. The farmer was evidently uncomfortable being placed in such a position, but responded: 'I am prepared to recommend that he [be] allowed until after the coming harvest to pay the arrears, without enquiring into his financial position'.[72]

Committees' and inspectors' judgements were not necessarily revealed to the settler, and in any case were most often sympathetic, generally emphasising their good character and capacity for 'hard work'. Inspectors' advice was usually brief and to the point. If they considered a settler's prospects to be 'hopeless' they would express it in just those terms. When the commentary was about an individual's character rather than their circumstances, inspectors were typically gentle. Assessments included statements such as: 'He seems a practical man and good worker', 'He is a hard worker and a very good type of settler' and 'He is … an industrious and deserving settler'.[73] The point though, is not that the reports were often positive, but that the settler was subject to the judgements of local agents, including other

---

70   Graeber, *Debt*, 121.
71   Director, Soldier Settlers, to Kenny, 28 February 1918, Soldier Settlement Loan File, 00072 (R. J. Kenny), NRS 8058, SARNSW.
72   Quoted in district surveyor to the under secretary for lands, 14 November 1925, Soldier Settlement Loan File, 3644 (N. H. Booth), NRS 8058, SARNSW.
73   Inspection of Returned Soldiers' Holdings, 28 November 1922, Soldier Settlement Loan File, 3644 (H. N. Booth), NRS 8058, SARNSW; District surveyor to the under secretary for lands, 3 March 1927, Soldier Settlement Loan File, 10406 (Barling); NRS 8058, SARNSW; Soldiers Settlements Appraisement Board to the under secretary for lands, 9 November 1927, Soldier Settlement Loan File, 7434 (C. Penfold), NRS 8058, SARNSW; Lake, *The Limits of Hope*, 76.

farmers. It could not be a relationship of equals. To the extent that fraternal relations did develop between soldier settlers and others, it was despite their unequal status as either debtors or adjudicators.

The *Farmers' Relief Act*

Soldier settlers' experiences of indebtedness might not have been typical of all farmers', but neither were they unique. Though wheat growers' returns recovered slightly from 1931 to 1932 with the assistance of government subsidies, they remained well below 1920s levels for several seasons.[74] Amid continuing low prices and high input costs, the Commonwealth government introduced a number of relief programs, administered through the states. Wheat growers received some support through bounties and remission of railway freight charges. Other relief was available more selectively. As the Advances to Settlers Board established 33 years earlier, the New South Wales Debt Adjustment Scheme under the *Farmers' Relief Act* of 1932 was designed as a temporary measure, this time to bridge a period of low world prices.[75]

Unlike previous programs designed to support farmers through hard times, this scheme's premise was not that farmers lacked a ready source of credit. Rather, it implied that some were not competent to manage their own way back to solvency, with a hint that their indebtedness also arose from self-indulgence. The scheme allowed farmers to apply for a stay order, which would prevent creditors from taking action in the event of default on a mortgage or other security, and encouraged farmers and their creditors, with the mediation of government-appointed supervisors, to negotiate voluntary adjustments to debt. The Act also limited the rate of interest that could apply to the farmer's liabilities.[76] The benefit for farmers was that they could continue in business with a better chance of trading out of debt. Creditors gained the prospect of retaining a farmer's continuing custom,

---

74 Commonwealth Bureau of Census, *Official Year Book of New South Wales, No. 53, 1950–51* (Sydney: Government Printer, 1955), 749. See also B. R. Davidson, 'Agriculture and the Recovery from the Depression', in *Recovery from the Depression: Australia and the World Economy in the 1930s*, ed. R. G. Gregory and N. G. Butlin (Cambridge: Cambridge University Press, 1988), 299–301; Dunsdorfs, *The Australian Wheat-Growing Industry*, 217–21.

75 Dunsdorfs, *The Australian Wheat-Growing Industry*, 284–5; New South Wales, *Farmers' Relief Act*, no. 33, 1932.

76 New South Wales, *Farmers' Relief Act*, section 9(2); *DL*, 2 May 1933, 1; Commonwealth Bureau of Census, *Official Year Book of New South Wales, 1934–35* (Sydney: Government Printer, 1937), 587–93.

3. 'MAKING A POOR MAN POORER'

with some assurance that the farmer's affairs were being put in order, in exchange for an adjustment to the outstanding debt. Over 60 Dubbo and Wellington farmers obtained relief under this scheme.[77]

For the farmers, the price of the scheme was that they became little more than employees or debt peons on their own properties. Supervisors had two main roles: to construct and manage a farmer's budget, and to intercede in relationships with creditors. They were appointed in each district, with powers to manage each enrolled farmer's business, and were paid a small percentage from each client's proceeds. Through a bank account opened jointly with the debtor, the supervisor received income due to the farmer and made disbursements on their behalf. The supervisor could sell the debtor's property and assets 'except his farm and such of his assets as are used in connection therewith'.[78] The supervisor could pay to the debtor from the farm's proceeds an annual amount of 7.5 per cent of gross proceeds, or £75, whichever was less, for the family's clothing and medical expenses and 'otherwise for his personal use'.[79] A supervisor's relationships with their farming clients' local creditors, including storekeepers, stock and station agents, and banks, were as important as that with the farmer. Inspectors sent out from Sydney to check on the supervisors' work would interview the chief executives of those main businesses. The confidence of the town was as important to the scheme as the farmers' compliance.

The government touted the scheme's decentralised administration, with each region to be run by 'a local man of standing in the district'.[80] Most supervisors were country town accountants, including 45-year-old, English-born Frank Keyworth of Dubbo. Leading citizens of the town and district supported his bid to be appointed in 1933, including the managing director of the Western Stores, the manager of the local branch of the Commercial Bank and a prominent Trangie grazier. He was successful and took on an area encompassing Gilgandra, Warren, Trangie and Narromine, as well as clients to the south-east almost as far as Wellington. By February 1934 he

---

77 Farmers Relief Act Files, NRS 19669, SARNSW.
78 New South Wales, *Farmers' Relief Act*, section 18.
79 New South Wales, *Farmers' Relief Act*, section 28. The Australian minimum weekly wage in 1932 was £3 3s, or £163 4s per year.
80 *WT*, 17 August 1933, 5.

was managing 27 farmers' accounts. At Wellington another accountant, John Muir, who had arrived in the town in around 1924, was appointed to manage the affairs of over 40 farmers.[81]

Scrutiny of a farmer's budget under this program was more intensely local than under the soldier settlers' schemes. Supervisors were expected to visit every client farmer several times each year to coincide with the main decisions to spend money, such as before sowing or at harvest. In collaboration with the farmer, they were to construct annual budgets for the board's approval, with an emphasis on minimising expenditure. One instruction from Sydney suggested that items 'desirable but not absolutely necessary' might include 'wages, domestic assistance, motor transport, telephones &c'.[82]

In response, farmers sometimes questioned town accountants' competence to judge farm management practices. The Gilgandra newspaper claimed that local people who had expected supervisors to be 'men with practical experience of land matters' were disappointed when poor or delayed decisions cost farmers valuable income because 'the person in control ... did not know which end a cow kicked with'.[83] Keyworth advised his manager in Sydney that the article was probably the work of an agent who coveted the supervisor's role, but a Dubbo bank manager agreed that, though Keyworth was a capable accountant, he lacked 'knowledge of practical operations'.[84]

Keyworth's manager recommended that he engage an advisor—'a competent practical man who will maintain direct contact with the farmers'. This was no doubt designed not only to improve the quality of advice the accountant received but also to maintain farmers' cooperation while intensifying surveillance. In January 1935, Keyworth recruited retired farmer and grazier William Yeo to inspect properties and advise him on each farmer's practices. Yeo's contribution enhanced the local office's advice on individual farmers' prospects, but it also came with a strong dose of judgement about both the debtors' competence and—what appeared to be equally as important—their moral qualities and general attitude.[85]

81   *DL*, 16 May 1935, 7; Keyworth to the director, Farmers Relief Board, 23 February 1934, Keyworth F. L., S.8001, NRS 13188, SARNSW; J. G. Muir statutory declaration, 13 October 1933, Muir J. G., S.8003, NRS 13188, SARNSW; *WT*, 8 October 1934, 6.
82   Deputy director to Keyworth, 7 December 1934, Keyworth F. L., S.8001, NRS 13188, SARNSW.
83   *Gilgandra Weekly and Castlereagh*, 21 September 1933, 8.
84   Report on F. L. Keyworth, 30 December 1935, Keyworth F. L., S.8001, NRS 13188, SARNSW.
85   J. W. Bennett to the deputy director, Farmers' Relief Board, Inspection of Supervisor Keyworth's Office, 22 March 1936, Keyworth F. L., S.8001, NRS 13188, SARNSW.

A good attitude, it seems, was a basic credential to participate in the scheme. The director of the Farmers Relief Board, addressing the annual conference of the Returned Soldiers and Sailors Settlers League in Wellington in August 1933, made it plain that to qualify for support under the scheme, financial considerations were only part of the equation. The board, he said, would make money available 'in every case where *the personal element* and seasonal conditions are satisfactory'; he also said that finance would be available to the farmer 'so long as he is reasonably industrious … and is prepared to play the game'.[86] Yeo had described one of Keyworth's clients as 'a lazy type of farmer & one whom it would be extremely difficult to rehabilitate'. Another assessment concluded that 'this man, as a farmer is "only fair"', and another that, 'although the settler is a good farmer, the Supervisor [Keyworth] and his practical adviser [Yeo] do not like the personal factor'.[87] The term 'personal factor' implied a willingness to cooperate with the prescribed terms of the relationship, and to present what one contemporary article represented as an 'agreeable exterior' reflecting 'the man within and … the expression of his force of character'.[88] The records are largely silent on client farmers' responses to surveillance and judgement, but the scheme's benefits must have been paid for with some loss of self-esteem, and perhaps of local standing.

Though supervisors were bound by conditions of confidentiality, the Debt Adjustment Scheme caused a farmer's finances to become public knowledge. Neighbours would have noticed a supervisor's visit down remote country roads. The Gilgandra newspaper was able to report accurately on cases involving three local farmers. Supervisors' assessments appear to have been informed by local opinion. One included the observation: 'Local reports are to the effect that the farmer is a hard worker.'[89] Supervisors also canvassed town creditors for their views on individual farmers' histories and prospects. We know that farmers generally resented local scrutiny of their finances because earlier, in 1919, 'many applicants' had declined support under a state government scheme of temporary relief rather than have 'their financial

---

86   *WT*, 17 August 1933, 5 (emphasis added).
87   Deputy director's inspection of F. L. Keyworth's office, 6 August 1937, Keyworth F. L., S.8001, NRS 13188, SARNSW.
88   *Central Queensland Herald*, 19 August 1937, 22.
89   *Gilgandra Weekly and Castlereagh*, 21 September 1933, 8; Memo to the deputy director, Farmers Relief Board, 22 March 1936, Keyworth F. L., S.8001, NRS 13188, SARNSW.

affairs known and discussed by local residents'. As a consequence, the following season they were given the option of sending their applications directly to Sydney rather than to local delegates.[90]

Like the Returned Soldier Settlement Scheme, being, virtually, a public arrangement, the Debt Adjustment Scheme created hierarchies of farmers, distinguishing between recipients and non-recipients. Some resented that participants under the scheme could receive advances to buy equipment. In 1937, neighbouring farmers who were not under the Act criticised a decision to finance the purchase of a new tractor by someone they regarded as 'a lazy settler'.[91] The visiting American rural sociologist Edmund Brunner observed more general resentment during that period, commenting that when farmers involved in closer settlement schemes had debts written off or postponed, it 'had a bad effect on the better type of settler who saw his less worthy neighbour profiting by concessions he believed to be undeserved'.[92] Critics were more inclined to blame the recipients than the policy. Thus, the scheme embedded distinctions within farming communities between the worthy and the unworthy: the farmer who was putatively competent and independent, and the one who relied on government support with the suspicion of ineptitude and an indifferent work ethic.

Conclusion

Debt in its various forms so pervaded farming people's lives that it can hardly have been an incidental experience consigned to an autonomous sphere of economic activity. Debt was laden with cultural meaning and moral judgement. That meaning, though, in terms of advancing our understanding of the roles of class and place in the farmlands, is complex. On the one hand, debt could affirm for farming people that they constituted a community bound by that common experience. It separated the rural indebted from the city as a place where ultimate power over access to credit resided, and where officials seemed not to understand the vicissitudes of

---

90   New South Wales, *Report of the Department of Agriculture for the Year Ended 30 June 1920*, in *Joint Volume of Papers Presented to the Legislative Council and Legislative Assembly*, vol. 1 (Sydney: Government Printer, 1920), 24.

91   Deputy director's inspection of F. L. Keyworth's office, 6 August 1937, Keyworth F. L., S.8001, NRS 13188, SARNSW.

92   Edmund de S. Brunner, *Rural Australia and New Zealand: Some Observations of Current Trends* (San Francisco: American Council, Institute of Pacific Relations, 1938), 21. See also Stephen Garton, *The Cost of War: Australians Return* (Melbourne: Oxford University Press, 1996), 130.

living with unpredictable seasons and commodity prices, compounded by debt. It was evident in the soldier settlers' exchanges with Sydney officials, but also tacitly reinforced every time a local bank manager deflected responsibility for a tough decision on extending credit by deferring to the policies of 'the bank' or the prerogatives of 'head office'. A sense of a common rural grievance against a distant city tormentor, of which debt was a significant element, found expression in the rise of rural-based political parties and other movements into the 1920s and 1930s, which are discussed in Chapter 5.

A second, perhaps more positive, side of farmers' common experience of debt was an ironic affirmation that, even though they were beholden to the city as a source of capital and markets, they remained part of the national project to populate rural Australia with productive smallholders. By the mid-1940s the Rural Reconstruction Commission would question the wisdom of indiscriminately supporting smallholders, but in the 1930s the vision still held sway.[93] For many, the merits of participating in that project were not worth its costs, but for those—like Albert Mawbey—who persisted even though they knew there were easier ways to make a living, there was an affirming national narrative of which they could feel a small part. The conspicuous presence of commercial banks in country towns and government schemes of financial support, linking farmers to vast flows of capital, were tangible evidence of their continuing faith in that story.

That experience involved lenders reinforcing a common set of values or qualities at the centre of an encompassing farming culture. People's 'subjective reality'—their socially constructed and maintained conceptions of themselves—must surely have absorbed authority figures' regular judgement on measures of 'character' and 'standing', and on matters so closely tied to their status as farmers.[94] Those indicators—that the worthy debtor be hardworking, honest, more steady than enterprising and sober in their ways—not only affirmed what it meant to be a 'good farmer' and a worthy citizen but also were consistent with and reinforced the idea of the 'yeoman farmer' at the centre of the agrarian idyll.

---

93 Australia, Rural Reconstruction Commission, *Rural Credit: The Commission's Fifth Report to the Honorable J. J. Dedman MP, Minister for Post-War Reconstruction* ([Canberra]: The Commission, 1945), 3.
94 Peter L. Berger and Thomas Luckmann, *The Social Construction of Reality: A Treatise in the Sociology of Knowledge* (Harmonsworth: Penguin, 1966), 169–74.

On the other hand, the different qualities of debt and sources of credit introduced the potential for the standards of (credit-)worthiness to emphasise difference and reinforce hierarchy within a local community of farmers. For some, debt was a manageable cost of expanding productivity, or of 'carrying on' while awaiting assured seasonal returns. A relationship with a commercial bank signified that one was worthy of access to credit on commercial grounds—a safe bet verified by the bank's network. In these circumstances, assessments of character could not only promote access to credit, but also the receipt of credit could be seen to affirm the recipient's character.[95]

For others, debt accumulated relentlessly and soaked up all productive energy—everything they had to show for each year's effort, and sometimes more. For those with limited capital, indebtedness to governments implied that the borrower received credit on something other than commercial terms, and the forms of oversight were more conspicuous and less sensitively managed. Government-sponsored credit could signify not just misfortune, nor even poor judgement or incompetence, but also a lack of moral worth. These differences would have been most acutely felt when both the town and, most tellingly, other more established and solvent farmers, were recruited as lenders' agents. Any sense of a cohesive local farming class must have been at least disrupted as one group formed part of the web of surveillance overseeing the other.

---

95 Finn, *The Character of Credit*, 19.

4

'A decent sort of a chap': Farmers and labour, 1880–1930

In 1932, soldier settler Albert Mawbey, by then 41, was still struggling to produce enough wheat and wool on his 430 acres to satisfy his creditors. As a single man, he provided as much of his own labour as he could, but was also obliged to hire workers, especially at harvest time. One year, as he once more sought leniency from his main creditor, the Department of Lands, he explained his expenses, pointing out that he had cut back by doing his own carting, and justified the remaining labour costs: 'although wages might seem high it's hard to ask a decent sort of a chap to put in long hours through the summer for a pittance'.[1] It is just one instance, but the statement stands in contrast with the stereotypical image of the hard, exploitative farmer, extracting as much labour at the least cost possible, from ill-used workers. It also seemingly contradicts this farmer's role as an active member of an FSA branch that, some years earlier, had voted in favour of lower rates of pay for rural workers and more control for individual farmers over labourers' conditions.[2]

---

1   Mawbey to the Department of Lands, 3 April 1932, Soldier Settlement Loan Files, 11139 (A. Mawbey), NRS 8058, SARNSW.
2   *DL*, 10 February 1914, 3. The farmers as exploitative: Charles Fahey, '"Abusing the Horses and Exploiting the Labourer": The Victorian Agricultural and Pastoral Labourer, 1871–1911', *Labour History*, no. 65 (1993): 96-114; [Joseph Jenkins], *Diary of a Welsh Swagman, 1869–1894*, abridged and annotated by William Evans (Melbourne: Sun Books, 1977), 29, 33–4, 36, 98, 101; Russel Ward, *The Australian Legend* (Melbourne: Oxford University Press, 1958), 198–9.

Australian farmers had been associated with conservative, non-labour politics for many years. From the early twentieth century, FSA branches in the Dubbo district regularly adopted an employer's perspective on labour relations. And yet the modes of wheat–sheep farming, on the scale that was most typical around Dubbo, were hardly a model that pitched employers and employees as clearly delineated oppositional groups. The interests of labour and capital were far from discretely and adversarially arranged. If class is a sense among people of shared interests and their common experience of the ways land, labour and capital entangle to produce goods and services, then how did farmers' class consciousness evolve around Dubbo in circumstances where these elements were thrown together in fluid, ever-changing ways? In an environment where individual farmers might simultaneously or at different times provide their own labour, employ labour from beyond the farm *and* sell their labour to others, how did class emerge at all as an aspect of farmers' cultural and political outlook?

This chapter examines two dimensions of the seeming dissonance that had emerged by the 1920s, between typical modes of production on the one hand, and farmers' political allegiances on the other. It explores the several ways labour was combined with land and capital in the half century from 1880. Into the 1930s, many farming people both worked beyond the farm and hired labour during seasonal peaks, such that any changes in class consciousness and attitudes towards labour cannot tidily be ascribed to changing modes of farm production. The second part of the chapter examines the broader political and industrial relations context between the turn of the century and World War I to show that farmers' attitudes towards labour, and their consciousness of themselves as a class, were influenced not only by their varied roles within the quotidian practices of farm production, but also by broader organisational responses to new compulsory industrial arbitration frameworks. Smallholders were more receptive to these influences because, when confronted with binary political choices, they identified with the class to which they aspired to belong, rather than one that their immediate interests and circumstances might have implied.[3]

---

3   I acknowledge the pioneering work on rural politics in New South Wales of Don Aitkin, *The Country Party in New South Wales: Membership and Electoral Support* (Canberra: Australian National University for the Australian Political Studies Association, 1965); B. D. Graham, *The Formation of the Australian Country Parties* (Canberra: Australian National University Press, 1966).

Though women were involved as farmers, workers and political actors, the arguments and narrative here are based overwhelmingly on men's stories. The challenge of properly representing women's roles is exacerbated by census managers' practice of labelling farming women's occupations as 'domestic duties', thus masking and demeaning the array of functions uniquely, or most often, performed by women.[4] The archive is also deficient because women were much less likely than men to be the official presence in exchanges with banks, creditors or government agencies. And, as their labour generally did not involve the exchange of cash, women's contributions were part of a less visible, taken-for-granted economy.

Farming and labour in the Central West

Three broad factors affected the demand for farm labour on small properties over the period from 1880 to 1930: mechanisation, the size of properties and the extent to which agriculture was combined with grazing. The mechanisation of agriculture tended to reduce the need for labour to cultivate and harvest a given area of land.[5] While this might have lessened aggregate demand for labour across a district, farms concurrently became bigger, therefore requiring more labour on each property than otherwise. The average size of properties on the Central Western Slopes increased from 642 acres in 1904 to 1,243 acres in 1921 and 1,585 acres in 1931.[6]

Though farms became bigger on average, enterprises continued to be relatively small—modest compared with properties further west—and the work was cyclical. Demand for labour peaked in certain seasons and for periods of relatively intense activity, each lasting from a few days to several weeks, and often at times that were dictated by the weather.[7] Wheat

---

4   Katrina Alford, 'Colonial Women's Employment as Seen by Nineteenth-Century Statisticians and Twentieth-Century Economic Historians', *Labour History*, no. 51 (1986): 1–10.
5   Bruce Davidson, *European Farming in Australia: An Economic History of Australian Farming* (Amsterdam: Elsevier, 1981), 180, 199; Edgars Dunsdorfs, *The Australian Wheat-Growing Industry, 1788–1948* (Carlton: Melbourne University Press, 1956), 409; Charles Fahey, 'Two Model Farmers: Ann and Joseph Day of Murchison', *Victorian Historical Journal* 71, no. 2 (2000): 118; Fahey, '"Abusing the Horses and Exploiting the Labourer"', 106–7.
6   Commonwealth Bureau of Census, *Official Year Book of New South Wales, 1904–05* (Sydney: Government Printer, 1906), 98; Commonwealth Bureau of Census, *Official Year Book of New South Wales, 1921* (Sydney: Government Printer, 1922), 835; Commonwealth Bureau of Census, *Official Year Book of New South Wales, 1931–32* (Sydney: Government Printer, 1933), 651.
7   Davidson, *European Farming in Australia*, 192; Fahey, '"Abusing the Horses and Exploiting the Labourer"', 98–9.

production was increasing, but generally on a relatively small scale. The average area of alienated land under cultivation per holding was 92 acres in the County of Lincoln in 1900, and 227 acres in the roughly equivalent Talbragar Shire by 1930–31.[8]

From the 1880s settlers increasingly complemented their acreages of grain with flocks of sheep. The rise of mixed wheat–sheep farming produced a new demand for seasonal labour associated with shearing and other tasks required in sheep husbandry. The scale of these operations, however, was utterly different from the archetypal pastoral stations further west, where sheds once had 80 or more stands—gathering places for dozens if not hundreds of shearers and shedhands during the season. There were a few substantial sheds closer to Dubbo, but they were at their zenith in the late nineteenth century, before closer settlement became firmly established. Nanima station near Wellington filled 16 stands in 1878, but by 1910 was employing only 10 shearers. Murrumbidgerie station engaged 32 shearers in 1893, 33 in 1896 (for over 120,000 sheep), and ran 20 stands in 1905, but just four (for 2,800 sheep) when it was a much smaller property in 1935.[9] In lists of over 600 New South Wales stations with shearing volumes large enough to warrant the attention of the Australian Workers Union (AWU) in 1914, Terramungamine's was the only shed in the Dubbo district nearer than Narromine. It had 24 stands at its peak; however, by 1934 it was reduced to half that number.[10]

The smaller-scale mixed farmers had their shearing and crutching done under contract at 'depot' sheds on the larger properties,[11] or managed the operation themselves, making do with infrastructure commensurate with the size of their holdings. Sheds might serve several purposes—storing machinery or grain for the most part, but able to be turned to shearing and crutching for a few days each year. They rarely contained more than three

---

8   New South Wales, *Statistical Register for 1900 and Previous Years* (Sydney: Government Printer, 1902), Table 53, 'Number and Extent of Alienated Holdings, in Area Groups etc.'; New South Wales, *Statistical Register for 1930–31* (Sydney: Government Printer, 1932), Table 86, 'Alienated Area, Capital Value and Crown Lands Occupied, 1930–31', 426, and Table 1, 'Area in Cultivation etc 1930–31 (Alienated Holdings Only)', 382.

9   *ATCJ*, 2 November 1878, 39; *Worker*, 28 September 1910, 5. On 1893: *Maitland Weekly Mercury*, 17 February 1894, 4. On 1896: *National Advocate*, 26 October 1896, 2. On 1905: *DL*, 11 October 1905, 4. On 1935 figures: *Australian Worker*, 9 October 1935, 17.

10   'Shearing Fixtures for 1914', *Australian Worker*, 19 March 1914, 26, 30 July 1914, 24; *DL*, 18 September 1934, 5. On the Terramungamine shed: *DD*, 28 November 1903, 4.

11   *DL*, 12 September 1911, 2; *DL*, 18 September 1934, 5; Harold Woodley (b. 1931), interview with author, Dubbo, 28 December 2018.

stands, or a mobile two-stand shearing plant could be moved to where it was needed. Bill Gorrie of Westella listed among improvements on his 520 acres a 'shed for shearing and general use' in 1931.[12] All in all, these were small, family-based cottage enterprises as compared with the industrial-scale wool factories of the Riverina and far west. At most they needed labour intermittently and for short periods. This in itself contributed to the itinerant, fractional and highly seasonal nature of local labour markets.

Sources of labour

Compounding the structural changes that reduced demand for rural workers, farming families themselves were stereotypically their own labour supply (see Figure 4.1).[13] The Board of Trade, which was briefly responsible for determining minimum wages in New South Wales in the 1920s, postulated the distinctive nature of farmers as labourers:

> The farmer is essentially a wage-earner, for he largely depends upon the return going to the labour factor of production ... The farmer has been well described as a labourer who buys himself a lifelong job ... The farmer's return, to be adequate, must reimburse the cost of his equipment, but his labour income is the true test of his success and efficiency. He ordinarily lays claim to no reward for management and organisation simply because he does not affect the position of the entrepreneur and because he is essentially *a fellow-labourer with those who assist him*.[14]

---

12 'Application for Postponement of ... Interest or Instalments', 30 June 1931, Soldier Settlement Loan File, 10142 (Gorrie, W.), NRS 8058, SARNSW.

13 Patricia Grimshaw, Charles Fahey, Susan Janson and Tom Griffiths, 'Families and Selection in Colonial Horsham', in *Families in Colonial Australia*, ed. Patricia Grimshaw, Chris McConville and Ellen McEwen (North Sydney: Allen & Unwin, 1985), 118–37; Lake Marilyn, 'Helpmeet, Slave, Housewife: Women in Rural Families 1870–1930', in *Families in Colonial Australia*, ed. Patricia Grimshaw, Chris McConville and Ellen McEwen (North Sydney: Allen & Unwin, 1985), 173–85; Kathryn M. Hunter, *Father's Right-Hand Man: Women on Australia's Family Farms in the Age of Federation, 1880s–1920s* (Melbourne: Australian Scholarly Publishing, 2004), throughout, but especially 138–75.

14 NSW Board of Trade, 'Declaration', *NSW Government Gazette*, no. 159, 28 October 1921, 6121 (emphasis added).

Figure 4.1: A farmer, 12 horses and a plough. Mo Cockerell, 'Valley Fields', Wongarbon, 1935.
Source: Mo Cockerell collection.

Evidence from the Dubbo district reinforces this impression. With most of their capital committed to acquiring land, stock and machinery, households undertook the core work of building and sustaining small farms. A visitor travelling towards Dubbo from Orange in 1880 noted that:

> people have settled on the soil with too little capital to work it to advantage, and to make comfortable dwellings for their families— each settler or selector having acquired as much land as the law would permit, and he was able to pay the first deposit of 5s per acre on, and then attempting to occupy and use more than he himself can work with plough and spade, being unable to employ paid labour, and not having even the means to buy sufficient stock to graze the land.

Though women's and children's labour was virtually invisible in official statistics, it was vital to farm production, the writer observing that the burden of working the land fell on the whole family: 'The women whom we saw … looked haggard and overworked; the children were strong and healthy, but wanted new wardrobes and boots, and more washing.'[15] A school inspector observed tenant farmers just west of Dubbo in 1893: 'They all appear to be hardworking, industrious people, and the women and children work at

---

15   *ATCJ*, 3 January 1880, 18.

fencing and clearing the land as well as the men'.[16] Gilgandra district farmer Alfred Richards observed in 1916 that 'most people do their own work on small farms'.[17] Reliance on a family's own labour continued throughout the first half of the twentieth century and beyond.

Around Dubbo, as elsewhere, women's contributions were integral to a household's maximal application of its own labour to farm production. The women who formally headed households are slightly more visible in the archive than the many who did not. They drew on older children's labour, though some also hired permanent workers. Ellen Kilfoyle of Beni was married to a farmer but had property of her own on which she grew wheat and ran 400 head of sheep in the early twentieth century.[18] Jane Bourke ran a farm at Eulomogo with the help of two sons, and then on her own when they enlisted in the First Australian Imperial Force (AIF); and Doris and Renie Dixon returned from boarding school to the family property near Coboco to help their mother run the place when their father died in 1917.[19] In the 1920s, Mary Neville ran a small wheat farm at Delroy near Dubbo, her son providing occasional labour as well as working on neighbouring properties and trapping rabbits for extra cash.[20] As a nurse who had served overseas during World War I, Mary Redfern Watt received support to acquire a closer settlement block on the Macquarie River just below Dubbo, where she built a dairy and grew wheat. She worked the land with the help of her sister and hired labour, and later engaged a sharefarmer, before leasing the land in 1926. However, her application to the Department of Lands to acquire, in addition, a milk run and associated equipment was declined, the inspector adjudging that 'the proposition is one more suitable to a man who has family labour'.[21] Farming widows frequently headed up households, often with the support of adult children. The Dubbo branch of the Bank of

---

16 Inspector to the chief inspector, 1 December 1893, Boogle Gumble School Administrative File, 5/15014.4, NRS 3829, SARNSW.

17 New South Wales, Royal Commission of Inquiry on Rural, Pastoral, Agricultural and Dairying Interests, *Commissioner's Report on All Matters Other than Dairying Interests* (Sydney: Government Printer, 1917), 594.

18 Series S01-0051, item 80-13-192, manager's information book, 1904, folios 23–4, Westpac Group Archives.

19 *DD*, 18 June 1918, 4, 6 September 1918, 1. Her husband lived with their son at Cobbora. See *WT*, 13 April 1922, 3; Gwenda Shearing, 'Mulwarree', in *A Compiled History of Coboco District*, ed. Pat Fisher, Robyn Healey and Sandra Burns (Narromine: Coboco CWA, 2002), 57–61.

20 Mary Jane Neville, statement to the Supreme Court, 14 June 1926, NRS 13655, SARNSW; M. J. Duffy and Sons to the official assignee, 14 July 1926, file no. 23986 (Neville M. J.), NRS 13655, SARNSW.

21 Inspector's memorandum to the director, Returned Soldiers Settlement Branch, 6 December 1923, Soldier Settlement Loan File, 8490 (Watt, M. R.), NRS 8058, SARNSW.

New South Wales had several customers in that situation in 1906, including Sarah Kilfoyle whom the manager considered 'a hard working woman, and quite able to manage the farm which is now her property'. 'Widow, grazier' Emma Johnstone was another customer: a 'very decent woman, [who] keeps the Balladoran Hotel and is farming a large area, with the assistance of her sons'.[22]

From an early age, children contributed to a farm's productivity. During seasonal peaks, in particular, demand for outside labour was modified by children's contributions.[23] Robert Patten, by then FSA vice-president and father of four boys aged between 13 and 18, noted in 1907 that 'the man with a family of boys is not taking great risks when he goes on the land, for boys are a wonderful help'.[24] As foreshadowed in Chapter 2, at least until World War I, schoolteachers in farming districts held little sway over older children's attendance during shearing and harvesting in the final months of the year. The Wellington district's 1883 report attributed lower attendance in the fourth quarter to 'the children being kept at home to water stock and to assist in harvesting'. In 1891, the Brocklehurst teacher explained low attendance thus:

> In September began the lambing followed by shearing, harvest and hay making when all the boys able to work were kept at home and the greater portion of scholars were 1st class and girls.

In November 1907, the teacher at Criefton, in accounting for low attendance, reported that two pupils 'will be continuously employed in harvesting operations for the next five or six weeks', and another two 'are often required to assist their parents'. As late as 1921, children were kept away from the Gollan school 'for four and five weeks in succession during busy times—such as ploughing and harvesting' (see Figure 4.2).[25]

---

22   Series S01-0051, item 80-13-192, manager's information book, [1904], folios 25–6, 69–70, Westpac Group Archives. See also Fahey, 'Two Model Farmers', 102–23.

23   New South Wales, *Parliamentary Debates*, second series, session 1915–16, vol. LX and vol. LXIII (Sydney: Government Printer, 1916), 6420–1.

24   *Farmer and Settler*, 18 October 1907, 3.

25   New South Wales, Department of Public Instruction, *Report of the Minister of Public Instruction upon the Condition of Public Schools Established and Maintained under the Public Instruction Act of 1880, for 1883, New South Wales*, in *Votes and Proceedings of the Legislative Assembly*, vol. VII, 1883–84 (Sydney: Government Printer, 1884), 866; Teacher to the secretary, Council of Education, 30 March 1880, Brocklehurst School Administrative File, pre-1939, 5/15094, NRS 3829, SARNSW; Teacher to the inspector, 8 November 1907, Criefton school Administrative File, pre-1939, 5/15566.3, NRS 3829, SARNSW; Teacher to the inspector, 10 October 1921, Gollan School Administrative File, pre-1939, 5/16063.1, NRS 3829, SARNSW.

Figure 4.2: Children helping with the harvest, c. 1930.
Source: Colleen Braithwaite collection.

Extended families were another source of unpaid labour during peak times of the year. Brothers, or parents and sons, worked adjoining properties, sharing machinery and their labour. John and Emily Callaghan and their son William used their jointly owned plant to work small adjacent blocks on the Glenara Closer Settlement Purchase Area in the 1920s.[26] Single men who took up blocks, including many under the soldier settlement schemes, adjusted for the absence of labour that a household would otherwise provide by living in primitive conditions (freeing up scarce capital for other purposes) or collaborating with extended family living nearby.[27]

Clearly, households took many forms, but the essential point in this context is that, in every case, the enterprise was the principal source of its own labour. Most farms were of a scale that allowed a household to supply the bulk of its labour, most of the time, with the exception of seasonal peaks

---

26 W. J. Callaghan to the under secretary, Department of Lands, 4 January 1924, Soldier Settlement Loan File, 5684 (W. Pile), NRS 8058, SARNSW.

27 Marilyn Lake, *The Limits of Hope: Soldier Settlement in Victoria, 1915–38* (Melbourne: Oxford University Press, 1987), 144; Bruce Scates and Melanie Oppenheimer, *The Last Battle: Soldier Settlement in Australia, 1916-1939* (Cambridge: Cambridge University Press, 2016), 57–9; E. Cahill to the secretary, Repatriation Committee, Narromine, Soldier Settlement Loan File, 00072 (R. J. Kenny), NRS 8058, SARNSW; District surveyor to the under secretary for lands, 10 September 1924, Soldier Settlement Loan File, 7303 (W. C. Clark), Soldier Settlement Loan File, NRS 8058, SARNSW.

in demand. Each farm was its own aggregation of land, capital and labour, but porous at its margins, needing (and sometimes supplying to others) supplementation from time to time.

Sharefarming

From the late nineteenth century, sharefarming further complicated the ways wage labour combined with land and capital, reduced demand for wage labour, and blurred the distinction between employers and employees. In most cases, it involved a landholder arranging with the owner of a plant (horses and machinery) to cultivate and harvest a crop on a portion of the landholder's property. The agreement could extend for one or several seasons, with the proceeds of the harvest to be divided between the parties, the proportion varying according to who contributed other inputs such as seed wheat, fertiliser and bags. Thus, a landholding farmer's need for outside labour was reduced by temporarily adding to the available land of another farmer, who would also accept responsibility for supplying any extra labour needed while the arrangement lasted. Sharefarming accounted for between one-fifth and one-third of the area under wheat in New South Wales for all but one year between 1906–07 and 1939–40.[28] Some observers attributed sharefarming's currency to a shortage of wage labour. According to the New South Wales statistician, in 1922, landholders 'could not obtain workmen to till large areas of their land'.[29] From another perspective, though, it could be argued that people with some capital in the form of horses and machinery were prepared to receive a lesser, or less certain, return than wage labourers, in exchange for less tangible rewards.

Sharefarming occurred in various circumstances—on large, established properties, and on small developing blocks. In 1917, Rudolph Van Heuckelum, manager of a 4,312-acre property near Gilgandra, cultivated some land himself but also assigned 800 acres in total to three sharefarmers.[30] At the other extreme, a settler with a new block that needed a substantial investment of labour and capital to bring it to its productive potential—clearing, fencing and conserving water—had limited capacity to simultaneously work those parts of the farm that *could* produce a crop.

28   Dunsdorfs, *The Australian Wheat-Growing Industry,* 246.
29   Commonwealth Bureau of Census, *Official Year Book of New South Wales, 1921,* 719.
30   New South Wales, Royal Commission of Inquiry on Rural, Pastoral, Agricultural and Dairying Interests, *Commissioner's Report on All Matters Other than Dairying Interests,* 602.

In those circumstances, some smallholders arranged to have a portion of the cleared land worked on the 'shares' system, effectively increasing the labour that was applied to the block to generate a more productive result. One advantage for the nascent landholder was that it was a cashless arrangement. The parties between them contributed inputs in-kind and took as their return an agreed proportion of the harvested grain. The landowner was probably indebted and could ill-afford to pay for their land to be cleared and fenced, but could arrange for a sharefarmer to produce a crop on the promise of a potential future return.

Some sharefarmers had land of their own, but not enough on which to apply all of their labour and machinery. John Lithgow owned a small 275-acre holding near Gilgandra, but by sharefarming on others' properties he increased his cropping to 500–700 acres until he expanded his own holding to 650 acres in 1915.[31] Returned soldiers and brothers Albert and Garnet Mawbey supplemented the crops on their own closer settlement blocks of 430 and 590 acres by sharefarming on adjoining properties between 1924 and 1928.[32] The arrangement could be represented as a melding of factors of production across two properties to achieve a mutually agreed equilibrium of land, capital and labour, and not an exchange of wage labour at all. In the words of Gilgandra landholder Warren Barden in 1916:

> My experience of share-farming really is this: that in many cases where a man has a small holding and is making a start for himself, if he is alongside of a man who has land and will allow him to go on it on the shares it has often helped him in that direction while he is waiting for his own land to come along; he gets perhaps 200 or 300 acres from the man alongside … If he is alongside his own place any spare time that he has got he can put into his own property.[33]

Sharefarmers without land at all generally saw it as a transitional phase, using their investment in plant and working stock to move towards acquiring a farm of their own. Farmer and stock and station agent Edward Townsend considered that 'most of the good share-farmers I know have not remained

---

31   Gilgandra landowner Walter Barden, before New South Wales, Royal Commission of Inquiry on Rural, Pastoral, Agricultural and Dairying Interests, *Commissioner's Report on All Matters Other than Dairying Interests*, 591.

32   District inspector to the under secretary for lands, 9 May 1925, Soldier Settlement Loan File, 5757 (G. L. Mawbey), NRS 8058, SARNSW; District inspector to the under secretary for lands, 27 December 1928, Soldier Settlement Loan File, 11139 (A. Mawbey), NRS 8058, SARNSW.

33   New South Wales, Royal Commission of Inquiry on Rural, Pastoral, Agricultural and Dairying Interests, *Commissioner's Report on All Matters Other than Dairying Interests*, 588.

share-farmers very long. They have generally been successful enough to get onto the land themselves.'[34] Wilson Powell, who came to the Gilgandra district from Victoria in around 1915 reveals the aspirations of such men. He got paid work ringbarking and clearing, but also sharefarmed with his brother:

> I am making share-farming a stepping stone to something better,
> I hope ... My present intention is to try and accumulate sufficient
> money to enable me to acquire a holding of my own.

Michael Wynne, also a sharefarmer, considered it 'a good thing for a man who wants to make a start'.[35]

On face value, sharefarming confounded the relationship between the parties to production in several ways so as to obscure any clear separation of class interests. The sharefarmer's return at the end of a season was so many bags of the wheat from the crop they had cultivated and harvested, exercising their own judgement and prowess, to sell when and to whom they chose. The sense of equivalence between landholder and sharefarmer, arising from the shared risk and reward of a poor or prosperous season, was further reinforced because cash did not change hands. The relationship could be construed as one between capitalist and aspiring capitalist, or between a larger and smaller capitalist, rather than between exploiter and exploited. So, to the extent that a farming household needed supplementary labour for agriculture, there were ways to obtain it that did not involve wage labour, and that disrupted any clear delineation between the local experiences of capital as compared with labour. Nevertheless, hired workers were still a common cost of farming production.

Paid labour

Any tidy demarcation between employers' and employees' interests in the farming economy was further confounded by the fact that many individuals were from time to time both hirers and suppliers of labour. John Thomson, the federal member for Cowper on the New South Wales north coast, observed in 1910 that:

---

34 New South Wales, Royal Commission of Inquiry on Rural, Pastoral, Agricultural and Dairying Interests, *Commissioner's Report on All Matters Other than Dairying Interests*, 598.
35 New South Wales, Royal Commission of Inquiry on Rural, Pastoral, Agricultural and Dairying Interests, *Commissioner's Report on All Matters Other than Dairying Interests*, 599, 609.

during certain seasons of the year young men who have embarked their capital in the agricultural industry are obliged to go out and earn money in another calling until they are in a position to make their land productive. Thus it is quite possible for an individual to be an employer and an employee at the same time.[36]

Farming families worked for neighbours, especially if they owned too little land to absorb their labour for the whole year. This might have been a delicate relationship to negotiate, as they were both peers and employees. William Bult, formerly of the 1st Australian Light Horse Regiment, supported himself by labouring locally after sowing was finished on his 635-acre farm near Narromine in 1921. Fellow returned soldier Robert Kenny had 1,200 acres near Narromine, but still got a job harvesting on a neighbour's property in 1920, and two years later took up a contract clearing timber regrowth (suckering) on an adjoining block.[37]

Shearing generally followed winter sowing, and concluded before the summer harvest, so farmers could provide much of the shearing labour both out west and closer to home. One witness testified before the federal Court of Conciliation and Arbitration in 1907 that 'when farmers and their sons got their crops in there was a slack time, and some of them put in the interval between seedtime and harvest in the shearing sheds'. Another witness observed that about 20,000 men across eastern Australia pursued shearing permanently, and another 10,000 'did casual shearing as "cockies" on the bosses' station'. Soldier settler Linden Minchin went contract shearing with a two-stand mobile plant when he was not working his 640-acre property near Balladoran in the late 1920s.[38]

In addition to the households' own labour, sharefarming arrangements and employment of other farmers and their families, smallholders still needed extra hired labour from time to time into the 1930s. Women are not

---

36 Commonwealth Conciliation and Arbitration Bill, second reading, 3 August 1910, Commonwealth of Australia, House of Representatives, *Parliamentary Debates* (Canberra: Government Printer, 1910), 1038.

37 Local Repatriation Committee to the Department of Lands, July 1921, Soldier Settlement Loan File, 10406 (Bult), NRS 8058, SARNSW; Kenny to the director, Soldier Settlements, 5 June 1920 and 14 March 1922, Soldier Settlement Loan File, 8944 (Kenny R.), NRS 8058, SARNSW.

38 *Worker*, 20 June 1907, 1, 11 July 1907, 17; District surveyor to the under secretary for lands, 20 February 1929, Soldier Settlement Loan File, 10157 (L. Minchin), NRS 8058, SARNSW. On farmers as shearers, see also C. E. W. Bean, *On the Wool Track* (Sydney: Angus & Robertson, 1969), 113; John Merritt, *The Making of the AWU* (Melbourne: Oxford University Press, 1986), 38, 42–52; Raymond Markey, *The Making of the Labor Party in New South Wales, 1880–1900* (Kensington: New South Wales University Press, 1988), 61.

conspicuous in the record but, still, they were taken on by some households with small children (see Figure 4.3).[39] Demand for male workers was mainly seasonal. In the Dubbo district, even farmers on relatively small blocks with little cash in reserve, including those on the verge of bankruptcy, counted wages among their expenses, and sometimes their debts. When Maryvale farmer Hobart Johnson was declared insolvent in 1879, his costs over the preceding December and January had included eight labourers' wages for four days to bind his hay, and 15 workers' wages for two days to thresh and bag wheat. Much later, one estimate put wages at around 10 per cent of the cost of producing an annual crop on 230 acres over the period 1915–16 to 1920–21. For George Condon, on 340 acres at Glenara, about 15 per cent of his expenses between March and December 1916 were for labour, though he would be bankrupt by 1918, with debts including nearly £50 in unpaid wages.[40] William Tomlinson of Eumungerie had a modest 634 acres of which he cultivated 335 acres for wheat in 1916, but still he could not do it entirely on his own: 'I generally do my own work except at harvest time. I get local men for harvesting.'[41] Garnet Mawbey on 590 acres paid out wages in 1923, 1924 and 1926. Douglas Yeo employed labour on his 500-acre property, most likely for short periods, in seven of the eight years between 1920–21 and 1927–28. Albert Mawbey's harvesting costs in 1932 included wages for one man for 50 days, and the equivalent of an additional casual hand for around 45 days.[42] Neither the Mawbeys nor Yeo had children of working age at that time, which might partly account for their need to hire labour. In all, hired labour was a common, but not necessarily a major expense, certainly as compared with the imputed value of a household's own labour, over the course of a whole year.

---

39 Harold Woodley (b. 1931), interview with author, Dubbo, 18 June 2017; Robert Woodley (b. 1937), interview with author, Isaacs (ACT), 20 December 2017.

40 Supplementary Schedule of Transactions, file no. 14849 (H. B. Johnson), NRS 13654, SARNSW; Commonwealth Bureau of Census, *Official Year Book of New South Wales, 1921*, 738; Form of accounts under rule no. 188, file no. 21390 (G. Condon), NRS 13655, SARNSW.

41 New South Wales, Royal Commission of Inquiry on Rural, Pastoral, Agricultural and Dairying Interests, *Commissioner's Report on All Matters Other than Dairying Interests*, 590.

42 Attachment to 'Application for Revision of Indebtedness', 7 October 1926, Soldier Settlement Loan File, 5757 (G. L. Mawbey), NRS 8058, SARNSW; A. Mawbey to the under secretary for lands, 3 April 1932, Soldier Settlement Loan File, 11139 (A. Mawbey), NRS 8058, SARNSW; 'Application for Revision of Indebtedness', 17 January 1929, Soldier Settlement Loan File, 3301 (D. H. Yeo), NRS 8058, SARNSW.

Figure 4.3: Farmer (Sam Condon) and domestic worker (Maggie McHattan), 'Rocklea', c. 1930.
Source: Condon family collection.

Beyond the farmer's own household and their farming neighbours, labour came mainly from itinerant workers and the nearby villages that clustered around the railway stations on the lines radiating from Dubbo, particularly Geurie and Murrumbidgerie/Wongarbon. At Dubbo's Overland Hotel in 1910, Tasman Lavender, a 15-year-old from Sydney on the lookout for work, noticed 'farmers ... looking around for likely young fellows to help them out with the harvest some two or three weeks ahead'.[43] Well into the twentieth century, workers' newspapers publicised regular advice on the districts where work was either plentiful or scarce.[44] With the railway close at hand, village dwellers could also find employment further afield. The villages were effectively labour dormitories. In 1898, 17 per cent of heads of households with children attending the Geurie school classified themselves as labourers (24 per cent if surrounding 'farmers' and a 'sheep owner' are excluded).[45] The teacher at Murrumbidgerie advised his department in 1905 that 'the majority of parents are labourers',[46] and though he would have been referring to railway employees as well as farm labourers, nevertheless rural work was plentiful and labour was mobile:

43   T. W. Lavender, 'Young Bill's Happy Days', unpublished manuscript, [1969], MS 8155, NLA.
44   For example, *Worker*, 12 April 1902, 2; *Australian Worker*, 14 December 1916, 19.
45   Petition, 26 July 1898, Geurie School Administrative File, 5/15981.A, NRS 3829, SARNSW.
46   Frederick Lovett to the senior inspector of schools, 13 March 1905, Murrumbidgerie School Administrative File, pre-1939, 5/17017.1, NRS 3829, SARNSW.

> The labour employed on those farms exhausts the labour market, and it is only those who do not require work that are idle at Murrumbidgerie to-day. Quite an influx of labourers from different parts came here, and all have received work.[47]

In 1911, the teacher described the village as consisting 'largely of rabbiters & farm hands'. Forty-five of Wongarbon's 110 men who were enrolled to vote in 1921 were recorded as 'labourers', 'farm labourers' or 'station hands'. Between 1915 and 1924, 37 per cent of families enrolling children at the Wongarbon Public School were from households where the breadwinner was identified as either a labourer, stockman or shearer.[48] So, while labourers might not have gathered in large numbers or for extended periods on farms, they were a concentrated presence in the nearby villages, which were thus potential incubators of working-class consciousness and community.

Figure 4.4: A farmer, neighbours and day labourers, lamb-marking, 1926.
Note: Standing: Henry Woodley, Gordon Condon, Sam Condon, Roy Arkell. Kneeling: Jim Arkell, Charlie Davidson, Norman McHattan.
Source: Colleen Braithwaite collection.

---

47   *WT*, 2 May 1907, 9.
48   Frederick Lovett to the chief inspector, 29 April 1911, Wongarbon School Administrative File, pre-1939, 5/18176.2, NRS 3829, SARNSW; Commonwealth of Australia, *Commonwealth Electoral Roll, New South Wales*, 1921; Registers of Admission to Wongarbon Public School, 1915–50 (copy), in possession of Colleen Braithwaite, Dubbo.

All in all, though farming practices changed in several ways between 1880 and 1930, hired workers remained a common element. But mostly it was only a seasonal component of a muddled mix of labour (see Figure 4.4). These were not self-evidently conditions likely to promote a strong sense of class antagonism. If labour, land and capital were so untidily entangled, then how and when did small farmers develop a distinctive class consciousness, involving an alignment with employers' interests, and an explicit antagonism towards advocates for labour?

Farming, labour and class consciousness

Farmers' day-to-day, personal engagements with (and as) labourers did not occur in isolation but, rather, were enfolded within a wider political world. I borrow here from Jonathan Zeitlin's argument that beyond individuals' direct experience of the struggle between capital and labour, formal institutions such as trade unions and employers' organisations influence people's consciousness of belonging to one class or another.[49] In this light, the FSA's role as an intermediary between farmers, trade unions and government deserves some attention.

Though some farmers might have had a strongly parochial perspective, hardly lifting their gaze beyond the farm gate (the FSA often alleged it was so), many were also aware of, if not directly connected with, matters playing out in state and federal parliaments, and in workers' and farmers' associations. The rise of organised labour and employer groups in the early twentieth century, prompted to some extent by the introduction of compulsory arbitration, decisively changed farmers' attitudes towards labour in ways that did not necessarily arise from, or become evident in, any actual engagements between farmers, as employers, and paid labourers. This contest challenged, and therefore served to define more explicitly, farmers' conceptions and consciousness of themselves as a class. It was evident in the emergence of the FSA and the Rural Workers Union (RWU), and the evolving industrial relations apparatus.

---

49   Jonathan Zeitlin, 'From Labour History to the History of Industrial Relations', *Economic History Review* 40, no. 2 (1987): 159–84.

Land policy and the rise of the Farmers and Settlers Association

Other than the two gatherings of a loose collection of local selectors' organisations in the late 1870s (discussed in Chapter 1), concerted collective action by New South Wales farmers dates from conferences held by Riverina settlers in Wagga in 1890 and 1892, at which they discussed access to land. A further conference in Cootamundra in 1893, which resolved to establish a Farmers and Settlers Association, was subsequently recognised as the organisation's genesis. The association developed a platform through debate and resolutions made at annual conferences attended by representatives of a growing branch network. For over 10 years it did not align with any one political party or faction, instead advocating on its members' behalf with all party leaders.[50]

The association tried to extend its influence and membership by holding annual conferences further north from 1898. The FSA chose Dubbo to host the 1904 conference, in part to stir interest in the district. With the largest stations being broken up for closer settlement and no longer an existential threat, people there were seemingly indifferent to farming politics. A few branches around the district had formed during the Federation drought; however, by 1903 several had fallen into abeyance and there were none close to the town.[51] In early 1904, the FSA's general secretary, Thomas Irving Campbell, visited the district to set wheels in motion. This energetic 42-year-old smallholder from Tabbita near the present-day town of Griffith pressed the defunct Bunglegumbie branch, just across the river and downstream from Dubbo, to re-form. A few willing members renamed themselves the Dubbo-Bunglegumbie branch and officially played host to the annual state conference. They called a town hall meeting and urged other dormant branches to re-form and engage, Campbell in the meantime working in the background to assemble the program for around 150 delegates.[52] In June, the Dubbo mayor welcomed them at the Masonic Hall flanked by Campbell and the FSA president, farmer and former carrier Jim McInerney of Gundagai. Affirming the district's previous indifference, the president

---

50   William A. Bayley, *History of the Farmers and Settlers' Association of NSW* (Sydney: Farmers and Settlers' Association, 1957), 43; Ulrich Ellis, *A History of the Australian Country Party* (Parkville: Melbourne University Press, 1963), 13, 16; Graham, *The Formation of the Australian Country Parties*, 56–7; *Catholic Press*, 21 June 1902, 22; *SMH*, 8 June 1904, 5.
51   Evidence on Dubbo district branch numbers is taken from various local newspapers for the period 1899–1914.
52   *DL*, 3 February 1904, 2, 17 February 1904, 2, 27 February 1904, 2, 13 April 1904, 2.

observed that the essential purpose of the meeting in the town was 'to arouse the interest of the farmers and settlers in the work of the Association, and to get them to take a deeper interest in their affairs'.[53]

Figure 4.5: Robert Patten (1859–1940).
Source: National Library of Australia.

---

53   *DL*, 8 June 1904, 2.

As well as highlighting local farmers' political apathy, as compared with their southern counterparts, the conference demonstrated that, at that stage, farm labour was of no concern to the broader organisation and its members. The FSA's annual report for 1903, presented at the Dubbo conference, referred to many concerns—the government's drought relief measures, the need for cheaper access to more land under secure forms of tenure, the problems of rabbit infestation and water conservation—but made no reference to farm labour. The association's platform, submitted for discussion at the conference, was also silent on such matters. None of the 56 resolutions debated over the eight days touched on farmers' relationships with workers.[54] This was despite the fact that compulsory industrial arbitration, which would become a touchpaper for agrarian discontent, had been in place in New South Wales since late 1901, and federal parliament was then debating the status of rural labour within a Commonwealth arbitration bill. The Dubbo gathering was also notable for Robert Patten's emergence in rural politics (see Figure 4.5). He had formed the Mitchells Creek branch just four years earlier and was elevated to the FSA executive at the conference. He had a persuasive command of political rhetoric and a knack for constructing just the right agrarian metaphor to engage a farming audience. In a short time he would exert substantial influence over the FSA through a decisive phase in the organisation's development.[55]

From around 1906, land tenure and taxation became more prominent planks in the FSA's platform. The issues gained traction with the rise of the Australian Labor Party. Like the farmers' organisation, Labor wanted more smallholders on the land. Drawing on Henry George's theory of a 'single tax', Labor's preferred mechanisms included, firstly, a progressive tax on land with an unimproved value set high enough to affect only the very largest landholders, and secondly, wider use of leasehold tenure. By leasing rather than alienating land, the party argued, wealthy landholders could be prevented from accumulating even larger tracts, and the public, through the state, would rightly retain the unearned appreciation in land values.[56]

54   Farmers and Settlers Association of NSW, *Reports—Annual Conference Held at Dubbo, June 1904* (Dubbo: [1904]) 5–9, reprinted from the *Dubbo Liberal*.
55   *SMH*, 11 June 1904, 15.
56   Jim Hagan and Ken Turner, *A History of the Labor Party in New South Wales, 1891–1991* (Melbourne: Longman Cheshire, 1991), 38; Frank Bongiorno, *The People's Party: Victorian Labor and the Radical Tradition, 1875–1914* (Carlton: Melbourne University Press, 1996), 87; Robin Gollan, *Radical and Working Class Politics: A Study of Eastern Australia 1850–1910* (Carlton: Melbourne University Press in association with The Australian National University, 1960), 206–7; *Worker*, 21 February 1907, 9; *DL*, 8 October 1910, 3.

As John Rickard has observed, while the Labor Party had remained a marginal presence in politics in the 1890s, farmers could regard it as a benign interest group and an occasional useful ally.[57] Between 1901 and 1910, though, Labor's increasing representation in state and federal parliaments enabled it not just to advocate for, but also to implement, its land policies. Its representation in the New South Wales lower house increased from 24 (of 125) seats in 1901 to 46 (of 90) in 1910, enabling it to win government. At the federal level, Labor's representation in the lower house increased from 16 to 43 (of 75) seats between 1901 and 1910, including 17 of 27 seats in New South Wales. Labor was no longer just an interest group with which to treat, but a formidable force that organisations opposed to its policies needed to confront politically.

In light of Labor's growing potential to legislate its land policies, the FSA's official position by the time Patten became president in 1909 was to support freehold title. 'Every man' should be 'allowed the opportunity to own the land he called his home', was one of Patten's standard lines.[58] The FSA also opposed a land tax even on the largest properties, arguing that if one were introduced, the threshold could be lowered later, eventually to encompass all landholders, no matter how insubstantial their assets.[59] On these issues, the FSA executive was positioning the association as diametrically opposed to Labor, which gave politicians such as state Labor member for Cootamundra William Holman the opportunity to allege, however dubiously, that the FSA was dominated by the old squatting class. Certainly, its views on land taxation provided the basis for closer political cooperation between small farmers and big pastoralists.[60]

The FSA's firm positions on land policy arose despite the membership, and even the executive, holding more diverse views. As late as 1904 the association was determinedly non–party political, and even proudly accommodated diverse opinions and allegiances. The Forbes farmer and founding member of the FSA Thomas Brown personified the association's eclectic early phase. This lay Presbyterian preacher, land tax supporter and

57   John Rickard, *Class and Politics: New South Wales, Victoria and the Early Commonwealth, 1890–1910*, (Canberra: Australian National University Press, 1976), 304.
58   *Corowa Free Press*, 26 March 1909, 3. See also New South Wales, Legislative Council, *Parliamentary Debates*, 24 November 1908, (Sydney: Government Printer, 1908), 2728.
59   *SMH*, 7 November 1906, 8; *DL*, 10 February 1909, 3.
60   *SMH*, 9 November 1906, 6, 16 November 1906, 3; *Worker*, 15 November 1906, 6; Graham, *The Formation of the Australian Country Parties*, 62; Hagan and Turner, *A History of the Labor Party*, 35–6.

federal Labor member for Canobolas spoke at the Dubbo conference in favour of branches being free to support whichever local candidate they chose, noting that members:

> were divided on party politics, and … it would be impossible to unite them on any given line of action, and the result would be the splitting of their members into sections.[61]

From 1905, office holders, members and branches holding positions aligned with Labor Party policy came under closer scrutiny, and either left the organisation or were voted from office. That year, Brown lost his position on the executive.[62] Then, at the 1906 conference, John Louis Treflé, who was also a founder of the FSA, was voted off the executive (Patten replaced him as vice-president) because of his continuing involvement with the Labor Party and his support for land taxation and leasehold tenure.[63] By November, Treflé had won a by-election for the state seat of Castlereagh, centred on Gilgandra, for the Labor Party, running against the FSA-endorsed candidate—a Quirindi farmer and former miner and shearer—John Perry. McInerney, the FSA president between 1902 and 1905, resigned rather than renounce his commitment to the Labor Party whose policies he considered were the most likely to enable his children to acquire land.[64] Ironically, and illustrating the fluidity of farmers' politics in this period, McInerney's successor as FSA president was Perry, who had been a member of the Labor Party before he resigned over the issue of land tenure.[65]

Though the FSA leadership was purged of Labor sympathisers and aligned more openly with the conservative side of politics, the rank and file were not necessarily so disposed. There was more clarity of conviction within the executive than across the organisation as a whole. Continuing, unresolved tensions were on display in 1907 when the annual conference debated a motion that members of the Labor Party should be debarred from joining the FSA. Responses affirmed the untidy mixtures of wage labouring and landholding, even within farming families. A Jerilderie delegate responded

61 Farmers and Settlers Association of NSW, *Reports—Annual Conference*, 27.
62 *Yass Evening Tribune*, 14 August 1905.
63 *Farmer and Settler*, 25 July 1906, 21; *ATCJ*, 1 August 1906, 17.
64 *SMH*, 2 August 1906, 10; *Gundagai Times and Tumut, Adelong and Murrumbidgee District Advertiser*, 7 August 1906, 2.
65 *Farmer and Settler*, 18 April 1906, 15; Parliament of New South Wales, 'Mr John [2] PERRY (1849–1935)', accessed 22 March 2024, www.parliament.nsw.gov.au/members/formermembers/Pages/former-member-details.aspx?pk=915. On this period, see also Graham, *The Formation of the Australian Country Parties*, 59–65.

that such a measure would 'cause disastrous splits in families the members of which included supporters of both organisations'.[66] Another report of the discussion stated that:

> farmers' sons had in many instances to leave home and go to the city, or shearing, and to do so they must join a union. The camp then became divided, the father on one side, and the children on the other.[67]

One delegate said that it would weaken the FSA in districts where the Labor Party was strong:

> In old settled districts people who have been on the land for years were conservative in their ideas, but in the newly settled districts, where some of the settlers had been labourers or shearers, different political ideas prevailed.[68]

The FSA leadership was seeking to persuade a still diverse membership of the merits of a narrowing set of policies and a more determined party allegiance.

Who were the FSA executive?

If farmers' views were so diverse, how and why did the FSA come to be so decisively aligned? At least part of the answer lies in the FSA executive's increasingly assertive role. Clearly, it could not act independently of the members, who voted on candidates for executive positions at each annual conference and who, through their branches, nominated motions for debate and decision at those forums. The executive needed a majority of members' support to shape the association's platform. But it did not simply respond passively to the members' direction. Rather, it became detached from those who put them in that position, as though to affirm Robert Michels's famous Iron Law of Oligarchy concerning political parties, and moved towards the orbit of the state's 'political class'. The FSA executive then disproportionately shaped the new orthodoxy, and enforced it on the whole organisation.[69]

---

66 *Daily Telegraph*, 11 July 1911, 9.
67 *Australian Star*, 11 July 1907, 7.
68 *SMH*, 11 July 1907, 4.
69 Robert Michels, *Political Parties: A Sociological Study of the Oligarchical Tendencies of Modern Democracy* (Glencoe Illinois: The Free Press, 1915), 405–9.

This was all the more curious because the individual officeholders did not have especially wealthy or privileged backgrounds. Between 1906 and 1913, the positions of president and vice-president (generally there were two of the latter) were filled by a very small group. Perry was president for three of those eight years, and vice-president for another two; John Wetherspoon was vice-president for six; the emerging Arthur Trethowan for three (he would go on to be president in 1916–20); and Patten an executive member for all eight years, including five as president. As a novice tenant farmer, Patten was not coming from a position of landed privilege, and both Wetherspoon and Perry had labouring backgrounds before they acquired land as selectors. Trethowan accumulated substantial property, though not through a long family association with the land.[70]

One characteristic they shared, though, was that at one time or another, they became members of either state or federal parliaments. This marks them as men of personal ambition, most likely articulate, and with connections to people with power and influence in non-Labor politics. They understood that what they took to be their constituents' interests were inextricably bound to the decisions of governments, which they could best advance by directly engaging in the adversarial, legislative process, not just seeking to influence from the sidelines. Being close to party politics, they would also have appreciated Labor's organisation and discipline: the strength it derived from its members' pledge of solidarity, its branch network and its connections to the trade union movement.[71] Patten expressed some qualified admiration for Labor in 1913, acknowledging the party as 'one of the most influential combinations in the Commonwealth'.[72]

A full-time general secretary who shared the new generation of officeholders' convictions on land policy and other matters also aided the executive's emergence as an influential body in its own right. Campbell became secretary in 1898, serving at first without remuneration. But by 1905, thanks to increased members' subscriptions, he was working from premises in Sydney with a salary and travel allowance.[73] Often he, rather than the president, was

---

70 Doug Morrissey, 'Trethowan, Sir Arthur King (1863–1937)', *Australian Dictionary of Biography*, National Centre of Biography, The Australian National University, published first in hardcopy 1990, adb.anu.edu.au/biography/trethowan-sir-arthur-king-8849/text15531.

71 Perry was the MLA for Liverpool Plains in 1904–07 and an MLC in 1920–22; Wetherspoon an MLC in 1908–28; Trethowan an MLC in 1916–37; Patten an MLC in 1908–10, before resigning to contest a lower house seat, and then serving in the federal parliament from 1910 to 1917 (see below).

72 *Land*, 31 January 1913, 12.

73 Bayley, *History of the Farmers and Settlers' Association of NSW*, 52–3.

the association's public voice. With his experience, continuity and sympathy for the executive's agenda, he was able to craft the association's direction by managing annual conference programs and communications with the branch network.

The executive was further strengthened when, in February 1906, it followed the labour movement's lead by launching its own newspaper, arranging with a private publishing company to produce the *Farmer and Settler* through which the executive could communicate directly with the broader membership. Campbell was the titular editor, probably to inspire confidence among the readership and advertisers. But that fraught relationship between the executive and the publishers ended acrimoniously in the courts in 1910 over interpretations of its financial aspects. Undaunted, early in 1911 the FSA launched its fully owned paper, the *Land*. With the organisation's growing maturity, it appeared better to understand the power of cultivating an imagined community of common interest by distributing uniform messages expressed in consistent language to its branches and members. The newspaper's importance to the executive, and the executive's increasingly forceful role in policing the organisation's platform, were illustrated when it admonished a member of the Coboco branch, north of Dubbo, for canvassing for the *Farmer and Selector*, which had become the rival rural paper.[74]

The executive's power had been consolidated at the 1907 conference that adopted Patten's motion to amend the constitution to allow the Executive Council to 'suspend or expel members and dissolve branches who are disloyal to the platform and constitution' of the FSA (see Figure 4.6).[75] Its assertive management of local issues was evident in 1911 when a member in Nevertire, north-west of Dubbo, complained that the executive was trying to establish an alternative branch in the district. According to one report in the rival newspaper:

> he had been a good secretary and a great worker in the cause of the man on the land, but he was guilty of being a believer in the platform of the Labor party, or was suspected of a strong leaning that way.[76]

---

74   *Farmer and Settler*, 7 February 1906, 3, 24 December 1909, 2, 19 May 1911, 1; Bayley, *History of the Farmers and Settlers' Association of NSW*, 34–85; *Land*, 27 January 1911, 11.

75   *Evening News*, 10 July 1907, 10.

76   *Farmer and Settler*, 19 May 1911, 1.

Figure 4.6: A branch official and the FSA executive.
Note: (L–R) Robert Patten, Arthur K. Trethowan, John Perry and Secretary Thomas I. Campbell.
Source: *Farmer and Settler*, 10 September 1912, 1.

Other branches had complained that their nominations for conference agendas were passed over by the executive without consultation.[77]

So, from 1905, the executive was becoming increasingly assertive in shaping and enforcing a narrow range of policies, particularly on land tenure and taxation, rather than reflecting the diversity of opinions and circumstances among farmers across the state. However, before 1907, neither within the association nor locally were farmers' relationships with labour sparking any great interest or concern.

77   *DD*, 22 June 1910, 2.

Arbitration and the rise of the Rural Workers Union

Labour relations would animate rural politics when farmers and their representatives felt threatened by compulsory conciliation and arbitration laws, and organisation among rural workers. The evidence from the rural sector bears out Rickard's contention that, by encouraging organisations to form and grow, on both employers' and employees' sides, and institutionalising an adversarial relationship between them, arbitration was one factor stimulating class consciousness in Australia in the early twentieth century.[78]

Though New South Wales had had such a law since late 1901, and the Commonwealth's Act (relevant to disputes that crossed state borders) was in force by the end of 1904, the effects were delayed in rural New South Wales for several reasons. First, farm labourers (as distinct from shearers and other workers in the pastoral sector) showed little inclination to organise so as to seek an award. Second, the Commonwealth Act excluded disputes involving workers engaged in 'agricultural, viticultural, horticultural, or dairying pursuits'.[79] Advocates for rural workers' exclusion asserted that farming was unique in its markets and modes of production, including the application of labour. They argued that, whereas industries selling domestically could adjust their prices in response to rising costs, farmers sold mainly into international markets and therefore were price-takers, unable to pass higher labour costs on to consumers. Farmers' advocates added that agriculture was too diverse an enterprise to be covered by a single award. Aspects they alleged were peculiar to farming included extreme peaks and troughs of seasonal work (and associated variations in wage rates and daily hours of work), and the fact that it accommodated little 'division of labour'. Rather, individuals undertook an array of tasks as the occasion required and were not tied to a narrow range of specialised work as might occur in a more orderly setting such as a factory, or even a shearing shed. In addition, conditions varied from one district to the next, and from one side of the country to the other, such that a more localised system of determining wages would work better.

78 Rickard, *Class and Politics*, 274–86.
79 Commonwealth of Australia, *Conciliation and Arbitration Act*, no. 13, 1904, para 4. Both the Commonwealth Act and the NSW Industrial Arbitration Act 1901 excluded domestic service.

Others argued that relationships between farmers and farm labourers were entirely amicable: that they worked side by side, almost as family, and therefore there were no disputes to arbitrate.[80]

The main arguments in support of agricultural labourers' inclusion emphasised that every worker was entitled to protection from exploitative employers and that independent and compulsory arbitration was a civilised alternative to strikes and lockouts. But agricultural workers' pivotal status in debates over the legislation suggests not only that farming involved unusual modes of production, but also that it possessed a sacrosanct status—not just an occupation but also a way of life supposedly untrammelled by social antagonism and class feeling. (Ironically, while the FSA and its supporters appropriated the idea that its membership constituted a 'class', apparently this did not manifest in their relationships with wage labourers.) Once agricultural labour's explicit exclusion was passed into law, it sat within the Commonwealth statute books as both a goad to advocates for rural workers' rights and arbitration, and also a caution to proponents of farmers' exceptionalism that the exclusion could be overturned by any future parliament dominated by a Labor Party backed by an increasingly ambitious union movement.

The arbitration system became more tangible in rural communities in 1907 when the AWU achieved a federal award for shearers and shedhands.[81] Then, in 1908, the RWU formed in Wagga and issued a log of claims setting out proposed rates of pay and conditions of employment and, as a body representing agricultural employees across New South Wales, sought to engage with the FSA. It is plausible that the RWU (like the FSA 15 years earlier) formed in the Riverina because of the relatively larger agricultural properties in that region, requiring larger teams of paid labour. In 1904–05, the average area of alienated holdings in the Riverina was almost 3,000 acres, as compared with around 1,900 acres on the Central Western Plains, and just 642 acres on the Central Western Slopes (Dubbo was on the border between the two).[82] Nonetheless, anxiety among farming communities, stoked by

---

80 Summarised from parliamentary debates of 1904 and 1910 on conciliation and arbitration bills: Commonwealth of Australia, House of Representatives, *Parliamentary Debates* (Canberra: Government Printer, 1904), 2 June 1904 (pp. 1914–51), 3 June 1904 (pp. 1985–2016), 7 June 1904 (pp. 2020–80), 30 November 1904 (pp. 7620–64), 1 December 1904 (pp. 7747–73); Commonwealth of Australia, House of Representatives, *Parliamentary Debates* (Canberra: Government Printer, 1910), 29 July 1910 (pp. 839–74), 2 August 1910 (pp. 882–922), 3 August 1910 (pp. 971–1055), 4 August 1910 (pp. 1139–66).
81 *SMH*, 22 July 1907, 3; *Worker*, 25 July 1907, 11.
82 Commonwealth Bureau of Census, *Official Year Book of New South Wales, 1904–05*, 98, 102, 104.

the FSA, spread across the state, and was heightened by developments in New Zealand where the union representing rural workers had cited 7,000 individual farmers to appear before that country's arbitration court.[83]

The focus on industrial relations sharpened again in April 1910 when the Labor Party under Andrew Fisher's leadership, as the first to achieve a majority in its own right in the federal parliament, came to power with both the enthusiasm and opportunity to implement its industrial policies. Fisher committed to amending the *Conciliation and Arbitration Act* to 'ensure fair and reasonable conditions to all classes of labour'.[84] The independent member for Gippsland, George Wise, claimed that during the campaign, at least in Victoria, non-Labor candidates had circulated the RWU's 'scale of wages' in country districts to injure their opponents. In June, an RWU delegation met with the prime minister, urging him to include rural workers in amended conciliation and arbitration laws. With a majority in both houses, the government's amendments were carried, including a provision for union preference. The RWU achieved status as a registered organisation under the revised *Conciliation and Arbitration Act* later in 1910, with around 10,000 members.[85]

From 1911, the union published further logs of claims and again sought to involve the FSA, whose strategy was to resist such engagement.[86] For an award to be created, either employees and employers (generally through their associations) had to reach an agreement, or the court had to determine that a dispute existed and then make a determination in the form of an award. The FSA executive declined the RWU's request to meet, stressing that it could not respond until all branches had had the opportunity to comment on the claims. Campbell asserted that there could not be a formal process of conciliation or arbitration because there was no dispute, and claimed that farmers could not participate in a meeting because of the

83   *SMH*, 2 September 1908, 8; *Farmer and Settler*, 7 August, 2, 18 September 1908, 7.

84   *SMH*, 5 March 1910, 15; Clem Lloyd, 'Andrew Fisher', in *Australian Prime Ministers*, ed. Michelle Grattan (Chatswood: New Holland Publishers, 2008), 73–86; John Uhr, '1910: Fisher Leads Labor to Victory', in *Elections Matter: Ten Federal Elections That Shaped Australia*, ed. Benjamin T. Jones, Frank Bongiorno and John Uhr (Clayton: Monash University Publishing, 2018), 26–44.

85   'Conciliation and Arbitration Bill', 4 August 1910, Commonwealth of Australia, House of Representatives, *Parliamentary Debates* (Canberra: Government Printer, 1910), 1158; *Age*, 16 June 1910, 8; *Worker*, 23 June 1910, 15; Commonwealth of Australia, *An Act to Amend the Commonwealth Conciliation and Arbitration Act 1904–1909*, no. 7, 1910; *Pastoralists Review*, 15 November 1910, 962; *Daily Telegraph*, 7 November 1910.

86   Graham, *The Formation of the Australian Country Parties*, 77; *Land*, 27 January 1911, 8; *Worker*, 22 February 1911, 5.

imminent harvest.[87] The association also declined to register with the court as an employers' organisation so that, if the RWU chose to prove a dispute, it would have to name individual farmers as parties, which it threatened to do.[88]

The perceived threat to farmers of rural workers' action can only have escalated in January 1913 when the RWU amalgamated with the much larger, industrially powerful and politically connected AWU to form one big rural union. As the union representing shearers and shedhands across the country, the AWU was well placed to extend its influence to the agricultural and dairying industries.[89] The FSA executive's very active role in seeking to shape the membership's response was evident in its 1913 annual report: 'the necessity for organisation to resist these [RWU] demands must be forcibly impressed on every agricultural or dairying settler'.[90]

Notwithstanding these developments, in the Central West farmers were not necessarily exercised about the threat of labour activism. FSA branches, including several in the Dubbo farmlands, had responded predictably when the FSA executive encouraged them to comment on the detail of the RWU's logs of claims, preferring lower to higher minimum wage rates, and favouring flexible rather than prescribed conditions of employment.[91] But the seeming indifference the FSA sought to turn around in 1904 was still evident a decade later. An FSA organiser touring the Dubbo district in 1914 encountered farmers who declined to contribute to the association's 'fighting fund', as he struggled to get them 'to see that there was any danger to their interests in the claims of the Australian Workers Union'.[92] The executive entreated the membership to take sides: to wake up from their alleged apathy and declare themselves loudly for employers' interests. Organisers and officeholders criticised the waverers, the indifferent, and the less-than-fully committed. A correspondent with the *Land*, seeking to explain the predominance of Labor-held seats in rural districts, fulminated that the 'overwhelming factor' was 'a tremendous and careless indifference to things political by the producer'.[93] The divide between the executive and

---

87   *Land*, 22 December 1911, 4, 18 October 1912, 6; *Daily Telegraph*, 4 February 1914, 9; *Land*, 22 May 1914, 7.

88   *DL*, 21 November 1911, 4; *SMH*, 28 November 1911, 6.

89   *Worker*, 22 January 1913, 1.

90   *SMH*, 2 May 1913, 7.

91   *Farmer and Settler*, 3 February 1911, 8; *DL*, 8 December 1911, 4.

92   *DL*, 25 September 1914, 2.

93   *Land*, 2 May 1913, 6.

some branches might also have been replicated in the separation between officeholders and other members at the local level, as executive members of the Dubbo branch were just as concerned about a lack of local enthusiasm:

> It is with … regret that your committee are compelled to refer to the apathy exhibited by the men on the land towards the local branch of the Association. They appear totally negligent as regards the necessity for that unionism, which is necessary during the present period of combinations and aggregations … [Y]our committee feel aggrieved that the support and assistance which the Association warrants … is so feebly and uninterestedly given.[94]

The association was framing, in stark, binary terms, arrangements that, arguably, admitted a 'half way', or rather a varied and complex set of gradations and conditions between farmers and labourers. The FSA executive was scoring a hard boundary across what was actually a messy and ambiguous set of relationships between labour, land and capital. Those in the middle were being challenged to pick a side—to make a definitive choice in the face of their more nuanced, day-to-day circumstances.

Opponents of trade unionism boldly claimed that a proportion of paid labourers was on their side of the divide by distinguishing between the aspirational worker, whom they cast as the least likely to join a union, and the rest. An FSA organiser attending a meeting of the Dubbo branch in 1913 suggested that 'almost every member of the community' should join the association, based on a rhetorical claim that:

> those who were not farmers now did not know when they would be working their own properties. It was certainly the aim of nearly every young man employed by landholders to become a farmer some day.[95]

Another FSA representative announced to a Dubbo audience in 1915 that the association planned to create its own union of workers to whom farmers could give preference, such that 'a bond of sympathy will spring up between the men on the land and the rural workers, who are the farmers of the future'.[96] A correspondent with the *Land* who claimed once to have been a rural worker dismissed those in the second category of labourers as being of little worth:

---

94   *Land*, 28 February 1913, 12.
95   *Land*, 30 May 1913, 12.
96   *Australian Worker*, 11 March 1915, 13.

One can easily divide the farm hands into two classes. The first and best are composed of farmers' sons and men who are working on the farm in the hope of some day owning a farm of their own; also the man who takes an interest in the farmer's work, his horses, bullocks, machinery, etc. The majority of this class will not join this union, unless forced to; but this second class of men will join the RWU ... They consist of the 'ne'er-do-well' the 'won't-do-well', the drunk, and the loafer.[97]

It is unlikely that all farmers shared such a decisive view, but the rise of unionism must at least have emphasised to farmers that their interests, and those of some paid labourers, did not necessarily coincide.

In the midst of the various parties' positioning in this period, there *were* instances in the Central West of potential and actual industrial disputes, and of labour assuming a political face. Workers in the more closely settled farming districts might have worked in relative isolation from other employees, but they were not immune from unionism. Indeed, the fluid exchange of labour across inland New South Wales probably meant that many people who lived or worked in the agricultural districts were familiar with, if not actively engaged in, the pastoral sector's longer experience of awards and industrial disputes. W. G. Spence, the AWU leader and Labor parliamentarian, claimed in 1904 that 'most of our farm labourers engage in shearing pursuits during the wool season', and by 1910 that the 'majority of the rural workers, who are now being organised, are also shearers and members of the Australian Workers Union'.[98] Each year, shearers from Murrumbidgerie/Wongarbon headed out to the earlier-starting sheds. An 1896 report stated that, by early August, 'farming operations are now completed and the majority of the young men have now gone shearing', and another in 1901 indicated that 'a number of our young men have gone out back shearing, where the season opens earlier than here', implying that they would return for later local shearing. This still occurred in the late 1920s: 'Shearing time is approaching, and the local shearers are preparing to migrate to the West.'[99] When they returned, they might also work as agricultural labourers. In Dubbo in 1910, Tasman Lavender encountered the fluid seasonal exchange between pastoral

97   *Land*, 13 April 1911, 10.
98   'Conciliation and Arbitration Bill', 30 November 1904, Commonwealth of Australia, House of Representatives, *Parliamentary Debates* (Canberra: Government Printer, 1904), 7637; 'Conciliation and Arbitration Bill', 29 July 1910, Commonwealth of Australia, House of Representatives, *Parliamentary Debates*, (Canberra: Government Printer, 1910), 840; Merritt, *The Making of the AWU*, 48–9; Hagan and Turner, *A History of the Labor Party*, 54.
99   *DL*, 1 August 1896, 2, 7 August 1901, 3; *WT*, 4 July 1929, 9.

and agricultural work: 'shearers and shed hands on the lookout for a job with the harvesting now that the shearing had "cut out"'.[100] Both itinerant and local labourers would have been able to compare conditions in the district with those in the western sheds, from 1907 regulated under a federal award.

Local disquiet from around the time the RWU formed was reported through the labour press. A correspondent to the *Worker* urged that a branch of the RWU be established at Wellington in 1908 on account of the 'scandalous conditions of farm labour in the central western districts'.[101] One correspondent reported on his experience of a farm near Dubbo, where he was carting and stacking hay in 1914:

> First, the hut accommodation here was nil, but we were to camp under a kurrajong tree in the paddock—no tent or any covering from the rain, if rain came. The tucker consisted of bread and salt beef, and we were to cook for ourselves in our spare time. No lunch allowed. Made a start and worked from 7 a.m. until half-past ten, and demanded lunch, and was asked to work on until dinner. That was the limit—passed the job in and left.[102]

By 1913, some workers in the Dubbo district were prepared to withhold labour in support of the unions' claims. Escalating workers' demands to receive union rates, sometimes leading to strikes, were reported near Narromine, Gilgandra and in the Wellington-Dubbo district at the beginning of that year's harvest. Their extent is hard to gauge as workers' advocates talked them up while farmers' supporters talked them down.[103] On the rich agricultural country around Ponto, though, farmers on larger properties were sufficiently affected to alter their cultivation practices for the following season, reducing the areas they cropped to an extent that they could manage without paid labour. Some arranged with sharefarmers to work the remainder.[104]

So farmers might well have been responding to actual contestation of pay and conditions in their local, day-to-day relationships, though the affected farms are likely to have been relatively large, and therefore employers of a comparatively substantial seasonal workforce. Fifteen farms in the

---

100 Lavender, 'Young Bill's Happy Days'.
101 *Worker*, 30 April 1908, 29.
102 *Australian Worker*, 19 November 1914, 19.
103 *Farmer and Settler*, 28 October 1913; *Land*, 31 October 1913; *Australian Worker*, 13 November 1913, 24, 20 November 1913, 23; *Leader*, 19 November 1913, 4.
104 *DD*, 3 March 1914, 4. See also *Wagga Wagga Advertiser*, 24 March 1908, 2.

Bodangora-Maryvale district each employed between 5 and 15 workers during the 1913 harvest. The more seasonal workers there were on a property, the higher the chance that they included people from beyond the district, and fewer who were otherwise farmers.[105] Thus, the conditions were more akin to those on larger grazing properties further west and in parts of the Riverina where the positions of labour and capital were more entrenched. Farmers would also have known that branches of the Political Labor League (PLL) were forming in the railway villages. Murrumbidgerie established a branch as early as 1903. With encouragement from the state Labor member, Thomas Thrower, branches formed at Geurie in 1912, Mogriguy and Eumungerie by 1913, and were resuscitated at Wongarbon and Beni also in 1913. Ballimore had a branch once the railway through there was completed, in 1918.[106]

By 1913, then, despite their often ambiguous roles as both employers and paid workers, farmers could hardly have avoided the rhetoric, if not the experience, of class, including via the urgings of the FSA executive as expressed through the pages of the *Land*, discussion within their local branches over the RWU's logs of claims, and the local presence of the RWU and the PLL. In the context of compulsory arbitration, and in response to the rise of the RWU, labour relations joined land policy among the FSA's principal platforms, with the FSA executive casting itself as the head of an industrial organisation, representing the employing class.

The 1913 federal election

The federal election of May 1913 proved that even the smallest farmers—those most likely to have recent or continuing roles as wage labourers—were aligning with the larger landholders and against advocates for labour. Historically, the New South Wales wheat belt had been a source of strength for the Labor Party, which Jim Hagan and Ken Turner attribute principally to land policies that favoured the struggling or aspiring smallholder.[107] By 1913, with the RWU and then the AWU promulgating further logs of claims and an election imminent, the FSA's executive had shed any

---

105 *Australian Worker*, 13 November 1913, 25; *DD*, 3 March 1914, 4.
106 *Australian Workman*, 12 December 1891, 3; *Evening News*, 19 April 1892, 6; *National Advocate*, 13 November 1893, 2, 24 January 1894, 3; *DL*, 24 January 1894, 2, 11 July 1894, 2, 6 December 1912, 2; *Worker*, 16 June 1894, 3; *DD*, 12 August 1903, 2, 6 May 1905, 3, 28 January 1913, 2, 31 January 1913, 2, 18 February 1913, 4, 21 March 1913, 4, 3 June 1919, 4, 1 July 1913, 2; *WT*, 12 December 1912, 7.
107 Hagan and Turner, *A History of the Labor Party*, 39.

pretence of being above parliamentary politics. 'It is no time for apathy', implored Patten: 'Every member should directly interest himself and others in our national politics.'[108] Running their own candidates in three-cornered contests under the 'first-past-the-post' voting system would have split the conservative vote, so delivering seats to their Labor opponents. Therefore, FSA branches were urged to work assertively with local Liberal Associations to select or endorse candidates for the forthcoming election.[109] Local branches endorsed Liberal candidates in eight rural seats held by Labor members or sympathisers. Though arrangements appear to have been relatively amicable, one participant in New England claimed that, by ceding the initiative, the local Liberal Association had become but a 'joint in the tail' of the FSA.[110] In Hume, held by the aged William Lyne, an independent with a record of supporting Labor, the local Liberal Association and FSA branch nominated Patten, by then the FSA's president of five years' standing and a past state legislative councillor. In the huge western electorate of Darling, which included Dubbo, the non-Labor associations endorsed Gilgandra branch president and farmer Edwin Townsend as the Liberal candidate. He was never likely to unseat Spence, who had won 65 per cent of the vote in 1910 with the strong support of the mining town of Cobar.[111]

The RWU's bids for coverage under an arbitrated award remained a conspicuous part of these candidates' pitch to rural constituents. Patten colourfully caricatured the prospect of farm labour being subject to 'nine-to-five' conditions: 'Let them go farming and leave a ripe crop to the tender elements from midday on Saturday till Monday morning, and see how rich they would get.'[112] A correspondent for the *Land* referred to the 'menacing purpose' of the RWU, and invited settlers to consider the question:

> To whom should I be most loyal, Sir William Lyne, whom I have voted for in the past, and who now is giving his support to the party which stands behind the RWU and its unreasonable demands, or my own interest as a tiller of the soil?[113]

---

108 *SMH*, 2 May 1913, 10.
109 Graham, *The Formation of the Australian Country Parties*, 93; Ulrich Ellis, *The Country Party: A Political and Social History of the Party in New South Wales* (Melbourne: F. W. Cheshire, 1958), 25; *Land*, 26 July 1912.
110 *Maitland Daily Mercury*, 29 March 1913, 4; *WT*, 6 March 1913, 5; *Daily Telegraph*, 27 February 1913, 8; *Goulburn Evening Penny Post*, 20 March 1913, 4; *Tamworth Daily Observer*, 1 February 1913, 3.
111 *DD*, 8 April 1913, 2; *Land*, 23 May 1913, 7.
112 *Land*, 11 April 1913, 7.
113 *Land*, 23 May 1913, 6.

Percy Abbott, the FSA-endorsed Liberal candidate for New England, while campaigning in Tamworth, said in relation to the prospect of a rural workers' award, that 'the Labor party would ultimately induce the farmer to throw up his land'.[114]

Six of the eight endorsed candidates were successful, including Patten in Hume. In the seat of Calare, which included farming country just east and south of Dubbo, the longstanding Labor member and former FSA vice-president Thomas Brown lost for the first time since entering the federal parliament in 1901. In Darling, a majority of voters in the east of the electorate, including the towns of Dubbo, Narromine and Gilgandra, voted for the FSA-endorsed candidate, but Spence prevailed with a reduced majority.[115] The New South Wales results, combined with Liberal victories in several non-metropolitan seats in Victoria, delivered the narrowest of defeats for the Fisher government.[116] One report claimed that the RWU log 'had a magical effect' in the Hume, Riverina, Indi and Werriwa electorates, and the *Land* editorialised that the campaign proved that 'the steady, solid country influence can save the State from political Trade Unionism'.[117] The election result showed that farmers were turning not only against the political advocates for wage labourers, but also, given the prominence of arbitration and union claims in the campaign, against labour more broadly, at least in its collective, unionised form.

The 1917 general transport strike

The general strike of August and September 1917 was a denouement in the contest between labour and capital for farmers' allegiances. It illustrated the extent to which farmers' conceptions of themselves as a class distinct from labour, and also from the city, were reinforced by broader societal perceptions. The confrontations between the FSA and the RWU/AWU had embedded the idea that 'labour' was now not just a group of more

---

114 *Tamworth Daily Observer*, 1 March 1913, 4; *Worker*, 20 February 1913, 5.
115 Colin A. Hughes and B. D. Graham, *Voting for the Australian House of Representatives 1901–1964* (Canberra: Australian National University Press, 1964); Commonwealth Electoral Office, *Statistical Returns in Relation to the Senate Election, 1913; The General Election for the House of Representatives, 1913*, in *Parliamentary Papers—General*, vol. II, 1913 (Melbourne: Government Printer, 1913), 155f.
116 *Land*, 6 June 1913, 6; Bongiorno, *The People's Party*, 92; Ross McMullin, *The Light on the Hill: The Australian Labor Party 1891–1991* (South Melbourne: Oxford University Press, 1991), 86; J. R. M. Murdoch, 'Joseph Cook: A Political Biography' (PhD thesis, University of New South Wales, 1968), 239–43.
117 *Albury Banner and Wodonga Express*, 6 June 1913, 46; *Land*, 6 June 1913, 6.

or less familiar people who supplemented a farm's seasonal workforce, but also a movement with form and discipline, and potential power defined under rules upheld by the state. But 'labour' took on an even more abstract, impersonal form when it referred to the workers and unions that farmers relied on to move their produce to markets on railways, wharves and ships. They were also associated mostly with the cities, and therefore could be objectified and contrasted with one's self, and an increasingly indurative farming class. The strike strengthened farmers' conviction that 'labour' was a remote and anonymous entity, insensitive to rural needs and values. This was borne out starkly in press depictions of strikebreakers from the country.

The wartime strike began with a dispute over the application of a card system for calculating labour productivity within the Government Tramway Workshops in Sydney, but spread to involve railway, mining and waterfront workers to become what was recognised at the time as 'the biggest industrial upheaval ever experienced in Australia'.[118] At its peak, at least 69,000 workers were on strike. Strikes, and protests in support of the unionists, extended beyond Sydney, but in their depictions of strikebreakers who arrived from the country, newspapers framed the conflict as being as much between city and country as between employer and employee, with 'country' being conflated with 'farmers'. Trethowan, by then a member of the Legislative Council, Dubbo landowner and FSA president, committed his association to support the state government, and organised strikebreakers to travel from country districts.[119] Men encamped at the Sydney Cricket Ground and Taronga Park Zoo.

Newspapers sympathetic to the strikebreakers attributed to the farmers a particular form of masculinity. The alleged country manner of the 'volunteer labourers', including a supposed capacity for hard work, was a point of distinction from the mainly urban, striking workers. 'It is amazing to a city dweller with what ease a country man will turn out in the morning', enthused the *Sun*: 'Long before the customary breakfast hour 300 of them

---

118 New South Wales Labour Council, *Report*, 31 December 1917, quoted in Ian Turner, *Industrial Labour and Politics: The Labour Movement in Eastern Australia, 1900–1921* (Canberra: Australian National University and Cambridge University Press, 196), 141. See also Dan Coward, 'Crime and Punishment: The Great Strike in New South Wales, August to October 1917', in *Strikes: Studies in Twentieth Century Australian Social History*, ed. John Iremonger, John Merritt and Graeme Osborne (Cremorne: Angus & Robertson in association with The Australian Society for the Study of Labour History, 1973), 51–80; Lucy Taksa, '"Defence Not Defiance": Social Protest and the NSW General Strike of 1917', *Labour History*, no. 60 (1991): 16–33.
119 *Daily Telegraph*, 8 August 1917, 7; *Land*, 10 August 1917, 13.

were at work on the wharves.'[120] Reports publicised the volunteers' home towns and localities, including Dubbo, Eulomogo, Wongarbon, Gollan, Bodangora, Tomingley and Wellington. These were not the typical centres of labour–capital confrontations of the 1890s. The references located the strikebreakers as being clearly from 'the bush', and also implied that small, identifiable communities were rallying to support a broader rural—indeed, farming—cause against labour, overlain in the context of the war with notions of patriotism.[121] A volunteer from Dubbo, 'horny-handed son of the soil' William Treece, became a celebrity in the sympathetic press when he allegedly beat off an assault by no fewer than seven striking workers while returning to camp one evening. Another report in the same edition extolled the country people:

> 'These coves from the country fairly beat anything', said a city man who has been officially connected with the camp. 'They go to work singing and whistling, and after a whole day's hard and rough toil on the wharves, or wherever they are sent, they come back to camp grimy of body but as fresh of spirit as when they kicked off their bed-clothes in the morning'.[122]

Though the labour press was obviously less flattering in its depictions of the strikebreakers, casting them as wealthy war shirkers, it nonetheless reinforced that they were farmers from the country, counterpoints to the urban unionists.[123] By 1917, then, whatever their local experience of engaging workers might have been, farmers were widely cast as the antithesis of organised labour: a trope encouraged not only in their own organisation's newspaper but also now in the labour and mainstream press.

Conclusion

In May 1914, the small Glenara branch of the FSA, with a high proportion of newcomers paying off very modest blocks on the local closer settlement purchase area, held their monthly meeting. They accepted five new members, thanked their secretary for his work in advocating for a local school and, on the motion of one of the smaller landholders, agreed that

---

120 *Sun*, 16 August 1917, 2. See also *Riverine Herald*, 16 August 1917, 2; *SMH*, 16 August 1917, 7; *DL*, 17 August 1917, 4.
121 *DD*, 24 August 1917; *SMH*, 18 August, 7, 27 August, 8, and 30 August 1917, 6.
122 *Land*, 31 August 1917, 12.
123 *Australian Worker*, 23 August, 19n, 30 August, 19, 6 September 1917, 1.

'only primary producers be accepted as members'.[124] It is not known what prompted the motion—whether it was a local initiative or a response to a direction from the FSA executive that branches should clarify their rules. But it was a clear statement of who this group considered themselves to be and who they were not.

A farming class consciousness had consolidated *despite* the complex ways land, labour and capital came together in the farmlands, with its economic base consisting predominantly of holdings small enough that households did the bulk of their own work with only occasional intermittent support from paid labour. It arose in opposition to an often abstract notion of labour, given force by the state and the rise of land taxation and industrial arbitration, all galvanised through the force of the FSA. And it was reinforced locally through the experience of people coming together as neighbours—fellow farmers—in these places increasingly dominated by a homogeneous economy and population. They gave local expression to the ideas and tropes issuing from the FSA through its newspaper and annual conferences: to assert that only primary producers be accepted as members (see Figure 4.7).

Figure 4.7: The farming class of 1924: Farmers and Settlers Association annual conference, Sydney, including Wongarbon branch delegates.
Source: Woodley family collection.

---

124 *DL*, 15 May 1914, 4.

5

'The farmers have been most loyal': Political allegiance in the farmlands

On a Thursday evening in June 1932, less than three weeks after the New South Wales governor, Philip Game, had dismissed Jack Lang's Labor government from office, the political ripples reached the railway village of Wongarbon. They were turbulent days. The state's unemployment rate had passed 30 per cent, the Labor Party had split into Lang's supporters on the one hand, and, on the other, those who sided with the federal parliamentary party's more moderate approach to managing the state and the country out of the Depression. A rally of Lang's followers three days later in Sydney's Moore Park would attract at least 200,000 people. George Wilson of the United Country Party was the first candidate standing for the seat of Dubbo at the imminent election to campaign in the village. On a shopkeeper's veranda, he was introduced to a gathering crowd by Albert Mawbey, president of the local branch of the FSA, which had by then utterly embraced parliamentary politics. Interjectors punctuated Wilson's long speech, one calling for 'three cheers for Jack Lang', to which the former premier's supporters responded heartily. Wilson in turn invited the gathering to give three cheers for his party's leader Michael Bruxner, which was as energetically accepted. The following evening a spokesperson for the sitting Labor member and Lang supporter in the recently dissolved Legislative Assembly, Alfred McClelland, addressed the villagers from the same spot, and he too was subject to the wags, one of whom 'counted him out', as though the candidate were a floored boxer. These were good-natured exchanges but they show that even these small communities were divided along political lines. They raise questions about the historian Don Aitkin's analysis of rural voting in New South Wales in which he concludes that between the 1930s and 1950s, communities of less than 600 people overwhelmingly supported the Country Party.[1]

In this chapter I look for voting patterns in the farmlands' small booths, but also at how parliamentary and municipal politics were experienced locally— on the hustings, at the ballot box and in the periods between elections. Did farmers organise locally? What was their relationship with candidates and local members? What qualities did they expect and encourage in a local member? Did politics matter? And, ultimately, what does their engagement with politics (or lack of it) say about people's alliance, either with a local community or broader farming class? I focus here on colonial/state and municipal politics because of the relative paucity of quantitative, local-level data for federal elections. Results were not officially published at booth level and, as Aitkin also concluded, subdivisional data are too coarse to support analyses of small communities' voting practices.[2] But also, for much of this period, federal politics was more remote and less relevant. Dubbo and its hinterland were always located on the fringe of huge electorates, encompassing diverse industries and economic interests so that the local farmlands vote counted for even less than in state contests.

1880–1903: Finding a voice

In the last decades of the nineteenth century many changes affected politics in the Dubbo district—in electoral boundaries and systems of representation, the evolution of political parties and the make-up of the population. The district experienced steady rather than spectacular economic and population growth. The depression of the early 1890s and the Federation drought at the turn of the century restricted investment. The town's population, which had grown substantially from 836 in 1871 to 3,199 in 1881, was still only 3,409 by 1901. At the same time, the railway, closer settlement schemes and the expansion of the wheat-growing frontier caused grain production to increase across New South Wales from the mid-1890s. Mixed wheat–sheep

---

1   Joan Beaumont, *Australia's Great Depression: How a Nation Shattered by the Great War Survived the Worst Economic Crisis It has Ever Faced* (Crows Nest: Allen & Unwin, 2022), 409; *SMH*, 6 June 1932, 8; *WT*, 9 June 1932, 4; Don Aitkin, *The Country Party in New South Wales: Membership and Electoral Support* (Canberra: Australian National University for the Australian Political Studies Association, 1965).
2   Aitkin, *The Country Party in New South Wales*, 18.

farming became the main mode of production in the Central West. Small villages formed along the new railway lines that also generated employment for wage labourers and contractors.[3]

The area within the vast western electorate of The Bogan was reduced in 1880 so that Dubbo made up a higher proportion of voters. The balance of population and power was shifting away from the pastoral west and towards the town, and though members of parliament were still drawn from relatively wealthy pastoralists, they were more likely than their predecessors of the 1860s and 1870s to live in the electorate.[4] Members of parliament were paid from 1889, making politics more accessible for those who were not independently wealthy.

In this late colonial period, political parties emerged, organised more or less coherently around policy platforms rather than allegiances to factional leaders, the 1887 election being the first contested by candidates aligned with the Free Trade and Protectionist organisations. Whereas in Victoria the Protectionists championed the nascent manufacturing sector and its workforce, in New South Wales, from 1894, the Free Trade Party leader George Reid reframed the contest between the two major parties such that the central issue became the source of government revenue. He cast his Free Traders as the party that would fund the government through redistributive direct taxes, including on land for those who could best afford them, rather than by imposing indiscriminate costs through tariffs on rich and poor alike. Thus, he represented his party as the liberal friends of the less well-off, and the Protectionists as the reactionary guardians of privilege. The Labor Party emerged at the 1891 election and, while it would flounder on the issue of members' obligations to support the caucus's majority positions (the 'pledge'), it gathered support in both the city and the country to become a potential alternative government by the early twentieth century.[5]

---

3   New South Wales, *Results of a Census of New South Wales Taken for the Night of the 31st March 1901* (Sydney: Government Printer, 1904), 546; Sir Samuel Wadham, R. Kent Wilson, Joyce Wood, *Land Utilisation in Australia*, 4th ed. (Parkville: Melbourne University Press, 1964), 108.

4   *ATCJ*, 7 April 1883, 17; *DD*, 15 April 1892, 3; *Sydney Mail and New South Wales Advertiser*, 23 April 1887, 842; *ATCJ*, 9 April 1887, 27.

5   P. Loveday and A. W. Martin, *Parliament Factions and Parties: The First Thirty Years of Responsible Government in New South Wales, 1856–1889* (Carlton: Melbourne University Press, 1966), 139; P. Loveday, A. W. Martin and Patrick Weller, 'New South Wales', in *The Emergence of the Australian Party System*, ed. P. Loveday, A. W. Martin and R. S. Parker (Sydney: Hale and Iremonger, 1977), 172, 175–81, 186–90; A. W. Martin, 'Free Trade and Protectionist Parties in New South Wales', *Historical Studies* 6, no. 23 (1954): 322; Jim Hagan and Ken Turner, *A History of the Labor Party in New South Wales, 1891–1991* (Melbourne: Longman Cheshire, 1991), 3. 'Labor Party' is used throughout as a generic term covering organisations that at various times were also known as the Labor Electoral League and the Political Labor League.

With Dubbo assuming greater importance within a redefined electorate, in 1891 Robert Booth became the first member for The Bogan to be closely associated with the town, where he practised as a solicitor and had served as mayor. In 1894, the new electorate of Dubbo closed even more tightly around the town and its increasingly agricultural hinterland, and excluded pastoral country to the north-west around Nyngan and beyond.[6]

The two main candidates contesting the new seat over the next decade were James Morgan and Simeon Phillips. It is difficult to judge what Morgan's success says about the electorate's social and political character. The president of the Peak Hill branch of the Amalgamated Miners Association, he had been elected as one of three members for The Bogan in 1891, and one of the new Labor Party's 35 candidates swept into office in the aftermath of the bitter Queensland bush workers' strike. In the schism that followed, over the 'pledge' and which of the fiscal policies (protection or free trade) were in the best interest of working people, Morgan lost the party's backing. For the remainder of the 1890s, he supported Protectionist policies and governments, arguing that import duties favoured local industry and workers. At face value, this placed him in the same camp as pastoral leaseholders who regarded Reid's policies favouring land tax as a threat to their estates. Morgan was re-elected, but as a Protectionist candidate, to the new single-member seat of Dubbo in 1894.[7]

Simeon Phillips, the second resident of Dubbo to represent the district, held the seat from 1895 to 1904. He had arrived in around 1878, established a business as a jeweller, and was mayor of the town from 1880 to 1889. At his first, unsuccessful attempt to enter the parliament in 1894, a 'requisition' signed by 300 supporters urged him to run on account of his 'liberal views' and 'sound practical knowledge of the want of the district'.[8] Despite his early commitment to be 'a thoroughly independent member, attached to no party'—a common boast among local members since 1856, but one decreasingly plausible as party discipline took hold—Phillips became a loyal supporter of George Reid's government, and from 1895 an endorsed candidate for the Free Trade Party.

6   *SMH*, 19 June 1891, 6; *DD*, 10 November 1916, 1; *Daily Telegraph*, 12 April 1894; *Truth*, 3 June 1894, 4; Eamonn Clifford, Anthony Green and David Clune, eds, *The Electoral Atlas of New South Wales, 1856–2006* (Bathurst: New South Wales Department of Lands, 2006).

7   Bede Nairn, *Civilising Capitalism: The Labor Movement in New South Wales, 1870–1900* (Canberra: Australian National University Press, 1973), 61–4; *Barrier Miner*, 23 June 1891, 2; *DL*, 7 February 1894, 2; Loveday, Martin and Weller, 'New South Wales', 175–81.

8   *DL*, 27 January 1894, 2.

Over the four general elections conducted between 1894 and 1901, the issues dominating candidates' pitches to voters in the electorate of Dubbo included federation, temperance, local infrastructure needs, reform of the Legislative Council, the relative merits of protection and free trade, and, above all, access to land. Over successive election campaigns, Morgan argued that he was the 'small man's' friend, but he could not shake off his opponents' assertions that he had supported the extension of pastoral leases, to the detriment of aspiring smallholders. Despite his protestations that his land policies and those of Phillips were identical, and that he was 'neither a squatter's nor a selector's man', his hesitancy on land taxes and closer settlement dogged his campaigns.[9] Phillips, on the other hand, was cast by a sympathetic local newspaper as a 'liberal land reformer'. He talked up the success of Reid's 1895 land laws that introduced perpetual leasehold tenure as an option for would-be farmers, and the lower costs of farm machinery arising from reduced import duties.[10] Electors applauded his claim in 1896 that:

> these leasehold areas should be at once thrown open for selection, so that everyone could select, and by the toil of his hands and the use of his brains not only add to the wealth and prosperity of Murrumbidgerie but also of the country generally.[11]

Figure 5.1: Hustings, Macquarie Street, Dubbo, c. 1880.
Source: State Library of New South Wales.

---

9   *DD*, 30 July 1895, 2; *DL*, 27 July 1898, 2.
10 *DL*, 14 July 1894, 2, 16 July 1898, 2.
11 *DL*, 25 March 1896, 3. See also *DL*, 13 July 1898, 3.

to assert that the village consisted mainly of 'freetraders', which might have been common local knowledge but would certainly have been affirmed by the newspaper's publication of election results for each booth.[18]

In the quarter century to 1904, small communities' political involvement extended beyond election campaigns and was not solely initiated by candidates and members. Suffrage for non-Aboriginal men had been in place in New South Wales for a generation, and for many who settled in the farmlands in this period, the principles and practices of representative government were familiar. Organisations with an explicitly political purpose would not emerge until the very end of the period, but specific local issues prompted people to seek their elected representatives' assistance, displaying a sophisticated understanding of the government process, and confidence in their own power to influence it. They readily sought local members' intervention in their exchanges with government officials or ministers. In 1883, residents of Beni, which was then a cluster of farms, a public school and a new church, sent a petition to one of the two local members, George Cass, seeking funds for a teachers' residence. When they did not receive what they considered a timely response, they wrote to The Bogan's other member, Patrick Jennings. Cass was also lobbied to have a school established at Geurie in 1886, and Eulomogo residents asked Phillips to intercede to have a teacher appointed locally in 1898.[19]

Communities did not necessarily need an immediate problem as a prompt to engage with a local member either. In 1896, the Murrumbidgerie Progress Association invited Phillips to the village before he returned to Sydney after a parliamentary recess. The event's chair surmised that Phillips 'might wish to see all the electors of the district, so that he could tell them what he had been doing'. The Bunglegumbie Progress Association also invited Phillips to a meeting in 1900, without identifying any specific issue for discussion.[20] These forums implied a closer relationship between a broader range of electors and their representatives than was the case before the late 1880s, and relied on the member being resident in the electorate. Communities were asserting a right not just to elect a representative, but also to impress on him their views, to seek his support for local causes and to hold him to account.

---

18 *DL*, 23 July 1898, 3.
19 T. A. Whalley to George Cass MLA, 7 August 1883, Beni School Administrative File, pre-1939, 5/14887.4, NRS 3829, SARNSW; W. Reynolds to George Cass MLA, 15 March 1886, Geurie School Administrative File, pre-1939, 5/15981, NRS 3829, SARNSW; F. Woodley to S. Phillips MLA, 31 January 1898, Eulomogo School Administrative File, pre-1939, 5/15848.1, NRS 3829, SARNSW.
20 *DL*, 25 March 1896, 3, 23 May 1900, 4.

Voting patterns were emerging in the farmlands by 1903.[21] Murrumbidgerie village, with its mix of railway employees, shearers and farm labourers, was distinctive. By providing nearly half its vote (47.6 per cent) to the Labor candidate in 1894, the village stood out from both Dubbo and the small rural booths.[22] Without an official Labor candidate in the field in 1895 and 1898, the village voted overwhelmingly for the Free Trade Party's Phillips, during a period when the parliamentary Labor Party was more closely aligned with Reid than with the Protectionists. When Labor endorsed a candidate for the seat of Dubbo again in 1901, Murrumbidgerie's support once more exceeded that of the town and the rural booths.[23] Voting in the rural booths was less definitive, showing marginally more support for the Protectionist Morgan in the elections of 1894 and 1895 before favouring the incumbent Free Trader Phillips in the subsequent polls, though again not by overwhelming margins. Without sharply distinguished platforms on land or farming policy to choose from, it is unremarkable that rural voters did not lean decisively one way or another in this period. Here was a loose collection of farmers, carriers and occasional wage labourers, assertive and literate in political matters, but without a distinct and coherent political voice.

1904–1919: Finding a party

Politics were no less dynamic in the period 1904–19. Women (so long as they were not Aboriginal) voted in New South Wales for the first time. Former adherents to either protectionism or free trade conjured with more meaningful ways to define their credos as the 'fiscal issue' became decreasingly relevant with the advent of the Federation. The Liberals emerged as a party of reform but also employers' interests and were increasingly defined as the alternative to a resurgent Labor Party. Labor formed government in 1910, before splitting over the conscription question when government passed in 1917 to a new Nationalist Party consisting of Liberals and pro-conscription former Labor members. In the country, farmers emerged as a more coherent political voice, but still without a dedicated representative in the state

21   Booth-level data in this section are taken from: New South Wales, *General Election, 1894*, in *Votes and Proceedings of the Legislative Assembly*, vol. I, 1894–95 (Sydney: Government Printer, 1895), 9; New South Wales, *General Election, 1895*, in *Votes and Proceedings of the Legislative Assembly*, vol. I, 1894–95 (Sydney: Government Printer, 1895), 9; *DL*, 30 July 1898, 2, 6 July 1901, 2.

22   The figures quoted in this chapter for 'small rural booths' include only booths within the electorate that encompassed Dubbo *at that time*, and is the subset of such booths I judge to be both rural and within the town's sphere of influence.

23   *DL*, 6 July 1901, 2; Loveday, Martin and Weller, 'New South Wales', 207–9.

parliament. The FSA's annual conferences regularly debated the merits of forming a country party, but the risk of splitting the non-Labor vote under a 'first-past-the-post' voting system meant that the association would only go so far as to agree that endorsed candidates could be put forward in negotiation with the Liberal or (from 1916) Nationalist parties.

In the Dubbo district, the town was expanding again, its population increasing from 3,409 in 1901 to 5,032 in 1921. In contrast, and despite governments' continuing promotion of closer settlement, the population of the surrounding Shire of Talbragar (formed in 1906) remained static, actually decreasing from 3,607 in 1911 to 3,584 by 1921. Thus, the town grew from being 23 per cent more populous than the shire in 1911 to having 40 per cent more residents by 1921. Nevertheless, and despite drought conditions through much of World War I, the rural population was becoming more productive, with wheat output increasing through a combination of more land being cultivated, more efficient machinery, better wheat varieties, the use of fertilisers and fallowing techniques, and mixed agricultural and grazing methods.[24]

Governments continued to mould rural development. Under closer settlement schemes, including those specifically for returned soldiers from 1916, larger properties were subdivided in places such as Glenara, Ridgeview, Drinane and Murrumbidgerie, and embedded the state government in the rural economy as a major creditor (see Chapter 3). During World War I, the government became the sole purchaser of the wheat harvest, so that marketing and price setting became sensitive economic and political issues in the country. Railway construction and maintenance continued to transform the economy, bringing navvies, sleeper cutters and permanent railway staff to villages that formed at Ballimore, Mogriguy and Eumungerie, thereby helping to make agriculture viable for the first time in many places (Chapter 6 examines railways' influence in more detail).[25] And, as the district's economic profile changed, so did its politics.

---

24 Commonwealth Bureau of Census and Statistics, *The First Commonwealth Census, 3rd April 1911* (Melbourne: Government Printer, 1911); Commonwealth Bureau of Census and Statistics, *Census of the Commonwealth of Australia Taken for the Night between the 3rd and 4th April, 1921* (Melbourne: Government Printer, [1921]); Edgars Dunsdorfs, *The Australian Wheat-Growing Industry, 1788–1948* (Carlton: Melbourne University Press, 1956), 188. Commonwealth Bureau of Census, *Official Year Book of New South Wales 1904–05* (Sydney: Government Printer, 1906), 289; Commonwealth Bureau of Census, *Official Year Book of New South Wales, 1930–31* (Sydney: Government Printer, 1932), 186.
25 Dalgety & Company, *Murrumbidgerie Estate* [sales brochure] (Sydney: S. T. Leigh and Co. Printers, 1901), 7; Wadham, Wilson and Wood, *Land Utilisation in Australia*, 108; Dunsdorfs, *The Australian Wheat-Growing Industry*, 214.

From 1904, both Dubbo and Wellington were the main centres in the new seat of Macquarie in a smaller Legislative Assembly, reduced from 125 seats to 90 with the advent of the federal parliament.[26] With these two towns containing a sizable proportion of the new electorate, it became a more marginal seat. The Labor Party had had a branch in Dubbo since at least 1891, and from the early twentieth century became increasingly active in the surrounding railway villages (see Chapter 4). Despite the Dubbo Political Labor League being described at the time as a 'numerically weak, uninfluential and somewhat distracted organisation', Labor's Thomas Thrower was the pre-eminent local member of the period. He defeated Phillips in 1904 and won three of the subsequent four general elections, including the 1917 poll, which he contested for the Labor Party as an anti-conscriptionist opposed to the new Holman-led Nationalist government. When the Trades and Labour Council of New South Wales was reconstituted in 1901 as the Sydney Labor Council, Thrower became the new entity's first president. In 1904, the 34-year-old from Sydney was a member of the New South Wales Labor Party's central executive committee. Though prominent in state Labor politics, he was virtually unknown in the Central West until he won preselection over men from Dubbo, Cobar and Gulgong.[27] He would move to the Central West once he was elected, but with no prior connections to the district, he first stood on the basis of his party's platform rather than claims of local affinity.

As land tenure and industrial arbitration began to animate the FSA's leadership, the association's branch network provided some focus for local political expression. However, with no party devoted to representing rural interests above all others, there were still no candidates specifically representing a farming vote during this period. Former bank manager and prominent Wellington landowner Charles Barton won the seat as a nominee of the Liberal and Reform Association in 1907. In 1910, Thrower returned, defeating Sydney-based James Burns who was considered a 'comparative stranger' in Macquarie.[28] A newly constituted FSA Macquarie Electoral Council endorsed Liberal nominee and Dubbo auctioneer Reginald Weaver in 1913, and Thrower's opponent in 1917 was a Wellington flour mill

26 Michael Hogan, '1904', in *The People's Choice: Electoral Politics in 20th Century New South Wales, Vol. One, 1901 to 1927*, ed. Michael Hogan and David Clune (Sydney: Parliament of New South Wales and University of Sydney, 2001), 29.
27 *DD*, 10 August 1904, 2; *Evening News*, 1 June 1904, 5; *Narromine News and Trangie Advocate*, 10 June 1904, 7; Bede Nairn, 'Thrower, Thomas Henry (1870–1917)', *Australian Dictionary of Biography*, National Centre of Biography, The Australian National University, published first in hardcopy 1990, adb.anu.edu.au/biography/thrower-thomas-henry-8807/text15447; *WT*, 18 August 1904; Hogan, '1904', 40.
28 *WT*, 22 August 1910, 3.

owner, Murdoch McLeod. Thrower died in office that year and was replaced at the by-election by another outsider with strong Labor Party connections, Patrick McGirr of Parkes. One of his brothers was already in the parliament, and another would become premier.[29] Whatever the political leanings of the successful candidates, voters in the Central West did not necessarily value a local connection.

But they did welcome candidates' direct attention. Local campaigning was just as intense in these years, with both Labor and non-Labor candidates canvassing in the villages and small rural localities. In 1904, Thrower committed to 10 local events in seven days. By then, there were still more booths, in places such as Buninyong and Bunglegumbie, on candidates' itineraries. Thrower spent a Saturday in Murrumbidgerie village before addressing a meeting in the evening. The effort to be present in these places seemed to count for as much as what the candidates had to say. A Minore correspondent noted: 'The present member seems to be the most in favour here, and a visit from him would further his prospects.' That year both Phillips and Thrower included on their itineraries the community of Ballimore, each addressing the local electors in the roadside inn, all to secure the 20 or so votes to be had in that place. In the 1917 by-election campaign, Labor's McGirr, the Nationalists' McLeod and a host of supporters engaged exhaustively with the outlying communities, holding meetings in halls and private residences.[30] McLeod and his entourage held meetings in every location that would host a polling booth.[31] Neither before nor subsequently were such communities so intensely duchessed.

From 1904, candidates conjured with how best to communicate with newly enfranchised women, who appear to have embraced electoral politics and campaigning. During the election campaign that year, women canvassed for both Liberal and Labor candidates, and were conspicuous at party rallies. At a Labor Party rally, women were well represented but still segregated, the gallery being 'one compact block of femininity'. Thrower appealed directly to the 'ladies' vote' in Wellington, supposing that 'womanly instincts' would lead them to identify with their sisters in the cities and support the party's efforts to shore up morality through its support of an early closing act (their opponents actually claimed to occupy the higher moral ground on

---

29   *DL*, 10 July 1907, 3; *WT*, 25 July 1910, 5, 12 July 1917, 8, 23 July 1917, 3; *SMH*, 5 December 1913, 6.
30   *WT*, 1 August 1904, 3; *DD*, 25 June 1904, 3; *DL*, 20 July 1904, 5, 23 July 1904, 2, 5, 6 July 1917, 2, 17 July 1917, 3; *National Advocate*, 9 July 1917, 2.
31   *DL*, 10 July 1917, 3, 17 July 1917, 3.

temperance issues), and efforts to secure for families a living wage. Phillips and Thrower held separate 'Ladies meetings' in Dubbo and Wellington, and a Miss Hall addressed electors on Labor's behalf. Thrower's meetings in Beni were attended by 'both ladies and gentlemen', and Phillips's meeting there was chaired by the local schoolteacher, Margaret Ryan.[32]

During the 1907 campaign, 28-year-old Selina Anderson left no doubt that women had a place in politics, not only as interested bystanders and voters but also as active participants. Born in 1878 near Hill End, she became a mover in labour affairs, including as a member of the organising committee of the Sydney Labour Council and the Labor Women's League. In 1903, she was the first woman to contest a seat in the federal House of Representatives when she stood for Dalley in Sydney. In 1907, she was staying with her mother and stepfather who owned an 800-acre farm on Mitchells Creek. She campaigned vigorously for Thrower at Spicers Creek, Goolma and Geurie. At Wongarbon, she addressed the crowd of 250 people for 2.5 hours—a performance punctuated with humour and willing exchange with the throng. Clearly, her assertive presence at such an event was novel, but the occasion also demonstrated that within just a few years, women were embedded in the idea of politics.[33] Some years later, a young woman's diary entry concerning polling day for the 1914 federal election at Coboco affirms that women participated as readily as men in what was both a political and a social event: 'There was nearly 100 voted altogether. The covered way was stacked with men and the front veranda with women.'[34] From the electoral data, it is not possible to conclude what effect candidates' overtures might have had, either on whether women voted, or for whom, but clearly they were prominent at electoral events, both as audience and campaigners.

Though campaigning at election time was often intense, and some residents engaged assertively with elected representatives, commentators were just as likely to note a lack of enthusiasm for politics among farmland voters. At the 1906 federal election, only about 100 of 243 electors enrolled at the Geurie booth voted, 'so it is evident that our electors either had enough appreciation of our glorious freedom or were too busy harvesting'. At Mogriguy in 1910 an observer noticed farmers in particular who, though 'hardly out of sight of

---

32   *DD*, 10 August 1904, 2; *WT*, 23 June 1904, 6; *DL*, 20 July 1904, 5, 4 August 1904, 5, 24 June 1904, 2, 3 August 1904, 5; Hogan, '1904', 4–9, 54–5.
33   *WT*, 28 March 1907, 4, 25 April 1907, 6, 9 May 1907, 6.
34   'Daisy' [Lilian] Fisher, 'From the Diary of Daisy Fisher', in *A Compiled History of Coboco District*, ed. Pat Fisher, Robyn Healey and Sandra Burns (Narromine: Coboco CWA, 2002), 96.

the polling booth ... had not interest enough in the elections to record their vote'.[35] This would remain a recurring theme in the farmlands, and not only among farmers. In 1904, a group of labourers chaff cutting near Eulomogo revealed to a local Labor organiser that they knew neither that an election was imminent, nor the identity of the Labor candidate, the famed union organiser W. G. Spence.[36]

Nevertheless, in the elections held between 1904 and 1917, the railway villages of Murrumbidgerie/Wongarbon, Geurie and, by 1917, Ballimore continued to support Labor candidates. Ballimore provides an indication of the sometimes rapid social and political change of the time. In 1913, in the predominantly farming community on the Dubbo to Cobbora road, Thrower received 8 of the 27 votes.[37] Four years later Ballimore was home to a railway construction camp. Thrower received 76 of the 92 votes recorded at the general election, and Labor's McGirr 88 of 112 at the subsequent by-election.[38] Whereas small rural booths had not shown any strong preferences before 1904, in this period patterns started to emerge, reflecting the class polarisation explored in the previous chapter. In contrast to the towns and villages, small rural booths generally gave 70 per cent of their vote to non-Labor candidates. In an increasingly homogenised political landscape, at the 1917 by-election, the entirely farming communities of Emagool and Terrabella recorded 26 of 30 votes, and 24 of 27 votes, respectively, for the Nationalist candidate.

Though predominantly farming communities strongly supported non-Labor candidates, they were not putting forward their own contenders. The towns' party organisations produced Liberal and Nationalist candidates, and there was no sign locally of the FSA's assertive promotion of favoured candidates that had characterised other parts of the state at the 1913 federal election (see Chapter 4). Patten's 'farming class' would not be unambiguously represented in the Dubbo farmlands until preferential voting was introduced after the war.

---

35 *WT*, 20 December 1906, 4; *DL*, 16 April 1910, 1.

36 *WT*, 9 May 1907, 6.

37 Electoral data for this section are drawn from: New South Wales, *General Election, 1904*, in *Joint Volumes of Papers, Presented to the Legislative Council and Legislative Assembly, Second Session of 1904*, vol. I (Sydney: Government Printer, 1905), 19; *DL*, 19 October 1910, 2; *DD*, 9 December 1913, 1; New South Wales, *General Election, 1917*, in *Joint Volumes of Papers Presented to the Legislative Council and Legislative Assembly, Second Session of 1917–18*, vol. III (Sydney: Government Printer, 1918), 28–9; *DD*, 31 July 1917, 2.

38 Inspector to the chief inspector, 15 May 1915, Ballimore School Administrative File, 1884–1920, 5/14763.2, NRS 3829, SARNSW.

1920–1929: Owning a party

The period between the end of World War I and the beginning of the Great Depression saw an assertive and influential farmers' party emerge, and its candidates represent the Central West for much of that time. Between 1920 and 1927, New South Wales reverted to a system of multi-member electorates. More significantly, the 1920 election saw the introduction of preferential voting, whereby candidates with the least number of votes were progressively eliminated, and their preferences distributed until one candidate had a majority or, in the case of multi-member electorates, when the requisite number of candidates had each attained a quota. One consequence was that non-Labor parties could run several candidates in the one electorate with less risk that it would advantage their opponents. The three-member seat of Wammerawa included Dubbo as well as towns as distant as Mudgee, Warren and Coonabarabran. Labor candidates William Francis Dunn and Joseph Alfred Clark won two of the three seats at each of the three elections contested in that period. Coonamble resident Clark was a tailor by trade, a longstanding alderman who had served two terms as mayor and been honorary secretary of the local Labor Party branch for 25 years. Dunn was a farmer who had resigned from his seat of Mudgee in 1910 rather than accept Labor's policy opposing conversion of leasehold to freehold title but then won it back at the following by-election after being assured that leaseholders' existing rights to convert would be retained. His pitch to voters at the western end of Wammerawa before the 1920 election emphasised 'his own practical experience' of wheat growing and pooling.[39] Barton aside—he was a bank manager for most of his adulthood anyway—Dunn was the first farmer to represent the farmlands in parliament. With the added appeal of being the minister for agriculture in the Storey government from 1920, if ever a Labor candidate were to attract farming communities' support on the basis of their association with the industry, it would have been Dunn.[40]

Immediately before that period of multi-member electorates, the FSA and the Graziers Association (GA) formed an electoral council of a new Progressive Party, to promote rural interests in collaboration with the Nationalists. New South Wales in fact lagged behind other jurisdictions in forming such a

---

39   *DD*, 11 July 1919, 3.
40   Bede Nairn, 'Dunn, William Fraser (1877–1951)', *Australian Dictionary of Biography*, National Centre of Biography, The Australian National University, published first in hardcopy 1981, adb.anu. edu.au/biography/dunn-william-fraser-6052/text10351; *Singleton Argus*, 1 August 1911, 2.

body, versions of a country party having emerged in Western Australia, Queensland, Victoria, South Australia and in the federal parliament since 1914. But the party soon attracted city members, so that its rural focus was diluted. The Progressives became more distinctly rural in outlook from 1921 when New England grazier Michael Bruxner and his colleagues (the 'True Blues') split from those inclined to form a coalition with the city-dominated Nationalists. The party—from 1925 the Country Party—supported the Fuller Nationalist government from the crossbenches until it lost office to Jack Lang's Labor Party in 1925, and formed a Nationalist–Country Party government under Thomas Bavin and Bruxner between 1927 and 1930.[41]

In the Dubbo district, the Talbragar Shire's population grew marginally, but stronger growth in the town meant that the farmlands' population continued to shrink as a proportion of the district's total. Dubbo went from being 40 per cent more populous than the shire in 1921 to having twice its population by 1933. In the aftermath of World War I, issues animating rural voters included the extension of closer settlement schemes to returned soldiers, and claims for compensation for farmers arising from wartime compulsory wheat pooling arrangements. By the end of the 1920s, falling wheat prices caused many participants in closer settlement schemes to founder.[42]

During this period, a Dubbo district farmer stood as a candidate for the Progressive/Country Party. For the first time, farmlands people had both a party standing for their interests above all others, and a familiar colleague to attract their vote. Harold Victor Campbell ('Vic') Thorby (see Figure 5.2) grew up on his Scottish Presbyterian grandparents' farm near Geurie, where he received his early education at the local primary school. He attended Sydney Grammar and later studied veterinary science and woolclassing through a technical college. Such an education set him apart from many of his contemporaries around Geurie, but he returned to farming at the age

41 Don Aitkin, *The Colonel: A Political Biography of Sir Michael Bruxner* (Canberra: Australian National University Press, 1969), 55–96, 103; Paul Davey, *The Nationals: The Progressive, Country and National Party in New South Wales, 1919 to 2006* (Annandale: The Federation Press, 2006), 9–10, 27–8; Michael Hogan, '1920', in *The People's Choice: Electoral Politics in 20th Century New South Wales, Vol. One, 1901 to 1927*, ed. Michael Hogan and David Clune (Sydney: Parliament of New South Wales and University of Sydney, 2001), 200–4; Minutes of a meeting of the Central Executive Council of the Progressive Party, 16 October 1919, Minute Books of the Central Council of the Progressive/Country Party (NSW) 1919–2005, New South Wales Nationals.
42 Australia, Department of Commerce, Royal Commission on Australian Wheat Industry, *Evidence Submitted by Mr E. McCarthy on Behalf of the Department of Commerce* (Melbourne: 1934), 61–2.

of 16, joined the local branch of the FSA, and later became its president. Thorby married into another local farming family in 1916, then served on the FSA's state executive between 1918 and 1921.[43]

Figure 5.2: Harold Victor Campbell Thorby (1888–1973), Sydney, June 1930.

Source: National Library of Australia.

---

43   Various undated biographical notes on Thorby in Ulrich Ellis Papers, box 1, MS 1006, NLA; Ian Carnell, 'Thorby, Harold Victor Campbell (1888–1973)', *Australian Dictionary of Biography*, National Centre of Biography, The Australian National University, published first in hardcopy 1990, adb.anu.edu.au/biography/thorby-harold-victor-campbell-8798/text15429; *DL*, 21 April 1914, 2, 13 November 1934, 6.

On the campaign trail in the 1920s, candidates continued to supplement town meetings, in halls and on street corners, with events in smaller surrounding communities. Cars made this easier. In 1925, a Progressive Party candidate spent a Tuesday at events at Barbigal (2 pm), Ballimore (4 pm) and Elong (8 pm). Conversely, in 1930, Thorby, by then a well-established member, took his time in the Wongarbon hall, where 'a large and representative gathering, including a number of lady voters, listened for over two and a half hours to a most interesting and instructive speech'.[44] Local political organisation was certainly limited, even precarious, between elections. Visiting Wellington in 1925, Bruxner criticised his party's lack of organisation in the 'small places', and those whose 'only thought was for a good season'.[45] But this did not necessarily reflect disenfranchisement or a lack of engagement with politics. People found ways to exert influence on issues that mattered to them. Farmland people's confidence and assertiveness in calling on their local members for support appears to have only increased as they embraced both a party explicitly representing farming interests and a local member with roots in the district. One wet Saturday afternoon in 1923, Thorby met with 40 farmers at Wambangalang at the invitation of the local FSA branch. They gathered in a private residence but otherwise it was a relatively formal occasion. A member of the press had travelled out with Thorby. A chair presided, resolutions were carried out, and the local member was invited to respond on matters including the wheat pool and the new Dubbo-Molong railway line being built through the district.[46] People in these places had engaged with local members for many years, but with such a close alignment between the association and the party, the relationship reached new levels of confidence and familiarity in this era.

Politics threw up another clue about the nature of rural society over this period: the connection between religious denomination and political preference. From the late nineteenth century, the Catholic press began to support the Labor Party as the anti-Imperialist opponents of privilege, while by 1906 Protestant voices were explicitly aligning with the Liberal Party.[47] Sectarianism re-emerged after the bitter debates over conscription

44 *DD*, 9 October 1930, 2.
45 *WT*, 23 April 1925, 3.
46 *DD*, 7 August 1923, 4.
47 Joan Rydon, R. N. Spann and Helen Nelson, *New South Wales Politics, 1901–1917: An Electoral and Political Chronicle* ([Sydney]: New South Wales Parliamentary Library and Department of Government, Sydney University, 1996), 21; Hagan and Turner, *A History of the Labor Party in New South Wales*, 22, 41; Frank Bongiorno, *The People's Party: Victorian Labor and the Radical Tradition, 1875–1914* (Carlton: Melbourne University Press, 1996), 168–70.

during the war, but was rarely, if ever, an explicit part of campaigning in the Dubbo district. Even the oblique comment made by Wongarbon shearer, farmer and Labor Party candidate Jack Ritchie during the 1925 campaign was unusual: he 'warned the electors to be on their guard against sectarian mongers'.[48] Around 28 to 30 per cent of Dubbo's population identified as Catholic between 1921 and 1947, a slightly higher proportion than across Australia as a whole. In the surrounding Talbragar Shire, fewer people identified as such, particularly from 1933 when the proportion declined to around one in four. In the predominantly Protestant farmlands, Beni stood out as a mainly Catholic community, having been settled by Irish immigrants, many of whose descendants intermarried.[49] It was also the only farming community with a Labor Party branch, and between 1904 and 1917 cast between 70 and 80 per cent of votes for Labor candidates. In the multi-member electorate period from 1920 to 1927, Thorby received just 3 Beni votes (of 49) in 1920, 2 (of 43) in 1922 and 4 (of 48) in 1925, when Ritchie gained 18.[50] Even if the large majority of rural voters were drawn to the Progressive/Country Party's platform and image, it might have had a tacit sectarian tinge, and therefore was not universally embraced.

Otherwise, from 1920, the rural booths voted strongly for Progressive and then Country Party candidates, and for Thorby in particular. In his case, at least, familiarity did seem to count. Though he was not elected that year, in a crowded field Thorby attracted 22.8 per cent of first-preference votes in the small Dubbo district booths as compared with 6.3 per cent in the town. As a local newspaper commented:

> He scored heavily, almost unanimously, among the anti-Labor voters in several places where he was well known—in the localities adjoining the district in which he has spent most of his life.[51]

Thorby worked on becoming better known among farmers and graziers across the electorate in 1922 and entered parliament at that election, receiving 34.2 per cent of the local small-booth, first-preference vote (as compared with 5.3 per cent in Dubbo). In 1925, his support in small booths increased to 42.1 per cent (as compared with the town's 9.9 per cent).

48 *Labor Daily*, 9 April 1925, 8.
49 Betty Hickey, *A Village that Disappeared: Beni Via Dubbo* (Dubbo: Orana Education Centre, 1987).
50 Electoral data for the remainder of this chapter are taken from the official returns contained in parliamentary papers, which are referenced in full in the bibliography. See New South Wales, *General Election for the Legislative Assembly*, [1920–50], *Statistical Returns*, in *Joint Volumes of Papers Presented to the Legislative Council and Legislative Assembly* [1920–50] (Sydney: Government Printer, [1921–1952]).
51 *DD*, 17 March 1922, 2.

The contrast now between the town and the farmlands consisted not only of differences in support for Labor (though that was increasingly plain), but also in farmers' support for the Country Party over Nationalist candidates who had a stronger following in the towns.

New South Wales reverted to single-member electorates for the 1927 election but retained preferential voting despite the Labor government's attempt to reintroduce a first-past-the-post system. Therefore, the non-Labor parties could continue jointly contesting seats without fear of advantaging their opponents, but then the Country Party had to contend with a redistribution, managed by the new electoral commission, which saw the ratio between city and country seats shift from 45:45 to 51:39 to reflect more accurately where people lived.[52] Dubbo and the farmlands were at the southern end of the electorate of Castlereagh, which extended north to Coonamble. Thorby won the seat from Labor's Joe Clark. The vote in the town of Dubbo was evenly split, but continuing his dominance of the farmers' vote, Thorby won more than three of every four votes at the small surrounding booths. He became minister for agriculture in a new Nationalist–Country Party coalition government. With their local farmer in the state cabinet, an influential 'farming class' was taking shape in political terms. It was reinforced through farmers' control of municipal government in the shires.

Local government

The farming population had gained new ways to influence politics and public administration from 1906 with the introduction of local government beyond the towns to previously unincorporated areas (other than the Western Division). The Talbragar Shire encircled Dubbo, and though it included the villages of Wongarbon, Eumungerie and Mogriguy with their assorted populations of labourers, railway workers, sleeper cutters, shopkeepers and schoolteachers, farmers quickly established firm control over this district. Talbragar was divided into three ridings, each represented by two councillors. Farmers immediately gained and maintained control of the council. A Eumungerie storekeeper, elected unopposed in 1914, was the only councillor who was not a farmer or grazier, and he resigned after

---

52   Kevin Cosgrove, '1927', in *The People's Choice: Electoral Politics in 20th Century New South Wales, Vol. One, 1901 to 1927*, ed. Michael Hogan and David Clune (Sydney: Parliament of New South Wales and University of Sydney, 2001), 334–9; Davey, *The Nationals*, 48.

one year due to 'pressure of private business'.[53] Once the first council had been elected (each riding was contested that year), there was only sporadic competition for positions.

In the earlier years, some candidates placed advertisements in local papers alerting voters that they intended to run, but nominees rarely campaigned for office. Nor were sitting councillors often challenged. In the 45 general elections that followed until 1950 (15 for each riding), 32 were not contested; nor were five of the seven by-elections. Most councillors served lengthy terms. William Baird was elected to the first council and remained until 1925, while fellow inaugural councillor George Graham did not depart until 1934. Graham's nephew was elected in 1947. A few families provided councillors for decades. A Wongarbon farmer and father-in-law to Vic Thorby, Alfred Morley, was a councillor from 1914 until he died in 1927. His place was filled by the only nominee, his brother Frederick, who also died in office in 1942, to be replaced by his son Wilfred, again the sole nominee. Two other father–son combinations served in this time (Godwin and Gavel), as did three generations of the Roberts family.[54]

The characteristics most valued in councillors were longevity of residence, being widely known and a reputation for being competent at one's occupation, which was overwhelmingly farming. On his appointment in 1915, Mogriguy farmer Bill Godwin was described as:

> a good man, in fact an ideal candidate … The gentleman needs no recommendation, for he has lived in the riding practically all his life, and all his interests are in the riding.[55]

Portraits of the candidates for C Riding in 1922 affirm the valued qualities:

> The three candidates are typical Western men of good standing, but competent judges put … 'Rick' Brownlow … as absolutely the best farmer in the district, and his personal popularity is unbounded. Mr T. H. Mathews enjoys the reputation of being one of those restless souls who cannot sit complacent with anything but strenuous effort. Mr A. F. Morley is capable and practical, and as full of work as any of them.[56]

---

53 *DD*, 12 January 1915, 1.
54 Talbragar Shire, *The Council of the Shire of Talbragar 1906-1966*, [Dubbo, 1966]; council election results were reported in relevant editions of the *DD* and the *DL*.
55 *DL*, 12 January 1915, 2.
56 *DL*, 17 November 1922, 2. Brownlow and Morley were elected.

Generally, 'successful' farmers were elected, with the scope to spend time away from their enterprises. They usually held several positions of local authority or responsibility, such as with a progress association, a branch of the FSA, the Pastoral, Agricultural and Horticultural Association, or the Pastures Protection Board. Several were members of a Masonic lodge, and most (if not all) were Protestant. No women sought office in this period.

These phenomena—of extended terms, family dynasties and the lack of competition for positions—say something about farming people in these places. First, small communities often place high value on avoiding overt conflict.[57] Most voters would have known or at least encountered councillors in the course of daily life, as neighbours, at FSA meetings, school events and so on—circumstances that could be disrupted by overt contests for public office. Second, local government's stability rested on a degree of apathy—a disinclination either to seek office or to vote. It is likely that very few people *wanted* office, even if the title came with a degree of status. If councillors were in any way a local elite, then they were as much self-selected as championed by their peers. Low participation rates were noted at several elections until voting became compulsory in 1947. Less than half the ballot papers were returned at a 1915 by-election.[58]

But both stability and apathy could only prevail while ratepayers considered that their interests were in safe hands. Until 1927, local government voting was restricted to property owners and those paying more than a minimum annual rent, so the constituency was even narrower and more homogeneous than the population as a whole. In 1906, even sharefarmers were ineligible to vote. Local councils (as well as the FSA and GA) strenuously opposed the 1927 amendment to extend the franchise to people who had resided in the local government area for at least six months.[59] Nonetheless, this form of government privileged property over labour, and permanence over itineracy. Local government affirmed and strengthened hierarchies within these communities.

---

57 Anthony P. Cohen, 'A Sense of Time, a Sense of Place: The Meaning of Close Social Association in Whalsay, Shetland', in *Belonging: Identity and Social Organisation in British Rural Cultures*, ed. Anthony P. Cohen (Manchester: Manchester University Press, 1982), 35.

58 *DL*, 18 January 1908, 4, 16 December 1947, 1; *DD*, 2 February 1915, 1.

59 *DL*, 19 September 1906, 3; Aitkin, *The Colonel*, 105–7; *Land*, 17 June 1927, 13.

1930–1941: Affirmation of a farming class

Throughout the 1930s, the New South Wales Country Party dominated rural politics, and for most of that time held power as a junior partner in a conservative coalition government. Around Dubbo, mixed wheat–sheep farming was entrenched as the dominant mode of production, and the basis of family and social life. Though farming people fared better than some during the Depression, they still faced subdued wheat prices and escalating debt (see Chapter 3). For those who survived, and despite years of closer settlement initiatives, properties were becoming larger on average, as unviable small blocks were absorbed. Land could be worked with less labour as machinery improved (see Chapter 4). Railway villages reached their peaks of population and influence in this period and the demand for wage labour on surrounding farms would soon begin to diminish. With cars by now common among farming households, people were more inclined to bypass the villages for commerce and recreation (see Chapter 6).

The town continued to consolidate its position relative to the hinterland. Though Dubbo's population barely increased from 12,295 to 12,805 between 1933 and 1947—a period of both low birth rates and low immigration—the shire actually shrank from 3,951 to 3,258. The town went from being little more than twice as populous as the shire to becoming nearly three times larger. Dubbo became host to families of unemployed workers who improvised crude dwellings on the town's fringe, including a large settlement on the eastern edge known as Tin Town that remained until at least 1938.[60]

In the midst of the Depression, the Labor Party returned to office decisively at the October 1930 state election under the leadership of the controversial Jack Lang. In rural areas, Labor's support for a compulsory wheat pool in the face of weak wheat prices contributed to its relatively strong performance.[61] Following another redistribution, the new seat of Dubbo saw the town once again united with Wellington and the places between. Thorby maintained his

---

60 Commonwealth Bureau of Census and Statistics, *Census of the Commonwealth of Australia, 30th June 1933* (Canberra: Government Printer, [1933]); Commonwealth Bureau of Census and Statistics, *Census of the Commonwealth of Australia, 30th June 1947* (Canberra: Government Printer, [1948]); *National Advocate*, 21 December 1934, 2, 24 June 1938, 4; Simone Taylor, 'Kerosene and Calico: The History of Dubbo's Tin Town', paper presented at the Western Plains Cultural Centre, 16 August 2018.
61 Geoffrey Robinson, '1930', in *The People's Choice: Electoral Politics in 20th Century New South Wales, Vol Two, 1930 to 1965*, ed. Michael Hogan and David Clune (Sydney: Parliament of New South Wales and University of Sydney, 2001), 47.

overwhelming support in the small rural booths, but could not resist Labor's former shearer and union organiser Alfred McClelland, who had previously represented the electorate of Northern Tablelands. He contributed to the Labor Party's landslide with the support of the towns and villages. Thorby entered federal parliament as a member for Calare the following year and would serve as a minister in several portfolios before losing his seat in 1940.

In rural New South Wales, one consequence of the Depression and that volatile and well-documented term of the Lang government was the resurgence of new states movements. Though they had minimal effect in the Central West, the experience nonetheless revealed something of farming people's attachments to class and place in the region. Movements seeking new, separate states in New England and Riverina had sparked briefly in the mid-1920s and reignited in the early 1930s. Their rhetoric repudiated Lang's threat to withhold interest payments to foreign lenders, and cast the regions as the ultimate source of all wealth, victims of an exploitative metropolis, and loyal stalwarts of decency and sanity in a political world endangered by Lang and Communists. A new state movement in the Central West formed in April 1931 as an offshoot of the Riverina Movement, spurred by frequent visits from the Riverina's animated and voluble chief protagonist Charles Hardy, and headed by Trangie grazier and merino-breeder Edmund Body. Whereas the New England movement was based on years of calculation and debate, and spurred by the strategic goal of gaining separate Senate and Loans Council representation for the region, Hardy's approach was more overtly populist, with a less thoroughly considered objective of replacing states with regional entities, and no clear idea about how to achieve it.[62]

At their peak, the movements did briefly upend grassroots rural political organisations. The combined New England, Riverina and Western organisations formed the United Country Movement in August 1931. Its proponents then effectively engineered a takeover of the New South Wales Country Party to form the United Country Party (UCP), leaving the FSA, in particular, unsettled about the prospect of losing a controlling influence over the party it had jointly created. Under Hardy's direction, the party created a military-style structure of regional divisions, groups based in

62   Sir Earle Page, *Truant Surgeon: The Inside Story of Forty Years of Australian Political Life* (Sydney: Angus & Robertson, 1963), 207–8; Ulrich Ruegg Ellis, *A Pen in Politics* (Charnwood: Ginninderra Press, 2007), 182–3; U. R. Ellis, *New Australian States* (Sydney: Endeavour Press, 1933), 207, 214–15; Aitkin, *The Colonel*, 138; *SMH*, 15 August 1931, 13.

the main towns, and subgroups in smaller locales.[63] In the Dubbo district, where farmland political organisation had consisted mainly of FSA and GA branches, the Talbragar Group formed with subgroups in Wongarbon, Ballimore-Elong, Beni, Rawsonville, Toongi, Coboco, Eumungerie, Mogriguy and Dubbo. The movement drew hundreds of people to conferences in Dubbo in 1931 and 1932. Once the governor had removed Lang from office in May 1932, local support for new states faded.[64] By 1935, the party's general secretary observed 'a certain amount of apathy and loss of interest in the organisation of the party', and the UCP's Western Division did not pay its annual financial contribution.[65] The movement's executive presented a case for a new western state before the Nicholas Royal Commission in 1934, essentially a slice west of the mountains flanked by the Riverina and New England claims. But most Dubbo district witnesses opposed the separation. Edwin Townsend of Gilgandra considered that proponents 'would have considerable difficulty getting a public meeting on this movement'.[66] No one complained when the Royal Commission subsequently concluded that there was insufficient basis for such a state.

Historians have questioned the extent of popular support for the Riverina and New England new states movements: by any measure, the relatively meagre response in the Central West was stark.[67] The movement floundered because it contradicted entrenched local perceptions of communities of interest. The new state movements' rhetoric emphasised the country's difference from Sydney, but their borders implied that one's regional identity as, say, a New Englander, predominated over one's allegiance as a farming class, or

63   Minutes of the Central Council of the Country Party of NSW, 24 September 1931, Minute Books of the Central Council of the Progressive/Country Party (NSW) 1919–2005; Ellis, *New Australian States*, 214–15; Ellis, *A Pen in Politics*, 182–3; Page, *Truant Surgeon*, 207–8; Aitkin, *The Colonel*, 138; Nancy Blacklow, '"Riverina Roused": Representative Support for the Riverina New State Movements of the 1920s and 1930s', *Journal of the Royal Australian Historical Society* 80, pts 3 & 4 (1994): 3, 18, 36; *SMH*, 15 August 1931, 13.
64   *DD*, 4 June 1931, 3, 6 July 1931, 1, 14 October 1931, 3; *DL*, 9 September 1930, 7; *SMH*, 12 October 1931, 10, 5 November 1932, 18.
65   ['General Secretary's Report for 1931'], 4 February 1932, 'General Secretary's Report for the Year Ending 31st December 1935', 7 February 1936, Minute Books of the Central Council of the Progressive/Country Party (NSW) 1919–2005.
66   New South Wales, New States Royal Commission, *Evidence of the Royal Commission Inquiry as to the Areas in New South Wales Suitable for Self-Government*, vol. 5 (Sydney: Government Printer, 1934), 1523.
67   Grant Harman, 'New State Agitation in Northern New South Wales, 1920–29', *Journal of the Royal Australian Historical Society* 63, pt. 1 (1977): 26–39; John Joseph Farrell, 'Opting Out and Opting in: Secession and the New State Movements', *Armidale and District Historical Society Journal and Proceedings*, no. 40 (1997), 143; John Joseph Farrell, 'Monster Demonstrations and Processions: The New State Petition Campaign 1921–1923', *Armidale and District Historical Society Journal and Proceedings*, no. 42 (1999): 41–9; Blacklow, 'Riverina Roused', 190.

a community of rural dwellers. This regionalism contradicted the bases of longer-standing and ultimately more enduring statewide institutions, such as the FSA, the GA and the Country Party, that had been formed on the principle that one's shared interests as a primary producer were paramount, irrespective of place.

For people in the Central West, the new states movements might also have exaggerated country regions' relationships with the metropole as being unremittingly exploitative and antagonistic. While each region related to Sydney as a source of political and financial power, of markets and as an entrepot, the relationship varied from one region to the next. The city's influence was central to people's experience but in nuanced and varied ways. The Riverina and New England movements' rhetoric, emphasising difference, disadvantage and self-determination, was typical of communities that regarded their remoteness from centres of power—their 'peripherality'— as being elemental to their culture.[68] One aspect distinguishing the experience of people in the western region from those to the north and south was that there was no obvious alternative to Sydney. One witness before the 1925 Cohen Royal Commission had considered that 'our people here, and the western district generally, are satisfied with the direction of traffic, and satisfied that Sydney is their market town: their established markets are there'.[69] Whereas the northern movement complained about railways and the lack of a closer deep-sea port, and the Riverina was more inclined to look towards Melbourne for markets and services, Sydney was the obvious destination for the west's products and source of its supplies. It was a direct and longstanding route, embedding a relationship where no other could be envisaged.

This, of course, did not obviate the potential for antipathy towards the city. Previous chapters have demonstrated that people often represented the city as wielding insensitive power over the country, to support arguments to receive better services or decisions. But, as the Gilgandra newspaper editor Patrick McManus had suggested to the Cohen Royal Commission in 1925, farmers were conscious of the symbiotic nature of the relationship:

---

68   Anthony P. Cohen, 'Belonging: The Experience of Culture', in *Belonging: Identity and Social Organisation in British Rural Cultures*, ed. Anthony P. Cohen (Manchester: Manchester University Press, 1982), 6–7.

69   New South Wales, New States Royal Commission, *Evidence of the Royal Commission of Inquiry into Proposals for the Establishment of a New State*, vol. 4 (Sydney: Government Printer, 1925), 2741, para. 68909.

He deals more with the city, and admits that the production of
... [machinery and other capital] goods somewhere else is for his
good, and there is more inter-relationship between the city and
the country.[70]

For the west, there was no sensible alternative relationship, and while it was
generally fraught, marked by an imbalance of power and frustrations over
distant officials ignorant of rural ways, few people seemed to regard severing
the relationship as an answer.

Finally, there was less of a sense of 'the West' as a coherent region with
clear natural and political boundaries. Looking east from the Central West,
there were the older, Labor-voting centres with a mining history, and the
country further west remained a pastoral landscape and economy, dotted
with its own mining centres. The Central West remained a liminal zone—
a crossroads sitting between other places. In short, the various iterations
of the proposed new western or central state had little meaning for many of
the people who lived there. It did not accord with their 'mental maps'—
the spaces and boundaries that helped to order their allegiances and sense
of belonging. It contradicted more entrenched ideas based on everyday
experience of economic and social exchange: of a common identity across
rural New South Wales; of a sometimes troubled but nevertheless valued
and essential relationship with Sydney; and a closer alliance to a town, such
as Dubbo or Wellington, and its hinterland, than to a more abstract and
disconnected 'West'.

As the new states movement faded, Country Party organisation in the
Central West reverted to a familiar dormancy between election campaigns.
An executive of the UCP's Western Division persevered in Dubbo until
1938, but Hardy's sub-branches do not appear to have continued in the
Dubbo farmlands beyond the return of a conservative coalition government
in 1932. In 1937, the administrator for the Western Division advised the
executive that there was an opportunity to collect subscriptions around the
district because, with both state and federal elections imminent, 'people will
be politically conscious and in a fitting frame of mind to be approached',
thus implying that on other occasions they were not.[71]

---

70   New South Wales, New States Royal Commission, *Evidence of the Royal Commission of Inquiry*,
2772, para. 69930.
71   Walpole to the Divisional Executive, [c.1937–38], Minute book of the United Western Movement
and the United Country Party, Western Division (1931–1938), PG2904, Page Research Centre Library,
Charles Sturt University Regional Archives, Wagga Wagga.

Candidates in this period did not delve as deeply into the smallest rural communities as their predecessors had. As transport and roads improved, and perhaps also as those communities formed smaller proportions of the voters, candidates favoured the towns and more substantial villages. Compulsory voting, which was introduced in New South Wales in 1928, also changed the nature of campaigning, there being less need to persuade constituents simply to vote.[72] However, as the scene that opened this chapter reveals, the contest of political ideas was still on display in the villages where candidates conducted meetings in the street and in halls. Fred Stroud, a farmer with a small property abutting Mogriguy, would wrangle with Labor supporters in that sleeper cutting centre in the 1920s. His daughter, Jessie, recalled: 'he had a lot of enemies—Labor enemies. He was proud of it. He used to have arguments.'[73] Along with the publication of each booth's count, these performances amplified the fact that politics were contested in these places.

In smaller, more uniformly rural places, electioneering was different. Aubrey Abbott's account of campaigning in the south of the federal electorate of Gwydir in 1925 portrays the contrast between the experience of campaigning in the towns on the one hand, and on the other in small community halls where he was least likely to encounter anyone but farming people. As a former student of The Kings School, captain in the Light Horse, owner of a substantial New England grazing property and prominent member of the GA, Abbott was used to keeping different company. As he and his wife drove towards the more agricultural southern end of the electorate, the patrician Abbott encountered 'stormy' meetings in towns where Labor had strong support, including Dubbo. But in the rural communities, the reception was quite different. He was surprised to find in one small locality that, though the local storekeeper had distributed leaflets, no one attended his meeting. Abbott had expected in those districts that 'the candidate for the Country Party would drive past little groups of supporters who would cheer and wave'. He was assured by the storekeeper that people would vote on polling day, but that 'nobody ever had a meeting ... in the day time. The people around here are all working. They work all day'.[74]

72   Christopher Monnox, 'Election Campaigns in Rural New South Wales and Victoria, 1910–22' (PhD thesis, Macquarie University, 2021), 18–19.
73   Jessie Woodley (née Stroud, b. 1907), interview with author, Dubbo, 24 June 1981.
74   'Family Background: The Upper Hunter Abbotts', undated manuscript, 288, CLA and Hilda Abbott Papers, box 9, MS 4744, NLA.

With modified expectations, Abbott worked his way around farming communities. Abbott wrote of such events, in general (not specifically of the Dubbo district), that he had 'never spoken to more dignified meeting[s] than to farmers and graziers at small country meetings'. In the small centres, people preferred to experience political rhetoric in a more formal setting, rather than to debate or contest it:

> Every day except Sunday the programme was practically the same. A meeting about 10 in the morning at a small hall in the bush; perhaps this would be only a friendly talk with two or three, but I found if there were more than five or six they liked to be addressed, so we would file into the hall, one of them would solemnly take the chair and introduce me and I would speak for half an hour or so.[75]

Abbott spoke at country dances, too, where he was given 15 minutes to address the gathering before the supper. These occasions reveal two things about these people and places. First, they emphasise these communities' homogeneity—that such a candidate might be accommodated at an open, social event without apparent concern that anyone might dissent, or at least express it in a disorderly manner. It spoke to the Country Party's thorough embeddedness in local social and civic life. Second, these occasions reflect an assured sense that people could exert influence through their associations. If they did not hold office in such bodies, then they knew people who did. They felt connected to decision-making on things that mattered to them. It was the understated self-assurance of people with a degree of power, however modest in each case, and confidence in the system that delivered it. This was, in part, a Country Party achievement.

At the landslide election of 1932 at which a Nationalist–Country Party government was installed, Forbes district grazier George Wilson regained the seat of Dubbo for the Country Party. He would go on to win the next three general elections. Wilson's background marked him as being somewhat removed from the average farmer of the region. He had been schooled at Scotch College in Melbourne and enlisted in the AIF in 1916. In 1924, as president of the Bland Shire Council and representative of the Lachlan District Council of the FSA, he had been a vocal supporter of a new Riverina state. In 1925, he toured Europe, the United States and Canada studying

---

75   'Family Background: The Upper Hunter Abbotts'.

'industrial and political conditions'.[76] Though Wilson had a more wealthy and landed background than Thorby, and was from a different region, he attracted even more support from the small rural centres for the Country Party through the 1930s. By then, the old animosity between selectors and squatters had long since passed, replaced by a phlegmatic adherence to a party and an encompassing rural class. Wilson attracted four of every five first-preference votes at these booths in 1935 and 1938, whereas the town and railway villages generally divided their votes evenly between the Country Party and Labor.

In his report to the Country Party's executive on the 1930 election, Abbott used the examples of rural booths around Dubbo to support his argument that, despite Lang's wheat marketing policies that year, 'the great majority of farmers have been most loyal to the Party'.[77] Though the district had joined in the brief flirtation with the new states movements and their elevation of regional identities, ultimately farmlands people reaffirmed their confidence in the Country Party's capacity to represent them, and their identification with broadly rural, rather than narrowly regional, interests.

1942–1950: Re-forming a party

Farming people continued to support the Country Party through the 1940s, even though it lost its way and returned to the opposition benches. Concurrently, they were dealing with drought conditions from the late 1930s and into the 1940s, and with wartime shortages of machinery, building materials and superphosphate, which dampened production and saw ageing infrastructure deteriorate, while petrol rationing restricted mobility.[78] Wool marketing was controlled, and wheat marketing became the responsibility of the Australian Wheat Board, formed in 1939. The federal Rural Reconstruction Commission drew attention to poor standards of housing and amenities in many parts of rural Australia. However, rather than perpetuate the old obsession with an agrarian fantasy, it recommended an economically rational, scientifically based approach to rural industry policy,

---

76 New South Wales, New States Royal Commission, *Evidence of the Royal Commission of Inquiry*, 2413; Parliament of New South Wales, 'Mr George Alan Lachlan Wilson (1895–1942)', www.parliament.nsw. gov.au/members/formermembers/Pages/former-member-details.aspx?pk=1565; *Wyalong Advocate and Mining, Agricultural and Pastoral Gazette*, 12 December 1924; *DD*, 29 April 1932; 'Wilson, G. A. L.', B2455, NAA.
77 C. L. A. Abbott, 'Report on the Recent State Elections', 1 November 1930, Minute Books of the Central Council of the Progressive/Country Party (NSW) 1919–2005.
78 Samuel Wadham, *Australian Farming 1788–1965* (Melbourne: F. W. Cheshire, 1967), 58–63.

divorced from what one of the commissioners, English-born agricultural scientist and academic Samuel Wadham, described as the 'fetish' of closer settlement and the family farm.[79] Postwar recovery was aided by better wheat prices and a strong demand for wool, the price of which by 1947–48 was three times higher than in 1939–40, and it would go still higher. People continued to move to the towns and cities. As properties expanded and production became less labour-intensive, the population of the Talbragar Shire fell by more than 17 per cent between 1933 and 1947.

The Country Party's extended term in government ended in 1941 as William McKell's Labor Party swept to power with the help of a healthy non-metropolitan vote. With Labor's schisms of the Lang years put to rest and the coalition tired and fractured, the Country Party was reduced from 21 seats to 12. McKell had targeted country regions. He toured the state and launched a detailed rural policy that included a commitment to dam the Macquarie River above Wellington for water conservation and irrigation. In the electorate of Dubbo, Wilson survived a significant swing to Labor with the help of preferences leaking from the Independent Labor candidate, and by distancing himself from the coalition, campaigning on the basis of his record of service to the electorate and his personal qualities rather than his political affiliations. One advertisement included the quotation: 'It's not the Party that matters, it's the Man that counts and George Wilson is that man! (quoted from the remark of an old Labor supporter)'.[80]

McKell understood the power of the established leadership in rural districts and so, in the *Sydney Morning Herald*'s words, selected candidates from among 'practical farmers, shire councillors, stock breeders and men from local families of long standing'.[81] When Wilson died less than a year later, one of McKell's 'practical farmers' regained the seat for Labor for the first time since 1932.[82] The Dubbo-born, 40-year-old Clarrie Robertson had been schooled in Dubbo and Wongarbon, and worked as a butcher, sharefarmer and railway employee. Having attended a small country school and worked locally both as a wage labourer and farmer, he had shared the

---

79 Quoted in Stuart Macintyre, *Australia's Boldest Experiment: War and Reconstruction in the 1940s* (Sydney: NewSouth Publishing, 2015), 171.

80 *DD*, 18 April 1941, quoted in Aitkin, *The Colonel*, 244n; David Clune, '1941', in *The People's Choice: Electoral Politics in 20th Century New South Wales, Vol. Two, 1930 to 1965*, ed. Michael Hogan and David Clune (Sydney: Parliament of New South Wales and University of Sydney, 2001), 195.

81 *SMH*, 1 May 1941, 9; *DL*, 1 May 1941, 5; Clune, '1941', 184–5, 188–9, 194–5; Christopher Cunneen, *William John McKell: Boilermaker, Premier, Governor-General* (Sydney: University of New South Wales Press, 2000), 127–8; Aitkin, *The Colonel*, 242, 247.

82 Aitkin, *The Colonel*, 248.

experiences of many smaller landholders. Many would have known him personally. On his election in 1942, he and his family ensconced themselves in the community. They moved from Dunedoo to Dubbo, and his wife became honorary secretary of the town's CWA branch.[83]

Small townships and villages remained on campaign itineraries in this period, but candidates no longer advertised visits to the least populous localities. Robertson nevertheless worked hard to meet voters face-to-face. At a time when candidates were increasingly using radio as a medium for connecting with voters, Robertson continued to campaign on the road. He told an audience in Wongarbon in 1944 that he travelled 1,000 miles each week to pursue his constituents' interests.[84] After a decade of Country Party ascendancy, he was not about to take his tenure for granted. He was the sort of local member a Country Party MLC somewhat snidely contrasted with his own party's more complacent representatives:

> Labor members, for the most part, are better off financially and in other ways than ever before in their lives. Consequently they live on the job, giving their whole time to it and missing no opportunity of cultivating local goodwill.[85]

With his energy and local background, Robertson seemed well-credentialed to persuade farmers to change their established voting habits.

Reflecting Labor's improving overall standing at both state and federal levels, Robertson did increase his vote, from 50.6 per cent to 58.7 per cent in the town of Dubbo between the 1941 election and the 1942 by-election, and from 34.7 per cent to 50.0 per cent in the villages. In the small booths, too, Robertson increased the Labor vote from roughly one in five in 1941, to one in four at the by-election and, once elected, to almost one in three in 1944, before it dipped again to one in four in 1947. In the end, though, these were marginal variations, and over this period the Country Party never secured less than two votes of every three in these booths. It confirmed as emphatically as ever these small communities' entrenched support for the party and the idea of a pan-farming class, no matter how familiar or empathic the candidate.

83 *DL*, 2 May 1944, 3 April 1947, 8; Parliament of New South Wales, 'Clarence Gordon Robertson (1902–1974)', accessed 23 March 2024, www.parliament.nsw.gov.au/members/formermembers/Pages/former-member-details.aspx?pk=1634; *Mudgee Guardian and North-Western Representative*, 27 February 1941, 7.
84 *DL*, 4 June 1942, 3, 18 May 1944, 2.
85 E. C. Sommerlad, 'A State Election Analysis: What of the Future?' [1944], Minute Books of the Central Council of the Progressive/Country Party (NSW) 1919–2005.

Other than at the ballot box, though, farmers in the Dubbo electorate continued to have little enthusiasm for party politics. In his annual report for 1941, the Country Party's general secretary blamed labour shortages and petrol rationing for members' disengagement from local party matters. The following year he was especially disappointed with the effort in Dubbo at the by-election: 'Our people were not interested, and would not, or could not, attend meetings or furnish finance, and, in consequence, this [central] office paid the bulk of the expenses incurred.'[86] It was consistent with a more general disillusionment that extended to the FSA. In its first two decades, the Country Party's central council had regularly debated the party's place in state politics. Throughout, there were existential tensions: between the FSA and the GA, which retained their own policies and policymaking structures; between promoting their members' interests and courting country town voters as farming populations declined; and with their sometime coalition partners, the Nationalists and the United Australia Party.

The Country Party was forced to fundamentally rethink its place when the FSA severed its formal links in August 1944, officially on the grounds that affiliation with any political party prevented the association from attracting members with all political views (a far cry from the bullish days before World War I when Labor sympathisers were hounded out of the organisation), but possibly as well so that it could negotiate with the Labor government as a lobby group, without a formal link to a party in opposition. The party, therefore, was deprived of the association's extensive branch network.[87] The cashed-up GA also withdrew in March 1945, thereby threatening the party's financial viability, and forcing it to build a membership base committed directly to the party rather than through affiliated producers' organisations.[88] The executive appointed an organising secretary to reinvigorate a network of field organisers set up to enrol members, collect subscriptions and form branches. Across the state they had some success, increasing financial membership from 3,266 across 348 branches in mid-1945 to 14,493 in 382 branches in 1948.[89] Some areas, at least, seemed able to sustain both producers' associations and a political organisation.

86   'Report for 1941 by the General Secretary', 3 February 1942, 'Report by the General Secretary for the Year Ending 31st December 1942', 11 February 1943, Minute Books of the Central Council of the Progressive/Country Party (NSW) 1919–2005.

87   *DL*, 5 August 1944, 1; *Land*, 11 August 1944, 1; Davey, *The Nationals*, 145–6; Aitkin, *The Colonel*, 252–3.

88   Minutes of a meeting of the Central Council of the Australian Country Party (NSW), 22 March 1945, Minute Books of the Central Council of the Progressive/Country Party (NSW) 1919–2005.

89   'Report by Organising Secretary—G. S. Millar', 26 July 1945, 'Report by the Central Executive', 14 February 1946, 'Total Subscribers All Electorates', [1948], Minute Books of the Central Council of the Progressive/Country Party (NSW) 1919–2005.

In the Central West, before the GA and the FSA severed their formal ties, there appeared to be little commitment to the Country Party, if the extent of financial membership meant anything. The party counted just two financial members in the Dubbo electorate in mid-1945, whereas most electorates in the Riverina and New England contained hundreds. But this was also a strength of the party—that people expressed their support through membership of the FSA while it remained a de facto shareholder in the Country Party, and consistently voted for the party whether they were financial members or not. The party was part of the rural landscape. Once organisers methodically recruited from the mid-1940s, Dubbo's membership grew to 396 by mid-1946, and to 507 across 10 branches by March 1948. In the town's immediate vicinity, branches formed in Eumungerie and Wongarbon in 1948, while still sustaining branches of the FSA.[90]

Conclusion

In the increasingly homogeneous farmlands, there developed quite uniform and consistent political preferences and clear definitions of a political community. People's dogged support for Country Party candidates from the party's inception aligned with their economic self-interest. The party's platforms strongly emphasised rural productivity, with slogans such as 'Production First', 'Production, Scientific Marketing and a Fair Deal', and 'Development and Increased Production'.[91] But fealty went beyond a mercenary calculation. Long after the early issues of industrial arbitration and land tenure had receded, farmers' allegiance to the Country Party was sustained irrespective of recent government performance, which party was in government, the state of the rural economy, or electoral laws of the day, even when the local party apparatus was in disarray, and with little regard for candidates' backgrounds or proximity. It coincided with a sense of persistent vulnerability arising from the steady decline of the farmlands population, in the shadow of the expanding town.[92] Voting patterns and the

90 'Total Subscribers All Electorates', [1948], Minute Books of the Central Council of the Progressive/ Country Party (NSW), 1919–2005; *DL*, 23 October 1948, 4, 6 November 1948, 30 July 1949, 3; *Gilgandra Weekly*, 5 August 1948, 1.

91 'Platform of the Progressive Party' ('Production First'), attached to minutes of the Central Electoral Council of the Progressive Party, 16 October 1919, 'The Progressive Party's 12 Points' ('Production First'), [1922], 'Country Party Platform', revised 10 June 1927 ('Development and Increased Production'); 'Australian Country Party's Fighting Points, Federal Election Nov 14th 1925', Minute Books of the Central Council of the Progressive/Country Party (NSW) 1919–2005.

92 Aitkin, *The Country Party in New South Wales*, 27–9.

more explicit theatre of political debate in the town and nearby villages were a regular reminder of how contested their political views were: how different the farmlands people were from others in those places, and how alike they were among themselves.

In the Central West, this devotion to the farmers' party did not translate into regular political engagement. One of the most consistent themes running through this period is people's apathy towards, or disengagement from, party politics. Politics was not a persistent aspect of most people's daily lives, and allegiances were rarely expressed other than by paying annual dues for some, and at the ballot box for all.[93] But apathy should not be read as disempowerment, because, just as remarkable, was people's literate and self-assured use of politics and politicians to change things that mattered to them, including through their control of local government. And they found strength in being part of a broader imagined community—a class—of 'primary producers', big and small, sharing the essential characteristic of being households that were also units of production, the family farm. In the farmlands, the Country Party's achievement lay in persuading such a high proportion of sheep and wheat farmers, no matter how wealthy or impecunious, that they shared an essential common interest and should act on it through the votes cast each election day.

93   Robert Woodley (b. 1937), interview with author, Isaacs (ACT), 20 December 2017.

6

'Tethered to the world': Transport, communication and imagining the farmlands

On Thursday 5 July 1900, snow fell in Beni, and also 10 kilometres away in Dubbo where it was said to be the first such fall since the town was a village.[1] It was a brief fall, and by the evening light rain had turned it to slush. Up the western railway line towards Sydney, however, between Orange and Katoomba, snow a metre deep covered the tracks and caused telegraph lines to collapse. Less than two decades after becoming accustomed to regular, reliable rail services, unusually harsh weather up to 300 kilometres away threw the Dubbo district into disarray for at least three days. Without telegraphic communication between stations along the line, trains could not run safely. Dubbo, Murrumbidgerie, Geurie and other stations up the line knew nothing of the expected trains' whereabouts. Communications between Dubbo and Sydney were patched together by telegraph lines running north through Tamworth and south via Forbes, to circumvent the broken lines to the east. As entrenched timetables and information flows foundered, the local press reported, almost breathlessly, the disruption and distress:

> Beyond Wellington there was for nearly two whole days an absolute terra incognita. What was transpiring eastward was absolutely unknown even to the best-informed. Where the incoming down

---

1 *DL*, 7 July 1900, 5; *DD*, 7 July 1900, 4, 11 July 1900, 2.

train [from Sydney] was or when it was likely to arrive—how far towards Sydney the duly dispatched up train had got; both were questions simply unanswerable.[2]

When the circuitous, improvised telegraph connections became congested, the newspaper related that:

> a long silence set in. By this time communication with Wellington had been broken at Maryvale, and nothing could be spoken east of Murrumbidgerie. The night found the town completely cut off from the outer world.

Local newspapers went to press without the usual instalment of colonial and intercolonial news. When trains did finally arrive, unannounced and with no orientation to schedules, people rushed to the post office to collect their delayed mail.

The contrast between the precision that people expected of train arrivals as part of daily life, and the disorientation that followed their suspension, is apparent in the report that:

> On Friday morning the down mail due at 8:52 was reported at Wallerawang, but thereafter for 16 hours all trace of it was absolutely lost in so far as Dubbo was concerned.

When another delayed train arrived, postal staff worked into the night to sort and dispatch mail:

> The mail coaches for the outlying centres were loaded almost simultaneously in the fast darkening evening. Timetables ceased to be for once; and coaches for Coonamble, Cobborah and Peak Hill, &c, simply blocked the main street of the town at the busiest hour on Saturday night.

The district's everyday dependence on its connection to the world beyond was most starkly felt when it was so decisively disrupted.

Historians of settler colonial societies, from Frederick Jackson Turner to Geoffrey Blainey to William Cronon, have long been alert to the effects of distance, and distance-modifying technologies, on economic, social

---

2   *DL*, 11 July 1900, 2. Subsequent references are from this source unless otherwise identified.

and political life.[3] In Australia, there is a common view that transport and communication in rural communities contributed to both the relative decline of the population and economy, and the dissipation of a distinct rural culture, as though the rail and telegraph lines were arteries bleeding, rather than invigorating, the bush.[4] I have a different emphasis here: that the society that evolved in the farmlands from around 1870, and which was the basis of the imagined rural idyll—the patchwork of productive agricultural households—could not have existed without those vital links to the city. They determined the work people did, what they produced, where they lived, the places they travelled to and the people they connected with. They also influenced how farmlands people imagined their communities.

John Hirst has argued that the land laws determined the nature of rural society.[5] While, as we saw in Chapter 1, I agree they were important, this chapter makes the case that transport and communications technologies were also fundamental. They were as much formative as transformative. Just as Sydney's place in the world was being transformed by faster ships and a submarine telegraph line spanning continents, settler society in the region was constructed with an essential relationship to an outside world through Sydney. All subsequent changes to the ways people moved goods, ideas, information and themselves only emphasised the centrality of that relationship to the existence and character of that evolving local society.

Changing transport and communications technologies also regularly disrupted ideas about what constituted local communities of place. Each technology performed this work in different, and often ambiguous and inconsistent, ways as successive waves of change shaped communities and the ways they were perceived and experienced. The remainder of the chapter deals with different technologies in turn, though their influences on settler society's politics, economics and ideas of place were entangled.

---

3   Frederick Jackson Turner, 'The Significance of the Frontier in American History', in *Annual Report for the Year 1893*, American Historical Association (Washington: 1894), 199–227; Blainey, Geoffrey, *The Tyranny of Distance: How Distance Shaped Australia's History* (South Melbourne: Sun Books, 1987); William Cronon, *Nature's Metropolis: Chicago and the Great West* (New York: W. A. Norton and Company, 1991).

4   Richard Waterhouse, *The Vision Splendid: A Social and Cultural History of Rural Australia* (Fremantle: Curtin University Books, Fremantle Arts Centre Press in partnership with Curtin University of Technology, 2005), 181; Graeme Davison, 'Fatal Attraction? The Lure of Technology and the Decline of Rural Australia 1890–2000', *Tasmanian Historical Studies* 9, no. 1 (2003): 40–55.

5   John Hirst, 'Transformation on the Land', in *Sense and Nonsense in Australian History* (Melbourne: Black Inc. Agenda, 2005), 114–22.

The mail

Postal services provided the region's squatters, managers, workers, government officials and missionaries with the first form of regular communication with Sydney and other settlements to the east. From 1848, even before a village there was gazetted, Dubbo had a post office receiving a weekly mail delivery from Wellington.[6] From the time free selection began to take hold outside the town in the 1870s, post offices competed with schools to be the first public infrastructure in the hinterland. Neighbours could host a post office if they were able to demonstrate the need. Usually, the post office was located in the house of a trusted and centrally located citizen, a woman of the house often running the post office (even if it was formally in the name of a male adult) in return for a modest stipend. Depending on the volume of mail the serviced community exchanged, the offices, in their most basic form, might only receive mail, or, at the other extreme, both receive and dispense mail, as well as sell stamps and money orders. By the 1920s, small facilities of this kind were being replaced by contractors delivering mail directly to farms' roadside mailboxes two or three times each week.[7]

Mail services were fundamental to settlers' experience of rural life, and their connectedness to the world beyond the farmlands, but it is difficult to judge the mail's precise effect.[8] The evidence is fragmentary. We cannot know what proportion of correspondence consisted of exchanges with nearby towns, as compared with Sydney, or how much involved business rather than social exchanges. Records from grazing properties further west, around Narromine and Trangie, indicate that the mail was an essential part of business for enterprises of that scale. The owners of Burraway station corresponded regularly, including with neighbours concerning their shared boundaries, with stock and station agents about buying and selling sheep, with workers about employment and with retailers about the supply of goods. In terms of social engagement, the fluency of surviving correspondence between local families and relatives enlisted in the First AIF indicates strongly that social letter writing was a very familiar part of many people's daily lives. Also, the volume of mail received and posted indicates that these services were an essential way to connect with the world. The 14 households served by the Rawsonville post office each posted on average 5.8 letters and packages per

---

6   *SMH*, 8 January 1848, 2; *Maitland Mercury and Hunter River General Advertiser*, 2 February 1848, 4.
7   *Commonwealth of Australia Gazette*, no. 104, 28 October 1926, 1760, no. 5, 26 January 1939, 129.
8   Alan Atkinson, 'Postage in the South-East', *The Push from the Bush; A Bulletin of Social History: Devoted to the Year of Grace, 1838*, no. 5 (1979): 20.

week in 1930–31, and received 10.6. The earnestness of people's petitions to have offices and deliveries established and maintained also speaks to the value that people attached to the service. That desire to connect, by whatever medium was available, would continue to be a constant and integral aspect of settler society in that district.[9]

The railways

No technology so fundamentally shaped the Dubbo farmlands' social, political and economic character as did the railways. This expensive infrastructure was the result of years, and sometimes decades, of consultation, deliberation, lobbying, debate and political horsetrading. The eventual routes were always contested, contingent on competing economic priorities and political heft. Arguments for favoured railway routes over this period included relative costs of construction and operation, revenue from traffic, the effect on established towns, access to timber suitable for sleepers, and the effects on agricultural settlement and production. The extension of the Great Western Railway to Dubbo in February 1881 occurred during a period of intense investment in New South Wales railways. Lines fanned out from Sydney on three main routes: to the north-west, the south-west, as well as the western line. To the west, once the slow and expensive course over the Blue Mountains had been accomplished, the pace of construction could quicken, with large injections of British capital, particularly between the late 1870s and the mid-1880s. The length of track across the colony increased from 402 miles in 1874 to 2,183 miles in 1889.[10]

Around Dubbo, railways were being built or undergoing labour-intensive upgrading for half the time between the mid-1870s and the mid-1920s. It had taken five years for the line to advance from Bathurst, with each section creating a new but temporary railhead for wool transported to Sydney markets. The railway historian Robert Lee assessed the decision

---

9   Burraway Letters, 1881–96, Narromine Library, Macquarie Regional Library; Lynette Harrison, comp., *Dear Da … : Letters from the Great War 1914–18, Written by and Concerning Jack Ison, 1565 3rd Battalion AIF, a Dubbo Boy Killed in Action 10/11/17*, assisted by Graeme Hosken (Dubbo: 1991); Phyllis Lynch letters [Wongarbon], PROO716, Australian War Memorial; District inspector to the senior inspector, 22 September 1931, Rawsonville Post Office File, 1903–47, SP32/1, NAA.

10   N. G. Butlin, *Investment in Australian Economic Development* (Canberra: Department of Economic History, Research School of Social Sciences, The Australian National University, 1972), 322, 324; Robert Lee, *The Greatest Public Work: The New South Wales Railways, 1848 to 1889* (Sydney: Hale and Iremonger, 1988), 81–3; John Gunn, *Along Parallel Lines: A History of the Railways of New South Wales* (Carlton: Melbourne University Press, 1989), 134–65.

to construct an extension of the line from Orange to Bourke as relatively straightforward but, still, there were competing views on how best to achieve the line's commonly agreed purpose—to divert the wool trade from western New South Wales towards Sydney rather than Adelaide and Melbourne.[11] Unlike subsequent lines, that railway's potential to promote agricultural settlement seems to have had little influence on the favoured route, much of its passage being across the western country considered unsuitable for such farming. Though a direct route to Bourke would have been the least expensive, it would also have been to the detriment of towns that would be bypassed. The question then became: which towns should be strung along the line? The joint claims of Wellington and Dubbo, which then had a combined population of almost 5,000 and served some rich pastoral country, had overwhelming, if not unanimous, support in the parliament.[12]

Even if the overriding purpose of the western route was to connect Sydney with the western wool trade, Dubbo thoroughly embraced its illustrious moment when John Robertson returned to mark the line's progress to the town in February 1881. It was a grand affair, with speeches, a banquet for 200 'gentlemen' and a ball in the evening.[13] In truth, the colony was alight with such celebrations. Albury and Narrandera would be connected to Sydney within the month, and lines to Tenterfield, Narrabri, Hay and Mudgee, and from Dubbo to Bourke, were in progress. For Dubbo though, it was no less momentous. In its first year, the station issued over 11,000 tickets and trucked out 44,216 bales of wool that would otherwise have been carried by wagon to other railheads. Wheat was not sufficiently relevant to be recorded in annual reports, but the new line itself would cause agriculture to flourish.[14]

Advocates for a line from Dubbo north through Gilgandra and on to Coonamble justified it as a means of bringing more land into agricultural production when construction began in 1902. No one seemed to dispute that the ultimate goal was to create a denser population of smallholders.[15] It cost about five times less to carry goods by rail as compared with horse-drawn wagons, but the advantage in getting goods to market quickly

11   Lee, *The Greatest Public Work*, 81.
12   It was represented as a long-settled question in parliamentary debates in 1877: *SMH*, 10 May 1877, 2. See also Gunn, *Along Parallel Lines*, 147.
13   *ATCJ*, 5 February 1881, 6.
14   'Annual Report of the Commissioner for Railways for the year 1881', in New South Wales, Legislative Assembly, *Votes and Proceedings of the Legislative Assembly*, vol. 4 (Sydney: Government Printer, 1882), 100.
15   *DD*, 4 July 1899, 2, 22 August 1899, 2; *DL*, 1 April, 10 June 1899, 5.

dissipated with the distance from the farm to the railway platform.[16] The distance over which it was viable to transport wheat varied with prevailing prices of the produce and of transportation, but during the era of railway construction, 20 miles (32 kilometres) was commonly regarded as a limit beyond which wheat growing became a precarious concern.[17] Railway routes were dotted with strategically placed platforms at which produce could be loaded, thus creating corridors at least 40 miles wide where agriculture became viable. Railway debates were also influenced by Dubbo's merchants who stood to profit from a growing, more densely populated and productive farming hinterland. Dubbo was selected as the point of connection with Coonamble in preference to Mudgee, Warren and Narromine, but its size and political influence were insufficient to gain a line south to Peak Hill in 1910. Instead, a route from Narromine—cheaper and through far better agricultural country—won the parliament's support despite lobbying from the Dubbo Railway and Progress Association.[18]

When momentum built to connect the western and northern railway systems, Dubbo's political weight was also in play.[19] The putative grounds for a line were to transport stock away from drought-affected districts in the west, but the expansion of agriculture again dominated debates about the precise route. A connection to the northern system at Werris Creek from either Wellington or Maryvale would also have passed through country with agricultural potential, but Dubbo's larger and more rapidly expanding population is likely to have made it a more attractive political choice. After another long debate, a line opened in 1918 from Dubbo, following the Talbragar River before crossing to Merrygoen, ultimately to connect through Werris Creek. The village of Ballimore formed around a station on that route, its streets named after contemporary wheat varieties as a testimony to its ultimate purpose. Agricultural expansion was the only consideration

---

16 Blainey, *The Tyranny of Distance*, 259–60.
17 New South Wales, Royal Commission as to Decentralisation in Railway Transit, *Report of the Royal Commission as to Decentralisation in Railway Transit*, in *Joint Volume of Papers Presented to the Legislative Council and Legislative Assembly*, vol. II (Sydney: Government Printer, 1911), 233; New South Wales, Standing Committee on Public Works, *Report Together with Minutes of Evidence, Appendix and Plan Relating to the Proposed Railway from Dubbo to Werris Creek*, in *Joint Volumes of Papers Presented to the Legislative Council and Legislative Assembly*, vol. III (Sydney: Government Printer, 1913), 62; Bruce Davidson, *European Farming in Australia: An Economic History of Australian Farming* (Amsterdam: Elsevier, 1981), 180.
18 *Peak Hill Express*, 22 February, 22 March 1907, 20.
19 New South Wales, Royal Commission as to Decentralisation in Railway Transit, *Report of the Royal Commission*, 235–42; New South Wales, Standing Committee on Public Works, *Report Together with Minutes of Evidence, Appendix and Plan Relating to the Proposed Railway from Dubbo to Werris Creek.*

when a second line to Molong, passing through rich wheat country west of the Macquarie, was opened in 1925 to complete the web of lines fanning from Dubbo.[20] After almost half a century of railway construction, by 1925 there were 15 stations and sidings within 35 kilometres of Dubbo (by rail) capable of loading wheat and wool, and little arable land more than 15 kilometres distant from at least one line.[21] As well as making agriculture viable across the district, the railways provided access to Sydney's live meat markets (see Figure 6.1).

Figure 6.1: Railway construction in the Dubbo region, 1881–1925.
Source: Flat Earth Mapping.

20   *DD*, 8 July 1921, 3; *SMH*, 20 July 1923, 12.
21   NSWRail.net, 'Timeline of Events', accessed 23 March 2024, www.nswrail.net/infrastructure/time line.php.

Figure 6.2: Harvesters delivered to Dubbo railway station, c. 1907.
Source: NSW Department of Lands, Annual Report, 1907.

Railways were not solely responsible for the expansion of agriculture and mixed farming over this period. Successive waves of land legislation were also material, notably the *Crown Lands Act* of 1884, which required that half of all pastoral leases be resumed at the lease's expiry and made available for selection, and the *Crown Lands Act* of 1895, which introduced new forms of leasehold tenure with low rents on areas of up to 1,280 acres, either for 28 years or in perpetuity. Then, from 1904, the state government could acquire land either voluntarily or (with the parliament's agreement) compulsorily, so that more people could settle on smaller portions. Under the *Closer Settlement Promotion Act* of 1910, three or more eligible people could come to an arrangement with a landowner, then approach the government to effect the conditional purchase through a series of annual repayments, the government thus becoming their financier. Finally, from 1916, soldiers who had served overseas with the First AIF gained certain entitlements under closer settlement.[22] But such inducements to take up land for agriculture would have foundered without the access to markets via the railways, which also delivered the new machinery (see Figure 6.2).

---

22   C. J. King, *An Outline of Closer Settlement in New South Wales, Part I: The Sequence of the Land Laws 1788–1956* ([Sydney]: Division of Marketing and Agricultural Economics, Department of Agriculture, [1957]), 91–107, 133–7, 187–215.

Under these stimuli, the area under crop in the County of Lincoln increased almost eight-fold between 1894 and 1921, and at more than twice the rate of the state as a whole.[23]

As well as being fundamental to the creation of a viable mixed farming economy, rail shaped the region's social and political character. The region's unique experience of railways included their construction and maintenance. The railways introduced villages with populations of contractors and wage labourers supporting the railways and rural production. Each wave of railway construction brought hundreds of men, living in tents and often accompanied by their families. A camp working on the western line between Wellington and Dubbo in 1878 was described as having:

> all the appearance of a goldfields rush, minus the sinking of shafts. Huts, tents, stores and boarding-houses are to be seen going up in all directions, which gives it an appearance of several months' permanency.[24]

Beyond the town's immediate surrounds, the first railways did not just stimulate agricultural farming but fundamentally created the farming landscape. The railways were there first. In January 1886, more than four years after the line had been completed, the Wellington postmaster wrote, concerning the platform at Geurie (then known as Ponto), that:

> the only Residents about this place is three or four Railway fettlers & the Porter in charge of the platform[.] [T]here are no farmers nearer than Maryvale [12 kilometres distant] … and the nearest Squatters place is about ten miles [16 kilometres] away.[25]

Later construction was more likely to disrupt some established farming communities, such as a major project to flatten the western line's grade between Geurie and Eulomogo, which employed 180 workers in 1895, and the new Dubbo to Coonamble line from 1900 (see Figure 6.3). At Ballimore in 1915, a railway camp caused enrolments at the local school, which had recently closed for want of pupils, to increase to 48.[26]

---

23   New South Wales, *Statistical Register for 1900 and Previous Years* (Sydney: Government Printer, 1902), 554; New South Wales, *Statistical Register for 1910 and Previous Years* (Sydney: Government Printer, 1912), 445; New South Wales, *Statistical Register for 1920–21* (Sydney: Government Printer, 1921), 744.

24   *ATCJ*, 2 November 1878, 39.

25   Wellington postmaster to the postal inspector, 18 January 1886, Geurie Post Office File, SP32/1, NAA.

26   Postal Inspector's memo, 4 November 1895, Eulomogo Post Office File, SP32/1, NAA; Inspector to the chief inspector, July 1914, 15 May 1915, Ballimore School Administrative File, 1884–1920, 5/14763.2, NRS 3829, SARNSW.

Figure 6.3: Railway workers on the Dubbo to Coonamble line, c. 1901.
Source: Local Studies Collection, Dubbo Regional Council.

Though the railway brought a new workforce to the region, its effect on the social and political character would be transitory or muted until construction on each line was completed. Some navvies did follow a trusted ganger from one job to the next, thus providing some degree of continuity of experience and comradeship, and allowing ideas of working-class unity to circulate from one location to the next. However, in the Dubbo district, the railway builders consisted of a combination of experienced workers from elsewhere and locals taking up opportunities for paid work. Jack Ison, a farmer's son from a property just east of Dubbo, worked on the Dubbo – Werris Creek line before enlisting in the First AIF; his ambition was to return to farming should he survive the war.[27] As Humphrey McQueen has observed, while itinerant workforces stimulated the exchange of ideas and experiences, leading to an evolving class consciousness spanning city and country regions, it also made the organising of strikes or unionism 'almost impossible'.[28]

---

27 Harrison, *Dear Da*, 33, 40; *DD*, 27 March 1914, 6, 2 March 1915, 1.
28 Humphrey McQueen, 'Improving Nomads', *Journal of Australian Colonial History* 10, no. 2 (2008): 223–50.

In more stable circumstances, once the lines were operating, station staff and fettlers were a more likely source of working-class consciousness in the district. As Greg Patmore and Lucy Taksa have argued, a shared place can be an important component of working-class formation, by fostering common experiences and the ready exchange of ideas of class.[29] And, as other chapters have shown, these villages did indeed stand out conspicuously, distinct from both the town and the surrounding farmlands, as centres of support for working-class politics. This was associated with a semipermanent railway workforce—those who were employed in various roles within the railway service as employees of the state, rather than the labourers who built the lines and carted sleepers while working for contractors. In the wake of the 1930 election, the Central Council of the New South Wales Country Party identified railway employees among those who voted to put them out of office.[30]

However, these places were a little more complex. Though I characterise them as 'railway villages'—the railways being the principal reason for their establishment—the railway workforce was only one part of a diversifying mix, as the villages expanded from being principally railway entrepots to providing services and labour to a growing farm population. In 1886, a year after the Geurie railway station opened, a school district inspector described the community thus: 'A few of the residents are farmers & lime burners—the remainder are employed on the railway line.' The applicants for a school there were the stationmaster and another railway employee. In time, the villages became more varied. By 1896, around 30 per cent of families with children at the school were farmers, about 20 per cent were employed by the railway, 30 per cent were labourers and others associated with rural industry, and the balance provided services from the village, including a hotelkeeper, storekeeper and blacksmith.[31] Railway workers did not usually dominate any village. Down the line towards Murrumbidgerie, in 1886 residents consisted of 'farmers, railway employees and timber getters'. By 1890, two years after the village was gazetted, 20 allotments were sold, and a hotel,

29   Greg Patmore, 'Working Lives in Regional Australia: Labour History and Local History', *Labour History*, no. 78 (May 2000): 1–6; Lucy Taksa, '"Pumping the Life-Blood into Politics and Place": Labour Culture and the Eveleigh Railway Workshops', *Labour History*, no. 79 (2000): 11–34.
30   Minutes of the Central Council, 19 November 1930, Minute Books of the Central Council of the Progressive/Country Party (NSW) 1919–2005, New South Wales Nationals.
31   District inspector's assessment of school application, 1 May 1886, petition supporting an application for a classroom, 26 July 1898, Geurie School Administrative File, pre-1939, 5/15981.A, NRS 3829, SARNSW.

store, public school and blacksmith's shop were in place.[32] The following year, the local schoolteacher described the village's recent progress, with its contrasting buildings indicating a mix of impoverished and somewhat better-off households:

> Some two years ago about two houses marked the intended township of Murrumbidgerie. Now within sight of the school may be seen 13 houses comfortably covered with iron roofs & several others of bark.[33]

Much of the Murrumbidgerie pastoral holding in the vicinity of the village had been sold for closer settlement by 1905, and by 1912 the railway station faced a growing array of commercial buildings that included three stores, a hotel, butcher's shop, a combined newsagency, barber's shop and billiards saloon, and a blacksmith's shop.[34] In that context, a small core of permanent railway employees were unlikely, by themselves, to instil an ascendant unionist culture. Nine of the 164 people registered to vote at the Murrumbidgerie/Wongarbon polling place in 1903 were men employed by the railway, and by 1921 they were 6 of 212.[35]

However, the railways attracted more than direct employees; they also brought sleeper cutters—between 250 and 300 north of Dubbo in the Gilgandra district in 1908. Such men were a potential source of strength for the Labor Party. In the interval between his terms as the member for Macquarie (1910–13), Labor's Thomas Thrower occupied himself as secretary of the local branch of the Western Sleeper Cutters and Carters Union.[36] But, as with itinerant navvies, the nature of their work militated against entrenched working-class consciousness. Some sleeper cutters were smallholders. One was on 40 acres at Beni and supplemented his farm

---

32   Inspector to the chief inspector, 28 May 1886, Murrumbidgerie School Administrative File, pre-1939, 5/17017.1, NRS 3829, SARNSW; F. Lovett to the postmaster general, 20 October 1890, Wongarbon [Murrumbidgerie] Post Office File, part 1, 1877–87, SP32/1, NAA.
33   F. Lovett to W. A'Beckett MLA, 10 February 1891, Wongarbon [Murrumbidgerie] Post Office File, part 2, 1890–1908, SP32/1, NAA.
34   F. Lovett to the senior inspector of schools, 13 March 1905, Murrumbidgerie School Administrative File, pre-1939, 5/17017.1, NRS 3829, SARNSW; Unnamed PMG Department memo, 30 November 1912, Wongarbon [Murrumbidgerie] Post Office File, part 6, 1911–12, SP32/1, NAA.
35   Voters registered at the 'Murrumbidgerie polling place' (1903), and voters giving 'Wongarbon' as their 'place of living' (1921). See Commonwealth of Australia, *Commonwealth Electoral Rolls, New South Wales,* Division of Robertson, 1903, and subdivision of Dubbo, Division of Darling, 1921.
36   New South Wales, Royal Commission of Inquiry on Forestry, *Minutes of Proceedings, Minutes of Evidence, and Appendix, Part II,* in *Joint Volumes of Papers Presented to the Legislative Council and Legislative Assembly, 1908 (Second Session),* vol. I (Sydney: Government Printer, 1909), 723; *DD,* 7 July 1909, 2; *DL,* 22 June 1917, 2.

income but was still unable to pay school fees in 1890. Another, in 1908, testified that he and his sons had been cutting sleepers for years.[37] In 1908–09, Anglican clergymen wandering in the dense ironbark forests north of Dubbo, in search of potential parishioners, located small groups of itinerant families:

> the camps are hard to find, they are there one month and gone the next. The timber suitable for sleepers is all cut, or the water supply has failed, and they have pitched in another part of the bush, perhaps 20 miles away.[38]

Nevertheless, the sleeper cutters did make their mark on villages closest to the Goonoo Forest. In 1911, a school inspector described Mogriguy as depending 'almost entirely upon the sleeper cutting industry' and, in 1915, as consisting of 'a few wheat farmers, some fettlers and a number of timber getters'. Another report from Mogriguy in 1915 highlights the precarious nature of the industry but also that, unlike shearers or farm labourers, sleeper cutters' ultimate employment relationship was with the government:

> Towards the end of the year the Railway Commissioners decided to buy no more sleepers, and as a result many families left the district. But a more recent decision to buy on a modified scale will cause some to return, though it is doubtful whether as many people will engage in this industry as formerly.[39]

In all, people associated with the railways were often prominent in local social and political life, and along with shearers and others contributed to the support for working-class politics that distinguished the villages from the surrounding farmlands. They were one of a range of factors defining the villages' political and social character: a leavening rather than a dominant political and social influence.

As well as altering the region's social and political make-up, the railways influenced how and to where people travelled, their mental maps and how they imagined the metropole, in ways that differed from other rural regions. In 1866, a journey from Sydney to Dubbo, even with the stage to Penrith being by rail, took 2.5 days, as compared with a rail journey in 1886 of less

---

37   Teacher to the district inspector, 25 August 1890, Beni School Administrative File, pre-1939, 5/14887.4, NRS 3829, SARNSW; New South Wales, Royal Commission of Inquiry on Forestry, *Minutes of Proceedings*, 726.
38   *Bush Brother* 4, no. 3, April 1908, 149.
39   Inspector to the chief inspector, 8 April 1911, March 1915, 15 January 1915, Mogriguy School Administrative File, pre-1939, 5/16886.2, NRS 3829, SARNSW.

than 14 hours, and, by 1931, of less than 12 hours.[40] We know that train travel became increasingly popular, including from the smaller platforms around the district. Dubbo's traffic increased by over 7 per cent each year, from 10,405 ticket sales in 1890 to 47,853 in 1911—a period when the town's population did not increase at all. Murrumbidgerie railway station's passenger business went from 1,094 in ticket sales in 1890 to 4,907 in 1911, while Geurie's increased from 969 to 11,558 over the same period. Both Geurie and Wongarbon were still selling more than 9,000 tickets in 1941. And, though ticket sales reveal nothing about people's destinations, from the early twentieth century and into the 1930s, Sydney was a popular destination for holidays or honeymoons, especially during vacation periods.[41] 'Countrymindedness'—Aitkin's distillation of an ideology at the centre of Country Party politics—had, at its core, a sharp, antagonistic separation between city and country. But in their choices of where to spend their leisure time, those who could afford it displayed a more nuanced relationship with Sydney. They sought out the city as a place of wonder and diversion. In May 1896, the *Liberal* anticipated that many people would take the train to the city for the holiday period:

> The metropolis is destined to present a most attractive appearance during the Easter week, the holiday events including the great Agricultural Show, Randwick races, the great theatrical spectacle at the Lyceum, the aquatic reception of [the Governor of Victoria] Lord Brassey, and amusements of every description.[42]

In the early 1930s, the Country Party held up the cost of building the Sydney Harbour Bridge as the foremost example of government investment favouring the city. The Dubbo Council refused to display posters advertising the opening because it would cause people to spend their money in the city rather than the town.[43] Nevertheless, one local newspaper observed that the opening ceremony was 'a great drawing magnet' for country dwellers:

40 *Empire*, 3 October 1866, 8; *NSW Government Gazette*, no. 516 (supplement), 14 September 1886, 6249; [New South Wales Government Railways], *Working Timetable for Passenger and Goods Trains, Western Division, from 31st May, 1931* [Sydney, 1931].

41 New South Wales, Department of Railways and Tramways, *Annual Reports of the Railway Commissioners for 1890, 1911 and 1941*, in *Votes and Proceedings of the Legislative Assembly*, vol. V, 1890, vol. III, 1911–12 (Sydney: Government Printer, 1941); *WT*, 30 May 1907, 5, 7 July 1921, 5, 14 January 1926, 5, 21 August 1930, 4, 17 March 1932, 1; *DL*, 2 February 1923, 7, 8 July 1927, 7; *DD*, 28 May 1904, 5, 21 March 1913, 4, 6 June 1913, 2.

42 *DL*, 21 May 1896, 3.

43 *DD*, 22 January 1932, 4.

A special excursion train passed through Wellington last night, having come from Bourke, and by the time it arrived at Wellington it was well crowded ... The total number of passengers from Wellington was 86, 21 from Geurie, 3 from Wongarbon and 2 from Maryvale.[44]

As discussed in Chapter 5, the western line seems to have contributed to a more benign attitude towards the city than was evident in other parts of New South Wales. People understood the farming economy's dependence on the city as a market and as a link to wider markets. In 1910, the Wellington farmer and former member for Macquarie Charles Barton told a Royal Commission on decentralisation: 'We have our business relationships already established with Sydney ... [which] will remain for all time our natural port, and our produce will always go in that direction.'[45] In addition, through their social and recreational choices, made simpler by their ready access to Sydney by rail, local people showed that difference did not necessarily imply disdain.

The Dubbo district's constant exposure to railway construction and upgrading could influence how people related not just to other places, but also to their immediate environment. Whereas roads made for coaches and wagons wound around the topography's contours, railways 'pushed through' the landscape.[46] New lines cutting through hills and spanning creeks can only have been a reminder of the technology's power, and governments' determination, to induce settlement and production. The technologies included the new, massive, modernist concrete wheat silos dotted along the lines. Whereas in the early 1880s wheat did not register as a significant item of rail cargo, from 1918 the state government invested in these facilities at 65 locations in the western and southern districts, with a total capacity of 12.6 million bushels. In 1920–21, the new Geurie silos took in more wheat than any other in the state.[47] Previously, wheat had been delivered to Sydney by rail in millions of hessian bags, but it could now be stored and transported in bulk. Vastly out of proportion to anything else in the

---

44   *WT*, 17 March 1932, 1.
45   New South Wales, Royal Commission as to Decentralisation in Railway Transit, *Report of the Royal Commission*, 228.
46   Wolfgang Schivelbusch, *The Railway Journey: The Industrialisation of Time and Space in the 19th Century*, (Berkley: University of California Press, 1986), 23.
47   New South Wales, *Report of the Department of Agriculture for the Year Ended 30 June 1919*, in *Joint Volume of Papers Presented to the Legislative Council and Legislative Assembly*, vol. 1 (Sydney: Government Printer, 1920), 6; *WT*, 27 January 1921, 5.

built environment, these structures in places such as Geurie, Minore, Eumungerie and Arthurville signified farming's dominance of the landscape and affirmed the state's commitment to that enterprise.

Rail had become a pervasive expression of people's capacity to subdue topographies and ecosystems, in the service of building vital connections to a wider world. The environmental and economic effects around Dubbo were akin to those the United States historian William Cronon observed in Chicago and its hinterland:

> The railroad left almost nothing unchanged … To those whose lives it touched, it seemed at once so ordinary and so extraordinary … that the landscape became unimaginable without it.[48]

Loan monies from the City of London financed the railways, which in turn allowed for the proliferation of broadacre farming by providing access to distant markets for wheat and livestock. Without the railways, towns and villages would not have formed and evolved as they did, and politics would have played out differently. Perceptions of the city as a malign, oppositional force were tempered by the ready social and economic exchange that the railways enabled. The railways showed that the landscape could be bent to the settlers' will in the service of productivity, wealth and the agrarian vision.

Automobility

A quarter of a century after rail's arrival, motor transport further modified the social landscape, and people's perceptions of space and time. Between 1890 and 1920, the bicycle was enormously popular in Australia, including in country districts where it had been adopted by shearers travelling to and between sheds. But its influence faded quickly once internal combustion engines became the motive power of choice for those who could afford them.[49]

Within 20 years of their arrival in the Dubbo district, cars were a staple on many farms. The first petrol-driven vehicle in Dubbo arrived from Sydney in 1901, its driver ambitious to reach Broken Hill. Newspapers were soon reporting record times for the Sydney to Dubbo run, and from Dubbo to

---

48 Cronon, *Nature's Metropolis*, 73.
49 Jim Fitzpatrick, *The Bicycle and the Bush: Man and Machine in Rural Australia* (Melbourne: Oxford University Press, 1980), 10, 192, 195, 209, 220.

Narromine. But motorbikes were as common as four-wheeled vehicles in those early years. A motorcyclist was seen towing two people on pushbikes along the road to Gilgandra in 1903. Dubbo had a 'cycle and motor' club by 1907, and the first garage west of Bathurst by 1909. Speed rather than utility captured people's imaginations, and for a short time, motorcycles and cars appeared to be solutions in search of a problem.[50]

With the advent of mass production in the United States and cheaper imports, better-off farmers around Dubbo were acquiring cars by around 1910. By 1914, an agent for Ford was advertising in the town.[51] Perhaps it was a sense of novelty, prestige and consequence of the technology that led Narromine farmer and stock and station agent Edward Cahill to record in his journal the mileage of *every* trip he took in his new car in 1913. In 1916, the McKillops of Buddah station, also near Narromine, drove a new Dodge home from Sydney, the purchase arranged by their agents Dalgety.[52] Smaller-scale farmers closer to Dubbo were buying cars by the 1920s, as motor transport proliferated across the country. In 1919–21, there were 44 people in Australia for every vehicle; by 1929–30, there were only 12.[53] Though cars were becoming a common sight in farming districts, local newspaper columns continued to report individual acquisitions. A 1917 report from Rawsonville was typical:

> Among those returning from the Easter show convinced that the gee-gee is behind the times is Mr HM Edmonstone of 'Willow Belah', who purchased a six-cylinder car—a real spic and span, handsomely finished show car.[54]

The extent to which rural districts had embraced the technology was on display at the 1923 Dubbo Show where ranks of more than 300 cars were parked at the southern end of the arena. Dealers exhibited cars at the show for the first time the following year. In a short time, they had become embedded in both the practice and performance of farm life.[55]

---

50   *DD*, 24 July 1901, 2, 29 June 1904, 2, 30 November 1907, 4 September 1909, 4; *DL*, 26 September 1903, 2.

51   *DL*, 3 November 1914, 7.

52   Edward Cahill Diaries, 1913, Narromine Library, Macquarie Regional Library; Ainslie McKillop, 'The McKillops of "Buddah"—Their History Briefly from 1811 to 1951', typescript, 1956–58, 59, McKillop and Sons Deposit, box 11, item 194, N385, Noel Butlin Archives Centre.

53   David Merrett and Simon Ville, 'Tariffs, Subsidies, and Profits: A Reassessment of Structural Change in Australia, 1901–39', *Australian Economic History Review* 51, no. 1 (2011): 58.

54   *DD*, 4 May 1917, 4. See also *DL*, 6 February 1925, 7.

55   *DD*, 1 May 1923, 4; *DL*, 9 May 1924, 2.

But cars were not evenly distributed among the rural population. A Dubbo journalist who was captivated by the display of cars at the 1929 show sought to describe a community of actual and aspiring car owners: 'As those who do not own a motor car are practically confined to those who aspire to ownership, there are few subjects commanding more widespread interest.'[56] The distinction, however, was starkly on display. By the mid-1920s, some cars were becoming more affordable. The prices of new cars displayed in a sample of advertisements in Dubbo newspapers in 1925 and 1926 varied markedly. They averaged £410, equivalent to 92 weeks' minimum wage, but at the cheaper end of the market, Ford and Overland models could be had for between £155 and £199, or well under a year's minimum wage. But the continuing costs of running a car (including registration, insurance and petrol) were onerous. Working-class residents of the town and villages, and the least-wealthy farming households, were less likely to own a car before the 1950s.[57]

Cars made little difference to a farm's productivity but held significant symbolic value. Historians have argued that the car's popularity in Australia arose not only from its functionality but also from its cultural meaning—the expression of progress and modernity, freedom, excitement, individualism, status, power and mastery over the physical world. In 1921, the *Liberal* noted the enduring fascination, affirming that cars' significance went beyond their novelty and basic functionality:

> Curiously enough many country papers continue to report the fact that someone has just purchased a motor car, as though the event was of such rare occurrence as to make it worth a par. Twenty years ago such an event was worth noticing, but to-day the appearance of a new sulky in the street is more uncommon than a new motor car.[58]

A 1929 editorial concerning that year's Dubbo Show took an utterly unsentimental view of the disappearance of 'heavy horse classes' and horse-drawn vehicles, representing the car as the 'magnificent triumph' of

---

56   *DL*, 10 May 1929, 2.
57   A sample of advertisements: *DL*, 2 January 1925, 7, 16 January 1925, 6, 29 January 1926, 6; *DD*, 26 November 1926, 2; John William Knott, 'The "Conquering Car": Technology, Symbolism and the Motorisation of Australia before World War II', *Australian Historical Studies* 31, no. 114 (2000): 5–7; Graeme Davison, *Car Wars: How the Car Won Our Hearts and Conquered Our Cities* (Crows Nest: Allen & Unwin, 2004), 7; Alan J. Holt, *Wheat Farms of Victoria: A Sociological Survey* ([Carlton]: School of Agriculture, University of Melbourne, 1946), 120.
58   *DL*, 8 March 1921, 2; Knott, 'The "Conquering Car"', 1–26; Davison, *Car Wars*, ix–xii.

human intellect over 'inanimate matter'.[59] Cars could signify relative wealth and achievement, and therefore be a point of distinction within a local community. They were also largely a male preserve. Georgine Clarsen has interpreted the phenomenon of female motorists undertaking extraordinary journeys through remote parts of Australia between 1925 and 1927 as part of the colonising project—as demonstrating Europeans' domination of the continent.[60] But another reading of the enthusiastic response to these women's iconoclastic achievements is that their experience was the exception, highlighting how widely motoring was held to be a masculine domain.

Whereas railways brought Sydney closer relative to local towns, cars increased people's contact with centres such as Dubbo, Narromine and Wellington. The town's reach expanded according to the speed of the motor car as compared to horse-drawn transport. One estimate put the average speed of horse-drawn travel at just under 10 kilometres per hour, and the range of a one-day return journey at around 40 kilometres. By comparison, the speed of cars in rural settings in the 1920s was between 40 and 65 kilometres per hour, at an average of around 48.[61] Even on the basis of the lowest estimated speed, cars caused the distances accessible to Dubbo at any given time to expand fourfold.

Cars influenced towns' and villages' relative sizes and functions by making them more accessible from surrounding farms. Whereas before the advent of motorised transport a journey to Dubbo from a distance of more than 20 kilometres might have involved an overnight stay, by car it became a comfortable day trip. People began to bypass the villages for the more distant towns with their wider choices of stores, services and entertainment.[62] While car ownership simultaneously curtailed the expansion of the railway villages, it also helped to consolidate Dubbo as the commercial and, to some extent, the social hub of an expanding hinterland. Between 1921 and 1933, when many rural households were buying their first cars, Dubbo's population increased by two-thirds. By the early 1930s, the town was the source of many services for rural customers, including 16 stock and station agents,

---

59   *DL*, 10 May 1929, 2.

60   Georgine Clarsen, *Eat My Dust: Early Women Motorists* (Baltimore: Johns Hopkins University Press, 2008), 120–39.

61   Norman T. Moline, *Mobility and the Small Town, 1900–1930: Transportation Change in Oregon, Illinois,* research paper no. 132 (Chicago: University of Chicago Department of Geography, 1971), 30, 97. Moline's estimates refer to the US, but concern conditions comparable to the NSW Central West.

62   On the general phenomenon, see also Davison, 'Fatal Attraction?', 51; Blainey, *The Tyranny of Distance*, 295.

a produce merchant, wool and skin merchants, and shearing contractors, as well as six accountants and seven banks. Two motor garages and a radio retailer supplied and supported the no longer novel technologies. Twenty-one refreshment rooms serviced an increasingly middle-class and somewhat leisured population, comfortably outnumbering the 12 hotels.[63]

Conversely, places like Geurie and Wongarbon bore out the Rural Reconstruction Commission's reckoning in 1945 that, in wheat districts, smaller towns struggled to survive within 32–40 kilometres of a larger one. They had flourished only briefly as commercial and social centres in the period bounded on the one hand by the arrival of the railways and consolidation of nearby agricultural settlement, and on the other the advent of motor transport. The Western Stores Limited retail chain across the Central West had businesses in both Geurie and Wongarbon from 1916. But in 1929, after years of profitable trading, a director of the company attributed the deteriorating business to the advent of the car. Both branches had been sold off by 1932. Ballimore formed in 1918 when cars were about to become commonplace, and therefore never developed as a significant commercial centre. Increased mobility contributed to these places' commercial life languishing, but the smaller towns continued to be an important component of local society, particularly while farmers still needed seasonal labour.[64]

Whereas railways effectively shrank space in specific directions and according to prescribed timetables—with the state itself the driver of all— cars placed owners in control of where and when to travel. For those who could afford them, cars expanded the possibilities for leisure and social engagement, bringing a much wider expanse of countryside within reach of a day trip. On a Sunday in 1924, a group departed from Mogriguy in five cars and collected another carload of people in Dubbo before travelling to the Wellington Caves. They stopped briefly in Wellington on the return trip before reaching Mogriguy that evening after a journey of around 150 kilometres—a customised day trip that could not have been achieved with

---

63   Commonwealth Bureau of Census and Statistics, *Census of the Commonwealth of Australia Taken for the Night between the 3rd and 4th April, 1921* (Melbourne: Government Printer, [1921]); Commonwealth Bureau of Census and Statistics, *Census of the Commonwealth of Australia, 30th June 1933* (Canberra: Government Printer, [1933]); Cooks Business Directories, *Business Directory of New South Wales, 1931–32* (Sydney: Interstate Business Directory Publishers, n.d.), 325–8.
64   Australia, Rural Reconstruction Commission, *Rural Amenities: The Commission's Seventh Report to the Honorable J. J. Dedman, MP, Minister for Post-War Reconstruction* ([Canberra]: The Commission, 1945), 77; T. H. Cameron, handwritten manuscript, 14 September 1929, history of the Western Stores Limited, typescript, ML MSS 6899, SLNSW.

any preceding technology.[65] Twelve-year-old Dorothy Morley went with her family from Wongarbon to the Ballimore soda springs, a journey of 32 kilometres, for the first time in 1926. She reported to the children's page of the *Land*:

> On Sundays, sometimes there are as many as 50 car loads of people, who have come from Dubbo and elsewhere ... We took our lunch so had a real day out.[66]

Technology was, again, modifying ideas of place.

By thus expanding people's social horizons, cars might have caused the smallest communities—those clustered around halls and one-teacher schools—to decline. However, before 1950 such communities actually flourished as cars became more common on rural properties. While people preferred centres such as Dubbo for shopping and to transact business, they organised much of their social lives closer to home. Cars made it easier to travel beyond a small community but also made those places more accessible for people from elsewhere. Social functions and competitive sports—tennis particularly—flourished among small communities within radii defined by the distance people could traverse in a comfortable return journey at each end of a function. It is remarkable that at least 10 country halls were built within 60 kilometres of Dubbo between 1918 and 1937, the era of the motor car.[67] This phenomenon is examined in more detail in Chapter 7.

Further change would follow, but not until the 1950s. Imports of new cars were suspended during World War II, and petrol was rationed for most of the time between 1940 and 1950. But, in a matter of decades, cars had changed the way many people experienced and imagined the farmlands, expanding social and recreational choices, and altering relationships with the town, the villages and local communities.

---

65 *DL*, 14 March 1924, 7.
66 *Land*, 26 February 1926, 19.
67 Gollan (1918), Ballimore (1920), Mogriguy (1924), Coalbaggie (1926), Ponto (1927), Coboco (1928, a rebuild), Rawsonville (1928), Toongi (1930), Westella (1935) and Comobella (1937).

Local newspapers

> Turning its pages, I am peculiarly at home … All the geography of
> the news is at my fingertips.[68]

Communities are shaped through the movement not only of people and
goods but also of words, images and ideas. The most influential vectors for
such exchanges in this period were newspapers. Benedict Anderson argued
that newspapers helped to create what he labelled 'imagined communities':
aggregations of people never likely to know each other, but bound by an idea
of a common identity. By juxtaposing, in regular editions, articles on events
occurring in diverse places, newspapers could create or affirm among their
readers ideas about what constituted *their* community, who was excluded,
and how their community related to a broader world. Newspapers could
also encourage a sense of common interest among their readership simply
by distributing one consistent message—in Alexis de Tocqueville's words,
placing 'the same thought at the same moment into a thousand minds'.
Newspapers also encouraged readers to imagine that they were a community
on the basis that they were participating in a regular ritual of consuming
a common product.[69]

Newspapers are likely to have been circulating in the district from the
beginning of European occupation. They were certainly present by the early
1860s when the grazier Henry Gwynne was subscribing to two English
journals. Petitioners seeking a post office at Comobella in 1878 stressed
the inconvenience of having to travel at least 10 miles to collect both letters
and newspapers. In 1891, six households at Eumungerie received 'about six
or eight' newspapers per mail delivery. At Gollan, 40 households received
136 newspapers over two deliveries in one week in 1908, equating to an
average of 3.4 papers per household per week. In the farming community of
Rawsonville, 14 households received 6,298 papers in 1930–31: an average

---

68 Writer commenting on local newspapers in *John O'London's Weekly* [undated], quoted in Ernest
C. Sommerlad, *Mightier than the Sword: A Handbook on Journalism, Broadcasting, Propaganda, Public
Relations and Advertising* (Sydney: Angus & Robertson, 1950), 111.
69 Benedict Anderson, *Imagined Communities: Reflections on the Origin and Spread of Nationalism*
(London: Verso, 2006), 62; Alexis de Tocqueville, *Democracy in America and Two Essays on America*,
trans. Gerald E Bevan (London: Penguin, 2003), 600.

of almost nine papers per household per week. Insolvent farmers often owed money for newspaper subscriptions, which suggests that papers were regarded as more than a discretionary expense.[70]

The particular communities that newspapers encouraged readers to imagine varied according to each title's content and circulation, and people in the farmlands consumed an eclectic assortment of local, specialist, metropolitan and international publications. Ken Inglis has highlighted the popularity of the weekly newspapers, such as the *Town and Country Journal* and the *Sydney Mail*, produced in the city for a country audience, although read in the cities as well. In 1907, Maryvale farmer William Craigie was receiving the *Sydney Mail*, the sports weekly the *Referee*, and Sydney's *Daily Telegraph*, along with the *Wellington Times*. Sydney's *Evening News* was among Glenara farmer George Condon's creditors in 1918, and he was also a *Wellington Times* reader. In the 1920s, Mogriguy farmer Fred Stroud read the *Bulletin* and the *Sydney Morning Herald*, as well as the *Farmer and Settler* and the *Land*.[71] Though people were connecting to broader communities and ideas, the remainder of this section focuses on the role of local papers in people's imagining.

Local newspapers were increasingly common in and around New South Wales rural towns from the 1870s. There was a newspaper for every 4,218 country dwellers by 1911.[72] Local papers included colonial, national and international news as part of their offering, but they understood their principal purpose and commercial advantage to lie in promoting and defining the region. With radio and the faster delivery of metropolitan papers threatening local newspapers' viability by the 1940s, E. C. Sommerlad, then the retiring secretary of the NSW Country Press Association, asserted that a paper's essential purpose was to identify with its local community:

> Country journalism is distinguished for its intimate contact with readers, for its friendliness, and for its attention to home-town affairs. It writes in a personal way of the average man's every-day

70   File no. 5200 (Gwynne), NRS 13654, SANSW; Petition to the postmaster general, [October 1878], Comobella Post Office File, SP32/1, NAA; Memo to the Dubbo postmaster, Eumungerie Post Office File, Part 1, 1891–1908, SP32/1, NAA; Postal inspector's memo, 11 May 1908, Gollan Post Office File, 1894–1914, SP32/1, NAA; District inspector to the senior inspector, 22 September 1931, Rawsonville Post Office File, 1903–47, SP32/1, NAA.

71   Ken Inglis, 'Questions about Newspapers', *Australian Cultural History*, no. 11 (1992): 120–7; File nos, 17321 (W. G. Craigie), 21390 (G. Condon), NRS 13655, SARNSW; Jessie Woodley (née Stroud, b. 1907), interview with author, Dubbo, 24 June 1981.

72   R. B. Walker, *The Newspaper in New South Wales, 1803–1920* (Sydney: Sydney University Press, 1976), 176–7.

experiences. It mirrors the life of the community and provides a
running day-to-day chronicle of the history of the territory in which
it is published … it is the authentic currency of the rural areas,
the friendly interplay of human activities of which country life is
essentially compact.[73]

Dubbo's papers pursued this principle enthusiastically.

The town acquired its first paper in 1866 when the brothers Manning arrived
from Bathurst to launch the weekly *Dubbo Dispatch*. The telegraph had
reached Dubbo just over a year earlier, so the new journal could both report
local affairs and compete with the Sydney papers, which arrived in the twice-
weekly mail, by publishing colonial, intercolonial and international news.
A succession of competing local newspapers were founded then failed from
1875, before the *Dubbo Liberal* (initially a weekly) took root and remained in
regular circulation from 1887. The *Dispatch* was produced biweekly by 1890,
as was the *Liberal* by 1900. Three editions of the *Liberal* were appearing each
week by 1940. Proprietors were wary of revealing their circulation, though
the *Liberal* claimed in 1930 that it issued three times as many papers in the
district as the bestselling city competitor, and twice as many as all the city
papers combined. That year the *Dispatch* claimed that, in the country, the
local press had 20 times the circulation of city papers. It is likely that most
newspaper-reading rural households consumed a local paper first, which was
sometimes supplemented by others from further afield.[74]

Having two local papers could help readers affirm their belonging to a
community of place, without necessarily having to align with one title's
politics. Almost without exception, country papers were politically
conservative but, still, Dubbo's papers were often distinguishable. The
Liberal typically took a more conservative stance, while the *Dispatch* was
generally more sympathetic to working-class politics. When the local
branch of the PLL supported the *Dispatch* in a libel case brought by the
Liberal in 1904, its representative justified the PLL's stance on the grounds
that, though the *Dispatch* was not 'in any way a labour organ', nonetheless

73   E. C. Sommerlad, 'What Is Ahead of the Country Newspaper?', address delivered to the 46th
annual conference of the NSW Country Press Association, Sydney, 23 October 1945, 6–7.
74   *Empire*, 14 September 1865, 5, 10 January 1866, 5; *DD*, 16 September 1887, 5; *DL*, 8 January
1910, 4, 21 October 1924, 1; Rod Kirkpatrick, 'Scissors and Paste: Recreating the History of Newspapers
in Ten Country Towns', *BSANZ Bulletin* 22, no. 4 (1998): 239; Rod Kirkpatrick, *Country Conscience:
A History of the New South Wales Provincial Press, 1841–1995* (Canberra: Infinite Harvest Publishing,
2000), 420–49; *DL*, 18 May 1930, 2; *Land* [quoting the *DD*], 21 March 1930, 4; Geoffrey Blainey,
Black Kettle and Full Moon: Daily Life in a Vanishing Australia (Camberwell: Viking, 2003), 108.

its proprietors 'always endeavoured to give the fairest of fair play'.[75] The papers took opposing sides on the conscription debates of 1916 and 1917: the *Liberal* for and the *Dispatch* against. Notwithstanding their differences, the papers uniformly promoted the town and district.

Local papers' scope to define a community was, to an extent, a function of the economics of establishing and sustaining a paper. That is, a paper needed a certain minimum number of readers to survive, though that number was not especially large. Printing presses cost as little as £200, and most country papers got by with a circulation of less than 500.[76] Consequently, places as small as Peak Hill (with a population of 1,557 in 1891) could support a paper, and therefore project the town as the centre of a community extending as far as its readership and the competition of neighbouring towns' papers would allow. On the other hand, an even smaller place such as Geurie, lacking its own paper, was more likely to be regarded as part of a hinterland—of Wellington or Dubbo—rather than as a community in its own right. It was easier to imagine a community that could attach a newspaper title to its name than one that could not. Just in the choice of one town's paper over another, readers effectively aligned with one imagined, town-centred community.[77]

But small places were far from invisible to the newspaper-reading public and, from around 1894, the Dubbo papers began to recognise the hinterland as a valuable source of copy and custom. The *Liberal* reminded 'readers in the country districts' that it was 'always pleased to publish any items of interest'. Columns appeared from places such as Bunglegumbie, Coalbaggie and Belarbigal, typically under the generic by-line 'Our correspondent'.[78] Papers in neighbouring towns—the *Wellington Times* particularly—did likewise, and if a locality sat on the boundaries of the adjacent towns' spheres of influence, its column might appear in both towns' papers. It is very likely that the regular contributors were known to the communities concerned, and there might even have been some broader agreement about who should take on that role. In 1935, the Westella Hall Committee, which had become the de facto forum in that district for discussing and resolving matters of communal interest, agreed that the local schoolteacher should be appointed as 'the Westella correspondent' to the *Liberal*.[79]

---

75   *DD*, 13 July 1904, 3.
76   Walker, *The Newspaper in New South Wales*, 176–8.
77   New South Wales, *Results of a Census of New South Wales Taken for the Night of 5th April 1891* (Sydney: Government Printer, 1894), 750.
78   *DL*, 3 January 1894, 4.
79   Minutes, 30 April 1935, Westella Hall Committee, Western Plains Cultural Centre, Dubbo.

The columns were the communities' own regular, performative renditions. They stressed consensus and harmony, and rarely conveyed conflict. The content was often comically quotidian, ranging from communal events such as dances and school picnics to the common preoccupation with the weather, the farming tasks of the season, and the fortunes of individual families including injuries, illness, vacations and birthdays. Correspondents would sometimes revel laconically in relating the mundane. A Mogriguy report of 1911 passed on the news that 'Mr Hudson lost a good milch cow last week, owing to a tree falling on her'.[80] These were events otherwise likely to be relayed over a fence, in passing on a country road, or at a local social function: experiences drawn from a common range available to people in those places, elevated to the status of 'news'.

Stripped of individuals' and families' names, the columns were remarkably uniform in their subject matter, yet the names and the specificity of individual events mattered. They affirmed who was acknowledged as part of that community and who, by their silent exclusion, was not. The columns conveyed the idea of the farmlands as consisting not of a uniform whole, but rather a patchwork of unique neighbourhoods, each with its own personality. If newspapers functioned to locate people as parts of a broader Dubbo district, a state, a nation and an empire, then they also affirmed and sustained the separate identities of these smallest of places, where the community was so tangible, so familiar, that the permanent residents did not need to imagine it at all.

Radio

From the beginning of official broadcasting in 1923, radio transcended spatial boundaries and thereby challenged the idea of communities of place. As one historian has observed, the medium could also 'cut deeply across individual, class, racial and ethnic experience'.[81] Like cars, radios were a symbol of modernity, being advertised in the Dubbo press from around 1927 as stylish adornments, relaying information and entertainment from distant places into the modern home. In 1925, the *Dispatch* enthused that radio

---

80 *DL*, 24 October 1911.
81 Michele Hilmes, *Radio Voices: American Broadcasting, 1922–1952* (Minneapolis: University of Minnesota Press, 1997), xvi.

'brings the ends of the earth together for the instruction, enlightenment and satisfaction of mankind ... The possibilities are limitless, the future rich with promise'.[82]

The federal government managed a national approach to radio, regulating the industry and collecting licence fees from its inception, and from 1932 the government-owned Australian Broadcasting Commission (ABC) assumed the role of national broadcaster. But radio was not experienced uniformly in every place. For over a decade after broadcasting began, radios were much less common in the country than in the city, access to particular broadcasters varied according to where one lived, and the distribution of commercial broadcasters was uneven. A few Dubbo radio enthusiasts received signals from Sydney from the time broadcasts commenced, but it was several years before radio sets were taken up by a more general population. By 1936, only half as many licences were issued, per head of population and per dwelling, beyond Sydney as in the city. Within 50 miles (80 kilometres) of Dubbo, there was a licence for every three dwellings, which was consistent with the non-metropolitan area as a whole.[83] In the early years particularly, the relative quality of reception might have been a factor, but also, for many households, receivers would have been prohibitively expensive. Radios offered as prizes in raffles and competitions in Dubbo papers in 1925 ranged in price from £72 to £125. By 1927, they were advertised at between £36 17s 6d and £45 (8–10 times the minimum weekly wage), and by 1937 at between £16 16s and £33 12s (4.6–9.2 times the minimum wage). So they were becoming more affordable but still beyond many people's reach.[84] As rural households did not have mains electricity, radios were powered by batteries, adding to their continuing expense.

Just how common radio was beyond the town is difficult to gauge. Whereas car ownership was highly visible, radios were as private as a new piano. A rare newspaper report in 1927 announced that two farming households near Wongarbon had listened to a broadcast of the opening of the new Parliament House in Canberra by the Duke of York. The newspaper's focus on the 'excellent day-time reception' received in these households suggests that these sets were, if not unique, then among a small number in the

---

82   *DD*, 6 March 1925; Lesley Johnson, *The Unseen Voice: A Cultural Study of Early Australian Radio* (London: Routledge, 1988), 15.

83   *DL*, 14 November 1924, 2; W. A. McNair, *Radio Advertising in Australia* (Sydney: Angus & Robertson, 1937), 288.

84   *DL*, 2 January 1925, 7, 6 February 1925, 3, 16 October 1925, 7, 23 August 1927, 3, 11 November 1927, 12; *Leader* (Orange), 30 April 1937, 3.

district. The account also suggests that people embraced the new medium's capacity to connect them with distant events in real time, extending experience into spheres one would not otherwise encounter, and affirming wider abstract communities—in this case of the nation and the empire— with an immediacy that newspapers could not match.[85]

From the mid-1930s, radio in the Central West began to encourage the idea that rural, farming households constituted a unified, abstract community. Farmers' groups recognised radio's potential to relay information quickly and broadly, to aid farming practices, such as through weather reports and stock prices, and to alleviate social isolation. The GA of New South Wales and some of its individual members launched a station, 2GZ, broadcasting from Orange in 1935. Around Dubbo, local GA branches sought better service from the station (and from others), indicating both a strong sense of proprietorship and also that the medium had become embedded as a routine part of rural life. The Dubbo District Council of the GA endorsed a recommendation in 1936 that the station should broadcast better programs, with 'additional subjects and information of value to the man on the land'. The Wellington branch also passed a strongly worded resolution that year, to the effect that 2GZ should be held to account for 'the incomplete report of the Wool Sales', and urging that the news service not commence before the farmer's long summer working day was over.[86] Dubbo's commercial station, 2DU, opened in 1936 with capital raised mainly from town professionals and graziers. By 1950, the station claimed coverage of a wide arc of territory, mainly to the north and west, encompassing a population of 6,000. As with local newspapers, its commercial interests prompted it to reach as much as possible into the farmlands (a third of its revenue came from the surrounding districts), providing another basis for defining a community of common interest and experience.[87]

The ABC established a relay station broadcasting into the Central West from Orange in 1936 to provide the region with better quality reception to a common national network, rather than a tailored service for rural listeners. Australian broadcasters were much slower than their counterparts in the

---

85   *WT*, 12 May 1927, 7.

86   Dubbo District Council, annual general meeting, minutes, 11 February 1936, Graziers Association of New South Wales, Deposit 1, E256/1481, Noel Butlin Archives Centre; Wellington Branch minutes, 25 January 1936, Graziers Association of New South Wales, Deposit 1, E256/1523, Noel Butlin Archives Centre.

87   'A Statement of Claim for a High Power License for Western and Far Western Listeners of New South Wales and Radio 2DU, Dubbo, July 1950', 25 and appendix XII, MP1170/1, 2DU4 part 1, NAA.

United States to target rural people as a unique audience. It took until 1943 for the ABC to broadcast the *Country Hour*, timed to coincide with farming people's midday meal.[88] The program was part of a continuing effort across governments to encourage primary producers to employ more scientific methods but also reinforced the idea of the sector having a unity of purpose and being. If newspapers could encourage people to imagine communities of simultaneous experience extending beyond their immediate sphere of knowing, then radio could apply new qualities to reinforce that sense. Unlike newspapers, radio resembled railways in imposing a discipline of time—any one broadcast was experienced simultaneously—so people heard in common the *Country Hour* at 1 pm each weekday whether the listener was in Tamworth, Wagga, Dubbo or Mogriguy.

Radio also influenced people's sense of one kind of community with its content and, especially, through serials, which, as Lesley Johnson observes, served to symbolise the shared experience of routines and ordinary preoccupations of everyday life. *The Lawsons* was the pre-eminent example, broadcast by the ABC between 1944 and 1949 on weekdays as part of the *Country Hour*.[89] Conceived as a complementary and surreptitious way to educate farmers, the series became valued by its audience more for its depiction of a farming household's daily life. *The Lawsons* created a sense of an imagined community through listeners' simultaneous, ritualised experience. It was enormously popular, including in the Dubbo district. Listeners wrote to the show's creator Gwen Meredith about the series' place in their daily lives, and how, especially for women, it became a shared event around which households' daily routines were organised. A Binnaway correspondent wrote:

> I am just one country woman voicing the expressed thoughts of a lot more country folk ... [The serial] is quite an 'institution' in many country homes ... [It] is the after dinner highlight in many homes—men, women & children of all ages listen to it almost as a last course of the meal.[90]

---

88   *Leader* (Orange), 7 May 1937, 7; Ian K. McKay, *Broadcasting in Australia* (Carlton: Melbourne University Press, 1957), 97–8; *Land*, 25 June 1943, 5; *Farmer and Settler*, 25 June 1943, 7.
89   Johnson, *The Unseen Voice*, 95. See also Michelle Arrow, '"Everything Stopped for Blue Hills": Radio, Memory and Australian Women's Domestic Lives, 1944–2001', *Australian Feminist Studies* 20, no. 48 (2005): 309; *Farmer and Settler*, 25 June 1943; Alan Thomas, *Broadcast and Be Damned: The ABC's First Two Decades* (Carlton: Melbourne University Press, 1980), 100–1, 153–4.
90   Gladys Hall to Gwen Meredith, 10 February 1947, Gwen Meredith Papers, box 10, MS 6789, NLA. See also V. to Gwen Meredith, 11 January 1945, Gwen Meredith Papers, box 9, MS 6789, NLA.

Meredith depicted a quite specific type of household, one that engaged two permanent employees, whereas a more typical farm in most parts of rural Australia would have employed labour only during seasonal peaks. In this way, she was evoking rural affluence and success—a rural middle class—even if on a modest scale. Meredith had connected with a broadly (though not universally) popular desire to claim, as nationally iconic, a particular (rural) social and political culture. Her characters also expressed explicitly conservative political views.[91]

The qualities with which the serial's many devotees valued and identified were evident in the cultural works with which they compared it. At least one correspondent contrasted Meredith's serials with Ruth Park's stark depiction of poverty, alcoholism and disability in *The Harp in the South* (1948), her story of a working-class, Catholic family in Sydney's Surry Hills.[92] The listener was most concerned about how 'Australians' were depicted, claiming the Lawsons as an essential national 'type', and as the antithesis of Park's characters, whom she considered 'give the rest of the world very wrong ideas of us all'. The Lawson family was also contrasted favourably with the simple and witless bumpkins portrayed in another popular radio serial, *Dad and Dave of Snake Gully* (1937–53), which one of Meredith's correspondents described as 'an insult to decent country people'.[93] When a production company asked Meredith to rework a script for a film, she was advised:

> We do not want to make the characters anything other than *normal*, middle-class people who live on the land and whom we would meet *any day* around the district—we do NOT want Dad and Dave types.[94]

Whereas the Snake Gully family were depicted as aspiring for respectability from a position of ignorance and relative poverty, the Lawsons were seen to have achieved and to exemplify it. The former were victims of their environment, whereas the latter were applying modern farming methods

91 *Daily Advertiser* (Wagga Wagga), 10 August 1946, 2; L. M. O'Neill to Meredith, 17 September 1950, Gwen Meredith Papers, box 10, MS 6789, NLA.
92 Philippa St Clair Maclardy to Meredith, 23 February 1949, Gwen Meredith Papers, box 10, MS 6789, NLA. See also Mrs A. Thorn Daniels to Gwen Meredith, 14 January 1950, Gwen Meredith Papers, box 8, MS 6789, NLA.
93 A. Heath to Gwen Meredith, 26 November 1945, Gwen Meredith Papers, box 8, MS 6789, NLA.
94 Supreme Sound System to Gwen Meredith, 5 April 1945, Gwen Meredith Papers, box 9, MS 6789, NLA (emphasis added).

to control it. As Megan Blair notes, audiences were invited to laugh *at* Dad and Dave but to laugh and empathise *with* the Lawsons as virtual acquaintances.[95]

Listeners responded to this household as 'typical' of a 'country', or even an 'Australian', outlook and way of life. The creators deliberately encouraged the audience's empathy by not locating the serial in a named place: it was nowhere specifically, so potentially anywhere in the listener's imagination. A Mendooran farmer found the serial to be 'very typical of country people & country conditions', and another correspondent considered that 'the characters are so real and might be just any family living on the land'. When Dubbo High School staged a Book Week in 1950, two students wrote to Meredith expressing sentiments that were common among her admirers. One wrote that *The Lawsons* consisted of 'real country folks, facing the hardships and joys of life', and the other described it as 'a typical Australian story ... about ordinary country families'.[96]

Like the other technologies examined in this chapter, radio affected people's perceptions of community in multiple, layered ways. As with local newspapers, it was in the Dubbo station's interest to foster in its listeners a sense of ownership and belonging in a region centred on and defined by the town. Conversely, with its network of relay stations, the national broadcaster allowed people to imagine much more extensive communities. One of the most pervasive effects was to allow rural dwellers to consider themselves part of a community of respectable, modern, but socially and politically conservative rural dwellers valorised as the epitome of a national type.

The telephone

Telephone technology had the potential to connect people faster and more intimately than any that had preceded it. How did they utilise this technology to connect, and how did it affect people's attachment to one community or another? As telephone services differed in cost, hours of

---

95   Megan Blair, 'Listening in to *The Lawsons*: Radio Crosses the Urban-Rural Divide', in *Struggle Country: The Rural Ideal in the Twentieth Century*, ed. Graeme Davison and Marc Brodie (Melbourne: Monash University ePress, 2005), 07.1–07.19.
96   Hector R. Luckie to Gwen Meredith, 1 January 1945, Valerie Jenkins to Gwen Meredith, 6 July 1950, J. W. to Gwen Meredith, 7 July 1950, Gwen Meredith Papers, box 8, MS 6789, NLA; [Unidentified at the ABC] to Gwen Meredith, 17 May [1944?], Gwen Meredith Papers, box 9, MS 6789, NLA; Margaret MacCallum, 'The Lawsons are Real People to the Listeners', *ABC Weekly*, 25 November 1945, 6.

operation and modes of connection, experiences are likely to have varied from place to place. Telephones were slow to reach the town of Dubbo, and slower again to connect with the farmlands. Sydney had its first private lines connecting city businesses with the Darling Harbour wool warehouses in 1880, and a government exchange by 1882, but Dubbo's exchange did not open until 1897, with 26 subscribers. At the official launch, as an early sign that telephones would become particularly relevant to women whose lives were more likely to centre on the household, 'ladies spoke through the telephone to friends, and received replies'. Telephones were gradually taken up in farming districts but were not as common as in the towns and cities. The federal government charged lower rental rates in the country, but many people could not afford the costs of installation in more sparsely populated districts. The Rural Reconstruction Commission estimated that, across rural Australia as a whole, no more than one household in three was connected to a telephone line by the early 1940s, though a more accurate comparison for the Dubbo district might have been a survey of the Victorian wheat belt that found just under four-fifths of farms connected at around that same time.[97]

Not only were phones less common beyond the towns, but also exchanges were not open as often. In the Dubbo farmlands, they operated only at specified times of the day and week unless a minimum number of subscribers had enrolled. In 1897, at least 15 subscribers were required to establish a 'day' service from a country exchange, while 25 subscribers warranted a 'day and night' service. A household could connect to an exchange up to 1 mile (1.6 kilometres) distance for an annual fee of £5, but each additional quarter mile (400 metres) of line cost an extra 10 shillings, so expenses could escalate quickly for subscribers beyond a town.[98] When an exchange opened at the Geurie post office in 1910, the government built lines extending 2 miles from the village, to which households could connect at their own expense. The Geurie exchange acquired enough subscribers to operate day and night from 1913. The Wongarbon exchange, which opened in 1911, only ever operated during post office hours, but locals pressed to have its hours extended in 1913 and 1916, so it was evidently a valued

---

97 Ann Moyal, *Clear across Australia: A History of Telecommunications* (Melbourne: Thomas Nelson Australia, 1984), 75, 78; *DL*, 17 November 1897, 2; Australia, Rural Reconstruction Commission, *Rural Amenities*, 44–5; Holt, *Wheat Farms of Victoria*, 122.
98 *DD*, 19 March 1897, 4.

service.[99] An exchange opened at Brocklehurst in 1913, and eight or nine Beni residents connected through a party line to the Dubbo exchange in 1916. That year, a Postmaster-General's Department official reported that 'the majority' of farmers in the vicinity of the Maryvale railway station were connected to either the Wellington or Geurie exchanges. However, farming households at Rawsonville were still being connected in 1923, and telephone services continued to be extended to households around the Dubbo district into the 1950s as pastoral stations were carved up into smaller blocks and new properties were established.[100]

People's own investment in this technology also shows that they valued it highly. Most farmland households with a telephone connected either through an individual or (most often) a party line. The costs of connecting to an exchange or government line could be defrayed if households—generally in groups of 5–10—collaborated to erect and maintain such a line. The McKillops were associated with Narromine more than Dubbo, but their experience in connecting to a party line was common among rural households. Between September and November 1907, they cut and erected 80 poles, fitted the insulators and strung the wire. The first call prompted an unusually effusive diary entry: 'Line works in a most satisfactory manner.' Likewise, the farmer Edward King recorded in his journal his family's completion of a line among the most noteworthy events of 1910.[101]

The significance of this enthusiastic adoption of the technology for community formation is difficult to gauge because it is less clear how phones were actually used. Some social scientists have argued that the telephone could create 'psychological neighbourhoods' that foster relationships based on mutual interests and personal needs, unconstrained by geography. Ann Moyal refers to the significance of the 'telephone neighbourhood' to women's lives, revealing a 'pervasive, deeply rooted dynamic feminine culture of the telephone', although her research was conducted on an era some considerable time after the period covered by this chapter. The American social scientist De Sola Pool has asserted that the party line system 'created a community',

99   Inspector's internal memo, 23 March 1909, Geurie Post Office File, SP32/1, NAA; Inspector's internal memo, 19 May 1913, A. V. Morley to the postmaster general, 19 February 1915, internal memo, 1915 [author and precise date obscured], Wongarbon Post Office File, part 7, SP32/1, NAA; *Evening News*, 17 September 1910, 5; *DD*, 24 January 1913, 2.
100 *DD*, 5 December 1913, 1, 19 May 1916, 1; Betty Hickey, *A Village that Disappeared: Beni Via Dubbo* (Dubbo: Orana Education Centre, 1987); Internal Postmaster-General's Department memo, November 1916, Maryvale Post Office File, part 2, 1908–17, SP32/1, NAA; *DL*, 13 April 1923, 4.
101 McKillop, 'The McKillops of "Buddah"'; Edwin Phillip King Diaries, 1893–1959, Narromine Library, Macquarie Regional Library.

but he also emphasises the technology's equivocal effects: 'No matter what hypothesis one begins with, reverse tendencies also appear.' For example, technology allowed people to initiate and control communication from their homes, but could also intrude into a space valued for its privacy.[102]

Relative costs favouring local use (flat-rate or untimed calls within the network of a local exchange) could have helped to strengthen more immediate community connection. However, the effects were more ambiguous, and indeed are unlikely to have changed substantially the ways people imagined their communities. The configuration of party lines bore little relationship to any other notion of communities of common interest. They consisted of blends of both cooperating neighbours and extended families, who favoured lines that connected their local, but not necessarily adjoining, households. Consequently, a locale might be crisscrossed by a web of unrelated party lines, with neighbours as likely as not to be on separate lines. By 1950, 52 households in the Gollan district were connected via nine party lines to three different exchanges.[103]

However, with the exception of extended families (both the McKillops and the Kings made their first calls on the newly erected lines to family members), even being a part of the same party line did not necessarily mean that the participants comprised a coherent community. The telephone could disturb a valued separation from surrounding households. The most obvious challenge was that anyone on a party line could eavesdrop on fellow subscribers' calls. As one Coboco resident recalled: 'everyone could hear. There was no privacy so business or anything of importance was never discussed.'[104] As a line could only be used by one subscriber at a time, there was also pressure to restrict calls. In 1939, a conference of the Central Western Districts of the Agricultural Bureau debated whether calls should be limited so as to avert 'the inconvenience and danger that might result from unduly prolonged conversation'.[105] The limits of people's willingness to collaborate was also evident in the widespread resistance to

102 Herbert S. Dordick, 'The Social Uses of the Telephone—an [sic] US Perspective', in *Telefon und Gesellschaft: Beitrage zu einer Soziologie der Telefoncommunikation*, ed. Ulrich Lange, Klaus Beck, Axel Zerdick (Herausgeber) (Berlin: 1989), 226; Ann Moyal, 'The Gendered Use of the Telephone: An Australian Case Study', *Media, Culture and Society* 14 (1992): 67; Ithiel de Sola Pool, 'Introduction', in *The Social Impact of the Telephone*, ed. Ithiel de Sola Pool (Cambridge: MIT Press, 1977), 4, 6.
103 *DL*, 20 September 1950, 2.
104 Jancie Fisher, '"Lara" (Fisher family)', in *A Compiled History of Coboco District*, ed. Pat Fisher, Robyn Healey and Sandra Burns (Narromine: Coboco CWA, 2002), 62.
105 Resolution discussed at the annual conference of the Central Western Districts of the Agricultural Bureau, Dubbo. See *WT*, 28 September 1939, 3.

the Postmaster-General's Department's practice of issuing a single bill to the parties to a shared line, rather than bill each individual subscriber, such that one subscriber was obliged to ensure that each household paid their dues. The Dubbo District Council of the FSA formally protested the practice in 1933, as did the CWA's Macquarie Group in 1934, and the Terramungamine CWA branch in 1935.[106] Connections beyond the party line also involved an operator's mediation. These were porous, often convenient, sometimes bothersome arrangements requiring some negotiation between and among private and public worlds, compared with those in cities connected through automatic exchanges.

In all, whereas newspapers and radio each extended and shaped communities by delivering an identical product to a wide audience, telephones consisted of a dishevelled tracery of thousands of bilateral connections. In 1945, the Rural Reconstruction Commission claimed boldly that the telephone enabled 'those on farms … [to] feel that they are a part of the nation and not merely its disconnected adjuncts'.[107] People clearly valued the facility. It probably made some local business transactions more efficient, and it strengthened already established relationships, possibly among women as Moyal argues, and certainly among extended families. Beyond that, there is little evidence that telephones had a uniform effect on ideas of communities, whether based on place, class or nation. If telephones did influence the formation of imagined communities, it was in creating the *potential* to connect with a wider world, one yet to be fully realised as late as the 1940s.

Air travel: A coda

Air travel came to Dubbo in the late 1920s and early 1930s, first as a novelty, and then as an elite form of transport. People could take a ride in a plane at the Narromine Show in 1928, and in 1931 and 1932 Charles Kingsford Smith sold joy flights in the *Southern Cross* from a paddock just outside Dubbo.[108] Commercial flights to and from Sydney for just a few passengers at a time began in 1935 but from Narromine rather than the larger town of Dubbo—a sign, perhaps, of the greater pastoral wealth to the west. Dubbo

---

106 *Western Age*, 24 November 1933, 1; *DL*, 6 October 1934, 5; Minutes, 6 March 1936, Terramungamine Branch of the CWA, Western Plains Cultural Centre, Dubbo.

107 Australia, Rural Reconstruction Commission, *Rural Amenities*, 44.

108 *Narromine News and Trangie Advocate*, 17 May 1928, 4; *Farmer and Settler*, 1 August 1931, 9; *National Advocate*, 21 May 1932, 5.

was added to the route sometime later. The one-and-a-half hour flight cost a little more than the minimum weekly wage. The experience was so novel that a list of the first 50 passengers was published in a local newspaper in May 1935.[109] A 21-seater began operating between Dubbo and Sydney in 1946 as Australian commercial air traffic expanded enormously from the mid to late 1940s.[110] But it would not be until the 1950s that air travel became more than a fantasy for most—a symbol of modernity and its possibilities rather than a common influence on the experience of time and space.

Conclusion

Henry Lawson, familiar with the western railway line from Sydney through Dubbo to Bourke, lamented towards the end of the nineteenth century that 'the mighty bush with iron rails is tethered to the world', as though rural New South Wales was newly constrained by this intrusive technology.[111] It was not just his view: in this instance, Lawson was invoking the broader trope of the virtuous and self-sufficient rural, threatened anew by the tainted and parasitic city. But this chapter has shown that, from the first incursion of colonists, the farmlands were always connected vitally to a broader capitalist economy. Indeed, the region's relationship to the world beyond was an essential reason for it to be, and to exist in the form that Europeans imagined and built it. One way or another, as a settler phenomenon, it was ever so. Railways, in particular, shaped the economic and social landscape, including the experiences and structures of class, such that the farmlands from 1881 onwards were unimaginable without them. Paradoxically, the agrarian idyll of a society consisting of a landowning, cultivating and independent citizenry could only be created and sustained if it was connected to the world through the ready exchange of produce, goods, people and ideas that technology increasingly enabled. Self-sufficiency was never a tenable element of the yeoman fantasy. As Hirst has argued, there *was* no age of splendid, self-sufficient isolation.[112] But I have challenged another of Hirst's views, that the land laws determined the nature of rural

---

109 *Narromine News and Trangie Advocate*, 31 August 1934, 4, 17 May 1935, 4; *DL*, 30 April 1935, 2.

110 *DL*, 18 May 1946, 1. Australian commercial air traffic increased threefold between 1943 and 1947, and fourfold by 1948. See C. Arthur Butler, *Flying Start: The History of the First Five Decades of Civil Aviation in Australia* (Sydney: Edwards and Shaw, 1971), 178.

111 Henry Lawson, 'The Roaring Days', *Bulletin*, 21 December 1889, 26. Lawson writes of the rail journey from Bathurst to Bourke in 'In a Dry Season', first published in the *Bulletin* in November 1892.

112 John Hirst, 'Distance—Was It a Tyranny?', in *Sense and Nonsense in Australian History* (Melbourne: Black Inc. Agenda, 2005), 24–37.

society. The land laws would have had little effect without operating in tandem with government investment in technologies as part of the agrarian project.

This chapter has also demonstrated that transport and communications were integral to the ways people experienced and imagined communities. They influenced who people engaged with, as well as how and how often; they altered the distances people travelled and the places they became familiar with. Ways to imagine communities could not readily settle. They were disrupted—distance and space were regularly warped—such that connections to a local place, town, the metropole, a class or a broader rural community were asserted or challenged with each new wave of change. Communities of place were always, in some way or another, new.

7

'All thoughts of depression were banished'[1]: Voluntary associations and the making of social spaces and communities

When he was not working his small, debt-encumbered farm between the wars, Albert Mawbey liked to join associations. He became president of the Wongarbon branch of the FSA and of the association's Dubbo district council. From the moment his local community decided to build a hall in 1934, Mawbey served as the committee's treasurer for 27 years. He was usually the first choice to act as master of ceremonies at hall functions. Though he was unmarried and had no children, in 1937 he served as president of the local school's parents and citizens association. Not everyone was so active in voluntary associations in the farmlands; however, from the late nineteenth century, voluntary associations were an increasingly common aspect of social life. The ways people organised their social time expressed their attachment to various communities; however, from the 1870s, it was sociability that most often defined and affirmed communities of place.

The voluntary associations that formed in the farmlands were an extension of a phenomenon that proliferated in Britain from the late eighteenth century. These were created, the historian R. J. Morris argues, by groups anxious to retain, accumulate or gain power in a changing and increasingly

---

1   *DL*, 15 May 1931, 4.

complex world. In Australia, such associations could affirm a common British cultural connection, though one that was modified in response to the local environment. Associations supported mutual aid, service to others, participation and advocacy. Through them, people showed that they amounted to more than work and home—that they were a part of something beyond themselves and held other allegiances and affiliations.[2]

People expressed aspects of their identities through a wide range of associations. Political groups, such as branches of the FSA and the Labor Party, were also forums for expressing companionship and mutual support. From 1913, the Gollan branch of the FSA organised annual sports days, with little explicit connection to the broader organisation's political purpose. Branches of the Manchester Unity International Order of Oddfellows (MUIOOF), formed in Geurie (1902), Eumungerie (1911), Wongarbon (1912) and Ballimore (1921), provided sickness and funeral benefits, as well as ritual and sociability. In 1922, 15 men—mostly farmers, but also teachers, a police officer, a station master, a shire clerk and others—established a Masonic lodge in Geurie, where members could feel part of an exclusive local conclave, participating in what Morris describes as the international order's 'common fund of ritual, rhetoric and experience'.[3]

Chapter 6 touched on the role of place and proximity in fostering a class consciousness among railway construction workers. And, as American historian Roy Rosenzweig has argued, social and cultural encounters—not just the relations of economic production—can illuminate understandings of class experience.[4] In this chapter, I examine the influence of place and associational life on people's consciousness of being a farming class beyond hours and sites of work, focusing on a few specific organisations—churches, sporting associations, the CWA and public hall committees.

---

2   R. J. Morris, 'Clubs, Societies and Associations', in *The Cambridge Social History of Britain 1750–1950, Volume 3: Social Agencies and Institutions*, ed. F. M. L. Thompson (Cambridge: Cambridge University Press, 1990), 395; Melanie Oppenheimer, '"We All Did Voluntary Work of Some Kind": Voluntary Work and Labour History', *Labour History*, no. 81 (2001): 2.
3   Morris, 'Clubs, Societies and Associations', 401; Minutes, 12 July 1913, Minute Book of the Gollan Branch of the FSA, 1907–15, in possession of Frank Rowe, Dubbo; *WT*, 14 August 1902, 4; *DD*, 1 December 1911, 4; *DL*, 28 April 1922, 5; Colleen Braithwaite, Rita Giddings, Pam Oates and Marie Tucker, *The History of the Wongarbon, Westella, Eulomogo and Pilewood Schools* (Dubbo: Development and Advisory Publications for the Wongarbon School Centenary Committee, [1987]), 144; Hazel Blekemore and Marylu Flowers-Schoen, *Ballimore Public School* ([Dubbo, 1984]), 30; Malcolm Hepburn, *The History of the Geurie Public School and District, Including the District Schools of Ponto, Maryvale, Comobella, Combo, Windora and Criefton* ([Geurie]: Malcolm Hepburn, 1986), 120.
4   Roy Rosenzweig, *Eight Hours for What We Will Do: Workers and Leisure in an Industrial City, 1870–1920* (Cambridge: Cambridge University Press, 1983), 1–5.

Churches and religious observance

People's identification with one religious denomination or another potentially complicated communities otherwise based on place or class. Around 49 in every 50 non-Aboriginal person in the Talbragar Shire identified as Christian between 1911 and 1947 and, as in most parts of Australia at that time, they aligned with one denomination or another. Religious practice and allegiance both drew people together and held them separate; it was a source of both unity and division that overlay other loci of the community. As noted in Chapter 4, in the shire, around 28 per cent of people identified as Catholic into the early 1920s. By 1933, that proportion had fallen to 21 per cent, possibly as farming wage labour became less common. Anglicans made up nearly half the farmland population throughout, Presbyterians around one in eight, and the remainder other Protestant denominations. But people's experience of religious community, and difference, was influenced by how the denominations were distributed across the district. Railway villages, with their preponderance of railway and rural workers, contained higher proportions of Catholic people, as did the community of Beni.[5] Otherwise, beyond the villages, communities containing more than one Catholic household were the exception. Often farming communities consisted solely of Protestant-identifying households or were predominantly associated with a particular Protestant denomination. The Boothenba district, for example, was described as a centre of the Presbyterian Church in 1938.

More people identified as Christian than regularly practised or demonstrated their allegiance, though this did not necessarily amount to what Bill Gammage described, in relation to the Narrandera district, as 'rampant nominalism'. Every district appears to have included people who gathered with fellow worshippers. By the 1890s, Catholic, Anglican, Presbyterian and Methodist churches based in Dubbo were sending clergy into surrounding districts to conduct Sunday services. Belarbigal had an Anglican Church in 1876 and Beni had a Catholic Church in 1882; however, until the late 1890s, they were the exception, with services elsewhere conducted mostly in private and improvised spaces. Public schools were explicitly prohibited

---

5   Roger C. Thompson, *Religion in Australia: A History*, 2nd ed. (South Melbourne: Oxford University Press, 2002), 22–3, 44; Commonwealth Bureau of Census and Statistics, *Census of the Commonwealth of Australia Taken for the Night between the 3rd and 4th April, 1921* (Melbourne: Government Printer, [1921]); Commonwealth Bureau of Census and Statistics, *Census of the Commonwealth of Australia, 30th June 1933* (Canberra: Government Printer, [1933]); Betty Hickey, *A Village that Disappeared: Beni Via Dubbo* (Dubbo: Orana Education Centre, 1987), [14–15].

from hosting religious events, but the occasional requests to allow a school to be used for these purposes—invariably from Protestant citizens or clergy—show that there was some significant thirst in the farmlands for communal religious observance.[6]

But sectarianism was never far from the surface of local consciousness. It was evident, for example, when the rules excluding religious ceremony from public schools were tested. In response to a request to use the Coalbaggie school for Anglican services in 1905, the school inspector advised that:

> although all the parents at present interested have signed the petition I am of the opinion that if the request be granted, it will lead to some unpleasantness locally and probably to some sectarian strife.

In 1894, a young teacher cautioned for allowing the Willandra school to be used for a Wesleyan fundraising event said that she had allowed it because the evening included no explicit religious instruction. A local landholder leased land to the Department of Public Instruction for the Boothenba school, allegedly on the condition that the building be available for Presbyterian services until the arrangement was challenged by the department in 1930.[7] These persistent overtures suggest a casual Protestant ascendancy that prevailed despite public schools being part of a putatively secular state.

In the late 1890s, some communities close to Dubbo built public halls in close association with Protestant churches based in the town. Dundullimal, which was both a property and the centre of a district of small-scale farmers, built a hall in 1899 initiated by the Presbyterian Church, and Bunglegumbie's new hall that year was intended for 'religious services, meetings, lectures etc'. The first event held in Eschol's new hall, also in 1899, was an Anglican service.[8] This nonchalant interchange between the secular and the sacred in public spaces was, again, a clear assertion of a

---

6   Bill Gammage, *Narrandera Shire* (Narrandera: Bill Gammage for the Narrandera Shire Council, 1986), 187; Minutes, 20 March 1893, 1 February 1897, 1 May 1899, Minute Book of the Parochial Council of Holy Trinity Anglican Church, Dubbo, 1883–1911, Holy Trinity Anglican Church, Dubbo; *DD*, 19 February 1892, 4, 10 October 1911, 2; *Freemans Journal*, 4 November 1882, 14; E. Tomlinson to the minister for education, 7 July 1898, Eulomogo School Administrative File, 5/15848.1, NRS 3829, SARNSW; Anglican Rector of Dubbo to the director of education, 29 May 1914, Ballimore School Administrative File, 5/14764.1, NRS 3829, SARNSW.

7   Inspector of Schools to the chief inspector, 24 October 1905, Coalbaggie School Administrative File, pre-1939, 5/15418.1, NRS 3829, SARNSW; Inspector to the chief inspector, 14 December 1894, Willandra School Administrative File, 5/18117.2, NRS 3829, SARNSW; Thorby to the minister for education, 27 May 1930, Boothenba school administrative file, 5/15029.4, NRS 3829, SARNSW.

8   *DL*, 18 February 1899, 2, 26 August 1899, 2, 20 December 1899, 2.

district's connection to an immanent Protestant faith. As another Anglican clergyman remembered, having just conducted a service in a public hall in the early twentieth century:

> I thought of the contrast—Westminster Abbey, the shrine of kings, and Coboco Hall, with the paper streamers from a dance on Boxing night still hanging from the roof; the glory and majesty, the hallowed traditions of one, the bareness and secularity of the other. But there the contrast ended. In spirit we were one.[9]

Church-building accelerated in the farmlands in this period as part of a wider Australian phenomenon, as church hierarchies became anxious about growing religious indifference, falling birth rates and a perception of deteriorating moral standards. Some sections of the Protestant churches urged that the state legislate to curb gambling, hotel trading hours, contraception and secular diversion on Sundays. The church-building era also coincided with a period of immoderate sectarian feeling, following a series of incidents and strident pronouncements by senior church figures in Sydney, including Presbyterian Minister Dill Macky and Catholic Cardinal Patrick Moran.[10] Around 400 people attended a meeting in Dubbo in February 1903, staged to form a branch of the Australian Protestant Defence Association, where women in particular were admonished to use their recent enfranchisement to elect representatives committed to a Protestant moral order.[11]

In this environment, church-building asserted a denomination's continuing relevance and strength.[12] Several villages, by then growing as commercial and residential centres, gained churches in this period. These included 'Union' churches built jointly by Protestant communities so as to share costs and at a time when those denominations' hierarchies considered collaborating to confront what they saw as the threats of Catholicism and secularism.[13] People built churches beyond the villages as well—wood and iron structures on donated land, in scrub clearings or surrounded by paddocks. Spicers

9   G. W. Lovejoy, 'In Journeyings Often': Being a Bush Brother's Record of Five Years Spent in the Australian Bush as a Member of the Brotherhood of the Good Shepherd, Dubbo (Dubbo: Brotherhood of the Good Shepherd, 1941), 54.

10   Richard Broome, Treasure in Earthen Vessels: Protestant Christianity in New South Wales Society, 1900–1914 (St Lucia: University of Queensland Press, 1980), 26–7, 95–161; Thompson, Religion in Australia, 44–7; Patrick O'Farrell, The Catholic Church and Community: An Australian History (Kensington: New South Wales University Press, 1985), 277–82.

11   Watchman, 14 February 1903, 3; DL, 11 February 1903, 2.

12   Broome, Treasure in Earthen Vessels, i.

13   Geurie (Union) 1897, Cobbora (Catholic) 1904, Wongarbon (Anglican) 1906, Geurie (Catholic) 1906, Geurie (Anglican) 1909, Wongarbon (Catholic) 1910; Broome, Treasure in Earthen Vessels, 73–80.

Creek had a Union church by 1902. The Reverend Joseph McDowell, an enthusiastic Presbyterian minister based in Wellington, energised people to build churches at Spicers Creek and Windora in 1905. A Baptist church opened at Gollan in 1908, the work of a handful of families. The Brotherhood of the Good Shepherd (the 'Bush Brothers')—an organisation within the Anglican Church based in Dubbo from 1903—held services in private houses and local halls, but also helped to found a church at Willandra in 1905 (see Figure 7.1). Belarbigal—by then renamed Rawsonville as an expression of fealty to sovereign and empire following a visit from the governor and former British naval officer Harry Rawson in 1903—replaced its old church in 1911.[14] These buildings were rare but pronounced statements of one form of community. An Anglican writer that year understood isolated church buildings' symbolic potential: 'Nor ought we to think that that little church, when it is standing locked and silent in the Bush, is useless, for it speaks its message to every passer-by.'[15]

Figure 7.1: 'Laying of the corner post' of the Willandra Anglican Church, 1905.
Source: *Bush Brother*, July 1905.

---

14   John Parker and others to the Baptist Union of New South Wales, 11 August 1902, Spicers Creek School Administrative File, 5/17652.1, NRS 3829, SARNSW; *WT*, 23 February 1905, 4, 27 April 1905, 5, 13 September 1906, 4; *WT*, 13 August 1908, 4; *Bush Brother* 1, no. 3, April 1905, 80; *Bush Brother* 1, no. 4, July 1905, 116; *Bush Brother* 2, no. 1, October 1905, 14–16; *DD*, 10 October 1911, 2; *National Advocate*, 8 August 1903, 2.

15   *Bush Brother* 8, no. 1, October 1911, 30.

In their personal beliefs and practices, people are likely to have held a range of positions, with the sternly devout who considered that their faith defined them at one end of the spectrum—particularly in contrast to those of other faiths. A stern sabbatarianism held sway in some communities around the turn of the century. For example, in 1902, the Scottish Presbyterian storekeeper and member for Yass, William Affleck, had introduced into the New South Wales parliament a bill 'to provide for the Better Observance of the Sabbath', containing a schedule of activities proscribed on Sundays, including dancing, cricket, football and tennis.[16] At that time, 37 people from Spicers Creek and the Baptist minister signed a petition protesting the 'nuisance and detriment' of people playing football on a ground forming part of the public school, as they worshipped in the adjoining Union church on a Sunday afternoon. In his advice to the Department of Public Instruction, the local schools inspector noted: 'It is, I regret to say, the custom for football, cricket and tennis matches between the neighbouring localities to be played on Sundays.' Perhaps emboldened by Affleck's bill then before the parliament, the inspector recommended that someone be empowered to take the names of transgressors in the future.[17] In this period, puritanical Protestants associated lax observance of the Sabbath with the Catholic Church, so the Spicers Creek congregation's stance was probably based on both sectarian partisanship and moral judgement. Twenty years later, though, tennis was routinely played across the farmlands on most Sundays throughout the season.[18]

Even in earlier years, those who had offended the Spicers Creek churchgoers with their noisy games might have been more typical of people in those places. In their regular publication, the Bush Brothers, of course, championed their evangelising work, but occasionally they also were frustrated by some settler communities' fickleness or outright indifference. They observed in 1910:

---

16   *DD*, 20 September 1902, 3; Parliament of New South Wales, 'Mr William Affleck (1836–1923)', www.parliament.nsw.gov.au/members/formermembers/Pages/former-member-details.aspx?pk=702.

17   John Parker and others to the Baptist Union of New South Wales, 11 August 1902; Baptist Union of New South Wales to the minister for public instruction, 10 September 1902, and inspector to the chief inspector, 13 September 1902, Spicers Creek School Administrative File, 5/17652.1, NRS 3829, SARNSW.

18   O'Farrell, *The Catholic Church and Community*, 282; Muriel Rosekelly, '"Parkdale" (Wheeler Family)', in *A Compiled History of Coboco District*, ed. Pat Fisher, Robyn Healey and Sandra Burns (Narromine: Coboco CWA, 2002), 39; Minute Books of the Westella Tennis Club, 1932–42, Western Plains Cultural Centre, Dubbo.

> Congregations at times improve amazingly and then melt away again.
> We suffer from a great number of conflicting interests occasioned by
> the land boom and prosperity still rapidly advancing. 'I will perform
> this or that religious duty supposing no other sensation or attractive
> engagement intervenes', that is the thought in some minds.

Stricter church discipline was needed, one clergyman wrote, rather than accommodating 'her message to the indolence and prejudice of those who desire an easy religion'. Disappointed with the number of confirmation candidates in Gilgandra, one writer concluded that 'our work in the town this year [1910] has been a complete failure'. There was a gendered aspect to it as well, with girls and women more likely to engage with the life of the church: 'Many of the young men fail to make use of the opportunities of public worship.'[19] Between the extremes many people attended services and engaged socially with fellow parishioners, perhaps more often than with others, though there was a conspicuously relaxed ecumenism among the Protestant denominations. Some rural households had their children baptised at home, into the church of whichever Protestant clergyman happened to be passing:

> [The Grandfather] was a Church of England, and Grandma was a
> Methodist ... [Their sons] the twins—they were baptised by the
> Church of England minister. But ... whichever minister came along,
> when there was a new baby or anything, then he'd baptize them, and
> some were Methodist and some were Presbyterian.[20]

Many years after this Federation-era example, at Coboco Hall, Presbyterian and Anglican people were attending each other's monthly services.[21] At least at Coboco, one of the conflicts of the seventeenth-century civil wars had been happily resolved. Church services and associated events were a significant part of social, as much as spiritual life. Even if somewhat sentimentalised, the following description of a scene as people arrived for a monthly service at a remote church in 1911 conveys the occasion's social (and gendered) dimensions:

---

19 *Bush Brother* 6, no. 3, April 1910, 206–7; *Bush Brother* 7, no. 1, October 1910, 33, 34; *Bush Brother* 6, no. 4, July 1910, 286.

20 Jessie Woodley (née Stroud, b. 1907), interview with author, Dubbo, 24 June 1981.

21 Joan B. Eggleton (Chapple), '"The Mount": Chapple Family History 1921–1945', in *A Compiled History of Coboco District*, ed. Pat Fisher, Robyn Healey and Sandra Burns (Narromine: Coboco CWA, 2002), 88.

The men sit or squat around a fallen tree trunk and, lighting their pipes, discuss the chances of rain or the condition of Old So-and-So's crop. The ladies sit on the church doorstep conversing over matters equally interesting to them, while the children play leapfrog or chase a 'goanna' … [I]t may be the only opportunity they have on busy times of meeting their neighbours at all.[22]

When people from Coboco individually recorded their recollections of living in that district between the wars, one of the most consistent memories was of Protestant church services held at the local hall:

The Presbyterian Church … [was] held there regularly once a month all dressed up in our very best clothes, ladies and girls complete with hats and gloves. I can tell you we really looked forward to the day.[23]

So it was both a social and a formal occasion, no doubt consistent with a pervasive ethos of respectability, and also an opportunity simply to experience the joy 'dressing up'.

An overt sectarian divide between Protestant and Catholic people might have been modified in the farmlands by the absence of denominational schools. Even if public schools could themselves become a focus of sectarian tension, as children mixed with all of their peers, there could perhaps have been less chance of embedding a sense of elemental difference. Moreover, where the predominant occupation was farming, which relied mainly on a household's own labour, there was less potential for competition and antagonism over preference in employment, as was more likely to occur in a town or city. There *was* an abiding sense of difference between Protestants and Catholics, but it was negotiated in different ways. People interpreted the churches' pronouncements according to their own circumstances. To give one example: in 1909 the Bush Brothers' journal asserted a fundamental difference between the denominations by cautioning non-Catholic families who were sending their children to a Catholic convent that 'the religious teachings of Rome' infused not only religious instruction but also reading and history teaching. The writer warned of an easy 'passage into the Roman fold', as well as the prospect of mixed marriages for those children who did not also attend the Anglican Sunday School.[24] However, the fact that

---

22   *Bush Brother* 8, no. 1, October 1911, 30.
23   Cecil Mawbey, 'Roseneath', in *A Compiled History of Coboco District*, ed. Pat Fisher, Robyn Healey and Sandra Burns (Narromine: Coboco CWA, 2002), 66.
24   *Bush Brother* 5, no. 3, April 1909, 150.

the Anglican Church felt the need to make the assertion indicates that Protestant people *were* sending their children to a Catholic school, in a time of swollen sectarian rhetoric.

It is conceivable that, as the historian of the Catholic Church in Australia Patrick O'Farrell surmised, 'mixed marriages' spanning the sectarian divide might have contributed to 'mutual understanding and tolerance'.[25] As often, though, they seem to have provoked stress arising from negotiations and decisions about which allegiances mattered most. Though people were more likely to marry someone of their own denomination, 'mixed marriages' were reasonably common: more than one in five in Australia between 1891 and 1961, according to one estimate.[26] In 1924, 25-year-old Lucy Stroud, who had been raised as part of an Anglican–Methodist household near Mogriguy, married a Catholic farmer, George Fallon, from north of Gilgandra. They wed in the Catholic Church in Dubbo, but in the sacristy rather than before the altar. Her Anglican father refused to attend the service because, in his view, 'the Catholic church did not think his daughter good enough'.[27]

An abiding attachment to religious difference was evident in private spaces, such as in 1918 when a Globelands resident offered to accommodate a teacher, but requested that they be a Protestant as services were held at the house, and 'a girl of Roman Catholic persuasion would be at some disadvantage'. In the same vein, in 1933, a teacher at Timbrebongie declined to board at one house because 'they are staunch Roman Catholics which would make this place unsuitable so far as I am concerned'.[28] The difference could play out in public spaces as well. In Geurie, if a prominent Protestant died, Catholic mourners, in accordance with the strictures of their church on participation in non-Catholic services, would wait at a distance from the church while the funeral service was conducted, before joining the cortège and the burial ritual at the cemetery.[29] Also in that place in the 1940s, men would emerge from a Catholic Sunday mass to enter the local hotel through a specific door (it happened to be green) to drink and talk among themselves, whereas men coming from Protestant services entered

25   O'Farrell, *The Catholic Church and Community*, 205.
26   Siobhan McHugh, 'Not in Front of the Altar: Mixed Marriages and Sectarian Tensions between Catholics and Protestants in Pre-Multicultural Australia', *History Australia* 6, no. 2 (2009): 42.2.
27   Nancy Wye, 'Family History of Frederick Stroud and Elizabeth Lawry Stroud', unpublished typescript (Dubbo: [2008]), n.p.; McHugh, 'Not in Front of the Altar', 42.13.
28   Inspector to the chief inspector, 19 July 1918, Globelands School Administrative File, 5/16055.3, NRS 3829, SARNSW; A. W. M. to the inspector, 8 November 1933, Timbrebongie School Administrative File, 14/7876, NRS 3829, SARNSW.
29   Harold Woodley (b. 1931), interview with author, Dubbo, 19 June 2017.

by a brown door to share each other's company in a different taproom. One man who grew up in the village interpreted this practice as signifying a bond within the groups rather than antagonism between them: 'It wasn't done in a nasty way or anything. It was just that they had *their* group, and they had *their* group. They were just good mates.'[30]

In all, the district's experience of religion was marked by two main features: a pervasive Protestantism, evident in the elision of clear boundaries between church, state and local institutions; and an undercurrent of sectarian division, such that religious affiliation was one of a range of layered loci of identity that influenced the spaces people occupied (or avoided), the company they kept and (as canvassed in Chapter 5) who they voted for.

Playing games

Sport was embedded in the farmlands' social life and shaped the ways local communities formed. Australian historians have tended to focus on elite, or at least formally administered, sport, rather than local, largely inclusive participation and its consequences for community formation.[31] This section examines four types of sporting or recreational gatherings to argue that, though some sporting associations were tied to class interests, in most instances they built and affirmed communities of place.

Horseracing

Horseracing had been a popular form of recreation in the district since the late 1850s. Dubbo hosted an annual race meeting from 1857. Beyond the towns, races were held from the 1870s at places such as Maryvale and Murrumbidgerie, which had a race club in 1900 with events conducted in the station's paddocks near the village. Geurie had a jockey club from 1901. The most local and popular events were the carnivals and gymkhanas, which attracted a democratic mix of locals. Footraces and other contests were held along with horseracing, with working horses pressed into service for the day's distraction. Geurie hosted an annual carnival from 1908, which by

---

30   Don Graham (b. 1932), interview with author, Wellington, 7 September 2017.
31   Brian Stoddart, *Saturday Afternoon Fever: Sport in the Australian Culture* (North Ryde: Angus & Robertson, 1986); Brian Stoddart, *Sport, Culture and History: Region, Nation and Globe* (Oxford: Routledge, 2008); Daryl Adair and Wray Vamplew, *Sport in Australian History* (Melbourne: Oxford University Press, 1997).

1912 was attracting around 2,500 people.[32] Schoolteachers in the 1920s applied for leave on carnival days, because every household attended them. Edgar ('Tib') Braithwaite's recollections show these events to have been among the most fondly recalled of his earlier life. His family moved to the Wongarbon district in 1925 and later bought a small 120-acre farm there. In that liminal world between small-scale farming and wage labouring, he also worked for neighbouring farmers at harvesting, lamb marking and digging out rabbits, but horses were his passion. Racing and other horse events could be as democratic as any form of recreation at that time. Around half a century later he could recall horses and moments:

> I remember leading him & the mare we bred to Eumungerie behind the sulky, I put him in 2 races[:] he won both & I won the Flag Race with the mare[;] about 70 miles the distance. Another time I led them to Ballimore, he won 2 races, I won the Flag race with the mare then two girls from here ... got 1st and 2nd on them in the Hack event.[33]

These events stood in contrast with the tightly controlled clubs but were typical of the ways most people came together for sport. Organisers were more likely to be larger-scale, established farmers, and some prestige might have been attached to their roles, but participation was very broad.

In other contexts, horseracing was a way to assert class as the basis of one form of community, most particularly in the guise of the Macquarie Picnic Race Club (MPRC). 'Picnic' race clubs began to appear in pastoral districts in New South Wales in the 1850s. They were based strongly on the British elite's ethos of amateurism: earnest preparation was either avoided or concealed, participation with flair (but not flamboyance) was revered, and success valued for the honour it bestowed rather than material gain. Amateurism was also treated as a point of moral distinction between its adherents and those who, by preference or for want of the means to indulge in sport without material return, chose a professional path. In a picnic racing club, this ethos merged with the complementary image of equestrian

---

32 *Bell's Life in Sydney and Sporting Reviewer*, 19 September 1857, 2; *SMH*, 30 December 1876, 7; *WT*, 15 February 1900, 4; *DL*, 25 February 1905, 5; Hepburn, *The History of the Geurie Public School*, 128, 131; *DD*, 22 October 1912, 2; Teacher to the chief inspector, Westella School Administrative File, pre-1939, 5/18090.3, NRS 3829, SARNSW; Teacher to the inspector, 22 September 1926, Gollan School Administrative File, pre-1939, 5/16063.1, NRS 3829, SARNSW.
33 Edgar Arthur Braithwaite (b. 1901), untitled manuscript, [1990], in possession of Colleen Braithwaite, Dubbo; Biographical detail supplied by Colleen Braithwaite, personal communication (email), 10 December 2020.

sport as a gentlemanly and chivalrous pursuit. People with sufficient land and leisure to breed, train and race horses for pleasure were at the centre of these clubs. Prominent members donated trophies (cash prizes were prohibited), and the riders were usually the owners themselves, or family members. Bookmakers could attend race meetings by invitation, but kept discrete accounts with their clientele rather than handle 'ready money' at the track.[34]

It was unmistakably an elite cultural form, involving closed networks well suited to the production and exchange of social capital and its returns in the form of prestige, respect, standing and obligation. [35] An account of the Braidwood picnic races in 1853 noted that the club's constitution was 'intentionally select': 'At the races none but gentlemen riders are allowed, and all is conducted in that manner most becoming and most agreeable to gentlemen.'[36] Balls and other social functions, exclusively for members and invited guests, were as integral as horseracing, and codified in clubs' rules.

The group that eventually formed the MPRC conducted its first race meeting at Warren in 1876 and held its events on pastoral properties before moving to the Dubbo course in 1885. Events were henceforth held adjacent to the town, but the club's executive committee and its cultural centre remained down the river in its pastoral heartland. These graziers were at the centre of protests in 1878 against changes to land tenure laws, and the shearers' strikes of the 1890s. The first president, Frank Todhunter, owned a 15,000-acre station that was running 20,000 sheep when it was sold in 1896. Another early member, Frederick Body, owned the 150,000-acre Bundemar station and represented the Dubbo district on the Council of the Pastoralists Union of New South Wales.[37] Clearly, there was a firm basis for class feeling arising from the everyday experience of pastoral production.

34   Richard Holt, *Sport and the British: A Modern History* (Oxford: Clarendon Press, 1989), 116; Norman Baker, 'Whose Hegemony? The Origins of the Amateur Ethos in Nineteenth Century English Society', *Sport in History* 24, no. 1 (2004): 1–16; Gordon Inglis, *Sport and Pastime in Australia* (London: Methuen and Co., 1912), 68.

35   Pierre Bourdieu, 'The Forms of Capital', in *Education: Culture, Economy, and Society*, ed. A. H. Halsey, Hugh Lauder, Phillip Brown and Amy Stuart Wells (Oxford: Oxford University Press, 1997), 46–58; Alejandro Portes, 'Social Capital: Its Origins and Applications in Modern Sociology', *Annual Review of Sociology* 24 (1998): 1–24; Alejandro Portes, *Economic Sociology: A Systematic Inquiry* (Princeton: Princeton University Press, 2010), 27–47.

36   *SMH*, 9 April 1853, 2.

37   Dorothy Baird, 'Macquarie Picnic Race Club', typescript [undated], Dubbo and District Family History Society; *National Advocate*, 2 July 1896, 2; *Pastoralists Review*, 16 August 1909, 605, 15 December 1910, 1096.

Through the rules and practices determining its membership and wider social circle, the MPRC privileged class over place. Whereas institutions such as the Dubbo Show, and later the Country Party, tended to obscure differences among landowners (see Chapters 8 and 5), the MPRC emphasised it. The MPRC's rules served to protect its elite standing, firstly by maintaining its race meetings' amateur status. Only members' horses could compete, and rules governing horses' preparation, their past winnings and jockeys' credentials as amateurs ensured that the club's racing avoided the apprehension of sordid monetary gain.

Picnic race clubs also maintained their standing by controlling club membership. A correspondent deeply familiar with that culture, in commenting on one of Gwen Meredith's scripts for the radio serial *The Lawsons* in 1947, observed: 'A Picnic Race Club is definitely a private Club ... [W]e ... consider it the Country person's private race meeting, for country landed people and their town friends', and 'most Picnic Race members would resent the intrusion of many would-be members'.[38] The correspondent was from Yass, but the picnic race clubs operated as a network of like-minded communities, coordinating race meeting dates, conferring on rule changes, providing concessions to neighbouring clubs' entrants and inviting their office holders to functions. Other than the club's founders, prospective members of the MPRC had to be nominated by two members, and their name, address and occupation submitted to the committee with a week's notice before the matter was considered. The committee rejected a nomination if it received more than one unfavourable vote in five, which would have made a successful nomination almost impossible if a core of executive committee members (between 11 and 15 in number) determined to oppose it. The club's surviving minutes indicate that, though most nominations were accepted, it was no certainty, with some deferred to a future meeting (presumably while the committee sought further information, or negotiations proceeded) and others rejected.[39]

Though the club's rules were very clear about the process for admitting new members, the criteria were tacit, resting on the committee's collective judgement of what constituted the right qualities in a prospective member. Women were not explicitly excluded, but the power of custom and hegemony

38 Kathleen Merriman to Gwen Meredith, 18 June 1947, Gwen Meredith Papers, box 9, MS 6789, NLA.
39 Rules 7–9 (1925 edition), notices of meetings and nominations, 26 April 1947, 1 May 1947, 6 May 1948, 27 April 1948, Minute Books, Rule Books and Miscellaneous Correspondence of the Macquarie Picnic Race Club, Dubbo and District Family History Society.

was such that women participated only as members' wives, daughters or invited guests. Many members were from the Warren-Trangie-Narromine-Dubbo region, but there were no strictures about location, and people joined from as far away as Mudgee, Bathurst, Bungendore, Gulargambone and Cumnock. Non-members' invitations to attend club functions were controlled as rigorously. All members' invited guests to specific functions had to be approved by the executive committee, and men from the district were explicitly excluded, even as guests, except with the agreement of the president and honorary secretary.[40]

Class implicitly defined this self-consciously bounded community, as reflected by the occupations of its members and invited guests. Guests in the mid-1920s included bank managers, representatives of Sydney wool broking firms, Protestant clergy, presidents of other amateur race clubs, the state governor, the premier and local members of parliament, as well as Sydney and local newspapers. A sample of records dating from the club's revival in 1947, after a 10-year hiatus, reveals that about three in four new members were 'graziers' or (less often) 'farmers and graziers', about one in five were town-based professionals (doctors, solicitors and bank managers mainly), and the balance were senior people in rural service industries, such as stock and station agents. The few whose nominations were rejected included the only nominee described simply as a 'farmer', and two retail managers from Dubbo.[41] 'Calling', it seems, was as important as character. This association was based only loosely on place, but exactingly on an idea of class that encompassed graziers (or those who chose to style themselves as such), the professionals they engaged with and regarded as social equals, and the conservative political and civic elite.

The MPRC might have regarded itself as existing for 'country landed people' (as Meredith's correspondent would have it), but its membership beyond the towns was much more confined. 'Landed' clearly signified something narrower than 'people owning land'. Membership stood at 220 in 1928 when there were around 1,200 rural holdings in the counties of Ewenmar and Narromine, where the majority of members lived.[42] And though

40   Membership rolls, 1913–15, 1921–37, 1947, and rules 41, 42 (1925 edition), Minute Books, Rule Books and Miscellaneous Correspondence of the Macquarie Picnic Race Club, Dubbo and District Family History Society.
41   From a sample of 81 successful nominations. See notices of meetings and nominations, 26 April 1947, 7 April 1948, 27 April 1948, 6 May 1948, Minute Books, Rule Books and Miscellaneous Correspondence of the Macquarie Picnic Race Club, Dubbo and District Family History Society.
42   New South Wales, *Statistical Register for 1920–21* (Sydney: Government Printer, 1921), 722.

the club undoubtedly included many people of means, membership was not necessarily based on actual wealth. Many retailers, as well as farmers engaged substantially in agriculture, are likely to have been as well-off, but were either excluded or, probably more often, neither aspired nor applied to become a part of that world.

Thus, through its rigorous regulation of admission, the MPRC shored up social capital among the pastoralist class. Though its relative economic power waned—as pastoral properties were broken up and the class arising from free selection and closer settlement gained economic and political strength—the MPRC survived as a persistent cultural practice. The continuing insistence on the club's rules of admission might have been a product of frailty, the material and symbolic returns derived from membership of the group being held more tightly as vestigial reminders of a once more prosperous and prestigious class. The club also defined some aspects of what the majority of farming people were not. They were not old money, nor the local elite. Their associations were based more firmly on place and on continuing face-to-face interaction.

Cricket and tennis

Like the gymkhanas and carnivals, cricket from the 1880s, and later tennis, were common and largely inclusive sports in the farmlands. Until the early twentieth century, there were no structured cricket competitions outside Dubbo and Wellington. Instead, teams bilaterally organised games with others from nearby communities. Cricket had the advantage that it could be played on any reasonably flat ground, very often on a private property, without a large outlay on equipment. It was almost entirely a male pursuit in these districts and had the attraction over football that people from a greater range of ages, spanning at least two generations, could participate. It could be sustained by small communities with a limited pool of players to call on.

Some historians have argued that the game in Australia was an explicit assertion of English heritage; however, beyond it being a part of settler society's cultural cargo, it is difficult to read people's participation at this level as such. Nor was it conspicuously a statement of Australian nationalism, as others have asserted. If it was an instrument of power and status, then that is also not borne out strongly by the evidence, except that the game compounded a highly gendered social structure. Class was neither a barrier nor an aid to participating at this level. In 1899, a Murrumbidgerie correspondent looked forward to the shearing season starting in the district, because returning shearers would bolster the local cricket team.[43]

Aboriginal men were not necessarily excluded from cricket teams, but settler Australians took race to be a ubiquitous marker of difference, so Indigenous players' participation was always on terms determined by whites. At Wellington, a team of Aboriginal men from Gobolion station beat the town team twice in 1883. Later, Aboriginal men played in local teams, though it probably counted that they were particularly talented. An Aboriginal man by the name of Mogil was an outstanding bowler for Wellington before he moved to Orange in 1905 to work as a police tracker. Another Aboriginal man named Baker top-scored, also for Wellington, against Stuart Town in 1906. The Governor brothers played at Breelong before 1900, though local white people assumed the prerogative to decide whether they could or not: 'as the Governors were fairly good cricketers they were allowed to play with the local Breelong team'. Nevertheless, some people objected, leading to speculation that this had precipitated the later tragic events (see Chapter 8) showing that, even at this level, sport was rigidly defining communities based on embedded cultural norms.[44]

Cricket in the farmlands was as much a social event as a contest of prowess. Consistently low scores indicate either that conditions for batting were poor or that players were generally unskilled—and probably both. Extended families fielded teams. Competition with surrounding communities was complemented by novelty matches. In 1899, when the Coalbaggie team did not arrive at Belarbigal for a match, the local married men played the single men, and won: 'The young fellows consoled themselves with a dance at the hall that night.' In general, women were involved only as spectators and in preparing refreshments. A match between a team of local women and the men's eleven at Dickygundi in 1904 was pointedly the exception. The men were obliged to wear either a skirt or a chaff bag and to bat and bowl with the non-favoured hand. The match was followed by a ball in the evening.[45]

---

43   Richard Cashman, 'Australia', in *The Imperial Game: Cricket, Culture and Society*, ed. Brian Stoddart and Keith A. P. Sandiford (Manchester: Manchester University Press, 1998), 34; Adair and Vamplew, *Sport in Australian History*, x; W. F. Mandle, *Going It Alone: Australia's National Identity in the Twentieth Century* (Ringwood: Allen Lane The Penguin Press, 1978), 24–46; *WT*, 7 September 1899, 4.

44   *ATCJ*, 17 February 1883, 36, 24 February 1883, 39; *WT*, 24 November 1902, 3, 25 January 1905, 4, 29 October 1906, 2; *DD*, 8 November 1912, 8.

45   *DD*, 23 February 1999, 4, 3 May 1899, 4, 2 March 1904, 3; *DL*, 29 October 1915, 2.

Was this a performance of entrenched paternalism or of inclusiveness? Either way, cricket was often taken lightly, as an excuse to share (mainly male) company rather than principally to compete.

One of the game's social functions was to reinforce the character of place, and a sense of belonging. Whereas schools and post offices prompted people to create names and boundaries, sporting teams later gave them an excuse to gather, often preceding a dance. Newspapers' local community columns regularly reported on the fortunes of 'our team'. One locality, still struggling to be recognised as an entity in its own right, listed having a cricket team as one of the usual markers of a bona fide community:

> It is a nice quiet little wool-growing district, intermingled with some farming. Of course we haven't got any cricket clubs, race meetings, progress committees, or anything of that kind here yet.[46]

By the first decade of the twentieth century, tennis was emerging as an equally popular pastime. It was a more costly game to stage, requiring ground to be prepared and maintained, netting fences erected, and nets and rackets procured. Cricket could bend around a resistant landscape, but tennis had to transform the terrain fundamentally: it was a more emphatic statement of settlement and possession of a place. Before communities could muster sufficient social and financial capital to create a public space for the game, it appeared first on the properties of better-off households. A tennis club formed in Murrumbidgerie in 1901, and at Geurie in 1908. Rawsonville and Brocklehurst were hosting matches by 1912, and by 1924 there were clubs at Windora, Westella and Ponto. As with cricket, there were no formal competitions, but rather clubs organised a season of matches with surrounding teams, with each tallying their score of wins and losses at season's end. Intra-club tournaments rounded out the season.[47]

---

46 *DL*, 21 March 1896, 3; Stoddart, *Saturday Afternoon Fever*, 42, 45.

47 Frank and Esma McIntyre, 'Yarrangrove', in *A Compiled History of Coboco District*, ed. Pat Fisher, Robyn Healey and Sandra Burns (Narromine: Coboco CWA, 2002), 94–5; Hepburn, *The History of the Geurie Public School*, 140; *DD*, 1 August 1900, 2; *DL*, 5 July 1912, 2; *WT*, 20 March 1924, 3; Minute Books of the Westella Tennis Club, 1932–42, Western Plains Cultural Centre, Dubbo.

Figure 7.2: Gathering at the Westella tennis courts, 1926.
Source: Woodley family collection.

Tennis had the advantage that women participated as readily as men, in playing as well as organising, though executive positions in club committees were still predominantly filled by men, and catering provided exclusively by women.[48] Perhaps even more so than cricket, tennis was first a social project, opening opportunities for mingling and courtship, complementing the local dances that tennis club committees also regularly organised. Though cricket and tennis emerged from England as middle-class pursuits, as practised in the farmlands they discarded some of those associations to become part of a relatively inclusive, and highly social, assertion of place (see Figure 7.2).

Women coming together: The Country Women's Association

By the end of the 1920s, no form of association was more common across the farmlands than the CWA. Within a few years of the organisation's foundation in 1922, it was drawing women together simultaneously to engage with its statewide program of fundraising to improve the lives of rural women and infants and to carve out new roles in hundreds of local

---

48   *DD*, 1 August 1900, 2; *WT*, 18 January 1906, 2; Minute Books of the Westella Tennis Club, 1932–42, Western Plains Cultural Centre, Dubbo.

communities. These were not the only women trying to improve the lives of country dwellers at that time. Only months later, Selina Siggins, who (as Selina Anderson) had campaigned so vigorously for Labor's Thomas Thrower in 1907, represented Wellington as the first woman to attend as a delegate the Farmers and Settlers Association's annual conference. In December she contested the federal seat of Calare at the general election, but whereas in her earlier life she had advocated for workers' rights, as an endorsed Country Party candidate her platform was remarkably similar to the new CWA's: pre-maternity education for country women, and care and education for country children. Country voters were unreceptive to a female candidate, though, and she finished with just 421 of more than 26,000 votes cast.[49] In contrast, rural society seemed to completely accept the idea of an association of women, advocating for rural amenity from a position ostensibly outside of politics, and it took root rapidly.

The association formed at a conference coinciding with the 1922 Royal Agricultural Show in Sydney, after several years of agitation in the Graziers Association's *Stock and Station Journal* to improve amenity for women in rural areas.[50] It was both a departure—a new way for women to effect change, *as women*—and an affirmation of the roles assigned to women as part of the colonising project; that is, as 'homemakers' and mothers, to help soften the landscape such that farming families could flourish. As one woman observed at the association's foundation, 'women want to impress upon the boys and girls the dignity of and independence of agriculture under proper conditions'.[51] Fundraising was to help alleviate the disproportionate rigours of country living in the form of holiday homes on the coast, women's restrooms and baby health centres in country towns, and maternity wards in rural hospitals.

A central executive presided over 24 regional groups, and within five years some 148 branches were scattered across the state.[52] The first president, Grace Munro, was an independently wealthy woman from a

---

49   *Land*, 25 August, 1922, 12; *Sydney Stock and Station Journal*, 8 December 1922, 10; *SMH*, 27 December 1922, 7.
50   Elizabeth Kenworthy Teather, 'Remote Rural Women's Ideologies, Spaces and Networks: Country Women's Association of New South Wales, 1922–1992', *Australian and New Zealand Journal of Sociology* 28, no. 3 (1992): 387; Helen Townsend, *Serving the Country: The History of the Country Women's Association of New South Wales* (Sydney: Doubleday, 1988), 4–8.
51   *Sydney Mail*, 26 April 1922, 45.
52   Country Women's Association of New South Wales, *The Silver Years: The Story of the Country Women's Association of New South Wales, 1922–1947* (Sydney: F. H. Johnston for the Association, [1947]), xiii; Teather, 'Remote Rural Women's Ideologies', 369.

New England grazing family. Consistent with her background, she had a strongly conservative political outlook, having helped to run the camp to accommodate strikebreakers travelling from the country during the general strike in 1917 (see Chapter 4). Jessie Sawyer, a founding vice-president, and president between 1928 and 1938, was part of a Cootamundra grazing family and, like Munro and her successor Ada Beveridge, received imperial honours. Women with these kinds of backgrounds dominated the early executive and shaped the organisation's rhetoric but, in contrast to the GA and FSA, the hierarchy did not necessarily have a strong influence on women's experience at the branch level. As compared with the Victorian Farmers' Union Women's Section, formed a few years earlier, the CWA was less explicitly a political organisation, and, to the extent that branches became involved in advocacy, it was generally for local causes.[53]

Through the CWA, women could align with a number of nested communities of common interest. First, it was a community of *women* exerting influence on public life, consisting mainly of rural branches, but also an active metropolitan group. The founding conference's organiser, Florence Gordon, had closed the first day's proceedings with the comment that:

> If this conference binds town and country women together by even the slenderest chains, we will have accomplished much. This will mean better understanding and comradeship which will link into a whole the lives of women workers of Australia for their ultimate good.[54]

Women contributed to statewide projects and gathered at annual conferences to debate and decide on common principles and actions. From its inception, the organisation was *only* for women, albeit reinforcing a very particular and conservative vision of women in action.[55] At hundreds of branch meetings

---

53   Jillian Oppenheimer, 'Munro, Grace Emily (1879–1964)', *Australian Dictionary of Biography*, National Centre of Biography, The Australian National University, published first in hardcopy 1986, adb.anu.edu.au/biography/munro-grace-emily-7686/text13451; Townsend, *Serving the Country*, 7; Julie Gorrell, 'Sawyer, Jessie Frederica Pauline (1870–1947)', *Australian Dictionary of Biography*, National Centre of Biography, The Australian National University, published first in hardcopy 2002, adb.anu.edu.au/biography/sawyer-jessie-frederica-pauline-11619/text20749; Country Women's Association of New South Wales, *The Silver Years*, 14, 16, 17; Heather Gunn, '"For the Man on the Land": Issues of Gender and Identity in the Foundation of the Victorian Farmers' Union Women's Section, 1918–1922', *Journal of Australian Studies* 18, no. 42 (1994): 32–42.

54   Quoted in Townsend, *Serving the Country*, 9.

55   Elizabeth Kenworthy Teather, 'The First Rural Women's Network in New South Wales: Seventy Years of the Country Women's Association', *Australian Geographer* 23, no. 2 (1992): 164, 167.

each month—from Mosman to Terramungamine to Bourke—devotion and loyalty to God, the monarchy and the nation were routinely reprised as members sang the national anthem and recited the CWA motto: 'Honour to God / Loyalty to the Throne / Service to the Country / Through Country Women / For Country Women / By Country Women'. So, while it was unambiguously a community of women, it more often affirmed than challenged the social and gendered order.

Notwithstanding that many city women supported the CWA, its early country members were quick to assert that it was essentially their organisation— a community of *country women* sharing a common experience of life beyond the metropole. Some early commentary emphasised both the value for local women of connecting with an overarching organisation and also that this was very much a rural-focused project:

> This is the day of combines and associations. Dingo Flat cannot establish its own Dingo Flat Farmers' Wives' Association, and do any good with it, because there are not enough of them; but, as a part of the Farmers' Wives' Association of NSW, or of Australia, or some other organisation of the kind, the greater will carry the smaller along on the principle of mutual help.[56]

Dubbo was well represented at the foundational Sydney conference. Victorian-born Ida Matchett of 'Wychitella' station on the Obley Road was a member of the association's first executive committee, but it was Kennedy Fletcher who formed a town branch six weeks later, in June 1922. The widowed 61-year-old was part of the landed Baird family. Her brother was William Webb Baird, a regular member of the Dubbo Show Association and founding councillor on the Talbragar Shire. She was Dubbo's nearest equivalent in social and economic standing to the group that had initiated the conference and the organisation.[57] Surrounding villages and localities were slower to act, but in the six years from 1925, at least six branches formed, at Eumungerie, Terramungamine, Geurie, Wongarbon, Coboco and Windora-Comobella.[58] The CWA branches emerged some years after

---

56 *Sydney Mail*, 26 April 1922, 45; Liz Harfull, *The Women Who Changed Country Australia: Celebrating 100 Years of the Country Women's Association of New South Wales* (Sydney: Murdoch Books, [2022]), 45–50.
57   *DL*, 9 June 1922, 17 September 1929, 3; Pat Dargin, *'It's Only an Old House': Dundullimal Homestead, Dubbo, New South Wales* (Dubbo: Development and Advisory Publications, 2011), 268; Harfull, *The Women Who Changed Country Australia*, 43, 82.
58   *DL*, 28 August 1925, 7, 28 May 1926, 2, 6 September 1927, 4; *WT*, 3 September 1931, 3; Geurie Country Women's Association, undated manuscript, Minute Books of the Geurie Branch of the CWA, 1932–47, Western Plains Cultural Centre, Dubbo; Minutes, 3 September 1927, Wongarbon CWA, in possession of the branch.

the peak period of FSA branch formation, and at a time when organisations advocating specifically for rural landholders' interests were an established part of political discourse. Women could travel more readily at this time too, with many farming households having acquired a car by the mid-1920s (see Chapter 6). Further, as birth rates declined, domestic responsibilities, though substantial and vital to most households' functioning, were also reducing.

On a third level, the CWA represented an even more particular vision of who 'country women' were. Consistent with that version of the national rural myth Hirst distilled and labelled the 'pioneer legend', she was the yeoman's partner and helpmeet. The initiating conference in 1922 had as its official aim: 'Improving the conditions of the woman *on the land*.'[59] While no one was formally excluded, this was an organisation implicitly designed for farming people. A speaker at the formative conference encapsulated these consistent themes:

> 'I don't think you city women have the slightest idea of what a drought means', said one delegate. 'You simply cannot understand what the women of the country have to face when the land dries up …'

> 'And yet', she persisted, 'I believe most of them would endure the hardships and toil rather than live in the cities'.[60]

At the CWA's core were the ideas that farming life was innately virtuous, that rural people's problems were unique and that they were poorly understood by town dwellers. Within that set of tropes was a role for women as essential guardians of that purer and nobler way of life. Through the organisation, women found new ways to advance the agrarian project. The speaker in 1922 went on: 'We would choose a life on the land for our sons, because we know it is a pure and manly life for them to live.' It was an assertively rural vision defined by place and class, and by very specific ideas about women's roles.

---

59   J. B. Hirst, 'The Pioneer Legend', *Historical Studies* 18, no. 71 (1978): 316–37; Flyer distributed at the Royal Agricultural Show, reproduced in Country Women's Association of New South Wales, *The Silver Years*, x (emphasis added).
60   *Sydney Mail*, 26 April 1922, 8.

Generally, the CWA's implicit emphasis on engaging with and benefiting farming women was reflected in branches' membership. In localities beyond the villages, such as at Terramungamine, Coboco and Windora-Comobella, membership was likely to have consisted entirely of women from farming households, reflecting the homogeneity of those places, and to have included someone from most households. Attendees at the Terramungamine branch's first meeting in 1926 agreed to write to another four women, inviting them to join, though there is no way of knowing if other local residents were overlooked.[61] Branches in the villages were drawn from a more diverse range of households, but farming women were still prominent. Of those members of Wongarbon's branch in its first year (1927) who can be identified, about half (10 of 22) were from farming households, the remainder being wives of labourers, store workers, a baker, a police officer and men employed by the railway (none of the women were in paid work themselves). Ten years later, almost 70 per cent of the identifiable members were associated with farming, and the rest were from the village, including just one from a labouring household. By 1947, four in five members able to be identified were from farming households.[62] This could have been influenced by economic and demographic change—the declining demand for rural labour and stagnation of the smaller villages—but it might also reflect a gradual sorting of people's priorities and perceptions of the organisation's, and each branch's, function and identity. Was it becoming even more clearly and narrowly defined as a forum where 'farming' women shared experiences and understanding of their particular way of life?

Finally, even as it expressed and reinforced rural women's connection across the state, the CWA strengthened members' attachment to a very local place. It brought women together for companionship and support. A 40-year member of the Coboco branch described it as 'our social meeting place to meet and see other ladies of the district'. Branches quickly established a local presence. From their inception, they asserted their own priorities, seeking a material stake in their locales by building meeting rooms and

---

61   Minutes, 23 April 1926, Terramungamine Branch of the CWA, 1926–45, Western Plains Cultural Centre, Dubbo.

62   Derived from membership summaries of the Wongarbon CWA branch, in possession of the branch; Commonwealth of Australia, *Commonwealth Electoral Rolls, New South Wales*; Registers of Admission to Wongarbon Public School, 1915–50 (copy), in possession of Colleen Braithwaite, Dubbo.

influencing local concerns. Dubbo district branches lent their weight to improving road, rail, school and telephone services.[63] A branch's support for a cause had meaning and heft.

In their distribution of funds, branches preferred local and independent action. Women used skills that were essential and empowering in a domestic environment to express their citizenship publicly. Cooking and needlework were always a part of the local CWA experience but did not represent the whole of women's activities. Branches organised the standard fundraising events—dances, balls, euchre parties and tennis tournaments. They booked venues and music, and assigned tasks to both women and men. Branches honoured their commitments to the broader organisation by supporting statewide projects, but regularly donated to local causes as well. Both the Coboco and Terramungamine branches raised money to acquire pianos for the respective halls, Wongarbon contributed to the cost of a gate for the village's cemetery and Windora-Comobella funded an end-of-year prize for children at the local school.[64] But branches particularly favoured local women's welfare. Between 1930 and 1938, the Wongarbon branch's annual expenses included contributions to women or families dealing with illness or house fires, as well as to 'necessitous cases'. The Windora-Comobella branch called a special meeting in 1943 solely to discuss ways to help a 'member in distress'. The beneficiaries' names did not appear in the record, out of respect for their dignity. Branch meetings were also forums to express sympathy and respect for a bereaved member, or to celebrate a member's engagement to be married.[65] Once the opening rituals of motto and anthem were dispensed with, each branch iteratively reinterpreted the organisation's purpose at each meeting.

63   Joan McFetridge, 'Eastern Hill', in *A Compiled History of Coboco District*, ed. Pat Fisher, Robyn Healey and Sandra Burns (Narromine: Coboco CWA, 2002), 42; Minutes, 3 March 1934, Wongarbon CWA, in possession of the branch; Minutes, 6 March 1936, and 'Terramungamine CWA History, 70th Birthday 1st May 1996', typescript [1996], Minute Books of the Terramungamine Branch of the CWA, 1926–45, Western Plains Cultural Centre, Dubbo; General secretary of the CWA to the Hon. D. M. Drummond MLA, 18 September 1935, Boothenba School Administrative File, 5/15029.4, NRS 3829, SARNSW.

64   Coboco CWA, extracts from CWA records, in *A Compiled History of Coboco District*, ed. Pat Fisher, Robyn Healey and Sandra Burns (Narromine: Coboco CWA, 2002),124; Minutes, 13 April 1927, Terramungamine Branch of the CWA, 1926–45, Western Plains Cultural Centre, Dubbo; Statement of receipt and payments, 1934, Wongarbon CWA, in possession of the branch; Minutes, 3 September 1943, Windora-Comobella Branch of the CWA, 1942–50, Western Plains Cultural Centre, Dubbo.

65   Statements of receipt and payments, 1934–8, minutes, 17 November 1927, 3 May 1930, 1 November 1930, 2 June 1934, Wongarbon CWA, in possession of the branch; Minutes, 27 March 1942, 14 April 1943, 17 October 1944, Windora-Comobella Branch of the CWA, 1942–50, Western Plains Cultural Centre, Dubbo.

This attachment to an immediate community was also expressed by asserting a claim on local space. Meetings were generally held in schools, halls or private homes; however, at its second meeting, the Wongarbon branch discussed joining with the local FSA branch to purchase a block of land in the village on which to build a meeting room, with conspicuous self-assurance for such a nascent organisation.[66] These were not the tentative, exploratory steps of a group unsure of its purpose, but, rather, a core of women well known to each other and assured of their standing and capacity to exert influence.

In the Dubbo farmlands, then, the CWA presented women with several overlapping communities with which to align. It gave women an imprimatur to come together regularly, in new combinations, but based on an established ideology that valorised a conservative, gendered, farming life. They could use the qualities that gave their private lives value and empowerment in a public and collective setting without challenging the established, gendered conventions of rural society. And for most members, the CWA was overwhelmingly a local experience, with women using the organisation's structures and standing to exercise agency among their own people—to affirm and strengthen the idea of a farming class in place.

Embedding communities of place: The case of the Westella Hall Committee

Many of the statewide, national or transnational organisations discussed so far provided ready structures and networks to support people as they came together. On other occasions, though, the process was more local and organic, even if people generally adopted established cultural practices. This section examines one such case: the process by which a group of farming households built and maintained a hall. Halls were a part of the process of defining a community of place, grounded as much in human relationships as in memory or experience of a physical space.[67]

---

66   Minutes, 22 September 1927, Wongarbon CWA, in possession of the branch.
67   D. W. Meinig, 'Introduction', in *The Interpretation of Ordinary Landscapes: Geographical Essays*, ed. D. W. Meinig (Oxford: Oxford University Press, 1979), 3.

Halls were a common cultural form, the template for building and managing them in rural districts being well established by the 1930s. The buildings were usually of corrugated iron over a cypress pine frame, the main space being a dance floor surrounded by fixed bench seating along the side walls, with a stage opposite the main entrance. Many included a supper room and kitchen.[68] In the villages of Geurie and Wongarbon, halls were sometimes in private hands, essentially a small business, or owned by the local MUIOOF branch. Beyond the villages, they were a cooperative venture. Other than that brief period of church-related hall-building in places relatively close to Dubbo in the late nineteenth century, the interwar years were the peak period of hall construction in the farmlands. What prompted people to build halls in this period? The example of Westella suggests that halls marked not the genesis of a community, but rather were the product of more mature and relatively stable localities, and involved the careful marshalling of accumulated social capital.[69]

On a Friday in June 1934, about six men met in the farming district of Westella and decided to build a public hall. They would have gathered in the provisional school or someone's house—there were no other choices—and, from that first meeting onwards, they recorded minutes in a school exercise book; they appointed a chair and secretary, identified people (all men) to form a committee and resolved to canvass the district for donations.[70]

Farms were being established at the place that later became known as Westella by the early twentieth century as land was set aside under conditional purchase and conditional leasehold arrangements, carved from the Murrumbidgerie pastoral station. A small half-time school was opened in 1906 for children from three households, but the settlement was not then dense enough to support it beyond 1908. That changed once the state government acquired an area of 5,020 acres (2,032 hectares) known as the Glenara Estate Purchase Area, and in 1913 sold it as 12 blocks ranging from 340 to 461 acres (138–187 hectares) under the *Closer Settlement Promotion*

---

68   Westella Public Hall File, 17/3394-2326, Ballimore Public Hall File, 17/3340-1489, Rawsonville Memorial Hall File, 17/3574-4355, NRS 15318, SARNSW.
69   C. J. Calhoun, 'Community: Toward a Variable Conceptualisation for Comparative Research', *Social History* 5, no. 1 (1980): 116.
70   Minutes, 1 June 1934, Westella Hall Committee, 1934–79, Western Plains Cultural Centre, Dubbo. Unless otherwise specified, evidence for the following text comes from these minute books.

Act of 1910. It was part of the latest scheme to put smallholders on the land that resulted in 3,134 farms being created covering over 300,000 acres between 1911 and 1914.[71]

For the next 20 years, the district was in a state of constant flux as dozens of people, each with their own trajectories—their 'stories-so-far'—sought to negotiate their way in that disrupted landscape. The newcomers included people with experience of local conditions, and others entirely unfamiliar with the place. Most were aged between 20 and 35 and came with some experience as sharefarmers or farm labourers. If there was a common thread binding them as a group, other than their desire to make an independent living on the land, it was that they all started there in debt, encumbered by their repayments to the government under the terms of their conditional purchases.[72]

Two of the Glenara Estate purchasers arrived as individuals, and the remainder as extended families sharing labour and plant across their adjoining blocks. The Condon family, consisting of a couple in their late fifties and four of their adult children, two with spouses, arrived from Omeo in Victoria's Gippsland region via Wagga Wagga in the Riverina to take up five blocks between them. Three blocks were purchased by the Mawbey brothers, who had been working locally; and two generations of the Callaghan family—parents and an adult son—arrived from southern New South Wales to claim the remaining two blocks. Roads were surveyed, houses and sheds built, and land cleared, fenced and cultivated. In the first season on the new blocks, one settler, David Renshaw, harvested an encouraging two tons of hay and seven bags of wheat per acre.[73] The burdens of debt were immediately apparent when the Department of Lands unconditionally postponed annual repayments for 6 of the 12 occupants for 1913. Some people moved on, but others took their place, children were born, and, in less than four

71   School's papers held on the file of the school with which it shared half-time status: Ballimore School Administrative File, 1884–1920, 5/14763.2, NRS 3829, SARNSW; *NSW Government Gazette*, no. 2, 8 January 1913, 128; New South Wales, *Thirty-Seventh Report of the Department of Lands, 1916*, in *Joint Volumes of Papers Presented to the Legislative Council and Legislative Assembly*, vol. I (Sydney: Government Printer, 1917), 7–8.
72   Doreen Massey, *For Space* (London: Sage Publications, 2005), 285. Sources for the following include NRS 8058, SARNSW; NRS 13655, SARNSW; NRS 13188, SARNSW; Ridgeview Estate, 10/13294, NRS 8052, SARNSW; Westella School Administrative File, pre-1939, 5/18090.3, NRS 3829, SARNSW; Harold Woodley (b. 1931), recording of an interview, Dubbo, 16 April 2020.
73   *WT*, 4 December 1913, 5.

years, there were 54 people living on the 12 farms. They had prepared three-quarters of the area for cultivation and made an average of £483 worth of improvements on each property.[74]

A self-defined community was forming there. Established and newly arrived people formed a Glenara branch of the FSA, meeting in members' homes from 1914. Residents must also have had some sense of themselves as a distinct community when they gathered to farewell two local men who had enlisted in the AIF and held dances in sheds on private properties. The district had its own regular column in the Dubbo and Wellington papers from 1915. With the influx of population to the closer settlement blocks, a provisional school opened on donated land in 1921, after some years of persistent lobbying from local people, as well as FSA branches and the local MLA.[75] As there was already a 'Glenara' school in the state, Westella became the name of the new school and the locale.

Further disruption ensued when another wave of settlers arrived that year. The Department of Lands purchased a property of 2,847 acres (1,152 hectares), referred to as the Ridgeview Estate and adjoining the Glenara blocks, for subdivision and sale of another five blocks. The slightly larger blocks of 520 to 629 acres (210–255 hectares) were still considered 'insufficient for home maintenance' when the district surveyor inspected them in 1929. The purchasers were all returned servicemen, but otherwise, again, were an eclectic mix, each with some experience of farm work. There was a fourth Mawbey brother, and three English-born brothers (one with a wife and child) who had sharefarmed around Wellington and occupied two blocks. Another English-born man with his wife and child, who had been sharefarming locally since his discharge from the army, took up a block, as did a local single man.[76]

74   Under secretary of lands to the chairman, Dubbo Local Land Board, 14 May 1914, Soldier Settlement Loan file, 5684 (W. Pile), NRS 8058, SARNSW; New South Wales, *Thirty-Seventh Report of the Department of Lands, 1916*, 8.
75   *Land*, 16 January 1914, 7; *DL*, 22 May 1914, 4, 16 May 1916, 2, 9 June 1916, 4, 15 August 1919, 2, 19 August 1933, 4; *WT*, 18 April 1924, 3; Secretary, Wongarbon branch of the FSA to the minister for education, 10 March 1919, and 'Inspector's Report upon the Proposed Provisional School Site at Glenara', 8 August 1919, Westella School Administrative File, pre-1939, 5/18090.3, NRS 3829, SARNSW.
76   *NSW Government Gazette*, no. 164, 4 November 1921, 6352; District surveyor to the under secretary for lands, September 1929, Soldier Settlement Loan File, (G. H. Carter), NRS 8058, SARNSW; Ridgeview Estate, 10/13294, NRS 8052, SARNSW; Soldier Settlement Loan Files: 6475 (C. N. May), 7434 (C. Penfold), 5757 (G. L. Mawbey), 7117 (G. H. Carter), NRS 8058, SARNSW; File no. 26353 (G. H. Carter), NRS 13655, SARNSW.

Change did not consist only of these waves of new settlement. By the time the Ridgeview settlers were moving in, three of the original Glenara households had departed, one of them bankrupted. Others were becoming more settled and integrated. Three people who had arrived among the original settlers in 1913 had married local people by 1919. In the 1920s, many of the new settlers struggled through some poor seasons and falling wheat prices.[77] Two of the five Ridgeview blocks changed hands by 1930, including another bankrupted settler's farm, which was subdivided and acquired by several of his neighbours. These were not the last of the departures. Some of those who bought the vacated Glenara blocks themselves left within a few years. Most who remained could only continue with the further postponement or forgiveness of debt to the state government; by sharefarming to supplement the produce of their own meagre acres; and, in one case, by working for the shire council. Several were protected from potential bankruptcy in the mid-1930s by having their affairs managed by a town accountant under the *Farmers' Relief Act* (see Chapter 3).

Some historians have argued that such patterns of new and disrupted settlement prevented people in new settler societies from developing an abiding sense of place and, specifically, an attachment to the land. The American historian Donald Worster considered that in the Oklahoma farmlands of the 1930s, where settlers had farmed intensively for 20 years, 'there had not been enough time for those things to develop'. And Donald Meinig wrote of the generic nineteenth-century settler in South Australia's wheat country: 'He had no emotional ties this land, he could not have—there was no heritage to bind him to this new and strange kind of country.'[78] Whether or not these broad assertions were reflected in the Dubbo farmlands, a sense of place and belonging *can* arise from social experience. Notwithstanding the frequent disruptions to the local population, by 1934 there was a 20-year history of farming people gathering, organising and advocating at Westella. A tennis team was competing on local courts by 1922. Such was the intensity of settlement that a second (subsidised) school—Pilewood—was established barely 5 kilometres distant from the small public school in 1926. The committee's minutes do not indicate why they were motivated to build a hall there and then, but the context suggests that there were enough households with a commitment to the project to bear the costs. Thirty-seven people, most

---

77   G. Mawbey to the Department of Lands, 10 May 1928, Soldier Settlement Loan File, 5757 (G. L. Mawbey), NRS 8058, SARNSW.
78   Donald Worster, *Dust Bowl: The Southern Plains in the 1930s* (New York: Oxford University Press, 2004), 87, 164; D. W. Meinig, *On the Margins of the Good Earth: The South Australian Wheat Frontier, 1869–1884* (Adelaide: Rigby Limited, 1972), 21.

likely from every household within what was already a commonly recognised area, each contributed between 10s and £5 to the first appeal for funds, which secured £87, equivalent to more than half a year's pay at the minimum wage. A separate appeal for bags of wheat or oats to sell raised more funds.[79]

People continued to arrive in the area, and others to depart, but most (probably all) households were known to each other. With the public school and the tennis club well established, there was a history of cooperation and achievement, such that a degree of familiarity, trust and tacit mutual obligation had developed. There was a critical mass of social capital: through their collective decision-making, people were confident that their investment of time and resources would be reciprocated in contributions or less tangible exchanges such as respect and standing. More people were drawn into the project after that first meeting in June 1934. The committee engaged a Wongarbon carpenter, the father of locally employed labourers, to build a hall on donated land adjacent to the tennis courts that, by then, had been in use for about 12 years. It was completed in early 1935 (see Figure 7.3). A shire councillor—a position of some local standing—officially opened the hall in March at a ball and euchre evening that attracted 300 people from as far away as Dubbo, Eumungerie and Wellington.[80]

Figure 7.3: Westella Hall, with skillion extension of 1955.
Source: Photograph by Peter Woodley, 2021.

79   *WT*, 16 December 1915, 5, 20 July 1922, 5; *DL*, 16 May 1916, 2; Returns and Enrolments for Subsidised Schools, 1924–46, NRS 4014, SARNSW; Braithwaite, Giddings, Oates and Tucker, *The History of the Wongarbon,* 89–95; Minutes, 1 June 1934, Westella Hall Committee, 1934–79, Western Plains Cultural Centre, Dubbo.
80   Minutes, 16 August 1934, Westella Hall Committee, 1934–79, Western Plains Cultural Centre, Dubbo; *DL*, 30 March 1935, 7; Westella Public Hall File, 17/3394-2326, NRS 15318, SARNSW.

A harmonious process was not inevitable in those circumstances. For example, in 1915 a school inspector recommended that the Department of Education allow a request from Rawsonville residents to meet and socialise in a disused school building, so long as they seek permission on each occasion as 'there is ... no apparent unanimity among the people'.[81] So, social capital had to be corralled and nurtured in various ways. The risk of conflict was reduced by the formal, structured and widely understood rules guiding how people came together. The committee's meeting procedures were of a form common across all associations in such places: FSA and CWA branches, political parties, progress associations and sporting clubs. No group was so small, its purpose so local or prosaic, that it did not warrant formal meeting procedure in settler communities. It was universally understood that such bodies operated under a chairperson's direction; proposals were canvassed through motions (moved and seconded) and motions to amend; matters were resolved through a vote of the majority of participants; all decisions were recorded and affirmed, or suitably amended, at a subsequent meeting; and the organisation determined the rules defining its own membership. The practice had two potential functions. First, by maintaining certain shared standards and cultural forms, people were asserting that, no matter how small or inconsequential their endeavour, they were participants in a wider civil society. Second, though the meeting procedure had a more extensive history and currency, it was implicitly a British tradition of decision-making procedure modelled on the Westminster parliament.[82]

The procedure's most important function though, in the context of small communities that valued harmony and equilibrium, was to allow discussions and decision-making about a common project to proceed with less risk of conflict and fracture. Competing views were heard, and matters resolved and recorded, with least chance of infringing on a person's dignity. The most prosaic matters were dealt with in this way. The following exchange was typical:

> Moved Mrs S. M. sec[onded] Mrs P. that the door fee be Ladies 2/- & Gents 3/-.
>
> Amend[ed] by Mrs E. P. G. sec[onded] Mrs W. that the door fee be 3/- all round.

---

81   Inspector to the chief inspector, 3 June 1915, Rawsonville School Administrative File, pre-1939, 5/17444.4, NRS 3829, SARNSW.
82   Judith Brett, *Australian Liberals and the Moral Middle Class: From Alfred Deakin to John Howard* (Cambridge: Cambridge University Press, 2003), 64–9; Wilbert van Vree, *Meetings, Manners and Civilization: The Development of Modern Meeting Behaviour*, trans. Kathleen Bell (London: Leicester University Press, 1999), 207–15.

Further amend[ed] by Mrs L. W. sec[onded] E. P. G. that the door
fee be Ladies 3/- & Gents 4/-.

1st amend[ment] <u>carried</u>.[83]

Stability was also evident in the composition of the executive. The same
three officeholders were routinely reappointed each year until the president
left the district in 1942. As with local government, public contests over
appointments could have been divisive. The incumbents were well-known,
middle-aged men who had owned land in the district for between 15
and 30 years, willing to take on the roles and otherwise unremarkable.
The 41-year-old inaugural president, Norman Hobden, had acquired one
of the modest Glenara blocks after it was forfeited by its original purchaser
in 1918, and built sheds on local properties to supplement farming
income. Then 44-year-old Albert Mawbey, on his closer settlement farm,
was treasurer. The 47-year-old secretary, Harold Woodley, had lived in the
district all his life and owned a relatively substantial property adjoining
the Glenara and Ridgeview blocks, which he had acquired in 1904 with his
father Henry's assistance.[84]

Though a small group of men took the first formal steps and tellingly
formed a committee consisting only of men, women soon became involved.
Their initial absence from these meetings suggests that there was not a
ready history there of men and women participating on public committees.
But women's subsequent engagement indicates that there was something
particular about *this* committee's purpose, and perhaps its timing. By 1934,
the CWA was a well-established forum where women initiated and managed
public events. Three local women had been part of the group organising
the first CWA ball in nearby Wongarbon in May 1934.[85] Women might
also have become involved in the Westella group because the hall was
regarded, not as a new public facility, so much as an extension of private
space—where women's involvement was entrenched—into the public
sphere. Nearly 20 years earlier, a public gathering on a private property for
departing servicemen had been organised by a committee consisting wholly
of local women.[86] Certainly, the continuing business of running a hall and
its social functions would call on many of the roles traditionally assigned

83   Minutes, 6 March 1935, Westella Hall Committee, 1934–79, Western Plains Cultural Centre,
Dubbo. Individuals' surnames appear in full in the original.
84   Closer Settlement and Returned Soldiers Transfer Files 1907–51, file 19/07640 (CN Hobden),
NRS 8054, SARNSW; Harold Woodley (b. 1931), interview with author, Dubbo, 16 April 2020.
85   Minutes, 24 March 1934, Wongarbon CWA, in possession of the branch; *DL*, 15 May 1934, 4.
86   *DL*, 16 May 1916, 2.

to women. The community was too small and connected for a separate 'women's auxiliary' to make sense, so people's authority to contribute to decision-making about the hall could rest on residency rather than gender. Still, there was not a complete dissolution of deeply embedded gender roles, with local men holding the three executive positions until a woman became secretary in 1959.

The inclusive Westella process extended to the two schools' teachers, and at least two wage labourers who were working on local farms, but whose permanent home was in Wongarbon. One of the labourers contributed £2 10s to the first fundraising drive, and another £1 10s: the equivalent of about four days and two and a half days pay at the minimum wage, respectively. The district's small scale would have made a choice not to participate more difficult than otherwise. Anonymity was not an option, and every resident—permanent or not—seems to have been swept up in the process at one time or another. Also, the vast majority of residents, being small- to medium-size landholders, could embrace a few temporary or non-resident members without feeling they were ceding control.

Having committed to creating and maintaining a communal space, people turned their attention to defining who constituted that community. One of the costs of generating and sustaining the exchange of social capital is containing, or at least defining, the community within which it circulates. Implied boundaries needed to be explicated. Who held responsibilities and privileges in relation to that space? At much the same time, the committee of the tennis club had contemplated this issue when it decided to construct two new courts with voluntary labour. In that case, the extent of the community was clear: it was the paid-up membership. But there remained the challenge of ensuring that members contributed equitably. The committee considered three proposals: that those not contributing labour be 'fined' 5 shillings; that all members make a small donation in addition to any fines; and, finally (the one that prevailed), that those not contributing labour make a 'small donation'. There was clearly an urge to protect with rules the fragile quantum of social capital the club was founded on, but it was equally important to maintain a sense of spontaneous communal effort by cloaking strictures in the language of voluntarism.[87]

---

87   Minutes, 15 July 1934, Westella Tennis Club, 1932–42, Western Plains Cultural Centre, Dubbo.

Over the following months, the hall committee conjured with similar issues, though the definition of 'membership' was less straightforward. The committee clearly felt that it needed the capacity to exclude—to define itself by its boundaries—and variously adopted rules based on people's location and their participation, before settling on voting rights being accorded to 'all those who had subscribed to the hall funds, their wives and families over the age of 20 years', with newcomers, most likely meaning new residents, to be admitted by ballot. As further statements of community based on participation and place, the committee determined that the three executive members were to be residents of 'Westella and Pilewood', while 'outsiders' wanting to hire the hall were to be charged twice the rate of local residents.[88] In the end, people moving to the district were formally but routinely admitted to the committee (without a ballot), and there is no evidence that they were ever denied. It was a form of admission to the social life of that place.

At face value, people built halls through impromptu collaboration. But Westella's experience shows that these processes were more likely to emerge in stable, homogeneous communities, relying on a managed process, hedged with rules, both overt and implied, governing the community of contributors and beneficiaries. Halls were simultaneously symbols of connection to a wider society and of a discrete community of place. The hall's events sustained these symbolic functions. The tennis club and the school's Parents and Citizens Committee met there; schools ran 'Christmas Trees' every year; the hall committee and the cricket and tennis clubs held dances; and more formal 'balls' were staged where people dressed up and bigger bands or 'orchestras' were booked. Birthdays were celebrated; 'gift evenings' were organised for women about to be married; people leaving the district were farewelled; and local recruits to the Second AIF were acknowledged before their departure, and welcomed home if they were lucky enough to return. An honour board, fashioned from the marble top of a washstand, recorded soldiers' names, marking the community as connected to the experience of the war and empire, and as distinct from other places (see Chapter 8).

Dances were the core social events in these districts. They were run according to standard and widely understood forms and procedures that required substantial coordination and participation, and were common across rural Australia. Karen Twigg and Helen O'Shea have observed such

88   Minutes, 16 August 1934, 6 March 1935, 11 April 1935, 25 February 1936, Westella Hall Committee, 1934–79, Western Plains Cultural Centre, Dubbo.

highly ritualised behaviours of country dances in other places, suggesting that, though details of dress and behaviour might have changed at the margins, these remained implicitly structured events. O'Shea, writing about the Golspie hall near Crookwell in southern New South Wales, notes that the 'codes and customs' of such events were widely understood, while Twigg, having interviewed people who went to dances in rural Victoria in the 1930s, argues that the 'strong normative pressures' governing the range of acceptable behaviours made explicit rules unnecessary.[89]

In the Dubbo farmlands these same forms applied. One-time Cobbora resident Lynne Burke, reflecting on her experience of hall functions there in the 1940s, recalled: 'No one was ever really excluded, I think it was pretty evident to everyone that there was a code of conduct, and it was adhered to.'[90] Organisers assigned men to certain roles, including doorkeepers, 'euchre markers' to run the card-playing part of the evening, and a master of ceremonies. Women were expected to supply and prepare food. Women and men gathered on the day of the event to prepare. Nancy Nott remembered the familiar reprise of preparing for hall functions, again at Cobbora in the 1940s:

> we would all go to the hall which had been swept and hosed down to get rid of the dust. We would decorate it with streamers & balloons, flowers and greenery. Then we would make the sandwiches with chicken, ham, eggs etc all from the farm.[91]

Discrete spaces allowed people to participate in different ways. Dancing occupied the main body of the hall, where the floor was carefully prepared to allow dancers to glide over the surface. People were generally familiar with a common lexicon of dances.[92]

89   Karen Twigg, 'The Role of the "Local Dance" in Country Courtship of the Nineteen Thirties', in 'But Nothing Interesting Ever Happened to Us ...': Memories of the Twenties and Thirties in Victoria, Victorian Branch of the Oral History Association of Australia, 1986, 17–27; Helen O'Shea, 'The Golspie Hall', Meanjin 47, no. 4 (1988): 701–8; Helen O'Shea, 'Country Halls', in The Oxford Companion to Australian Folklore, ed. Gwenda Beed Davey and Graham Seal (Melbourne: Oxford University Press, 1993), 73–8; Emma Dewson, 'Off to the Dance: Romance in Rural New Zealand Communities, 1880s–1920s', History Australia 2, no. 1 (2004): 05-1–05-9.
90   Lynne Burke (b. 1941), personal communication (email), 22 December 2020.
91   Nancy Nott (b. 1918), 'The Cobbora Hall 1915–1996', manuscript, [2011], in possession of Penny Stevens and Rob Ingram, Cobbora.
92   Harold Woodley (b. 1931), interview with author, Dubbo, 16 November 2020.

The dance provided opportunities for mingling with people of the opposite sex and for courtship. Norms guided how one dressed, where one stood or sat between dances, and who one danced with. Pride and status attached to one's dancing ability and appearance. Pearl Evans, born in around 1900, recalled dances at Brocklehurst in her youth:

> It was quite an ordeal getting ready for a dance. We had to sneak the starch and crush it to face powder, and get red paper and wet it to put colour in our lips.

Her one observation of a large family in the district was simply that they were 'all good dancers'. Stern standards of behaviour applied:

> It would be considered a shame on a young man if he didn't walk around the ballroom and slightly bow and ask could I have the pleasure of the next dance. To dance with the one partner was an unforgiveable sin.[93]

Tacit conventions in the more populous and diverse villages might have been more difficult to maintain but were enforced nonetheless. In 1936, a man was fined £1 with costs after he had been heard to use 'indecent language in a loud voice' at a dance in Wongarbon while standing at the hall doorway with other young men.[94]

Dancing was not the only activity available at these functions, and the dance floor not the only space. Euchre tournaments, generally but not exclusively popular with older locals, were another form of highly managed sociability. Players rotated through contests, changing after a set time announced by the ringing of a small bell, guaranteeing fair competition and that everyone engaged with all other players. A third shared space was outside the hall, around a fire used to boil water for tea, but also serving as a place where men—it was a gendered space—could talk, or just be anonymous, without the distractions of the dancing, flirting and card playing going on elsewhere.[95]

Halls, then, were the setting for a common social vernacular of imported cultural practices, which were narrow in range, but therefore widely understood. Social norms were no less firm for being unspoken, but it is

93   Pearl Evans, Speech Delivered at the 80th Anniversary of Brocklehurst School, manuscript, [1958], Western Plains Cultural Centre, Dubbo.
94   *DL*, 19 May 1936, 2.
95   Harold Woodley (b. 1931), interview with author, 16 November 2020.

difficult to avoid the conclusion that these halls were, in effect, a district's living room. At the same time, they signified attachment to both a wider cultural community, and to a local and formally secular place.

Conclusion

We have seen that people in these places shared a common experience of relationships with government, labour and the city, that bound them as a self-proclaimed, pan-rural class of farmers, in ways that were independent of where they lived and worked, and who they encountered from day to day. This chapter has explored the ways that local, and particularly social, experiences modified people's sense of the communities they belonged to. It has shown that, in the places where they lived, people identified in diverse ways—through religious observance, advocacy, self-help and recreation. Whether they formed branches of statewide, national or global associations, or gathered to share common cultural practices, they nevertheless adapted them in local forms. This did not occur spontaneously but required a careful nurturing of social capital in increasingly stable communities. For the most part, these social lives tended to blur, if not completely efface, distinctions of class and faith. Through social and visceral experience, they cultivated micro-communities of place. However, this sense of community was also a local expression of the other claim on people's identity—the idea of a pan-rural class. The two ideas were not only compatible but also mutually reinforcing.

8

'The tales of the pioneers are told': The place of the past in local consciousness

In 1893, 16-year-old Edwin King arrived in Narromine with his parents and siblings, having travelled from Castlemaine in Victoria to take up a property on the Tomingley Road. Twelve years later, in early 1905, King paused to write, in a few pages, about the family's time in that place: 'a review of our feelings, experiences and our general knowledge of farming, our happy times and our sorrows and the ups and downs of our lives on Neath Estate'.[1] This rare glimpse into one person's origin story of living in that district makes no mention of their lives to that point, but records the precise date of their arrival, marking this as a momentous time—a genesis: 'On the 28th day of August 1893 we arrived in Narromine absolute strangers and everyone looking at us as at something foreign.' The story of their trek from the town to the farm includes detail of individual family members' parts— who walked, who rode on the dray, and how they crossed the creek. The profusion of names and personal pronouns marks this as an intimate, family tale. It is not a triumphal narrative, but rather a string of self-deprecating anecdotes of early naivety and inexperience.

In 1907, King's younger sister's wedding prompted further reflection. Heading his thoughts 'The tales of the pioneers are told', he framed the occasion as an emphatic end to a chronicle, each of the people who had arrived in 1893 having by then broken a connection—through death or

---

1   Edwin Phillip King Diaries, 1893–1959, diary of 1905, ff. 131–6, Narromine Library, Macquarie Regional Library.

departure—with the original selection: 'the curtain is rung down for ever[.] The History of the King family comes to an end as they lived at Neath.'[2] In fact, King would live in the district for the remainder of his life, but in his telling the story speaks loudly of that time as embedding a connection between family and place: the family is transfigured, from being 'something foreign', to belonging through a process consecrated by their work to make the land productive.

No doubt farming households nurtured many such stories, though most often they were shared and passed on orally rather than written down: private yarns of arrival and settlement, enlivened with anecdotes of hardships, endurance and innocent embarrassments. Consistent with the ways these places were most often occupied in the colonising era, they were stories of families—groups of related households at most. Like King's, the narratives were also linked to place as people gave their farms names—as signifiers of occupation, ownership and belonging. The names and stories emphasised a shared experience and served a purpose, in Greg Dening's words, of making 'a boundary about the group', rather than being about a broader community.[3] On the whole, the stories remained private and are therefore mainly beyond the reach of the historian.

This was not a unique phenomenon. In more recent times, historians have shown emphatically that, for many people, history evokes meaning most often when it relates to the familiar and the familial.[4] However, these intimate, settler histories were complemented by broader public— but still local and vernacular—narratives. Local histories were shaped and reinforced in customs, language and everyday conversation, and the evidence survives in formal and sometimes ritualised places: in newspapers, monuments, reports and images of public performances, and through the annual rendition of the Dubbo Show. They consist of shared stories of a place's past—sometimes referred to as social, collective or cultural memory, or history/historical consciousness—and exist between officially received historical narrative on the one hand, and individual or family memory on the other. Storytelling satisfies a fundamental urge to locate oneself and

---

2   Edwin Phillip King Diaries, 1893–1959, 3 September 1907, Narromine Library, Macquarie Regional Library.
3   Greg Dening, *Performances* (Carlton South: Melbourne University Press, 1996), 50.
4   Paula Hamilton and Paul Ashton, 'At Home with the Past: Initial Findings from the Survey', *Australian Cultural History*, no. 23 (2003): 5–30; Roy Rozenzweig and David Thelen, 'The Presence of the Past: Popular Uses of History in American Life', in *The Public History Reader*, ed. Hilda Kean and Paul Martin (London and New York: Routledge, 2013), 30–55.

one's immediate community in a larger narrative. It is a process of making sense of, or justifying, the present by connecting it to a coherent past. As Doreen Massey has argued, stories are fundamental to ideas of place as well: claims to establish the identity of a place depend on a reading of its history. In so doing, historical consciousness contributes powerfully to community formation by—as Canadian historian Peter Seixas writes—defining 'a boundary between members who share the common past and those who do not'. So storytelling has a powerful political purpose as well: it can form part of the scaffolding of a social order.[5]

There follow three aspects of local historical consciousness and storytelling. They each involve conjuring with the meaning of performances in one form or another, using what the influential anthropologist Clifford Geertz called 'thick description': the close observation of nuance—in gestures, text, behaviour, inclusions and omissions—to reveal something of people's sense of their communities, and of a local social and political order.[6] The first section investigates the emergence of a local version of the story of the first settlement, focusing on the Dubbo Show, which became one of the main vehicles for performing as well as historicising a particular order of local rural society. The second explores the ways that commemorations of World War I introduced new emphases to historical consciousness, connecting local experiences to a wider world. The third part explores the place that European Australians assigned to Aboriginal people in their constructions of the district's history, and how that reflected the colonisers' own sense of the values underlying local settler society. Finally, those threads come together in a reflection on the state of a local historical narrative in the aftermath of World War II, with Dubbo's centennial celebrations of 1949 as its focus. I do not presume to interpret in detail Aboriginal people's constructions of post-contact history in that place—this is an analysis of settlers Australians—but, in not addressing that matter, I also do not deny that their perspectives were profoundly felt.

5   Doreen Massey, 'Places and Their Pasts', *History Workshop Journal*, no. 39 (1995): 182–92; Peter Seixas, 'Introduction', in *Theorizing Historical Consciousness*, ed. Peter Seixas (Toronto: University of Toronto Press, 2004), 6. See also Anna Clark, *Private Lives Public History* (Carlton: Melbourne University Press, 2016), 4–5, 55–7; Kate Darian-Smith and Paula Hamilton, 'Introduction', in *Memory and History in Twentieth-Century Australia*, ed. Kate Darian-Smith and Paula Hamilton (Melbourne: Oxford University Press, 1994), 1–2; Tom Griffiths, *Hunters and Collectors: The Antiquarian Imagination in Australia* (Cambridge: Cambridge University Press, 1996), 1; Paul Readman, 'The Place of the Past in English Culture c. 1890–1914', *Past and Present*, no. 186 (2005): 147–99.
6   Clifford Geertz, 'Thick Description: Toward an Interpretive Theory of Culture', in *The Interpretation of Cultures: Selected Essays*, ed. Clifford Geertz (New York: Basic Books, 1973), 3–30.

The show and a local pioneer legend

> Races, balls and all these things are very well in their way. They, however, are only indulged in by a limited number. The Show, on the other hand, gets the patronage of all ... The Show is a different performance altogether.[7]

Settlers in the Dubbo district had no common foundation story before 1914. An article in a local newspaper in 1897 claimed (wrongly) for the Dulhunty family the distinction of being the first Europeans in the district, but was otherwise generally a loose collection of personalities and first occurrences.[8] A journalist visiting the town in 1898 found no evidence of historical memory there:

> As I am unable to obtain more than disjointed snaps of the early history of the place, I must leave the past to the imagination of my readers, and dwell upon the Dubbo of today.[9]

By the early twentieth century, with few people remaining who could recall the era of pastoral occupation preceding the town's foundation in 1849, an anonymous writer produced 10 articles reminiscing about the period to 1865. While that series was often anecdotal and lacked a strong narrative thread, the author introduced the idea that the present arose from, and could only be understood in the context of, the past through the familiar trope of 'the pioneers', represented as people selflessly enduring hardship such that later generations should feel a sense of connection and obligation:

> It is to the strong men of the past, the pioneers of the early days, that we must turn when we seek ... the real source, from which will spring the new prosperous Australian Commonwealth.[10]

But whereas the Dulhunty story had valorised the early pastoralists, this writer exalted the more utilitarian carriers who delivered supplies to pastoral runs and returned to the coast or railheads with wool—an early indication that 'pioneer' could be a contested idea. His story had more to say about the place of the town and the farming settlers who so often had started out as carriers.

---

7   *DD*, 6 May 1887, 4.
8   *DD*, 28 May 1897, 3.
9   *ATCJ*, 24 December 1898, 28.
10   *DL*, 6 April 1904, 2. The series began on 12 March 1904 and concluded on 8 October 1904.

From 1915, newspaper articles valorising the first Europeans in the district appeared more frequently, often linked explicitly with the Dubbo Show. They located the show as the culmination of an unfolding narrative of place. As both a shared experience and the focus of a common history for many European Australians, the show affirmed a community's sense of embeddedness, entitlement and belonging in that place. To understand why the show became a catalyst for the construction of the district's history, it is instructive to examine its form and the particular vision of a rural society that it embodied.

The Dubbo Show, first staged in 1873, was modelled on a well-established formula of annual exhibitions of rural produce designed to encourage contemporary scientific practice and competition among farmers. The Agricultural Society of New South Wales had held its first show at Westmead in 1824, foundered in the 1830s, but then revived in 1859. Beyond Sydney, a show in the Bathurst district was first held in 1860, and the Hunter River Agricultural Association began staging regular events in Maitland that same year.[11] Dubbo's show was founded by the district's western pastoral elite over several meetings in Sydney and Dubbo in 1871 and 1872. They settled on Dubbo as the 'commercial and recognised centre' of communities along the Macquarie, Castlereagh, Bogan and Lachlan rivers, and named their organisation the North-Western Pastoral, Agricultural and Horticultural Association (PA&HA). Though the committee was said to comprise 'squatters, storekeepers and agriculturalists', the pastoralists—men wealthy enough to travel routinely to Sydney after the shearing—were best placed to devote time and money to the venture.[12]

The show continued to be run by western graziers even after agriculture became established in the district and the relative wealth and influence of the pastoralists had declined. In 1896, one correspondent, commenting on the PA&HA committee's dominance of the broader membership, and alluding to its bias towards the pastoral districts west of the town, described the committee disparagingly as the 'Narromine-cum-Bogan Annual Circus and Picnic Race Society', consisting of people 'able to count a flock of sheep, or draw out an agreement with a few Chinamen for a ringbarking contract,

11   Gilbert Mant, *The Big Show* (North Sydney: Horwitz Publications, 1972), 24; Brian H. Fletcher, *The Grand Parade: A History of the Royal Agricultural Society of New South Wales* (Paddington: Royal Agricultural Society of New South Wales, [1988]), 13; Bathurst Agricultural, Horticultural and Pastoral Association, *100 Bathurst Shows, 1968: A History of the Bathurst Show* ([Bathurst: 1968]), 17; *Maitland Daily Mercury*, 22 March 1910, 6.
12   *Sydney Mail and New South Wales Advertiser*, 23 December 1871, 1349; *ATCJ*, 2 March 1872, 389.

or train a horse for a picnic races', but incapable of running a public association.[13] The writer probably had Frank Mack in mind, in many ways a typical example of the association's leadership and its connections with other local institutions. Mack was originally from Victoria, bought Narramine station with a colleague in the mid-1880s, and later acquired Weemabah station as well. He was a stud-sheep breeder but is also credited with introducing wheat farming to the Narromine district in the 1890s. Mack was chair of the Narromine Branch and Dubbo District Council of the GA and was active in the Macquarie Picnic Race Club and the Narromine Polo Club: two organisations strongly associated with the pastoral elite. Mack served as president of the PA&HA from 1892 until 1896 and then again from 1903 to 1924. He was typical of prominent graziers who formed the bulk of the committee and who held the presidency throughout the show's first 75 years.[14]

Notwithstanding its elite genesis and leadership, the show was broadly popular as a place for gathering as well as exhibiting. As the town and the immediate agricultural surrounds developed, the show became more closely connected to Dubbo. From 1885, it was held at a dedicated site adjoining the town itself, and by 1886 the association had inserted 'Dubbo' in its title, in place of 'North-West'. A public holiday on one of the two annual show days was established in 1885. At show time that year, there was not a bed to be had in Dubbo's 31 hotels. Each year, the committee negotiated with the railway authorities to offer concessional return fares from as far away as Sydney and Bourke. One report claimed that almost 12,000 people attended the 1900 show, including 1,100 who arrived by rail, at a time when Dubbo's population was around 3,400. Despite several interruptions, the show became an integral pulse in the district's annual cadence.[15]

The show presented a particular vision of rural society. Whereas in other contexts farmers' representatives asserted their status and claimed rights as a class with distinct needs, disadvantages and values, the show's organisers claimed the event to be an inclusive, classless and non-political expression of

---

13 *DL*, 4 January 1896, 3.

14 *Daily Telegraph*, 26 May 1926, 11; *Land*, 28 May 1926, 15; *Narromine News and Trangie Advocate*, 26 May 1926, 3; Branch minutes, Narromine, 256/1510, District Council minutes, Dubbo, Graziers Association of New South Wales, Deposit 1, E256/1481, Noel Butlin Archives Centre; *DL*, 11 May 1939, 2.

15 *Evening News*, 4 June 1885, 3; *SMH*, 4 June 1885, 8; *DL*, 18 April 1900, 2, 12 May 1900, 2; Commonwealth Bureau of Census, *Official Year Book of New South Wales, No. 51, 1947–48* (Sydney: Government Printer, 1950), 187.

the rural. There might have been a continuing emphasis, even a privileging, of pastoral exhibits, but there was a place for almost every rural enterprise. Its evolving narrative, if not strictly its form, was egalitarian: a melting pot of primary production and related industry. One report on the first show expressed disappointment that 'the farmers around took very little advantage of that portion of the schedule set apart for their particular interest'; nevertheless, the agriculturalists and mixed farmers were included in the program. 'Smallholders' had their own categories, to ensure fairer competition, and by 1900 there was a well-patronised farm produce section. Acknowledging that soldier settlers often struggled to carve out productive farms next to more established neighbours, they were accorded their own separate section in the wheat competition in 1923.[16] Chinese people, who worked market gardens on the river flats by the town, regularly won prizes in the horticultural section. Reports did not always refer to the winners by name, but rather as 'Celestials' or 'resident Chinese gardeners'. Their involvement and its reporting suggest that they occupied an equivocal position in local society: a distinct, somewhat anonymous group whom European Australians defined by their race, but then also acknowledged for their ability to make the land productive.[17] Exhibits of crafts that were universally women's work—cooking in the home and needlework—augmented the agrarian ideal of a self-sufficient farming class. 'Fancy work' suggested that farming women were not just productive components of an independent household, but also members of an aspirational middle class, participating in what American historian Catherine E. Kelly has described as 'the democratisation of refinement'. Commenting on the miscellaneous throng at the 1911 show, one commentator claimed: 'At the show they were on an equality … It was not a time for class distinction'.[18]

But the show revealed a more nuanced picture of the community it purported to represent, one that was neither classless nor apolitical. Paid labour, for example, did not necessarily fit neatly within the agrarian idyll, and here the Dubbo Show indicated where the peripheries of the vision lay. Sleeper-squaring, though clearly not a skill associated with landowners,

---

16   *Sydney Mail and New South Wales Advertiser*, 29 March 1873, 389; *DD*, 11 May 1900, 4; *Sydney Mail*, 9 May 1923, 31.

17   *DD*, 8 May 1909, 6. See also 12 May 1906, 4; *DL*, 3 May 1902, 2; Michael Williams, 'Vegetables Varied and Excellent, Chiefly from a Celestial Garden', *History: Magazine of the Royal Australian Historical Society*, no. 153 (2022): 9–11.

18   Catherine E. Kelly, '"The Consummation of Rural Prosperity and Happiness": New England Agricultural Fairs and the Construction of Class and Gender, 1810–1860', *American Quarterly* 49, no. 3 (1997): 574–602; *DL*, 13 May 1911, 4.

was an event at the 1901 show. That such work was most often undertaken by contractors, as piece work, and was not farm work, represented a nod, perhaps, to the importance of railways to the local economy.[19] But the most conspicuous absence from the show was shearing, even though many smallholders were also shearers either on their own properties or as part of the broader shearing workforce, and the district was home to perhaps hundreds of professional shearers. Shearers' exclusion might have reflected deep-seated antagonism between the shearers' union and the class of GA-affiliated graziers that dominated the association's committee, as discussed in Chapter 4. Bag sewing and sheaf tossing—essential skills in agricultural production—were only included after World War II. By then new technologies (hay balers and bulk wheat handling) meant that they were on the verge of becoming redundant—nostalgic echoes of a passing era—and increasingly likely to be undertaken by farming households themselves rather than by paid labour.[20]

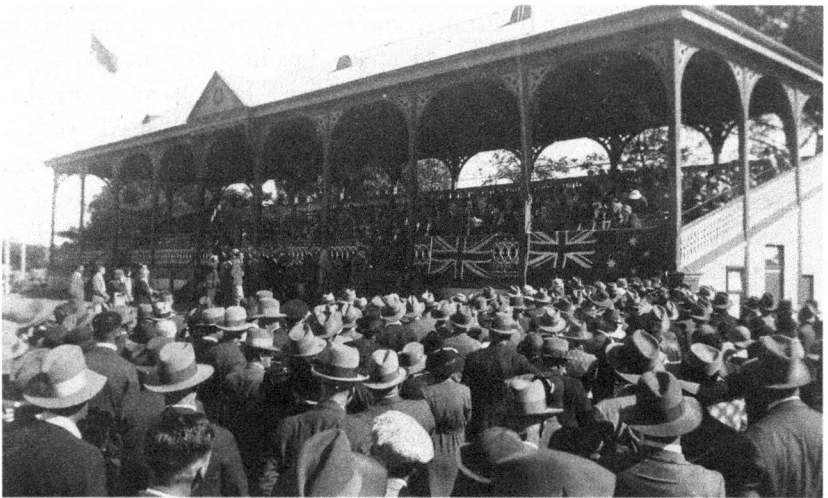

Figure 8.1: The governor of New South Wales opens the Dubbo Show, 1934 or 1935.

Source: Mo Cockerell collection.

19   *DL*, 11 May 1901, 2.
20   *DL*, 27 April 1946, 1, 11 May 1946, 4, 24 April 1947, 8, 28 February 1948, 4, 13 April 1948, 3, 4 May 1948, 3, 25 April 1950, 3.

So the show could be represented as classless, but only by including a selective range of rural endeavour, and some activities that had passed from necessary labour to skills for their own sake—a more refined expression of a distinct identity. The exclusions were made starker by the inclusion of town-based industry. Buggy- and machinery-building and saddlery were a part of the show in the late nineteenth and early twentieth centuries.[21] Thus, the exchange of urban- or town-sourced products was acknowledged as an essential part of rural production, but not paid farm labour. All in all, the show was an expression of one vision of a putatively inclusive, classless and apolitical society, aspiring to respectability, but from which the rural working class was silently excluded (see Figure 8.1).

For about a decade from around 1914, the show took on an extra function as the focus of an annually reiterated narrative of the district's history. Local newspaper reports and editorials moved seamlessly from commentary on that year's show to placing it in the van of a broader story. As a regular event conducted according to a set of standard procedures, the show was susceptible to becoming a ritualised connection with the past. It was a point of continuity and assurance: in Eric Hobsbawm's terms, an 'invented tradition'.[22] By then, many of the participants in the first show were ageing. An era was passing from living memory, perhaps prompting an urge to write it down and valorise it. Don Aitkin has written about the increasing insecurity of rural towns following the long boom of 1860–90 and the tardy subsequent recovery in rural areas.[23] The interruptions of war, influenza and drought, which prevented shows from being held in 1916–17 and 1919–20, might also have contributed to a sense of vulnerability, inducing some writers to reflect on the show as tradition. In that context, it could also have reflected a heightened impulse to assert an entitlement to that place, such that the performance of an inclusive and productive society was nourished by the assurance and justification of historical depth: as Heather Goodall has expressed it, 'to try to fix white history to the earth'.[24]

Local newspapers' show-inspired stories contained several persistent and familiar elements, common across rural Australia. Most of the narratives from this period are not anchored in names, dates and places. It is a

21   *DL*, 30 April 1898, 2; *DD*, 8 May 1901, 2.
22   Eric Hobsbawm, 'Introduction: Inventing Traditions', in *The Invention of Tradition*, ed. Eric Hobsbawm and Terence Ranger (Cambridge: Cambridge University Press, 1983), 1–14.
23   Don Aitkin, '"Countrymindedness"—The Spread of an Idea', *Australian Cultural History* 4 (1985): 38.
24   Heather Goodall, 'Telling Country: Memory, Modernity and Narratives in Rural Australia', *History Workshop Journal* 47, no. 1 (1999): 168.

mythologised past but with implied historical veracity.[25] The story consists, initially, of the first white men (and occasionally women) harnessing qualities of endurance, persistence and courage, with their cattle and sheep to take possession of the western plains. It shares a consistent thread that Ann Curthoys has identified in popular Australian historical narratives, one that emphasises white settlers' exile and suffering as victims of an unjust or impoverished old world, or of a harsh environment.[26] A 1915 account, within a story about that year's show, was typical:

> The last century was well advanced before the first of the pastoralists moved West from Wellington, the man who was destined to become a sort of patriarch, a modern Abraham or Moses, seeking the Land of promise in the West ... And so it was that the history of the district began.[27]

The environment they encountered was variously represented as hostile, and therefore eliciting courage and endurance, or untouched, benign and awaiting the predestined attention of the newcomers' science and persistence: 'the vast areas of the fertile Western plains have yet to be turned to the use for which Nature intended them'.[28] Curthoys also argues that the emphasis on settler colonists' suffering in the face of an unforgiving environment effectively displaced, or left no room for, Aboriginal people as victims in this process. Consistent with the general tenor of history-telling by European Australians at the time, if Aboriginal people were acknowledged to have been present at all, they were represented as the antithesis of the first European intruders. Aboriginal people's place in European Australians' historical imagination in this district is examined more extensively below.

The idea of the 'pioneer'—a term used liberally through these stories—was central to narratives of European occupation. Tom Griffiths has observed, in relation to the Victorian town of Beechworth, that the term was historically contingent, its meaning shifting according to such factors as a person's date of arrival in the colony or their connection with working the land. At the

---

25   The exception to these anonymous stories was the Dulhunty family whose descendants kept their story in the public eye: *DD*, 5 May 1916, 3; Beryl Dulhunty, *The Dulhunty Papers: Chronicle of a Family* (Sydney: The Wentworth Press, 1959).
26   Ann Curthoys, 'Expulsion, Exodus and Exile in White Australian Historical Mythology', *Journal of Australian Studies* 23, no. 61 (1999): 1–19.
27   *DL*, 14 May 1915, 3.
28   *DL*, 8 May 1914, 2, 14 May 1915, 33.

same time, however, it also defined a quite exclusive group.[29] In contrast, in the commentary surrounding the Dubbo Show, the term was liberally assigned, applying in some instances to the first white people to depasture stock in the district, but in others to any white settler who gave their best endeavour to some enterprise or other. Pioneers could be associated with the town; they could be of the past, the present or even the future. In 1915, a local newspaper bemoaned the lack of a pioneers' association, as one would be 'an inspiration to the pioneers of today and the pioneers of the future'; in 1923, it was asserted that 'every man and woman who does his work in the West faithfully and well now is a pioneer equally with the pioneers of old'.[30] Thus, the 'pioneer' trope was as inclusive and democratic as the show, though set in contrast to Aboriginal people, and still without explicit reference to anyone unambiguously of the working class.

The show itself also entered that narrative, the first event of 1873 being characterised by 1914 as 'a pioneers' effort, [with] a humble and yet ambitious beginning'. It became the central uniting symbol, binding past to present to future, squatter to farmer, town to hinterland, even district to empire and race. Just attending the show, according to one report, inspired affinity:

> Everything was big. We felt a sense of greatness in ourselves. We were pleased to be component parts in a great whole ... [W]e feel the pride of race[,] and the spirit of local patriotism permeated our very beings, and we were greater and better men and women for it.[31]

In 1933, the PA&HA president, Les Clark, conflated the show's and the district's pasts, claiming that 'the history of the Association is the history of Dubbo', as though the district's history began and ended with the stories of settler achievement that the show embodied and celebrated.[32]

It is hard to say whether people in Dubbo's hinterland embraced these narratives of the show's and the district's history, or whether they were the isolated musings of a handful of speech-makers and local journalists. Few probably expressed these sentiments themselves, but people kept turning up. Edwin King's diary entries were laconic to a fault, but over the years

---

29   Tom Griffiths, *Beechworth: An Australian Country Town and its Past* (Richmond: Greenhouse Publications, 1987), 57–72; *DL*, 7 May 1915, 2.

30   *DL*, 7 May 1915, 4 May 1923, 2.

31   *DL*, 8 May 1914, 2.

32   *DL*, 18 May 1933, 4. He repeated the claim six years later: *DL*, 11 May 1939, 2.

he often recorded that he 'Went to the Dubbo show'.[33] By the late 1880s, the Department of Public Instruction had recognised the significance of country shows by granting schools one day's holiday each year to enable families to attend. That concession was taken up universally around Dubbo. Outlying villages' columns in the Dubbo press congratulated local prize winners or simply noted that most people in the locale had attended. One journalist claimed in 1914 that, for many people, 'the Show is the only holiday season of the year', and that 'most interested and excited' patrons were people from the surrounding district—the 'horny-handed sons of toil and the yeomanry of the rural centres'. The Eulomogo schoolteacher reported in 1931 that 'all the parents and children attended'; likewise, on show day in 1935, Eumungerie 'was deserted ... the whole population going to the Dubbo show'.[34]

People's emphatic participation in the show might not have reflected their sense of self or local history, but there were few, if any, obvious alternative narratives. By 1918, if Dubbo had a foundation story, it was consistent with what the historian James Belich has described as an ideology of 'settlerism', consisting of a vague and anonymous procession of essentially peaceful occupation, characterised less by specific events and personalities than by a general tenor of purpose and worthiness derived from work, struggle and transforming the land.[35] It attached historical roots and legitimacy to a particular social order, of which the annual show was a contemporary expression.

World War I

Rhetorical references to the Dubbo district's 'pioneer' roots were appearing less often by the mid-1920s, though they never vanished. Speeches at Dubbo Show functions invariably referred to the first show and the district's history. The ageing William Webb ('Billy') Baird, as the last surviving participant in the first show, became a prompt for newspapers to reflect on connections

33   Edwin Phillip King Diaries, 1893–1959, 10 May 1899, 8 May 1901 and 11 May 1904, Narromine Library, Macquarie Regional Library.
34   DL, 8 May 1914, 2; Elizabeth Kennedy to the district inspector, 21 August 1889, and L. Clark to the inspector of schools, 8 May 1931, Eulomogo School Administrative File, pre-1939, 5/15848.1, NRS 3829, SARNSW; DL, 25 May 1935, 4.
35   James Belich, *Replenishing the Earth: The Settler Revolution and the Rise of the Anglo-World, 1783–1939* (Oxford: Oxford University Press, 2009), 153–65.

to a pioneering past, until he opened his last Dubbo Show in 1936.[36] In the meantime, the disruption of World War I caused people to position the district, as well as smaller places, in new, locally crafted historical narratives.

As for much of the nation, Dubbo farmlands people had responded in the early months of the war with enthusiastic declarations of loyalty to nation and empire, and disdain for Germany and its allies. The sentiment was imperial, but the action was determinedly local. In April 1915, the Glenara Farmers and Settlers Association branch organised a social to raise money for the Belgium Relief Fund, its members' contributions including a pig, a bag of wheat and a pair of fowls to be auctioned for the cause. In August, Wongarbon staged an Australia Day procession that included young women dressed to represent the allied nations, and vehicles decked out as battleships. Three costumed characters representing the German Kaiser, a Turkish Sultan and the Emperor of Austria-Hungary animated the onlookers. Six men used the occasion to announce that they would volunteer to enlist, and the event raised £430 for the war effort—equivalent to more than three times the annual minimum wage. In October, the privately organised 'Coo-ee' recruitment march left Gilgandra—one of at least eight staged across New South Wales in 1915–16—to be wholeheartedly welcomed in the village on its way to Sydney. A dinner provided for the proto-recruits and local people in the hall had to be staged over several sittings to accommodate everyone. Twelve men joined the march, and others said they would enlist after the harvest. People in small communities could hardly avoid being drawn into the war effort, one way or another. Long lists published in newspapers identified donors to comfort funds. Well-attended gatherings in village halls and farm sheds honoured departing recruits and then welcomed those who returned. In this early phase, people emphasised the war's capacity to unify. At a soldier's farewell in Wongarbon in early 1916, one speaker said that in those circumstances 'all differences, political or religious or otherwise, were sunk, and all had united in a common cause'.[37]

There were few early signs of public dissent from this full-throated patriotism, but once the early surges in recruitment had passed and casualties accumulated, unity began to dissipate. In August and September 1915, the federal government's census of manpower, and a subsequent questionnaire

---

36 *DL*, 14 May 1936, 4.
37 *DL*, 9 April 1915, 2, 7 January 1916, 5; *WT*, 9 August 1915, 3, 12 August 1915, 5; *DD*, 15 October 1915, 1; John Meredith, *The Coo-ee March, Gilgandra–Sydney 1915* (Dubbo: Macquarie Publications, 1981), 33–4; L. L. Robson, *The First AIF: A Study in its Recruitment* (Carlton: Melbourne University Press, 1982), 57–88.

asking all males aged between 18 and 45 about their intentions to enlist, would have reached almost every household.[38] A correspondent to the *Liberal*, anticipating every reason someone might choose not to enlist, singled out farmers and graziers for special attention:

> The fat young landholder, who says he can't go to war, but will subscribe £2 or perhaps £5 ... the farmers' sons, who are afraid— not of war, of course—but that the crops won't be able to be got in without them; the most dutiful and loving sons who are afraid—not of war, of course—but of what might become of their mothers—all these and all the others who won't stand up besides the Australians at the war,
>
> *Are They the Australians?*
>
> or are they true Germans ... doing everything but helping their own country and their own men[?][39]

The plebiscites on conscription for overseas service in 1916 and 1917 forced people into opposing positions. Dubbo's two newspapers each took a side. Men and women expressed themselves not only at the ballot box but also very publicly through anti-conscription committees that held fundraising functions and hosted speakers in centres of relatively strong Labor support. In Ballimore, then host to a large railway construction workforce, one could buy a button displaying the slogan 'Labour and No-conscription' for a shilling. Not to be outdone, pro-conscriptionists staged meetings in the railway villages of Wongarbon and Mogriguy.[40]

In 1916, the rural 'no' vote was relatively high in New South Wales, as well as South Australia, but conscription was especially unpopular in the Central West. Only 66.2 per cent of enrolled voters in the subdivision of Dubbo, and 65.8 per cent in the subdivision of Wellington, participated in the poll. This was far lower than the rates for their respective electorates of Darling and Calare, and for the state as a whole, in which 80.9 per cent of enrolled voters turned up. Less than one in four enrolled voters in Dubbo voted 'yes' at either plebiscite, again significantly fewer than in the electorate of the Darling as a whole, and the state. In Wellington, support was even lower,

38 John McQuilton, *Rural Australia and the Great War: From Tarrawingee to Tangambalanga* (Carlton South: Melbourne University Press, 2001), 40–1.
39 *DL*, 8 October 1915, 2.
40 *DD*, 9 March, 23 March 1917, 1, 20 November, 1, 30 November 1917, 2.

where fewer than one in five enrolled voters voted 'yes'.[41] A comparison between the 1914 federal election results and the 1916 plebiscite reveals that a significant proportion of non-Labor voters did not support conscription. Whereas the Liberal candidate for the Darling, William Kelk, obtained 51.2 per cent of the Dubbo subdivision's vote at the general election, only 35.6 per cent of those who voted in 1916 supported conscription. The same patterns were even starker at the 1917 plebiscite (see Figure 8.2). It is not possible to distinguish how farming households voted, as compared with others in the district. But at the time, many, including the state minister for railways, Henry Hoyles, held farmers responsible, claiming that they feared conscription would diminish the rural labour force.[42]

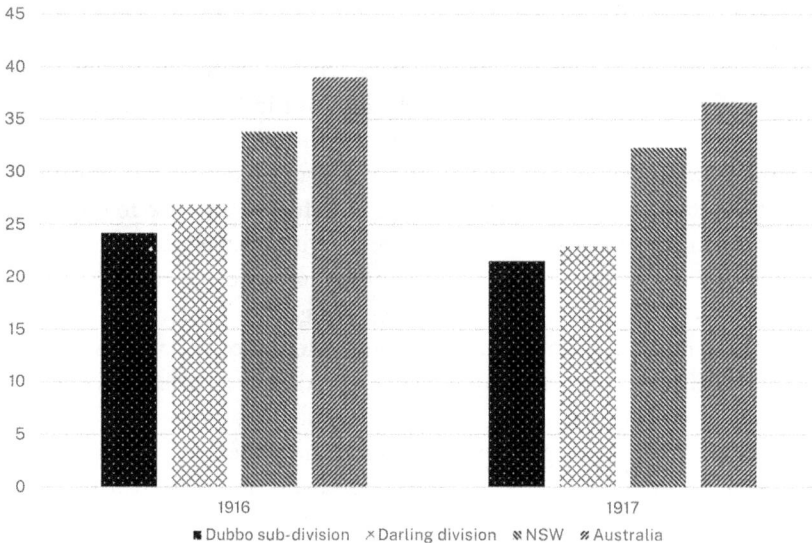

Figure 8.2: Conscription plebiscites, percentage of enrolled voters who voted 'yes'.

Source: Compiled from Commonwealth Parliamentary Papers.

41 Commonwealth Electoral Office, *Statistical Returns in Relation to the Submission to the Electors of the Question Prescribed by Section 5 of the Military Service Referendum Act 1916*, in *Papers Presented to the Parliament 1914–15–16–17*, vol. II (Melbourne: Government Printer, 1917); Commonwealth Electoral Office, *Statistical Returns in Relation to the Submission to the Electors of the Question Prescribed by Regulation 6 of the War Precautions (Military Service Referendum) Regulations 1917*, in *Papers Presented to the Parliament 1917–18–19*, vol. IV (Melbourne: Government Printer, 1918).
42 *DD*, 8 September 1914, 1; Jenny Tilby Stock, 'Farmers and the Rural Vote in South Australia in World War I: The 1916 Conscription Referendum', *Historical Studies* 21, no. 84 (1985): 391–411; Murray Goot, 'The Results of the 1916 and 1917 Conscription Referendums Re-examined', in *The Conscription Conflict and the Great War*, ed. Robin Archer, Joy Damousi, Murray Goot and Sean Scalmer (Clayton: Monash University Publishing, 2016), 133–5; *DD*, 31 October 1916, 1.

On face value, exemption court hearings in Dubbo in 1916 show that farmers were concerned to at least suspend, if not reject, enlistment so as to maintain farm production. The federal government had anticipated a 'yes' vote at the 1916 plebiscite, and so had called up eligible men for service within Australia, but enlistees could seek exemptions on various grounds. In the Dubbo district, around half of those who were passed fit applied to be spared. About 90 of the claims reported in local newspapers were from farmers, almost all seeking exemptions to bring in the imminent harvest.[43] Those farmers from the district who did enlist over the course of the war were more likely to join up between January and March, after the harvest season and before the following agricultural cycle began. August, when sowing was complete and haymaking was still to come, was also a more common month for farmers to enlist.[44]

But decisions not to enlist are likely to have been more complex, particularly in light of the continuing pressure applied by political and civic leaders, and some sections of local communities. By leaving decisions to enlist or to remain at home in the hands of every man of military age, the plebiscites' defeat served to sustain division, ensuring that those who chose to stay home would continue to have their courage and values challenged. Wongarbon maintained a recruitment association throughout the war, chaired by the local storekeeper.[45] Every farewell to a departing recruit was an opportunity to draw attention to those in the district who had not come forward. As Bart Ziino has also concluded, it was often a question of balancing a range of competing obligations, to the state, one's family and one's self. He singles out farmers as negotiating financial pressures and opportunities, with duties to family, and a rationale that producing food and fibre were contributions in themselves to the war effort. After all, as we have seen, there was an ideology that valorised rural production, and agriculture in particular, that war could not necessarily neutralise. But whatever individuals' reasons were, in the context of constant urging, the choice not to enlist was also not one that could be dealt with and then put aside; rather, it had to be continually re-examined for the war's duration.[46]

---

43 *DD*, 24 October 1916, 6, 31 October 1916, 3; *DL*, 31 October 1916, 2.
44 Based on recruits named on memorials in Wongarbon, Gollan, Geurie and Rawsonville whose service records have been identified. John McQuilton, 'Doing the "Back Block Boys Some Good": The Exemption Court Hearings in North-Eastern Victoria, 1916', *Australian Historical Studies* 31, no. 115 (2000): 237–50.
45 *WT*, 5 August 1915, 5.
46 Bart Ziino, 'Enlistment and Non-enlistment in Wartime Australia: Responses to the 1916 Call to Arms Appeal', *Australian Historical Studies* 41, no. 2 (2010): 217–32; J. N. I. Dawes and L. L. Robson, *Citizen to Soldier: Australia before the Great War—Recollections of Members of the First AIF* (Carlton: Melbourne University Press, 1977), 12–20.

In all, Dubbo district farmers experienced the same pressures to enlist as those across Australia, and they were no more inclined to enlist than their peers. There do seem to have been differences from one community to the next, though, that might indicate that peer pressure was a factor. Wongarbon had a substantial farming hinterland but only 6 of 38 whose names were recorded on the memorial (and who can be linked to military records) identified as farmers, whereas 22 of 29 recorded in the entirely rural community of Rawsonville so identified. Pressure to enlist was not the only issue bearing on people in the Dubbo farmlands during the war of course. Drought, disruptions to wheat and wool marketing, and government schemes to regulate it might have given people as much concern, and, as discussed in Chapter 4, the strike of 1917 drew the attention of many rural people. The point, though, is that the divisions that were either created or exacerbated, along lines of class and religion over people's choices and contributions, were all the more personally experienced in smaller communities.[47]

Memorialisation and historicisation

Communities that created memorials at the end of World War I were very consciously not only commemorating but also constructing history. Wellington's memorial included female figures described in 1920 as representing Victory, Fame and, next to them, History, 'recording the deeds of the men'.[48]

By 1918, Wongarbon was one of many communities planning to memorialise those residents who had enlisted. It was not only a form of public, communal remembering, but also signified a locality's connection to a much larger drama. Other than the innumerable headstones and adornments marking individuals' passing, Wongarbon's was probably the first public monument or memorial created by European Australians in the Dubbo district. A Soldiers' Memorial Committee arranged with a firm of Dubbo funeral directors to design and construct a reinforced concrete obelisk, the single most common form among Australian memorials of that

---

47   Michael McKernan, *Australians at Home: World War I* (Scoresby: Five Mile Press, 2014), 178.
48   *WT*, 26 April 1920, 2; Ken Inglis, assisted by Jan Brazier, *Sacred Places: War Memorials in the Australian Landscape* (Carlton: Melbourne University Press, 2008), 164–5; Graeme Davison, *The Use and Abuse of Australian History* (Crows Nest: Allen & Unwin, 2000), 38.

war. Like hundreds of communities around Australia, in the words of Ken Inglis, they 'negotiated their own communal understandings of the meaning of war' in that place.[49]

The monument's simplicity and scale (around 4.6 metres in height) and the surrounding ornamental concrete and iron fence denote a space both secular and sacred (see Figure 8.3).[50] Except for a small silhouette of crossed rifles on the pediment, there is nothing to draw the eye other than the text, in inlaid lead on white marble panels. One panel announces plainly, 'The Great War 1914–1919', anchoring the structure, and through it the locale, to a time and monumental event. Another proclaiming 'They heard the call and answered', recognises that those listed had joined a volunteer force. A small panel on another face records that the memorial had been 'Erected by the citizens of Wongarbon and district', and also depicts the Union Jack and the Australian flag, thus connecting all the people of that place to the nation and the empire. The largest and most conspicuous panels display the local recruits' names—surname and one initial—in democratic alphabetical order, with no reference to rank or unit, and just a small cross against the names of those who had died. A few are credited with military decorations.

Like just over half of Australian memorials to that war, by including the names of both the living and the dead, the village affirmed volunteering as the act most worthy of honour. The names also made the memorial intimate and unique to that place. Fred Lovett, who had been the principal at the school for many years and whose son had been killed in France, spoke emotionally at the unveiling of the familiar names of those he had taught there. By locating the memorial in the village's school grounds, the committee demonstrated, firstly, a claim of communal ownership of the space, and, secondly, a conviction that the commemoration had an educative function. It reinforced the idea that the memory of the people and event it commemorated should endure, not just in the structure but also in the historical consciousness of that place. A speaker at the unveiling predicted: 'Their children's children will read the names.'[51]

---

49   Inglis, *Sacred Places*, 122; obelisks as the most common form, 153–4.
50   K. S. Inglis, 'World War One Memorials in Australia', *Guerres mondiales et conflits contemporains*, no. 167 (1992): 51–8.
51   *DD*, 8 April 1919, 3; *DL*, 8 April 1919, 4; Inglis, *Sacred Places*, 174.

Figure 8.3: Wongarbon war memorial.
Source: Photograph by Peter Woodley, 2021.

That ceremony, under a clear sky on an autumn Saturday in 1919, revealed the tension between abstractions of nation and empire on the one hand, and the local and personal intimacy of visceral loss on the other. The memorial was draped in the flags of Australia and Britain, reinforcing a symbolic connection to nation and empire. Many women wore black, and a wreath was placed by 'a woman with kindly thought'. In this performance, as elsewhere, women—through their attire particularly—were expected to represent the 'emotional burden of loss'.[52] The speeches affirmed that this was a self-conscious exercise in both community- and history-making. The Australian flag that was removed in the unveiling had been carried by a Wongarbon recruit during the 'Coo-ee' recruitment march four years earlier: 'a historical bit of bunting', according to one speaker. The one clergyman to speak, of the Dubbo Presbyterian Church, tied Wongarbon's 'sons' to themes of empire and 'the virtues of Christianity'. Others spoke of the proportion of deaths among the enlistees as being higher than 'from any other town', and the memorial as being 'one of the first ... on the western line'.[53] It was as though not only the nation had been 'born in a day at Gallipoli', but also the village and district of Wongarbon. Whereas established historical narratives such as those surrounding the show had located a community of the Dubbo district in a past untethered from specific names and events, the war prompted more localised and personal statements of place embedded in history.

This was not the end of Wongarbon's memorialising. Across Australia, the distribution of thousands of captured German artillery pieces, trench mortars and machine guns also prompted communities to contemplate how war should be remembered. Trophy committees in each state allocated these souvenirs to councils and some schools, and smaller locales could apply to receive one. Reactions to the offers revealed divergent views on the commemoration of war. Some councils, including Redfern and the City of Sydney, declined the trophies on the basis that they celebrated militarism rather than sacrifice or righteous endeavour. Other places were disappointed if their allotted trophy was too insubstantial, or if, like the rural community of Gollan, they were assessed to be too small to receive one.[54]

---

52   Tanja Luckins, *The Gates of Memory: Australian People's Experiences and Memories of Loss and the Great War* (Freemantle: Curtin University Books, 2004), 77, also 15–16, 51–76.
53   *DL*, 8 April 1919, 4.
54   *SMH*, 16 December 1920, 7, 20 January 1921, 10, 15 February 1921, 6, 29 August 1921, 10; *Sunday Times*, 18 September 1921; Inglis, *Sacred Places*, 170–1.

Members of the Wongarbon community were eager to supplement their obelisk with a war trophy, and in July 1920 were allocated a machine gun through the Talbragar Shire Council.[55] However, before the gun could be installed, the New South Wales minister for education in the new Labor government, Thomas Mutch, instructed that such weapons should not be displayed on public school property. The Wongarbon committee entrusted with the trophy was determined to proceed anyway, and its chair, returned serviceman Samuel Armstrong, mounted it beside the obelisk despite the teacher's protestations on behalf of his minister. It was unveiled on Empire Day in May 1921 by Emma Lovett, the wife of the former principal, and the mother of a man killed in the recent war. However, due to pressure from the Department of Education, the gun was removed in August.[56]

The significance of the trophy to this community could be interpreted in several ways. Was it regarded as evidence that local recruits' sacrifices had been rewarded, a counterbalance to the loss recorded on the memorial? Or did it make more tangible the imagined ties between the community and the distant battlefields where local men might have died? An important adjunct to each piece of hardware was that they were not random relics of unknown origin. Each was accompanied by a short description of its provenance—the military unit that had captured it, and the place and campaign in which that had occurred—linking the community to a specific time, place and sortie. People's experiences of the war were diverse, their contributions contested, and so too were ideas about how the war and each locale's place in it was remembered.

Other localities were slower to respond, but nevertheless marked local people's participation in the war as a reason to define the district, each with slightly different emphases. Gollan unveiled its own near facsimile of Wongarbon's obelisk in March 1920.[57] In many places throughout Australia at that time, the dilemma was whether to commemorate with a monument or a structure more generally useful.[58] Mogriguy (1924) and Rawsonville (1929) each chose to build a hall memorialising local volunteers and featuring honour

---

55   [Allotment of 1914–1918 War Trophies] Wongarbon, NSW, item 719193, AWM194, Australian War Memorial.
56   Memos, W. A. Oldham to the chief inspector of primary schools, 9 May, 25 May, 1 June, 2 July, 5 August and 10 August 1921, Wongarbon School Administrative File, pre-1939, 5/18176.2, NRS 3829, SARNSW; *DL*, 30 July 1920, 2, 20 May 1921, 2, 7 June 1921, 2; *DD*, 13 May 1921, 1.
57   *DL*, 30 March 1920, 3.
58   Inglis, 'World War One Memorials in Australia', 51–8; Inglis, *Sacred Places*, 131–8.

boards.[59] Thus, they combined a statement of place through the memory of the locality's contribution to the war with a continuing expression of, and means of affirming, the community through a public building (see also Chapter 7).

Commemoration of the war was not always so local. As people became more mobile and the town a larger proportion of the district's population, it became easier to conceive of Dubbo and its hinterland as one. The Dubbo war memorial, unveiled before 4,000 people on the tenth anniversary of the Gallipoli landing, was meant to represent Dubbo *and district*. As such, it is a less intimate monument than those in the surrounding places, far more imposing in scale, being dedicated to 'the fallen' rather than all who enlisted, and with the individuals' names confined to a roll stored within the structure.[60]

In Wongarbon, the memorial had certainly been an exclamation of a place and its location within a broader story of nation, empire and race, but its force was not as sustained as its creators might have hoped. As Dening has observed, the meaning of commemoration changes over time: 'That is the problem of history, of myths, of signs and symbols. They are all in time. They cannot be set in stone or in gold.'[61] The memorial's continuing potency might have been eroded by the fact that several of the names inscribed on it were misspelt or the initial mistaken, indicating that in the rush to lay claim to an impressive quantum of local recruits, the committee had included people with tenuous connections to the place. They included labourers from elsewhere who might never have returned to the village after the war, and without local relatives to correct the record. Also, its force as a symbol of a new, unifying local narrative was compromised from the beginning by the fact that, through the years of fervour, grief, dissent and often bitter contest over how one should contribute to the war effort, people had experienced the war in different ways. In smaller communities, those differences were rawer and more personal.[62] As the foundation of a unifying, shared narrative of place, war had its limits. In time, the memorial ceased to be a focus for Anzac Day services. If there were ceremonies held there after 1933, they were not recorded in the local press.

---

59 *DL*, 19 September 1924, 4; *DD*, 1 August 1929, 1.
60 *DL*, 28 April 1925, 4; *DD*, 28 April 1925, 2.
61 Greg Dening, 'Anzac Day: An Ethnographic Reflection after Reading Bruce Kapferer', *Social Analysis: The International Journal of Anthropology*, no. 20 (1990): 62.
62 McKernan, *Australians at Home*, 178.

Aboriginal people and settler historical consciousness in the Dubbo district

In 1882, Edwin Newbold Blacket, auctioneer, land agent, railway enthusiast and amateur artist, produced a delicate and detailed drawing of a Dubbo scene (see Figure 8.4). A woman and child sit beside a small garden rotunda. A church roof and spire are visible beyond a high, tidy fence. It is a picture of domestic orderliness and tranquillity, balanced on the left, within the garden, by a large tree, probably a eucalypt. New growth sprouts from its base, but the tree is dead. Its trunk is adorned with extensive and ornate carving, rendered in detail by the artist, but the meaning of those scars to their Wiradjuri creators is most likely entirely unknown to the newcomers.[63]

Years later, in 1916, an anonymous writer in the *Dubbo Dispatch* admitted to using some licence in describing the Dulhunty brothers' arrival in the 1830s at the place that became Dubbo. The author imagined the season (placing them there in spring), the landscape and even the newcomers' response to what they found (it was 'inspiring and animating'), but such musings did not extend to including Wiradjuri people in the story. The writer pictured the settlers experiencing 'a life in which old Pan was the only but cheery companion':

> The lowing of their cattle was heard in the bush lands, or the birds twittered in the budding shrubs, and fleecy clouds moved across the sky, while the waters of the Macquarie scintillated in the brilliant day, as the ripples and rills gurgled and crooned and purled over the gravelly beds. The voice of Nature was heard by these intrepid men of the back woods. They came to stay in the West, and 'far from the madding crowd'.[64]

Another article from 1921 asserted that:

> trackless spaces that had long been pining for the civilising influence of the white man, became sheep and cattle walks, while the ring of the settlers' axe was heard in the woods.

63 *DL*, 1 August 1908, 4.
64 *DD*, 5 May 1916, 3.

Figure 8.4: Edwin Newbold Blacket sketch, Dubbo, c. 1882.
Source: Local Studies Collection, Dubbo Regional Council.

Settler colonists were always aware that Aboriginal people had lived on that land for more years than the newcomers could know. However, they struggled to incorporate the fact of dispossession, and of Aboriginal people's continuing presence and claims, in their own historical narrative—their story so far, in that place. Blacket found a way to acknowledge, but also to graphically absorb and supersede First Nations people's presence, assigning it to memory and artefact. The *Dubbo Dispatch* writers in 1916 and 1922 indulged in an extreme, almost wilful, arcadian fantasy, imagining away First Nations people through silence. Still, the silence was not complete. Evidence can be teased out, in historical accounts and in various local performances, to reveal settler Australians' constructions of Aboriginal people's place in the district's history, and what that indicates in turn about the colonisers' conceptions of themselves.[65]

This section examines the ways in which text and performance represented Aboriginal people: as momentary impediments to colonisation; as figures of ridicule; and as primitive, essentially distant and irrelevant 'others'. It explores reactions to murders committed at Breelong in 1900, as a recurring statement of settler Australians' construction of race over the following 50 years. Ultimately, it asks what these silences and narratives said (and say) about the colonisers and their concepts of themselves. First, though, it is instructive to consider the diverse ways Aboriginal people were negotiating their continuing presence over this period.

Aborigines Protection (later Welfare) Board censuses recorded 55 people in the town of Dubbo in 1898, 74 in 1915 and 50 in 1940, but officials are likely to have underestimated the Aboriginal population.[66] Aboriginal people's choices were constrained, certainly, by shrinking employment opportunities arising from the district's transition from pastoralism towards smaller-scale agriculture and mixed farming—an economy less dependent on wage labour—and by governments' escalating attempts from the 1880s to control their lives. But Aboriginal people still found work (see Chapter 1).[67] In 1898, the colonial government gazetted a reserve of 19 acres at the

65   *DD*, 20 May 1921, 6; Tom Griffiths, 'The Frontier Fallen', *Eureka Street*, March 2003, 25; Chris Healy, *Forgetting Aborigines* (Sydney: University of New South Wales Press, 2008), 11.
66   New South Wales, Aborigines Protection Board, *Aborigines (Report of Board 1898)*, in *Votes and Proceedings of the Legislative Assembly*, vol. V, 1899 (Sydney: Government Printer, 1900), 4; New South Wales, Aborigines Welfare Board, *Aborigines Welfare Board (Report for the Year ended 30th June 1940)*, in *Joint Volumes of Papers Presented to Both Houses, 1941–42*, vol. I (Sydney: Government Printer, 1942), 5.
67   New South Wales, Aborigines Protection Board, *Protection of the Aborigines (Report of the Board for 1891)*, in *Votes and Proceedings of the Legislative Assembly*, vol. VII, 1892–93 (Sydney: Government Printer, 1893), 301.

junction of the Talbragar and Macquarie rivers, north of Dubbo, amid a general policy across the state to put Aboriginal people at a distance from towns and villages, while ensuring that they remained available as a labour source. When a camp of Aboriginal people at Murrumbidgerie was 'broken up' in 1906, some of the residents moved onto the Talbragar Reserve. In 1910, young Aboriginal women were in demand as domestic servants in the town. Into the 1940s, Aboriginal people also found contract work on the bigger properties north-west of Dubbo.[68]

Many local Indigenous people appear to have chosen not to live on the reserve, though records are sparse and mostly reveal only people who came into contact with the courts. They lived in camps on the riverbank, along with itinerant and indigent non-Aboriginal people. In 1899, an Aboriginal woman by the name of Louise Hunter was charged with being 'an idle and disorderly person' and was accused of prostitution. Though she had no fixed place of abode, she refused to live with 'the general body' of Aboriginal people receiving rations from the board. An unknown number in the surrounding districts made a life as part of predominantly European Australian communities, including Sarah Knight, daughter of an Aboriginal mother from Mudgee, who married a non-Aboriginal man and farmed at Lincoln near Wellington, as Sarah Collins, until her death in 1919.[69]

Aboriginal people sustained and adapted their culture as well. In 1891, 300 or 400 people turned up to see a 'corroboree' on a river flat by the town, where the performers controlled the event, sending a hat around the audience, adjusting the energy of their performance in proportion to the generosity of the donors on each pass.[70] Sometimes Aboriginal people were politically vocal, asserting a narrative of dispossession and unceded sovereignty, such as the man at Wellington railway station in 1882 who, when someone complained that Aboriginal people received free rail passes,

---

68 *NSW Government Gazette*, no. 956 (supplement), 5 November 1898, 8750; Peter Kabaila, *Survival Legacies: Stories from Aboriginal Settlements of Southeastern Australia* (Canberra: Canprint Publishing, 2011), 167; Peter Rimas Kabaila, *Wiradjuri Places: The Macquarie River Basin and Some Places Revisited* (Jamison: Black Mountain Projects, 1998), 50–9; *Bush Brother* 3, no. 2, February 1907, 23; *DL*, 14 September 1910, 2, 17 September 1910, 4; J. K. Scott, 'Merinong', in *A Compiled History of Coboco District*, ed. Pat Fisher, Robyn Healey and Sandra Burns (Narromine: Coboco CWA, 2002), 72; D. N. McLean, 'Wallawallah', in *A Compiled History of Coboco District*, ed. Pat Fisher, Robyn Healey and Sandra Burns (Narromine: Coboco CWA, 2002), 90.
69 *National Advocate*, 30 January 1903, 3; *SMH*, 8 December 1925, 11; *DL*, 11 February 1941, 4, 26 May 1942, 4; *DL*, 16 December 1899, 5; Kabaila, *Survival Legacies*, 166–76; *Mudgee Guardian and North-Western Representative*, 30 October 1919, 17; Australian Institute of Aboriginal and Torres Strait Islander Studies, 'Diana Mudgee', accessed 25 March 2024, aiatsis.gov.au/diana-mudgee.
70 *Maitland Mercury and Hunter River General Advertiser*, 26 September 1891, 4.

reportedly replied: 'All, all my country! You nobody!' In 1920, an unnamed Aboriginal man appeared on the back of a lorry about to serve as a platform for Progressive and Nationalist party candidates campaigning for the forthcoming state election. On behalf of 'his countrymen', he 'inveighed against those who robbed them of their country without compensation'. They engaged with state politics: residents of the Talbragar Reserve attended an Australian Labor Party (ALP) meeting in Dubbo at which the premier, Jack Lang, spoke in 1931.[71] This diversity of experience and forms of resilience and protest contrasted starkly with the places that settler Australian texts and performances assigned to Aboriginal people in the district's past.

Returning to the accounts of early European occupation of the district, those who acknowledged Aboriginal people's presence portrayed them as one of a number of inconvenient and expensive impediments to progress. A 1911 article on early pastoralists noted:

> these men who opened up the country, fought fever and blacks, and made it possible for us to make homes on the land which they had conquered with the loss of their health and lives.

A 1918 article prompted by that year's show was in a similar vein, depicting Europeans as both victims and victors:

> The pioneers had to be continually on guard ... in constant dread of unprovoked attack by the implacable aborigines ... [I]n spite of every opposing force settlement spread and gradually the whole country was brought under pastoral occupation.[72]

Though these accounts acknowledge their assertive presence, they do not recognise that Aboriginal people might have had a legitimate grievance. Instead, their resistance is represented as irrational hostility or 'savagery'.[73]

There were at least hints that the place had a violent history, even if the dominant narratives have Aboriginal people as either invisible or a transient and irrational hindrance to Europeans' occupation. As Amanda Nettelbeck and Robert Foster observe, the 'great Australian silence' concerning Aboriginal people's presence, and interracial violence, was often more likely

---

71   *ATCJ*, 16 September 1882, 39; *DL*, 16 March 1920, 5, 10 December 1931, 6.
72   *DD*, 5 August 1911, 4; *DL*, 14 May 1915, 3.
73   Robert Foster, Rick Hosking and Amanda Nettelbeck, *Fatal Collisions: The South Australian Frontier and the Violence of Memory* (Kent Town: Wakefield Press, 2001), 7.

to be broken in local oral and written histories than in larger narratives.[74] One rare account appeared in the 1904 series of articles on the district's history, written by 'an old inhabitant'. Most of the articles describe the early history of the town, and stories of squatters, bushrangers and other outlaws, but one in particular gives a frank account of frontier violence:

> In order to be prepared for an attack by the blacks, due precaution was taken in the erection of the huts on clear ground, making loopholes on all sides of the hut, so that under cover the inmates might, and did, defend themselves. It frequently happened during the absence of the stockman and hutkeeper, raids were made on the huts and rations stolen. In one instance the hutkeeper (Walters), anticipating an attack, left the hut to their mercy, but before doing so he emptied a bottle of strychnine into the bag. I leave my readers to contemplate the result. Men, women, and children were poisoned by this inhuman wretch.[75]

There is no indication of where the incident occurred, but it suggests that in the early twentieth century, people were aware that the country they occupied had witnessed violent dispossession, even if it was not widely propagated as part of most public storytelling.

Another local story hints at a more complex and confrontational past. On face value, it conforms to one of the standard narratives, rehearsing the story of the settlement of the west by 'the early pioneers' and paying tribute to the 'indomitable pluck and enterprise by which they penetrated into the unknown wilds'. It tells how, on Bunglegumbie station in the 1830s, near present-day Dubbo, through the 'courage and commanding influence' of the squatter Moore Campbell, 'the large number of aboriginals were subdued, and kept docile without cruelty or inhumanity':

> On one occasion when the blacks were getting troublesome, he appeared suddenly in Highland costume, and by a well-timed solo on the bagpipes sent them scattering in all directions, and never had any trouble with them.[76]

---

74 Amanda Nettelbeck and Robert Foster, 'Commemorating Foundation: A Study in Regional Historical Memory', *History Australia* 7, no. 3 (2010): 53.3.

75 *DL*, 19 March 1904, 6.

76 *DL*, 4 January 1918, 2.

The strong implication is that this was an exceptional incident in a place where the suppression of Aboriginal resistance was more often cruel and inhumane. The tale is also so improbable that it allows for an interpretation that displacement is at play: that Campbell's weapon of choice might not have been the bagpipes at all.

There *were* recorded instances of interracial violence—of massacres of Aboriginal people—that had the potential to be incorporated into social memory in the 1840s, though they occurred north-west of present-day Dubbo and probably no nearer than Mount Hopeless beyond what became the town of Nyngan on the Bogan River, around 200 kilometres distant. There, in 1841, three European stockmen were killed after the cattle in their care had deprived local Aboriginal people of their waterholes. In revenge, at least 12 Ngiyampaa people were indiscriminately killed. That event became part of Nyngan's public memory, though in an inverted form in which an inflated number of Europeans died, while reference to Aboriginal deaths was erased entirely.[77] It does not appear, even in its corrupted form, in popular accounts of Dubbo's history, perhaps being sufficiently removed in time and place to be ignored or discounted. In any event, there were towns formed nearer the incidents to mythologise it as part of *their* local folklore.

When Aboriginal people were acknowledged to be a part of the district's past and present, the purpose was often to provide a contrast that brought into sharper relief the colonisers' 'progress'. The narrative required that the people they were trying to usurp were inferior: less worthy of being in that place and incapable of understanding or embracing the westerners' idea of civilisation. A report on the 1912 show included the observation that:

> the Dubbo of today is no more like the village which then existed [at the time of the first show] than is the modern villa to the aboriginal's bark humpy.[78]

As the twentieth century unfolded, the positioning of Aboriginal people as a counterpoint to white 'civilised' society was often achieved through casually dismissive ridicule. In 1935, the Rural Bank produced a series of audio recordings commemorating the histories of towns where the bank

---

77 Cameron Muir, *The Broken Promise of Agricultural Progress: An Environmental History* (Oxford: Routledge, 2014), 10–22. The University of Newcastle's Colonial Frontier Massacres in Australia, 1788–1930, project records two other massacres in the same general area: at Mount Foster in September 1845 and on the Bogan River in August 1846. See 'Colonial Frontier Massacres, Australia, 1788 to 1930', accessed 25 March 2024, c21ch.newcastle.edu.au/colonialmassacres/map.php.

78 *DL*, 3 May 1912, 2.

had opened branches. The episode on Dubbo features a dramatisation, without any evident archival foundation, including the character of an early squatter in the district saying 'the blacks are either cowering away in fear of us or just running, panic-stricken'.[79] The recording included an Aboriginal man being astonished at the first train to arrive in Dubbo, perplexed that it was not pulled by horses.

Representations of Aboriginal people as pejorative racial stereotypes within European Australians' local performances were a staple of popular culture. In 1906, a boy appeared as 'Toby the Aboriginal' in a fancy dress event staged by the Bodangora PLL branch.[80] A 'comic and fancy dress procession' in Geurie to raise funds for the war effort in 1918 included two men dressed as 'Aboriginal and Lubra' and others as 'Coon' and 'Lubra'. The report noted, matter-of-factly, that the 'procession caused much merriment, especially among the small fry'. In 1925, a dance at Mogriguy to raise funds for the Sydney Children's Hospital included a children's fancy dress parade, with one boy dressed as 'lubra Kate', after a brand of motor oil. In 1937, a man dressed as 'Katie, Queen of Aboriginal Alley' won the prize for 'Most Comical Woman' at the Eumungerie CWA's fancy dress ball. The fact that in every case the performers were males strengthens the impression that these crude stereotypes were meant to convey otherness and inferiority, the performer and character separated by gender as well as race.[81] This casual objectification of Aboriginal people and their culture was not so much a silence as an entrenched ambient din.

Performances by Aboriginal people themselves were included in the Back to Dubbo celebrations of 1935, but on highly prescribed terms that illustrate the limited ways Aboriginality could be expressed in contexts controlled by whites. They performed at the instigation of local labourer and ALP member William Ferguson, who was born on the Warangesda mission near Darlington Point on the Murrumbidgee in 1882. This son of a Scottish-born shearer and boundary rider, and an Aboriginal former housemaid, worked in shearing sheds around the Riverina before moving to Gulargambone, north of Gilgandra, in 1916. There he continued to work in the sheds as well as labouring and delivering mail, and was prominent

79   National Film and Sound Archive of Australia, 'The Grand Parade, Episode 26, Dubbo', no. 415949, Macquarie Broadcasting Services for the Rural Bank, c. 1935.
80   *WT*, 30 May 1907, 5.
81   *DL*, 18 October 1918, 5, 11 September 1925, 7; *Gilgandra Weekly and Castlereagh*, 1 July 1937, 1; Liz Conor, 'The "Lubra" Type in Australian Imaginings of the Aboriginal Woman from 1836–1973', *Gender and History* 25, no. 2 (2013): 238.

in local ALP affairs. In 1933, he and his family settled in Dubbo. Ferguson identified strongly as Aboriginal and was one of the pre-eminent advocates for citizenship, working with John Patten, Pearl Gibbs, William Cooper and Doug Nicholls. He formed the Aborigines Progressive Association in Dubbo in 1937 and managed its development into a statewide body advocating for the abolition of the Aborigines Protection Board (APB) and the extension of full citizenship status to Indigenous people.[82]

From 1934 until at least 1937, Ferguson sponsored what appear to have been relatively dynamic performances by Aboriginal people that included dancing, music and fire-lighting demonstrations, but he left few clues about his motives.[83] As someone with both European and Aboriginal heritage, he appears to have moved readily within a predominantly white, working-class world. He was never subject to the APB's control, but the board's draconian, arbitrary and incompetent actions would increasingly animate his activism. As unemployed workers gravitated towards Dubbo during the Depression, he saw first-hand that Aboriginal people were receiving lower levels of welfare relief than white workers. The performances, though, suggest that Ferguson's urge to advocate for citizenship rights might have been complemented by ideas of Aboriginal people deserving recognition and rights not just as citizens, but also as the First Australians. We know that Ferguson was aware of Fred Maynard's Australian Aboriginal Progressive Association and its assertion of the value of traditional civilisation. So, at that particular moment in the evolution of his thinking, we might suppose he was concerned to assert an innate Indigenous worth, and a place for Aboriginal people in Australian history and culture in their own right, rather than as mere context for a Eurocentric story.[84]

But whatever Ferguson was hoping to achieve, in Dubbo, and in 1935, he is likely to have been quite constrained in the type of performance that the other organisers would countenance. As part of Melbourne's 1934 centenary parade, he had organised a group—in the language of the time—of 'full-blood' Aboriginal people to appear on a float (they won the 'best

---

82   *SMH*, 1 July 1937; Jack Horner, *Vote Ferguson for Aboriginal Freedom* (Sydney: Australian and New Zealand Book Company, 1974), throughout; John Maynard, 'Fred Maynard and the Australian Aboriginal Progressive Association (AAPA): One God, One Aim, One Destiny', *Aboriginal History* 21 (1997): 1–13; Jack Horner, 'Aborigines and the Sesquicentenary: The Day of Mourning', *Australia 1938: A Bicentennial History Bulletin*, no. 3 (1980): 44–51.

83   *DL*, 6 January 1937, 6; *WT*, 11 January 1937, 3.

84   John Maynard, *Fight for Liberty and Freedom: The Origins of Australian Aboriginal Activism* (Canberra: Aboriginal Studies Press, 2007), 5; Horner, *Vote Ferguson for Aboriginal Freedom*, 27.

historic entry' award for 'a magnificent and realistic bush scene, with four aborigines').[85] Had Ferguson not pursued the 1935 Back to Dubbo Week committee to secure performances for his group, it is unlikely that the week would have included Aboriginal people at all: they were generally excluded from such celebrations.[86] The committee arranged for Ferguson to have the use of a lorry to bring the participants to Dubbo, but the report was silent on who the performers were or where they were from, only stating that they were not local. As individuals, they were never named.

More generally, performances staged for non-Aboriginal audiences were used assertively by Aboriginal people for a number of purposes, including, in Anna Haebich's words, 'to express their humanity to doubting colonists and to openly celebrate their sovereignty and identity'. However, in this case, the performers' motives were never disclosed, and probably never sought.[87] A list in a local newspaper of the floats to be included in the parade stressed that Ferguson's was to consist of 'full-bloods only'.[88] The newspaper also published a photograph of two of the group, with headpieces and painted bodies, confronting each other and brandishing boomerangs: 'one of the "encounters" in the aboriginal corroboree and pageant, to be staged at Back to Dubbo Week'.[89] Either journalists were incurious, or the performers' anonymity was an integral part of the unspoken terms of their participation.

But why were these particular depictions of Aboriginality entertained at this event, and what does it say about the ways European Australians located Aboriginal people in history? Maryrose Casey offers an interpretation of the type of scenario that unfolded in the celebrations in her argument that Aboriginal performance was constrained by an 'economy of authenticity', whereby performances were only credited with being authentic if they were distant in time and place, and anonymous, without engagement between performer and audience: 'savage and absent, something from the past, temporally and spatially distant'. This also denied validity to Aboriginal people who lived in proximity to white people.[90] Similarly, Lynette Russell argues that Aboriginal people were commonly depicted as unchanging,

---

85 *Herald* (Melbourne), 26 October 1934, 1; *Gilgandra Weekly and Castlereagh*, 24 January 1935, 15.
86 Helen Wendy Doyle, 'Australia Infelix: Making History in an Unsettled Country' (PhD thesis, Monash University, 2005), 253.
87 Anna Haebich, *Dancing in Shadows: Histories of Nyungar Performance* (Crawley: UWA Publishing, 2018), 67.
88 *DL*, 19 September 1935, 6, 31 October 1935, 6.
89 *DL*, 24 October 1935, 6.
90 Maryrose Casey, 'Colonisation, Notions of Authenticity and Aboriginal Australian Performance', *Critical Race and Whiteness Studies* 8 (2012): 1–18. See also Haebich, *Dancing in Shadows*, 71.

occupying no specific time or place, and therefore having no history: what she terms the 'homogeneity paradigm'. In this form, Aboriginal people were represented as playing no part in the dominant narrative of Western civilisation and progress, as relics of another time. A corollary of this depiction of 'full-blood' people as the distant but only truly authentic Indigenous people is that the majority of Aboriginal people from nearer the town who were of mixed heritage were denied authenticity.[91]

In that context, Ferguson's float took its place alongside fire engines, scout troops, marching bands, 'Queen of Dubbo' contestants and the Buninyong Agricultural Bureau's display of local produce. At the rear was a late entrant: a bullock team and wagon laden with wheat entered by the Baird family, 'descendants of one of the first pioneers', proceeding 'on the track blazed so long ago by the first agriculturalists of the district'. The same report again emphasised that Ferguson's float consisted of 'full-blooded aborigines' with 'dark-hued bodies', standing before a 'gunyah' and carrying spears.[92] Static and silent, abstracted and anonymous, as though museum exhibits, they could be viewed as utterly dissociated from national and local history.

That evening the group was included in a performance at the showground with some pretence of being historical that further illustrated how European Australians located Aboriginal people in local folklore. As a prelude, the bullock wagon entered the arena and 'paraded the ground', this time depicting the arrival of the explorer and surveyor John Oxley's party in the district in 1818, and setting up camp around a blazing fire that lit the night. The Aboriginal troupe then emerged to perform what the newspaper described dismissively as 'two weird corroborees' before dispersing passively into the dark, leaving Oxley's party as the pageant's final image.[93] On a superficial level, the performance was an advance on the abstracted, ahistorical representation of Aboriginality in the parade, in that it acknowledged Aboriginal people's presence at the time of Europeans' incursion: Aboriginal and European people cohabited the arena. However, the fact that the pageant began with the wagon's entry allowed the myth that Europeans arrived into an empty landscape; they controlled—indeed, through fire, created—the visible space before the Aboriginal performers

91   Lynette Russell, *Savage Imaginings: Historical and Contemporary Constructions of Australian Aboriginalities* (Melbourne: Australian Scholarly Publishing, 2001), 3–14; Henry Reynolds, *Nowhere People: How International Race Thinking Shaped Australia's Identity* (Camberwell: Viking, 2005), 3–14.
92   *DL*, 5 December 1935, 1.
93   *DL*, 7 December 1935, 7.

emerged, and then remained after the performers simply vanished without cause or provocation as though remnants of a doomed people melting away in the face of British civilisation.

Ferguson's group's participation in the December events appears to have been a rushed but considered plan. It was known as early as September; in late November, advertisements alerted audiences that an 'Aboriginal corroboree and boomerang throwing' event, and, separately, an 'Aboriginal pageant' would follow the sports event.[94] There was no reference to the bullock wagon until the report on the parade, which suggests that it may have been a last-minute innovation, effectively wrapping the Aboriginal performance in a vernacular and local foundation story. Thus, Ferguson might have achieved a purpose of reinserting Aboriginal people within representations of local history, and on terms that did not involve overt ridicule. But it was nevertheless constrained in ways that either distanced Aboriginal people from history or placed them in a subordinate position. And, paradoxically, given Ferguson's own heritage, it also tacitly delegitimised those of mixed heritage living in the vicinity of the town.

Breelong

The various ways that European Australians constructed Aboriginal people's place in Australia's past and present were vividly on display in reportage surrounding what became the pre-eminent historical story involving Aboriginal people sustained in the Dubbo district through the first half of the twentieth century. It involved the murder of five members of a settler household on a property at Breelong in July 1900. Brothers Jimmy and Joe Governor evaded police and civilian pursuers for three months, in which time they killed another three people, before Jimmy was captured, and Joe was shot dead near Singleton. A third man, Jackie Underwood, had been arrested near Elong within days of the murders. He was summarily tried, found guilty and executed in Dubbo. Jimmy Governor met the same fate later in Sydney. The essential elements of the story are that the Governors had both Aboriginal and European heritage; Jimmy was working for the Mawbey family cutting fence posts; and his white wife worked in the Mawbey household where, according to several accounts, she was taunted

---

94   *DL*, 30 November 1935, 7.

for having married an Aboriginal man and borne a child with him.[95] These events have been examined extensively by historians, generally as evidence of the nature of racism and the relationship between colonisers and Indigenous peoples. They have also become national cultural property through Thomas Keneally's 1972 novel *The Chant of Jimmie Blacksmith* and the subsequent (1978) Fred Schepisi film. But they were already embedded in local history as the emblematic social memory of race relations among European Australians in the district.[96] The question here is, how did the reportage and public remembering of this episode harden European Australians' constructions of Aboriginal people in general as alien?

News of the murders spread quickly. Households on isolated farms retreated to villages for protection in places as far away as Wongarbon, some 90 kilometres from Breelong. Even people in the town of Dubbo felt threatened:

> The capture and trial of the notorious Breelong Blacks has had the effect of restoring Dubboites to a feeling of security. A few weeks ago every door was securely barricaded, and every sleeper was armed with pistols, cudgels or some other formidable weapon of defence.[97]

Reportage repeatedly emphasised the fugitives' Aboriginality, their most common epithet being the 'Breelong blacks'. This was not just a fixation of newspaper writers. A teacher at a small, isolated school explained to her inspector that children would not be attending because of the risk of encountering the fugitive 'black murderers', also referring to them as 'those aboriginals'.[98] The murders were widely considered to be evidence of an innate, instinctual irrationality and violent disposition. This pervasive emphasis on the fugitives' Aboriginality was also evident in reports that referred to the groups of pursuers as 'whites'. An article described a

---

95   Laurie Moore and Stephen Williams, *The True Story of Jimmy Governor* (Crows Nest: Allen & Unwin, 2001). Governor's name was recorded as James on his marriage certificate, but he signed himself 'Jimmy', so that is how I refer to him.

96   Meg Foster, 'The Forgotten War of Jimmy Governor and the Aboriginal People of Wollar', *Australian Historical Studies* 50, no. 3 (2019): 305–20; Katherine Biber, 'Besieged at Home: Jimmy Governor's Rampage', *Public Space: The Journal of Law and Social Justice* 2 (2008): 1–41; Marilyn Wood, 'The "Breelong Blacks"', in *Race Matters: Indigenous Australians and 'Our' Society*, ed. Gillian Cowlishaw and Barry Morris (Canberra: Aboriginal Studies Press, 1997), 97–120; Meg Foster, 'Murder for White Consumption? Jimmy Governor and the Bush Ballad', in *Archiving Settler Colonialism: Culture, Space and Race*, ed. Yu-ting Huang and Rebecca Weaver-Hightower (London: Routledge, 2018), 173–89.

97   *DL*, 25 August 1900, 2; *Molong Argus*, 7 December 1900, 3.

98   Teacher to the district inspector, 30 July 1900, Dapper School Administrative File, 5/15644.3, NRS 3829, SARNSW; Meg Foster, *Boundary Crossers: The Hidden History of Australia's Other Bushrangers* (Sydney: NewSouth Publishing, 2022), 155.

confrontation during the pursuit thus: 'the blacks ... had rifles, while the whites had only an old double-barrel gun', and another: 'The blacks then fired upon the advancing whites.'[99] The implication was that everything they, as Aboriginal men, were seen to stand for—irrationality, violence, unpredictability, untrustworthiness, primitivism—was the antithesis of their pursuers, and European Australians generally. Other reports emphasised the Governors' mixed heritage, which was interpreted pejoratively as rendering them less civilised than whites and drawn to savage behaviour. One report pondered:

> Whether the murder was premeditated, or whether the outrage was due to one of those customary relapses into savagery, peculiar to the partly-civilised black, which forced them to deeds of outrage on 'White Mary', can only be conjectured.[100]

They speculated that 'impure' lineage was the cause: 'Civilisation has deteriorated rather than improved their original nature ... they had engrafted on their primitive instincts some of the worst passions of the white man.'[101]

The events of 1900 echoed in local public memory for years, assuming a significance well beyond the families who were directly and tragically affected. The Breelong murders were cast as a stain on all Aboriginal people. Several times, Indigenous men appearing before judges and magistrates in the Central West were enjoined not to follow in the Governors' footsteps. In 1902, an Aboriginal man in Dubbo was sentenced to a term of five years for inflicting grievous bodily harm, the judge remarking that if he 'attempted to imitate Jimmy Governor's crime he must expect a heavy sentence'; and at Trangie, police placed an Aboriginal man, charged with robbery and assault, in leg-irons, interpreted by one newspaper report as 'evidently treating him as one of the Governor class'.[102]

Public memory was regularly refreshed through newspaper articles, prompted by anniversaries of the events, or by the retirements or deaths of people associated with them. Into the 1940s, obituaries of people with any connection, however tenuous, referred to their association with the episode, implying that it was one of the defining aspects of their lives, and that a whole (white) community was allied through connections either to

---

99 *DD*, 4 August 1900, 4; *Scone Advocate*, 7 September 1900, 5.
100 *Truth*, 22 July 1900, 3. 'White Mary' appears to have been a term European Australians attributed to Aboriginal vernacular, meaning a non-Aboriginal women.
101 *Sunday Times*, 20 January 1901, 6.
102 *DL*, 1 February 1902, 2, 21 June 1902, 2. See also Foster, *Boundary Crossers*, 147.

victims or to the hundreds of pursuers. They included survivors, but also the victims' relatives, the wife of a police officer involved in the pursuit, and a nurse who had attended to the victims. Twenty-seven years after the murders, an advertisement for a touring wax works exhibition in Dubbo encouraged people to see 'the life-like representations of famous Australian characters, including The Breelong Blacks'. The lingering presence in public (white) memory suggests that the episode served to regularly reassert the positioning of Aboriginal people outside the boundaries of European Australian society.[103]

In short, the constant retelling of the tragic events at Breelong in 1900 was one of the most distinctive aspects of local public memory in the district. The incident struck a jarring chord and, while it lingered in living memory, reinforced a deep sense of separateness from, and superiority to, Aboriginal people. In other regards, Indigenous people appear not to have been accorded as conspicuous a place in white people's historical consciousness in the Dubbo district as elsewhere across rural New South Wales. In newspaper accounts of the district's past, though there were isolated hints of awareness of a violent dispossession, generally the Aboriginal population was treated variously as absent, comically primitive or irrationally violent. The sense of Aboriginal people's 'otherness' hardened in the 1930s as the Depression, reductions in paid labour on the land and policies of the APB forced people into the towns. By then, there were two essential stereotypes applied by European Australians to Aboriginal people: anonymous, timeless and place-less, inhabiting an imagined pre-contact world; or, in Russell's words, a 'degraded and diluted hybrid'.[104] In either form, these representations served as antitheses of white Australians' constructions of themselves and their history.

Continuity and change: Local historical consciousness by 1949

In December 1949, the centenary of Dubbo's gazettal as a village again encouraged people to fashion and perform a local history. It is in the nature of such commemorative landmarks to invite contrast between then and

---

103 *DD*, 20 May 1924, 2, 12 October 1931, 3; *Gilgandra Weekly and Castlereagh*, 11 February 1932, 2; *DL*, 3 June 1927, 6, 25 March 1943, 4; Betty Bartley, comp., *The Mawbey Murder Papers* ([Dubbo: n.d.]).
104 Russell, *Savage Imaginings*, 14.

now, old and new, aspiration and fulfilment. Compared to 1935, for most of the settler population at least, it was a more optimistic time. War was over, the rural economy was in better shape, and consumer goods were more available and conspicuous in the shops and catalogues. In that very month, a rejuvenated conservative Liberal–Country Party government came to office in Canberra, with the promise to finally end petrol rationing.

Dubbo's Anzac Day ceremony earlier that year, at its imposing cenotaph, was reported to be 'the most impressive … seen for some years'.[105] With another global conflict only recently past, war continued to be a significant part of local remembering, but was not so central to historical narratives in small communities as it had been 30 years earlier. As many people enlisted from Wongarbon in World War II as in World War I but it was commemorated differently. Returning servicemen were welcomed home at a ceremony in the local hall in September 1946, where they each (or a relative on their behalf) received an ornately illustrated testimonial and a wallet of bank notes.[106] But only the names of the four who had died were inscribed on a small plaque, which was attached to the 1919 memorial without an epitaph: only mentioning that they were 'killed'. As compared to World War I, not everyone who served overseas was a volunteer, and on the home front the distinction between civilians and soldiers was blurred as more people were involved in wartime production, and many service personnel—both men and women—never left the country. But it is also likely to have signified that the conflict had a different meaning: that both the nation and the locale (along with so many others) had had its foundational moment in the earlier conflict. There could only ever be one, and everything else was an addendum.[107]

The district's Aboriginal past and present were almost completely absent from the December celebrations. Bill Ferguson was just as active in advocating for Aboriginal people's rights; however, by 1949, he was so disillusioned with even his own party's inertia that he ran as an independent for the seat of Lawson in the federal election. He received 1 per cent of the vote and died weeks later at the age of 60.[108] When the Bulgandramine reserve near Peak Hill (Wiradjuri Country) closed earlier in the decade, people moved to Dubbo, but the council, the police and the APB attempted to exclude them.

---

105 *DL*, 26 April 1949, 1.
106 *DL*, 26 September 1946, 6.
107 Inglis, *Sacred Places*, 332, 345.
108 *DL*, 22 December 1949, 1; *WT*, 12 January 1950, 8; Horner, *Vote Ferguson for Aboriginal Freedom*, 155–69.

Amendments to the *Aborigines Protection Act* in 1940, which Peter Read identifies as the zenith of legalised repression in the state, made it easier for the authorities to do so.[109]

Four articles on Dubbo's history published in a local newspaper to mark the centenary contained no references to Wiradjuri owners. A speech delivered by the deputy Labor premier, Joe Cahill, at an official council function, related the sequence of pastoral and then agricultural incursions into the district, but referred to Aboriginal people only by selectively quoting Oxley's description of 'the virgin land', and particularly his observation that: 'We have yet seen no inhabitants and very few signs that the country was inhabited at all.' It served only to reinforce a version of the place's history that had Aboriginal people melting away in the face of the intruders. The one reference to Indigenous people in the climactic parade, on a council float displaying the boon of gas cooking, reverted to treating First Nations people as objects of ridicule and the antithesis of Western society:

> Two girls … attired in immaculate white dresses and standing next to gleaming modern stoves, contrasted with a white-bearded aborigine, who squatted among the branches next to a smouldering stick fire—with a badly scorched rabbit for company.

Whether European Australians were performing their history or their modernity, their persistent and demeaning representation of Aboriginal people and culture demonstrated the trope's centrality to white people's constructions of themselves and their progress.[110]

Veneration of the still anonymous 'early pioneers', so pronounced earlier in the century, was revived during Dubbo's centenary as the premier unveiled a plaque in their honour, but it is unclear who it was intended to communicate with, being discreetly installed in a hallway of the council chambers.[111] Dubbo was to receive its own official history, commissioned by the council from the prolific Sydney-based local historian James Jervis. It is unlikely to have been a local initiative, but rather pressed on the council by the MLA Joseph Jackson who had grown up in the Wellington and Dubbo districts. Jervis also published four articles in the *Liberal*, dealing with the earliest squatters, the establishment of the town, and a series of first

---

109 Peter Read, *A Hundred Years War: The Wiradjuri People and the State* (Canberra: Australian National University Press, 1988), 85.
110 *DL*, 5 October 1949, 1, 4 October 1949, 1.
111 *DL*, 5 October 1949, 1.

occurrences, from municipal government through to water and sewerage infrastructure. Jervis had a very thorough command of primary sources in the state archive, and though his story had a much firmer basis in evidence than the romanticised fantasy that had passed as history in some previous pieces published in local newspapers, his writing was based on a well-worn formula that treated local history as a project of unerring, harmonious progress.[112]

Reflecting on research conducted in a later period, Anna Clark has concluded that people are less likely to connect to a formal narrative that is independent of their personal histories.[113] If people read Jervis's articles, they might have been impressed that someone considered the district's white settler history to be worthy of being told, but few are likely to have connected with it as their own. What is perhaps most significant, as an indication of the district's interest in its past, was not that the history was commissioned, but that it was received and never published, being most likely a temporary enthusiasm that sat low among the council's priorities before it was forgotten altogether.

The centenary organisers encouraged a more vernacular reflection on Dubbo's history when they gave the parade the theme of 'past and present'. Some entrants responded, but the parts of their displays representing former times were generically 'of the past', serving mainly as an amusing benchmark from which to measure conspicuous progress. A building company's float consisted of an 'old-time bark hut, contrasting with a modern civic centre'. Many of the commercial floats dispensed with the past altogether, simply displaying the latest fashions or products a modern household should contain (see Figure 8.5). One featured a 'modern all-tile bathroom … a setting to delight the heart of any home lover'. Car dealerships paraded the latest models of Fiats and Studebakers, and the new homegrown Holden. There were 10 Singer sports cars in a range of colours, and each:

> carried a number of attractive feminine passengers dressed in various sports attire to suggest that the Singer was an ideal car for the sports—whether he or she favoured golf, swimming [or] tennis.

---

112 *DL*, 7 September 1948, 1, 26 May 1949, 2, 27 September 1949, 2, 28 September 1949, 2, 29 September 1949, 2, 1 October 1949, 2; James Jervis, 'History of Dubbo 1818 to 1949', unpublished manuscript, [1949], Macquarie Regional Library, Dubbo; Philip Geeves, 'In Memoriam—James Jervis', *Journal and Proceedings of the Royal Australian Historical Society* 49, part 1 (1963): 74–8.
113 Clark, *Private Lives Public History*, 40.

Figure 8.5: Dubbo's Centenary Parade, Macquarie Street, October 1949.
Source: Local Studies Collection, Dubbo Regional Council.

The Dubbo FSA branch represented the rural parts of the district, its float featuring a cornucopia from which the farming produce of the district spilled, beneath a banner reading, 'Dubbo, Land of Plenty'.[114] In an atmosphere of lightness and humour, the parade evoked a district grown tired of reflecting on history. By the late 1940s, people appeared to be much more interested in the prospect of an exotic, affluent future than the baggage of a humdrum, local past.

Conclusion

Clearly, conceptions of the past *were* called on, from time to time, to provide context and justification for the present. For the most part, though (the Oxley pageant aside), European Australians did not display a sustained public curiosity about a specifically local past: there was no elevation of, or connection to, individuals or events in a specific time and place. Instead, there were occasional expressions of Hirst's 'pioneer legend'—negating class and conflict, and politically conservative—but with barely discernible

114 *DL*, 4 October 1949, 1.

foundations in communal storytelling of local people and events.[115] There was a firmer attachment to a settler class and country-minded ideology in historical consciousness than there was to the past of any particular place.

Throughout, in this settler trope, Aboriginal people were either excised, denied authenticity and history, or cast as the antithesis—the ultimate 'other'—to the legend. This is a reminder that history writing is itself a performance in which the writer brings preoccupations and questions from the present that shape their interrogation of the past in ways that might have puzzled or offended their subjects. As Dening notes, 'history cannot be divorced from the circumstances of its telling'.[116] War inspired local storytelling and memorialisation; however, as this was based on diverse, sometimes conflicting experiences and responses to war, there were limits to its enduring effect.

The nearest any of the participants in the 1949 centenary parade came to representing something relating, however imprecisely, to the district's past was a bearded man dressed as an 'old time bushman' walking beside a horse-drawn dray in which sat, according to one report, 'Mum and the kids'. There was a lightness to it (it won the humorous section award); more importantly, in its simplicity, its ordinariness and its assignment of gender roles, and by representing a family rather than an individual or some other grouping, it would have been entirely recognisable to many spectators in town for the day. It tacitly referenced the popular *Dad and Dave of Snake Gully* radio series and might have brought to mind the hundreds of farmers' miniature autobiographies appended to the *Australian Men of Mark* series published in 1889–90, with their emphasis on modest and hard-won success.[117] It also could have been a tableau vivant of Edwin King's family going to their new farm 56 years earlier. Perhaps what dominated local historical consciousness were the thousands of such private fragments of memory, inscribed in family Bibles, reprised and embellished at clan gatherings, and tidied in eulogies.

115 J. B. Hirst, 'The Pioneer Legend', *Historical Studies* 18, no. 71 (1978): 316–37.

116 Dening, *Performances*, 50.

117 Charles F. Maxwell, *Australian Men of Mark*, 2 vols (Sydney: Charles F Maxwell, [1889–90]).

Conclusion

Fifty woolgrowers gathered in Dubbo on Friday 22 September 1950 to protest the federal government's plan to place an impost on wool exports. The government had been concerned about the inflationary effects of booming wool prices and export earnings that had been stimulated by the Korean War. The Australian National University's influential and outspoken vice-chancellor, Douglas Copland, a leading economist, had recommended a substantial tax on wool exports in preference to currency appreciation. Though the government announced a modified version of his proposal in the September budget, involving the Taxation Department holding aside a substantial proportion of wool export earnings from which future tax liabilities would be extracted, farmers were unhappy.[1]

Sixty-one-year-old Vic Thorby was in the chair that Friday in Dubbo. By then he had been a decade out of parliament, but continued to serve as honorary secretary of the Wongarbon FSA branch. Recently, as an indication that the distinction between the grazier and the farmer had become blurred, if not completely effaced, Thorby had joined the Dubbo branch of the GA.[2] Albert Mawbey, 59 and president of the Wongarbon FSA branch for the past 30 years, shared the podium with him.[3] The soldier settler had survived the Depression, and over the years had supplemented his wheat earnings by producing a few bales of wool each season. Sheep grazing had long become a staple of farm production, and wool was no longer the preserve of the large pastoralists. These people who made their living by working the land to produce food and fibre had adopted various terms to express a common identity—primary producers, 'the man on the land'—but, echoing the early years of the century, the language of 'class' was resurrected over the issue of a

---

1   *SMH*, 12 September 1950, 4, 30 September 1950, 1, 7 October 1950, 1; *Land*, 6 October 1950, 2.
2   *DL*, 23 September 1950, 1.
3   *DL*, 30 July 1949, 3.

tax on wool exports. The general secretary of the GA described woolgrowers as a class, and the FSA's equivalent regarded the tax proposal as 'class discrimination'.[4]

In this book, I have sought to expand on the historiography of rural New South Wales that has either emphasised the contest over land as the central theme, with the story ceasing by the twentieth century, or interpreted the twentieth-century experience as consisting predominantly of struggle, degradation, decline and nostalgic remembering. I have argued for different emphases, seeking to understand the continuing processes of community formation in farming places by focusing on people's everyday exchanges with creditors, wage labour, government, formal politics and each other. I have considered people's complex interactions with Sydney and with their imagined collective past. What emerges is a tangle of influences—of gender, religious denomination and ethnicity, and of deep imported and adapted cultural traditions. Without denying the complexity of these factors, I have sought to distil the influences of class and place on forming and shaping communities.

What of Patten's 'farming class'? Was it a mere rhetorical flourish or *did* these people constitute a 'class' arising from the common everyday experience of engaging with competing interests through the production process? Had it survived into the 1950s? Who did it consist of, what did they value and had they changed since the late nineteenth century? At the time of the selectors' conferences in the late 1870s, the central relationship beginning to define this group was with established pastoralists with whom they contested ownership of the land. But that contest soon receded and, as landholders more often produced both wheat and wool, the distinctions between the old squatting and selecting classes became muddied. The graziers and the selectors found enough common ground to form and then sustain a successful political party.

For the majority of farmers in this district, relationships with wage labour were a regular but relatively minor aspect of production, and insufficient in themselves to be the basis of a strong sense of class, particularly as many moved back and forth in that liminal space between farmer, sharefarmer and wage labourer. They nonetheless possessed at least one element constituting a class in that they had an increasingly common relationship with the means of production. That is, their principal resource, even if it might often have

---

4   *SMH*, 19 September 1950, 2; *Newcastle Sun*, 30 September 1950, 3; *Land*, 1 December 1950, 8.

been formally in the hands of creditors, was land to which, for the most part but not exclusively, they applied their own labour. But if class consists in relationships involving an imbalance of power, and the experience of competing interests in the context of processes of production, this group's status is less clear. The central relationship through which they sought to increase or retain power was with the government as the essential agent of an agrarian economy and society, whether by legislating compulsory pooling, taxation, tariffs, the acquisition of land and industrial arbitration, or providing public infrastructure. That is, most often this community of broadly common economic interests defined itself in relation to the state as much as against other sectional interests with which it had a direct relationship in the production process.

This persistent project of government to create a rural society of smallholders occupying just enough country to sustain a household mainly with their own labour was interpreted as a compact by those who took up those opportunities, and was used to exert political influence. It was regularly reprised by a sector under constant pressure: farming production and wealth expanded, but the sector formed a shrinking part of the economy and the population. So farmers had a rhetoric of class, as well as one of family, along with the industrial and political institutions to advance their interests.

There *were* differences in class experience within this population, certainly, that were not based on simple gradations of wealth. There was the experience of prospering on one's own farm returns, as compared with that of being obliged to supplement farm income with paid work elsewhere. There was the experience of borrowing capital from commercial lenders so as to expand wealth, as compared with needing government capital simply to hang on. And the old status of a squatter class never quite disappeared, but persisted in some social and industrial associations. All in all, though, when under pressure or confronted with a choice, such as at the ballot box, such distinctions were often subsumed by the shared experience of working and owning the land and being country people.

This class position also manifested in the values and culture of agrarianism, which included a belief in an innate worthiness of working the land and producing food, and of primary production as the ultimate source of all wealth. Work itself was ennobling, not necessarily as a value unique to this farming class, but nevertheless reinforced by the terms on which most people came into possession of the land: as purchases extended on condition that they effected 'improvements'. For capital-poor purchasers, this translated into ringbarking trees, erecting fences, excavating tanks, cultivating land—transforming the landscape with their labour. As Grace Karskens has observed, this work was not only a practical necessity but also 'freighted with enormous imperial and moral implications'.[5] In the case of conditional purchasers, it was their part of the contract with the government, regularly reinforced by the judgements of financiers and their agents, public and private. In return, farmers asserted claims for the latitude to continue even if their labour was insufficient to generate adequate returns. This culture of venerating landholding, cultivation, work and stability also encouraged in the farming class the pervasive practice of caricaturing Aboriginal people and culture as the ultimate 'other'.

Attachment to a pan-rural farming class was both leavened and reinforced through the influence of where people lived—by place. I have argued that local communities of place were fragile in the face of a rapidly changing economic and social geography. Settlement was not a discrete stage in the region's formation as a settler project. Many people and households left either through failure or finding better opportunities elsewhere, and, in any event, under the influence of government land policy and infrastructure investment, new settlements unfolded in waves that extended even into the 1940s. Any stable notion of place was also disrupted throughout by the rapidly changing ways people travelled and communicated. In that environment, it is unremarkable that local historical consciousness consisted most often of individual households' stories of first arrival.

Notwithstanding these challenges, the seeds of communities of place were created, again, in response to government, as people came together to solve a common problem and assert what they argued were entitlements under the terms of the implied compact with the state to realise the agrarian vision. Communities of place were experienced and sustained as social as well as physical spaces, enriched through a shared social life. These were places, after all, of intensive daily experience, where people lived and worked and came together.

In the end, people will identify with one form of community or another in response to changing pressures and circumstances. I do not argue that either class or localism were predominant influences for farming people.

---

5   Grace Karskens, *People of the River: Lost Worlds of Early Australia* (Crows Nest: Allen & Unwin, 2020), 193; James A. Montmarquet, *The Idea of Agrarianism: From Hunter-Gatherer to Agraraian Radical in Western Culture* (Moscow: University of Idaho Press, 1989).

Rather, they were mutually reinforcing in these increasingly homogeneous landscapes. A sense of place arising from easy sociability and familiarity was aided by the fact that the majority of people who were in the same economic circumstances shared a comfortable notion that they occupied a one-class position. At the same time, in their social lives and incidental local gatherings—either casually or as members of wider industrial and political associations—their sense of class was constantly refreshed and reaffirmed.

This study arose from questions posed by a landscape, about the people who had scored it and lived on it over the 80 years to 1950. It sought answers mainly in the archive—the places where those people's voices might be heard and interrogated for clues about who they were, why they were there, who they considered constituted their communities and what that place meant to them. Throughout, it has been clear that they were participating in a bigger project, a state-empowered vision for rural Australia with deep roots in Western and British culture that provided the motivation, moral justification, leverage and the means to shape the landscape in just such a way; indeed, this is one of the constant themes of the book. It is also clear that abstractions such as class, community and agrarianism only have meaning in the everyday—in the routine and commonplace ways people came together and made choices in those places.

Bibliography

Published

Adair, Daryl and Wray Vamplew. *Sport in Australian History*. Melbourne: Oxford University Press, 1997.

Adams, Nancy. 'Forlonge, William (1811–1890)'. *Australian Dictionary of Biography*, National Centre of Biography, The Australian National University. Published first in hardcopy 1966. adb.anu.edu.au/biography/forlonge-william-2054/text2549.

Aitkin, Don. '"Countrymindedness"—The Spread of an Idea'. *Australian Cultural History* 4 (1985): 34–41.

Aitkin, Don. *The Colonel: A Political Biography of Sir Michael Bruxner*. Canberra: Australian National University Press, 1969.

Aitkin, Don. *The Country Party in New South Wales: Membership and Electoral Support*. Australian Political Studies Association, monograph no. 8. Canberra: Australian National University for the Australian Political Studies Association, 1965.

Alderman, Derek H. 'Place, Naming and the Interpretation of Cultural Landscapes'. In *The Ashgate Research Companion to Heritage and Identity*, edited by Brian Graham and Peter Howard, 196–213. London: Routledge, 2008.

Alford, Katrina. 'Colonial Women's Employment as Seen by Nineteenth-Century Statisticians and Twentieth-Century Economic Historians'. *Labour History*, no. 51 (1986): 1–10. www.liverpooluniversitypress.co.uk/doi/10.3828/27508793.

Anderson, Benedict. *Imagined Communities*. London: Verso, 2006. First published 1983.

Arrow, Michelle. '"Everything Stopped for *Blue Hills*": Radio, Memory and Australian Women's Domestic Lives, 1944–2001'. *Australian Feminist Studies* 20, no. 48 (2005): 305–18. doi.org/10.1080/08164640500304322.

Atkinson, Alan. 'Local History: The Next Step'. *Locality* 11, no. 3 (2000): 4–7.

Atkinson, Alan. 'Postage in the South-East'. *The Push from the Bush; A Bulletin of Social History: Devoted to the Year of Grace, 1838*, no. 5 (1979): 19–28.

Australia. Department of Commerce. Royal Commission on Australian Wheat Industry. *Evidence Submitted by Mr E. McCarthy on Behalf of the Department of Commerce*. Melbourne, 1934.

Australia. Rural Reconstruction Commission. *Rural Amenities: The Commission's Seventh Report to the Honorable J. J. Dedman, MP, Minister for Post-War Reconstruction*. [Canberra]: The Commission, 1945.

Australia. Rural Reconstruction Commission. *Rural Credit: The Commission's Fifth Report to the Honorable J. J. Dedman MP, Minister for Post-War Reconstruction*. [Canberra]: The Commission, 1945.

Baker, D. W. A. 'The Origins of Robertson's Land Acts'. *Historical Studies: Australia and New Zealand* 8, no. 30 (1958): 166–82. doi.org/10.1080/1031461580859 5111.

Baker, Norman. 'Whose Hegemony? The Origins of the Amateur Ethos in Nineteenth Century English Society'. *Sport in History* 24, no. 1 (2004): 1–16. doi.org/10.1080/17460260409414732.

Barcan, Alan. *A History of Australian Education*. Melbourne: Oxford University Press, 1980.

Bartley, Betty, comp. *The Mawbey Murder Papers*. [Dubbo: n.d.].

Bathurst Agricultural, Horticultural and Pastoral Association. *100 Bathurst Shows, 1968: A History of the Bathurst Show*. [Bathurst: 1968].

Bayley, William A. *History of the Farmers and Settlers' Association of NSW*. Sydney: Farmers and Settlers' Association, 1957.

Bean, C. E. W. *On the Wool Track*. Sydney: Angus & Robertson, 1969. First published 1910.

Beaumont, Joan. *Australia's Great Depression: How a Nation Shattered by the Great War Survived the Worst Economic Crisis It Has Ever Faced*. Crows Nest: Allen & Unwin, 2022.

Belich, James. *Replenishing the Earth: The Settler Revolution and the Rise of the Anglo-World, 1783–1939*. Oxford: Oxford University Press, 2009.

Bell, Colin and Howard Newby. *Community Studies: An Introduction to the Sociology of the Local Community*. London: George Allen & Unwin, 1971. doi.org/10.4324/9781003213765.

Berger, Peter L. and Thomas Luckmann. *The Social Construction of Reality: A Treatise in the Sociology of Knowledge.* Harmonsworth: Penguin, 1966. doi.org/10.1007/978-3-658-37354-2_11.

Biber, Katherine. 'Besieged at Home: Jimmy Governor's Rampage'. *Public Space: The Journal of Law and Social Justice* 2 (2008): 1–41. doi.org/10.5130/psjlsj.v2i0.785.

Blacklow, Nancy. '"Riverina Roused": Representative Support for the Riverina New State Movements of the 1920s and 1930s'. *Journal of the Royal Australian Historical Society* 80, pts 3 & 4 (1994): 176–94.

Blainey, Geoffrey. *Black Kettle and Full Moon: Daily Life in a Vanishing Australia.* Camberwell: Viking, 2003.

Blainey, Geoffrey. *Gold and Paper: A History of the National Bank of Australasia Limited.* Melbourne: Georgian House, 1958.

Blainey, Geoffrey. *The Tyranny of Distance: How Distance Shaped Australia's History.* South Melbourne: Sun Books, 1987. First published 1966.

Blair, Megan. 'Listening in to *The Lawsons*: Radio Crosses the Urban-Rural Divide'. In *Struggle Country: The Rural Ideal in the Twentieth Century*, edited by Graeme Davison and Marc Brodie, 07.1–07.19. Melbourne: Monash University ePress, 2005.

Blekemore, Hazel and Marylu Flowers-Schoen. *Ballimore Public School.* [Dubbo: 1984].

Bolton, Geoffrey. *Spoils and Spoilers: A History of Australians Shaping Their Environment.* 2nd ed. Sydney: Allen & Unwin, 1992.

Bongiorno, Frank. *The People's Party: Victorian Labor and the Radical Tradition, 1875–1914.* Carlton: Melbourne University Press, 1996.

Bonyhady, Tim and Tom Griffiths. 'Landscape and Language'. In *Words for Country: Landscape and Language in Australia*, edited by Tim Bonyhady and Tom Griffiths, 1–13. Sydney: University of New South Wales Press, 2002.

Bourdieu, Pierre. 'The Forms of Capital'. In *Education: Culture, Economy, and Society*, edited by A. H. Halsey, Hugh Lauder, Phillip Brown and Amy Stuart Wells, 46–58. Oxford: Oxford University Press, 1997.

Bourdieu, Pierre. *Outline of a Theory of Practice*, translated by Richard Nice. Cambridge: Cambridge University Press, 1977.

Braithwaite, Colleen, Rita Giddings, Pam Oates and Marie Tucker. *The History of the Wongarbon, Westella, Eulomogo and Pilewood Schools*. Dubbo: Development and Advisory Publications for the Wongarbon School Centenary Committee, [1987].

Brett, Judith. *Australian Liberals and the Moral Middle Class: From Alfred Deakin to John Howard*. Cambridge: Cambridge University Press, 2003. doi.org/10.1017/cbo9780511481642.

Briggs, Asa. 'The Language of "Class" in Early Nineteenth-Century England'. In *History and Class: Essential Readings in Theory and Interpretation*, edited by R. S. Neale, 2–29. Oxford: Basil Blackwell, 1983.

Broome, Richard. *Treasure in Earthen Vessels: Protestant Christianity in New South Wales Society, 1900–1914*. St Lucia: University of Queensland Press, 1980.

Brunner, Edmund deS. *Rural Australia and New Zealand: Some Observations of Current Trends*. San Francisco: American Council, Institute of Pacific Relations, 1938.

Butler, C. Arthur. *Flying Start: The History of the First Five Decades of Civil Aviation in Australia*. Sydney: Edwards and Shaw, 1971.

Butlin, N. G. *Investment in Australian Economic Development*. Canberra: Department of Economic History, Research School of Social Sciences, The Australian National University, 1972. First published by Cambridge University Press, 1964.

Butlin, N. G. and A. Barnard. 'Pastoral Finance and Capital Requirements, 1860–1960'. In *The Simple Fleece: Studies in the Australian Wool Industry*, edited by Alan Barnard, 383–400. Parkville: Melbourne University Press in association with The Australian National University, 1962.

Butlin, S. J. *Australia and New Zealand Bank: The Bank of Australasia and the Union Bank of Australia Limited, 1828–1951*. Croydon: Longmans, 1961.

Buxton, G. L. *The Riverina 1861–1891: An Australian Regional Study*. Carlton: Melbourne University Press, 1967.

Calhoun, C. J. 'Community: Toward a Variable Conceptualisation for Comparative Research'. *Social History* 5, no. 1 (1980): 105–29. doi.org/10.1080/03071028008567472.

Campbell, Craig and Helen Proctor. *A History of Australian Schooling*. Crows Nest: Allen & Unwin, 2014.

Carnell, Ian. 'Thorby, Harold Victor Campbell (1888–1973)'. *Australian Dictionary of Biography*, National Centre of Biography, The Australian National University. Published first in hardcopy 1990. adb.anu.edu.au/biography/thorby-harold-victor-campbell-8798/text15429.

Carter, Paul. *The Road to Botany Bay: An Exploration of Landscape and History*. London: Faber and Faber, 1987.

Casey, Maryrose. 'Colonisation, Notions of Authenticity and Aboriginal Australian Performance'. *Critical Race and Whiteness Studies* 8 (201): 1–18.

Cashman, Richard. 'Australia'. In *The Imperial Game: Cricket, Culture and Society*, edited by Brian Stoddart and Keith A. P. Sandiford, 34–54. Manchester: Manchester University Press, 1998. doi.org/10.7765/9781526123824.

Clark, Anna. *Private Lives Public History*. Carlton: Melbourne University Press, 2016.

Clarsen, Georgine. *Eat My Dust: Early Women Motorists*. Johns Hopkins University Press, Baltimore, 2008. doi.org/10.1353/book.60154.

Clayton, Iris and Alex Barlow. *Wiradjuri of the Rivers and Plains*. Port Melbourne: Heinemann Library, 1997.

Clifford, Eamonn, Anthony Green and David Clune, eds. *The Electoral Atlas of New South Wales, 1856–2006*. Bathurst: New South Wales Department of Lands, 2006.

Clune, David. '1941'. In *The People's Choice: Electoral Politics in 20th Century New South Wales, Vol. Two, 1930 to 1965*, edited by Michael Hogan and David Clune, 167–201. Sydney: Parliament of New South Wales and University of Sydney, 2001.

Cohen, A. P. *The Symbolic Construction of Community*. Oxford: Routledge, 2015. First published 1985.

Cohen, Anthony P. 'A Sense of Time, a Sense of Place: The Meaning of Close Social Association in Whalsay, Shetland'. In *Belonging: Identity and Social Organisation in British Rural Cultures*, edited by Anthony P. Cohen, 21–49. Manchester: Manchester University Press, 1982.

Cohen, Anthony P. 'Belonging: The Experience of Culture'. In *Belonging: Identity and Social Organisation in British Rural Cultures*, edited by Anthony P. Cohen, 1–17. Manchester: Manchester University Press, 1982.

Commission on Country Life. *Report of the Commission on Country Life*. New York: Sturgis and Walton, 1917. First published 1911.

Commonwealth Bureau of Census and Statistics. *Census of the Commonwealth of Australia Taken for the Night between the 3rd and 4th April, 1921.* Melbourne: Government Printer, [1921].

Commonwealth Bureau of Census and Statistics. *Census of the Commonwealth of Australia, 30th June 1933.* Canberra: Government Printer, [1933].

Commonwealth Bureau of Census and Statistics. *Census of the Commonwealth of Australia, 30th June 1947.* Canberra: Government Printer, [1948].

Commonwealth Bureau of Census and Statistics. *Official Year Book of New South Wales.* Sydney: Government Printer, 1906–1964.

Commonwealth Bureau of Census and Statistics. *The First Commonwealth Census, 3rd April 1911.* Melbourne: Government Printer, 1911.

Commonwealth Electoral Office. *Statistical Returns in Relation to the Senate Election, 1913; The General Election for the House of Representatives, 1913.* In *Parliamentary Papers—General.* Vol. II, 1913. Melbourne: Government Printer, 1913.

Commonwealth Electoral Office. *Statistical Returns in Relation to the Submission to the Electors of the Question Prescribed by Section 5 of the Military Service Referendum Act 1916.* In *Papers Presented to the Parliament 1914–15–16–17.* Vol. II. Melbourne: Government Printer, 1917.

Commonwealth Electoral Office. *Statistical Returns in Relation to the Submission to the Electors of the Question Prescribed by Regulation 6 of the War Precautions (Military Service Referendum) Regulations 1917.* In *Papers Presented to the Parliament 1917–18–19.* Vol. IV. Melbourne: Government Printer, 1918.

Commonwealth of Australia. *An Act to Amend the Commonwealth Conciliation and Arbitration Act 1904–1909.* No. 7 of 1910.

Commonwealth of Australia. *Commonwealth Electoral Roll, New South Wales.* 1903, 1921.

Commonwealth of Australia. *Conciliation and Arbitration Act.* No. 13 of 1904.

Commonwealth of Australia. *Historical Records of Australia: Series I, Governors' Despatches to and from England.* Vol. XX, Jan 1819 – Dec 1822; Vol. XII, June 1825 – Dec 1826; Vol. XIII, Jan 1827 – Feb 1828; Vol. XV, June 1829 – Dec 1830; Vol. XXI, Oct 1840 – Mar 1842; Vol. XXV, Apr 1846 – Sept 1847; Vol. XXVI, Oct 1847 – Dec 1848. Sydney: Library Committee of the Commonwealth Parliament, 1917–1925.

Commonwealth of Australia. House of Representatives. *Parliamentary Debates.* Canberra: Government Printer, 1904.

Commonwealth of Australia. House of Representatives. *Parliamentary Debates*. Canberra: Government Printer, 1910.

Commonwealth of Australia. *Report of the Royal Commission Appointed to Inquire into the Monetary and Banking Systems*. In *Parliamentary Papers*. Vol. 5. Canberra: Government Printer, 1937.

Commonwealth of Australia. *Royal Commission on the Wheat, Flour and Bread Industries, Supplement to the First Report of the Commissio*n. In *Papers Presented to Parliament*. Vol. 4. Canberra: Government Printer, 1934.

Conor, Liz. 'The "Lubra" Type in Australian Imaginings of the Aboriginal Woman from 1836–1973'. *Gender and History* 25, no. 2 (2013): 230–51. doi.org/10.1111/1468-0424.12016.

Cook, Pavla, Ian Davey and Malcolm Vick. 'Capitalism and Working Class Schooling in Late Nineteenth Century South Australia'. *ANZHES Journal* 8, no. 2 (1979): 36–48.

Cooks Business Directories. *Business Directory of New South Wales, 1931–32*. Sydney: Interstate Business Directory Publishers, n.d.

Cosgrove, Kevin. '1927'. In *The People's Choice: Electoral Politics in 20th Century New South Wales, Vol. One, 1901 to 1927*, edited by Michael Hogan and David Clune, 334–9. Sydney: Parliament of New South Wales and University of Sydney, 2001.

Country Women's Association of New South Wales. *The Silver Years: The Story of the Country Women's Association of New South Wales, 1922–1947*. Sydney: F. H. Johnston for the Association, [1947].

Coward, Dan. 'Crime and Punishment: The Great Strike in New South Wales, August to October 1917'. In *Strikes: Studies in Twentieth Century Australian Social History*, edited by John Iremonger, John Merritt and Graeme Osborne, 51–80. Cremorne: Angus & Robertson in association with The Australian Society for the Study of Labour History, 1973.

Crawford, R. M. 'Foreword'. In *Echuca: A Centenary History*, by Susan Priestley, v–vi. Brisbane: Jacaranda Press, 1965.

Crenshaw, Kimberle. 'Demarginalizing the Intersection of Race and Sex: A Black Feminist Critique of Antdiscrimination Doctrine, Feminist Theory and Antiracist Politics'. *University of Chicago Legal Forum* (1989): 139–68.

Cronon, William. *Nature's Metropolis: Chicago and the Great West*. New York: W. A. Norton and Company, 1991.

Cunneen, Christopher. *William John McKell: Boilermaker, Premier, Governor-General.* Sydney: UNSW Press, 2000.

Cunningham, P. *Two Years in New South Wales; A Series of Letters, Comprising Sketches of the Actual State of Society in That Colony; Of Its Peculiar Advantages to Emigrants; Of Its Topography, Natural History &c &c, in Two Volumes.* Vol. I. London: Henry Colburn, 1827.

Curthoys, Ann. 'Expulsion, Exodus and Exile in White Australian Historical Mythology'. *Journal of Australian Studies* 23, no. 61 (1999): 1–19. doi.org/10.1080/14443059909387469.

Dalgety & Company. *Murrumbidgerie Estate.* [Sales brochure]. Sydney: S. T. Leigh and Co. Printers, 1901.

Dargin, Pat. *'It's Only an Old House': Dundullimal Homestead, Dubbo, New South Wales.* Dubbo: Development and Advisory Publications, 2011.

Darian-Smith, Kate and Paula Hamilton. 'Introduction'. In *Memory and History in Twentieth-Century Australia*, edited by Kate Darian-Smith and Paula Hamilton, 1–2. Melbourne: Oxford University Press, 1994.

Davey, Paul. *The Nationals: The Progressive, Country and National Party in New South Wales, 1919 to 2006.* Annandale: The Federation Press, 2006.

Davidson, B. R. 'Agriculture and the Recovery from the Depression'. In *Recovery from the Depression: Australia and the World Economy in the 1930s*, edited by R. G. Gregory and N. G. Butlin, 273–88. Cambridge: Cambridge University Press, 1988. doi.org/10.1017/cbo9780511597206.013.

Davidson, Bruce. *European Farming in Australia: An Economic History of Australian Farming.* Amsterdam: Elsevier, 1981.

Davis, Michael. '"I Live Somewhere Else but I've Never Left Here": Indigenous Knowledge, History, and Place'. *Counterpoints—Indigenous Philosophies and Critical Education: A Reader* 379 (2011): 113–26. doi.org/10.3726/978-1-4539-0131-1/13.

Davison, Graeme. 'Fatal Attraction? The Lure of Technology and the Decline of Rural Australia 1890–2000'. *Tasmanian Historical Studies* 9, no. 1 (2003): 40–55.

Davison, Graeme. *Car Wars: How the Car Won Our Hearts and Conquered Our Cities.* Crows Nest: Allen & Unwin, 2004.

Davison, Graeme. *The Use and Abuse of Australian History.* Crows Nest: Allen & Unwin, 2000.

Davison, Graeme and Marc Brodie. 'Introduction'. In *Struggle Country: The Rural Ideal in Twentieth Century Australia*, edited by Graeme Davison and Marc Brodie, ix–xvi. Melbourne: Monash University ePress, 2005.

Dawes, J. N. I. and L. L. Robson. *Citizen to Soldier: Australia Before the Great War—Recollections of Members of the First AIF*. Carlton: Melbourne University Press, 1977.

Dawson, Barbara. *The Bibbenluke Estate and the Robertson Land Acts, 1861–1884: 'One of the Finest Properties in New South Wales (If Not the Best)'*. Weetangera: Barbara Dawson in conjunction with Bombala and District Historical Society, 2016.

Dewson, Emma. 'Off to the Dance: Romance in Rural New Zealand Communities, 1880s–1920s'. *History Australia* 2, no. 1 (2004): 05-1–05-9. doi.org/10.2104/ha040005.

de Sola Pool, Ithiel. 'Introduction'. In *The Social Impact of the Telephone*, edited by Ithiel de Sola Pool, 1–9. Cambridge (Massachusetts): MIT Press, 1977.

de Tocqueville, Alexis. *Democracy in America and Two Essays on America*, translated by Gerald E. Bevan. London: Penguin, 2003.

Dening, Greg. 'Anzac Day: An Ethnographic Reflection after Reading Bruce Kapferer'. *Social Analysis: The International Journal of Anthropology*, no. 20 (1990): 62–6.

Dening, Greg. *Performances*. Carlton South: Melbourne University Press, 1996.

Dordick, Herbert S. 'The Social Uses of the Telephone—an [sic] US Perspective'. In *Telefon und Gesellschaft: Beitrage zu einer Soziologie der Telefoncommunikation*, edited by Ulrich Lange, Klaus Beck, Axel Zerdick (Herausgeber), 221–38. Berlin, 1989.

Dormer, Marion. *Volume I, Dubbo to the Turn of the Century: An Illustrated History of Dubbo and Districts, 1818–1900*. Dubbo: Macquarie Publications, 1981.

Dormer, Marion. *Volume II, Dubbo: City of the Plains, 1901–1980*. Dubbo: Macquarie Publications, 1988.

Doyle, Helen Wendy. 'Australia Infelix: Making History in an Unsettled Country'. PhD thesis, Monash University, 2005.

Dulhunty, Beryl. *The Dulhunty Papers: Chronicle of a Family*. Sydney: The Wentworth Press, 1959.

Dunsdorfs, Edgars. *The Australian Wheat-Growing Industry, 1788–1948*. Carlton: Melbourne University Press, 1956.

Eggleton (Chapple), Joan B. '"The Mount": Chapple Family History 1921–1945'. In *A Compiled History of Coboco District*, edited by Pat Fisher, Robyn Healey and Sandra Burns, 85–9. Narromine: Coboco CWA, 2002.

Ellis, U. R. *New Australian States*. Sydney: Endeavour Press, 1933.

Ellis, Ulrich. *A History of the Australian Country Party*. Parkville: Melbourne University Press, 1963.

Ellis, Ulrich. *The Country Party: A Political and Social History of the Party in New South Wales*. Melbourne: F. W. Cheshire, 1958.

Ellis, Ulrich Ruegg. *A Pen in Politics*. Charnwood: Ginninderra Press, 2007.

Fahey, Charles. '"Abusing the Horses and Exploiting the Labourer": The Victorian Agricultural and Pastoral Labourer, 1871–1911'. *Labour History*, no. 65 (1993): 96–114.

Fahey, Charles. 'Two Model Farmers: Ann and Joseph Day of Murchison'. *Victorian Historical Journal* 71, no. 2 (2000): 102–23.

Farmers and Settlers Association of NSW. *Reports—Annual Conference Held at Dubbo, June 1904*. Dubbo: [1904]. Reprinted from the *Dubbo Liberal*.

Farrell, John Joseph. 'Monster Demonstrations and Processions: The New State Petition Campaign 1921–1923'. *Armidale and District Historical Society Journal and Proceedings*, no. 42 (1999): 41–9.

Farrell, John Joseph. 'Opting Out and Opting in: Secession and the New State Movements'. *Armidale and District Historical Society Journal and Proceedings*, no. 40 (1997): 139–48.

Ferry, John. *Colonial Armidale*. St Lucia: University of Queensland Press, 1999.

Finn, Margot C. *The Character of Credit: Personal Debt in English Culture, 1740–1914*. Cambridge: Cambridge University Press, 2003.

Fisher, 'Daisy' [Lilian]. 'From the Diary of Daisy Fisher'. In *A Compiled History of Coboco District*, edited by Pat Fisher, Robyn Healey and Sandra Burns, 95–7. Narromine: Coboco CWA, 2002.

Fisher, Jancie. '"Lara" (Fisher Family)'. In *A Compiled History of Coboco District*, edited by Pat Fisher, Robyn Healey and Sandra Burns, 61–3. Narromine: Coboco CWA, 2002.

Fisher, Pat and Robyn Healey and Sandra Burns, eds. *A Compiled History of Coboco District*. Narromine: Coboco CWA, 2002.

Fitzpatrick, Jim. *The Bicycle and the Bush: Man and Machine in Rural Australia.* Melbourne: Oxford University Press, 1980.

Fletcher, Brian H. *The Grand Parade: A History of the Royal Agricultural Society of New South Wales.* Paddington: Royal Agricultural Society of New South Wales, [1988].

Fletcher, J. J. *Clean, Clad and Courteous: A History of Aboriginal Education in New South Wales.* Carlton: J. Fletcher, 1989.

Foster, Meg. 'Murder for White Consumption? Jimmy Governor and the Bush Ballad'. In *Archiving Settler Colonialism: Culture, Space and Race*, edited by Yu-ting Huang and Rebecca Weaver-Hightower, 173–89. London: Routledge, 2018. doi.org/10.4324/9781351142045.

Foster, Meg. 'The Forgotten War of 1900: Jimmy Governor and the Aboriginal People of Wollar'. *Australian Historical Studies* 50, no. 3 (2019): 305–20. doi.org/10.1080/1031461x.2019.1623272.

Foster, Meg. *Boundary Crossers: The Hidden History of Australia's Other Bushrangers.* Sydney: NewSouth Publishing, 2022.

Foster, Robert, Rick Hosking and Amanda Nettelbeck. *Fatal Collisions: The South Australian Frontier and the Violence of Memory.* Kent Town: Wakefield Press, 2001.

Fry, Ken. 'Soldier Settlement and the Australian Agrarian Myth after the First World War'. *Labour History*, no. 48 (1985): 29–43.

Gammage, Bill. 'A Dynamic of Local History'. In *Peripheral Visions: Essays on Australian Regional and Local History*, edited by B. J. Dalton, 1–7. [Townsville]: Department of History and Politics, James Cook University, 1991.

Gammage, Bill. '*Historical Reconsiderations VIII*: Who Gained, and Who Was Meant to Gain, from Land Selection in New South Wales?' *Australian Historical Studies* 24, no. 94 (1990): 104–22. doi.org/10.1080/10314619008595834.

Gammage, Bill. *Narrandera Shire.* Narrandera: Bill Gammage for the Narrandera Shire Council, 1986.

Garton, Stephen. *The Cost of War: Australians Return.* Melbourne: Oxford University Press, 1996.

Geertz, Clifford. 'Thick Description: Toward an Interpretive Theory of Culture'. In *The Interpretation of Cultures: Selected Essays*, edited by Clifford Geertz, 3–30. New York: Basic Books, 1973.

Geeves, Philip. 'In Memoriam—James Jervis'. *Journal and Proceedings of the Royal Australian Historical Society* 49, part 1 (1963): 74–8.

Gollan, Robin. *Radical and Working Class Politics: A Study of Eastern Australia 1850–1910*. Carlton: Melbourne University Press in association with The Australian National University, 1960.

Goodall, Heather. 'Telling Country: Memory, Modernity and Narratives in Rural Australia'. *History Workshop Journal* 47, no. 1 (1999): 161–90. doi.org/10.1093/hwj/1999.47.160.

Goodall, Heather. *Invasion to Embassy: Land in Aboriginal Politics in New South Wales, 1770–1972*. Sydney: Sydney University Press, 2008. First published 1996. doi.org/10.2307/jj.130855.

Goot, Murray. 'The Results of the 1916 and 1917 Conscription Referendums Re-examined'. In *The Conscription Conflict and the Great War*, edited by Robin Archer, Joy Damousi, Murray Goot and Sean Scalmer, 111–46. Clayton: Monash University Publishing, 2016.

Gorrell, Julie. 'Sawyer, Jessie Frederica Pauline (1870–1947)'. *Australian Dictionary of Biography*, National Centre of Biography, The Australian National University. Published first in hardcopy 2002. adb.anu.edu.au/biography/sawyer-jessie-frederica-pauline-11619/text20749.

Graeber, David. *Debt: The First 5,000 Years*. Brooklyn: Melville House, 2014.

Graham, B. D. *The Formation of the Australian Country Parties*. Canberra: Australian National University Press, 1966.

Granovetter, Mark. 'Economic Action and Social Structure: The Problem of Embeddedness'. *American Journal of Sociology* 19, no. 3 (1985): 481–510. doi.org/10.1086/228311.

Gray, Nancy. 'Bettington, James Brindley (1796–1857)'. *Australian Dictionary of Biography*, National Centre of Biography, The Australian National University. Published first in hardcopy 1969. adb.anu.edu.au/biography/bettington-james-brindley-2989/text4367.

Griffiths, Tom. 'Introduction'. In *George Seddon: Selected Writings*, edited by Andrea Gaynor, 1–19. Carlton: La Trobe University Press in conjunction with Black Inc., 2019.

Griffiths, Tom. 'The Frontier Fallen'. *Eureka Street*, March 2003, 24–30.

Griffiths, Tom. *Beechworth: An Australian Country Town and its Past*. Richmond: Greenhouse Publications, 1987.

Griffiths, Tom. *Hunters and Collectors: The Antiquarian Imagination in Australia*. Cambridge: Cambridge University Press, 1996.

Grimshaw, Patricia, Charles Fahey, Susan Janson and Tom Griffiths. 'Families and Selection in Colonial Horsham'. In *Families in Colonial Australia*, edited by Patricia Grimshaw, Chris McConville and Ellen McEwen, 118–37. North Sydney: Allen & Unwin, 1985.

Gunn, Heather. '"For the Man on the Land": Issues of Gender and Identity in the Foundation of the Victorian Farmers' Union Women's Section, 1918–1922'. *Journal of Australian Studies* 18, no. 42 (1994): 32–42. doi.org/10.1080/14443059409387184.

Gunn, John. *Along Parallel Lines: A History of the Railways of New South Wales*. Carlton: Melbourne University Press, 1989.

Haebich, Anna. *Dancing in Shadows: Histories of Nyungar Performance*. Crawley: UWA Publishing, 2018.

Hagan, Jim and Ken Turner. *A History of the Labor Party in New South Wales, 1891–1991*. Melbourne: Longman Cheshire, 1991.

Hamilton, Paula and Paul Ashton. 'At Home with the Past: Initial Findings from the Survey'. *Australian Cultural History*, no. 23 (2003): 5–30.

Hancock, W. K. *Australia*. New York: Charles Scriber's Sons, [1930].

Hancock, W. K. *Discovering Monaro: A Study of Man's Impact on His Environment*. London: Cambridge University Press, 1972.

Harfull, Liz. *The Women Who Changed Country Australia: Celebrating 100 Years of the Country Women's Association of New South Wales*. Sydney: Murdoch Books, [2022].

Harman, Grant. 'New State Agitation in Northern New South Wales, 1920–29'. *Journal of the Royal Australian Historical Society* 63, part 1 (1977): 26–39.

Harrison, Lynette, comp. *Dear Da ...: Letters from the Great War 1914–18, Written by and Concerning Jack Ison, 1565 3rd Battalion AIF, a Dubbo Boy Killed in Action 10/11/17*, assisted by Graeme Hosken. Dubbo: 1991.

Haskell, Thomas L. and Richard F. Teichgraeber III. 'Introduction: The Culture of the Market'. In *The Culture of the Market: Historical Essays*, edited by Thomas L. Haskell and Richard F. Teichgraeber III, 1–39. Cambridge: Cambridge University Press, 1993.

Healy, Chris. *Forgetting Aborigines*. Sydney: UNSW Press, 2008.

Henry, David. 'Lord, George William (1818–1880)'. *Australian Dictionary of Biography*, National Centre of Biography, The Australian National University. Published first in hardcopy 1974. adb.anu.edu.au/biography/lord-george-william-4037/text6417.

Hepburn, Malcolm. *The History of the Geurie Public School and District, Including the District Schools of Ponto, Maryvale, Comobella, Combo, Windora and Criefton.* [Geurie]: Malcolm Hepburn, 1986.

Hickey, Betty. *A Village that Disappeared: Beni Via Dubbo.* Dubbo: Orana Education Centre, 1987.

Hilmes, Michelle. *Radio Voices: American Broadcasting, 1922–1952.* Minneapolis: University of Minnesota Press, 1997.

Hirst, J. B. 'The Pioneer Legend'. *Historical Studies* 18, no. 71 (1978): 316–37. doi.org/10.1080/10314617808595595.

Hirst, John. 'Distance—Was It a Tyranny?'. In *Sense and Nonsense in Australian History*, by John Hirst, 24–37. Melbourne: Black Inc Agenda, 2005. First published in *Historical Studies*, 16, no. 64 (1975): 435–47. doi.org/10.1080/10314617508595515.

Hirst, John. 'Transformation on the Land'. In *Sense and Nonsense in Australian History*, by John Hirst, 114–22. Melbourne: Black Inc. Agenda, 2005.

Hobsbawm, Eric. 'Introduction: Inventing Traditions'. In *The Invention of Tradition*, edited by Eric Hobsbawm and Terence Ranger, 1–14. Cambridge: Cambridge University Press, 1983. doi.org/10.1017/cbo9781107295636.001.

Hogan, Michael. '1904'. In *The People's Choice: Electoral Politics in 20th Century New South Wales, Vol. One, 1901 to 1927*, edited by Michael Hogan and David Clune, 29–55. Sydney: Parliament of New South Wales and University of Sydney, 2001.

Hogan, Michael. '1920'. In *The People's Choice: Electoral Politics in 20th Century New South Wales, Vol. One, 1901 to 1927*, edited by Michael Hogan and David Clune, 181–232. Sydney: Parliament of New South Wales and University of Sydney, 2001.

Holder, R. F. *Bank of New South Wales: A History.* 2 vols. Sydney: Angus & Robertson, 1970.

Holt, Alan J. *Wheat Farms of Victoria: A Sociological Survey.* [Carlton]: School of Agriculture, University of Melbourne, 1946.

Holt, H. T. E. 'Josephson, Joshua Frey (1815–1892)'. *Australian Dictionary of Biography*, National Centre of Biography, The Australian National University. Published first in hardcopy 1972. adb.anu.edu.au/biography/josephson-joshua-frey-3873/text6167.

Holt, Richard. *Sport and the British: A Modern History*. Oxford: Clarendon Press, 1989.

Horner, Jack. 'Aborigines and the Sesquicentenary: The Day of Mourning'. *Australia 1938: A Bicentennial History Bulletin*, no. 3 (1980): 44–51.

Horner, Jack. *Vote Ferguson for Aboriginal Freedom*. Sydney: Australian and New Zealand Book Company, 1974.

Hoskins, W. G. *English Landscapes*. London: British Broadcasting Corporation, 1973.

Hughes, Colin A. and B. D. Graham. *Voting for the Australian House of Representatives 1901–1964*. Canberra: Australian National University Press, 1964.

Hunter, Kathryn M. *Father's Right-Hand Man: Women on Australia's Family Farms in the Age of Federation, 1880s–1920s*. Melbourne: Australian Scholarly Publishing, 2004.

Inglis, Gordon. *Sport and Pastime in Australia*. London: Methuen and Co. Ltd, 1912.

Inglis, K. S. 'World War One Memorials in Australia'. *Guerres mondiales et conflits contemporains*, no. 167 (1992): 51–8. www.jstor.org/stable/25730856.

Inglis, Ken. 'Questions about Newspapers'. *Australian Cultural History*, no. 11 (1992): 120–7.

Inglis, Ken. *Sacred Places: War Memorials in the Australian Landscape*. Assisted by Jan Brazier. Carlton: Melbourne University Press, 2008. First published 1998.

Jeans, D. N. *An Historical Geography of New South Wales*. Sydney: Reed Education, 1972.

[Jenkins, Joseph]. *Diary of a Welsh Swagman, 1869–1894*. Abridged and annotated by William Evans. Melbourne: Sun Books, 1977. First published 1975.

Johnson, Lesley. *The Unseen Voice: A Cultural Study of Early Australian Radio*. London: Routledge, 1988. doi.org/10.4324/9781315457253.

Jones, Rebecca. *Slow Catastrophes: Living with Drought in Australia*. Clayton: Monash University Publishing, 2017.

Kabaila, Peter. *Survival Legacies: Stories from Aboriginal Settlements of Southeastern Australia*. Canberra: Canprint Publishing, 2011.

Kabaila, Peter Rimas. *Wiradjuri Places: The Macquarie River Basin and Some Places Revisited*. Jamison: Black Mountain Projects, 1998.

Karskens, Grace. *People of the River: Lost Worlds of Early Australia*. Crows Nest: Allen & Unwin, 2020.

Karskens, Grace. *The Rocks: Life in Early Sydney*. Carlton: Melbourne University Press, 1997.

Kelly, Catherine E. '"The Consummation of Rural Prosperity and Happiness": New England Agricultural Fairs and the Construction of Class and Gender, 1810–1860'. *American Quarterly* 49, no. 3 (1997): 574–602. doi.org/10.1353/aq.1997.0047.

King, C. J. *An Outline of Closer Settlement in New South Wales, Part I: The Sequence of the Land Laws 1788–1956*. [Sydney]: Division of Marketing and Agricultural Economics, Department of Agriculture, [1957].

Kirkpatrick, Rod. 'Scissors and Paste: Recreating the History of Newspapers in Ten Country Towns'. *BSANZ Bulletin* 22, no. 4 (1998): 232–46.

Kirkpatrick, Rod. *Country Conscience: A History of the New South Wales Provincial Press, 1841–1995*. Canberra: Infinite Harvest Publishing, 2000.

Knott, John William. 'The "Conquering Car": Technology, Symbolism and the Motorisation of Australia Before World War II'. *Australian Historical Studies* 31, no. 114 (2000): 1–26. doi.org/10.1080/10314610008596113.

Lake, Marilyn, 'Helpmeet, Slave, Housewife: Women in Rural Families 1870–1930'. In *Families in Colonial Australia*, edited by Patricia Grimshaw, Chris McConville and Ellen McEwen, 173–85. North Sydney: Allen & Unwin, 1985.

Lake, Marilyn. *The Limits of Hope: Soldier Settlement in Victoria, 1915–38*. Melbourne: Oxford University Press, 1987.

Lawrence, Jon. 'The Culture of Elections in Modern Britain'. *History: The Journal of the Historical Association* 96, no. 324 (2011): 459–76. doi.org/10.1111/j.1468-229x.2011.00529.x.

Lawson, Henry. 'The Roaring Days'. *Bulletin*, 21 December 1889, 26.

Lee, Robert. *The Greatest Public Work: The New South Wales Railways, 1848 to 1889*. Sydney: Hale and Iremonger, 1988.

Lloyd, Clem. 'Andrew Fisher'. In *Australian Prime Ministers*, edited by Michelle Grattan, 73–86. Chatswood: New Holland Publishers, 2008.

Loveday, P. and A. W. Martin. *Parliament Factions and Parties: The First Thirty Years of Responsible Government in New South Wales, 1856–1889*. Carlton: Melbourne University Press, 1966.

Loveday, P., A. W. Martin and Patrick Weller. 'New South Wales'. In *The Emergence of the Australian Party System*, edited by P. Loveday, A. W. Martin and R. S. Parker, 172–248. Sydney: Hale and Iremonger, 1977.

Lovejoy, G. W. *'In Journeyings Often': Being a Bush Brother's Record of Five Years Spent in the Australian Bush as a Member of the Brotherhood of the Good Shepherd, Dubbo*. Dubbo: Brotherhood of the Good Shepherd, 1941. First published 1940.

Luckins, Tanja. *The Gates of Memory: Australian People's Experiences and Memories of Loss and the Great War*. Freemantle: Curtin University Books, 2004.

Lydon, Jane and Lyndall Ryan, eds. *Remembering the Myall Creek Massacre*. Sydney: NewSouth Publishing, 2018.

'Lyth' [Lambert, K.]. *The Golden South: Memories of Australian Home Life 1843–1888*. London: Ward and Downey, 1890.

MacCallum, Margaret. 'The Lawsons Are Real People to the Listeners'. *ABC Weekly*, 25 November 1945, 6.

Macintyre, Stuart. 'The Making of the Australian Working Class: An Historiographical Survey'. *Historical Studies* 18, no. 71 (1978): 233–53. doi.org/10.1080/10314617808595589.

Macintyre, Stuart. *Australia's Boldest Experiment: War and Reconstruction in the 1940s*. Sydney: NewSouth Publishing, 2015.

Macintyre, Stuart. *Little Moscows: Communism and Working-Class Militancy in Inter-War Britain*. London: Croom Helm, 1980.

Mandle, W. F. *Going It Alone: Australia's National Identity in the Twentieth Century*. Ringwood: Allen Lane the Penguin Press, 1978.

Mant, Gilbert. *The Big Show*. North Sydney: Horwitz Publications, 1972.

Markey, Raymond. *The Making of the Labor Party in New South Wales, 1880–1900*. Kensington: New South Wales University Press, 1988.

Martin, A. W. 'Free Trade and Protectionist Parties in New South Wales'. *Historical Studies: Australia and New Zealand* 6, no. 23 (1954): 315–23. doi.org/10.1080/10314615408595001.

Martin, A. W. 'Pastoralists in the Legislative Assembly of New South Wales, 1870–1890'. In *The Simple Fleece: Studies in the Australian Wool Industry*, edited by Alan Barnard, 577–91. Parkville: Melbourne University Press in association with The Australian National University, 1962.

Massey, Doreen. 'Places and Their Pasts'. *History Workshop Journal*, no. 39 (1995): 182–92. doi.org/10.1093/hwj/39.1.182.

Massey, Doreen. *For Space*. London: Sage Publications, 2005.

Mawbey, Cecil. 'Roseneath'. In *A Compiled History of Coboco District*, edited by Pat Fisher, Robyn Healey and Sandra Burns, 65–7. Narromine: Coboco CWA, 2002.

Maxwell, Charles F. *Australian Men of Mark*. 2 Vols. Sydney: Charles F. Maxwell, [1889–90].

Maynard, John. 'Fred Maynard and the Australian Aboriginal Progressive Association (AAPA): One God, One Aim, One Destiny'. *Aboriginal History* 21 (1997): 1–13. doi.org/10.22459/ah.21.2011.01.

Maynard, John. *Fight for Liberty and Freedom: The Origins of Australian Aboriginal Activism*. Canberra: Aboriginal Studies Press, 2007.

Mayne, Alan. 'Outside Country'. In *Outside Country: Histories of Inland Australia*, edited by Alan Mayne and Stephen Atkinson, 1–88. Kent Town: Wakefield Press, 2011.

McCalman, Janet. 'The Originality of Ordinary Lives'. In *Creating Australia: Changing Australian History*, edited by Wayne Hudson and Geoffrey Bolton, 86–95. St Leonards: Allen & Unwin, 1997.

McDonald, D. I. 'Serisier, Jean Emile (1824–1880)'. *Australian Dictionary of Biography*, National Centre of Biography, The Australian National University. Published first in hardcopy 1976. adb.anu.edu.au/biography/serisier-jean-emile-4559/text7479.

McFetridge, Joan. 'Eastern Hill'. In *A Compiled History of Coboco District*, edited by Pat Fisher, Robyn Healey and Sandra Burns, 42. Narromine: Coboco CWA, 2002.

McHugh, Siobhan. 'Not in Front of the Altar: Mixed Marriages and Sectarian Tensions between Catholics and Protestants in Pre-Multicultural Australia'. *History Australia* 6, no. 2 (2009): 42.1–42.22. doi.org/10.2104/ha090042.

McIntyre, Frank and Esma. 'Yarrangrove'. In *A Compiled History of Coboco District*, edited by Pat Fisher, Robyn Healey and Sandra Burns, 94–5. Narromine: Coboco CWA, 2002.

McKay, Ian K. *Broadcasting in Australia*. Carlton: Melbourne University Press, 1957.

McKernan, Michael. *Australians at Home: World War I*. Scoresby: Five Mile Press, 2014.

McLean, D. N. 'Wallawallah'. In *A Compiled History of Coboco District*, edited by Pat Fisher, Robyn Healey and Sandra Burns, 89–90. Narromine: Coboco CWA, 2002.

McMullin, Ross. *The Light on the Hill: The Australian Labor Party 1891–1991*. South Melbourne: Oxford University Press, 1991.

McNair, W. A. *Radio Advertising in Australia*. Sydney: Angus & Robertson, 1937.

McQueen, Humphrey. 'Improving Nomads'. *Journal of Australian Colonial History* 10, no. 2 (2008): 223–50.

McQuilton, John. 'Doing the "Back Block Boys Some Good": The Exemption Court Hearings in North-Eastern Victoria, 1916'. *Australian Historical Studies* 31, no. 115 (2000): 237–50. doi.org/10.1080/10314610008596129.

McQuilton, John. *Rural Australia and the Great War: From Tarrawingee to Tangambalanga*. Carlton South: Melbourne University Press, 2001.

Meinig, D. W. 'Introduction'. In *The Interpretation of Ordinary Landscapes: Geographical Essays*, edited by D. W. Meinig, 1–7. Oxford: Oxford University Press, 1979.

Meinig, D. W. 'Reading the Landscape: An Appreciation of W. G. Hoskins and J. B. Jackson'. In *The Interpretation of Ordinary Landscapes: Geographical Essays*, edited by D. W. Meinig, 195–244. Oxford: Oxford University Press, 1979.

Meinig, D. W. *On the Margins of the Good Earth: The South Australian Wheat Frontier, 1869–1884*. Adelaide: Rigby Limited, 1972. First published 1962.

Meinig, Donald W. 'Spokane and the Inland Empire: Historical Geographic Systems and the Sense of Place'. In *Spokane and the Inland Empire: An Interior Pacific Northwest Anthology*, edited by David H. Stratton, 1–31. Pullman: Washington State University Press, 1991.

Meredith, John. *The Coo-ee March, Gilgandra-Sydney 1915*. Dubbo: Macquarie Publications, 1981.

Meredith, Louisa Anne ('Mrs Charles'). *Notes and Sketches of New South Wales, during a Residence in that Colony from 1839 to 1844*. London: John Murray, 1844. Facsimile edition, 1973. doi.org/10.1017/cbo9780511783784.

Merrett, David and Simon Ville. 'Tariffs, Subsidies, and Profits: A Reassessment of Structural Change in Australia, 1901–39'. *Australian Economic History Review* 51, no. 1 (2011): 46–70. doi.org/10.1111/j.1467-8446.2011.00324.x.

Merritt, John. *The Making of the AWU*. Melbourne: Oxford University Press, 1986.

Michels, Robert. *Political Parties: A Sociological Study of the Oligarchical Tendencies of Modern Democracy*. Glencoe Illinois: The Free Press, 1915.

Moline, Norman T. *Mobility and the Small Town, 1900–1930: Transportation Change in Oregon, Illinois*. Research paper no. 132. Chicago: University of Chicago Department of Geography, 1971.

Monnox, Christopher. 'Election Campaigns in Rural New South Wales and Victoria, 1910–22'. PhD thesis, Macquarie University, 2021.

Montmarquet, James A. *The Idea of Agrarianism: From Hunter-Gatherer to Agrarian Radical in Western Culture*. Moscow (Idaho): University of Idaho Press, 1989.

Moore, Laurie and Stephen Williams. *The True Story of Jimmy Governor*. Crows Nest: Allen & Unwin, 2001.

Morris, R. J. 'Clubs, Societies and Associations'. In *The Cambridge Social History of Britain 1750–1950, Volume 3: Social Agencies and Institutions*, edited by F. M. L. Thompson, 395–443. Cambridge: Cambridge University Press, 1990. doi.org/10.1017/chol9780521257909.009.

Morrissey, Doug. 'Trethowan, Sir Arthur King (1863–1937)'. *Australian Dictionary of Biography*, National Centre of Biography, The Australian National University. Published first in hardcopy 1990. adb.anu.edu.au/biography/trethowan-sir-arthur-king-8849/text15531.

Moyal, Ann. 'The Gendered Use of the Telephone: An Australian Case Study'. *Media, Culture and Society* 14 (1992): 51–72. doi.org/10.1177/016344392014001004.

Moyal, Ann. *Clear across Australia: A History of Telecommunication*. Melbourne: Thomas Nelson Australia, 1984.

Muir, Cameron. *The Broken Promise of Agricultural Progress: An Environmental History*. Oxford: Routledge, 2014. doi.org/10.4324/9781315849676.

Murdoch, J. R. M. 'Joseph Cook: A Political Biography'. PhD thesis, University of New South Wales, 1968.

Murphy, Kate. *Fears and Fantasies: Modernity, Gender, and the Rural-Urban Divide.* New York: Peter Lang, 2010. doi.org/10.3726/978-1-4539-0023-9.

Nairn, Bede. 'Dunn, William Fraser (1877–1951)'. *Australian Dictionary of Biography*, National Centre of Biography, The Australian National University. Published first in hardcopy 1981. adb.anu.edu.au/biography/dunn-william-fraser-6052/text10351.

Nairn, Bede. 'Robertson, Sir John (1816–1891)'. *Australian Dictionary of Biography*, National Centre of Biography, The Australian National University. Published first in hardcopy 1976. adb.anu.edu.au/biography/robertson-sir-john-4490/text7337.

Nairn, Bede. 'Thrower, Thomas Henry (1870–1917)'. *Australian Dictionary of Biography*, National Centre of Biography, The Australian National University. Published first in hardcopy 1990. adb.anu.edu.au/biography/thrower-thomas-henry-8807/text15447.

Nairn, Bede. *Civilising Capitalism: The Labor Movement in New South Wales, 1870–1900.* Canberra: Australian National University Press, 1973.

Nettelbeck, Amanda and Robert Foster. 'Commemorating Foundation: A Study in Regional Historical Memory'. *History Australia* 7, no. 3 (2010): 53.1–53.18. doi.org/10.2104/ha100053.

New South Wales. Aborigines Protection Board. *Aborigines (Report of the Board for the Protection of, for the Year 1898).* In *Votes and Proceedings of the Legislative Assembly*. Vol. V, 1899. Sydney: Government Printer, 1900.

New South Wales. Aborigines Welfare Board. *Aborigines Welfare Board (Report for the Year ended 30th June 1940).* In *Joint Volumes of Papers Presented to Both Houses, 1941–42.* Vol. I. Sydney: Government Printer, 1942.

New South Wales. *An Act for Regulating the Alienation of Crown Lands.* No. 26a of 1861.

New South Wales. *An Act for Regulating the Occupation of Crown Lands.* No. 27a of 1861.

New South Wales. *An Act to Make Better Provision for Public Education* (the *Public Schools Act*). No. 33a of 1866.

New South Wales. *An Act to Make More Adequate Provision for Public Education.* No. 23 of 1880.

New South Wales. *Census of 1881.* In *Votes and Proceedings of the Legislative Assembly*. Vol. VIII. Sydney: Government Printer, 1884.

New South Wales. *Crown Lands (Held under Pastoral Occupation), 1865–66*. In *Votes and Proceedings of the Legislative Assembly*. Vol. III, 1865–66. Sydney: Government Printer, 1866.

New South Wales. *Crown Lands under Lease or License beyond the Settled Districts, 1859*. In *Votes and Proceedings of the Legislative Assembly*. Vol. III, 1859–60. Sydney: Government Printer, 1860.

New South Wales. Department of Public Instruction. *Report of the Minister of Public Instruction for the Year 1880*. In *Votes and Proceedings of the Legislative Assembly*. Vol. II, 1880–81. Sydney: Government Printer, 1881.

New South Wales. Department of Public Instruction. *Report of the Minister of Public Instruction upon the Condition of Public Schools Established and Maintained under the Public Instruction Act of 1880, for 1882, New South Wales*. In *Votes and Proceedings of the Legislative Assembly*. Vol. VII, 1883–84. Sydney: Government Printer, 1884.

New South Wales. Department of Public Instruction. *Report of the Minister of Public Instruction upon the Condition of Public Schools Established and Maintained under the Public Instruction Act of 1880, for 1883, New South Wales*. In *Votes and Proceedings of the Legislative Assembly*. Vol. VII, 1883–84. Sydney: Government Printer, 1884.

New South Wales. Department of Public Instruction. *Report of the Minister of Public Instruction for the Year 1887*. In *Votes and Proceedings of the Legislative Assembly*. Vol. IV, 1887–88. Sydney: Government Printer, 1888.

New South Wales. Department of Public Instruction. *Report of the Minister for Public Instruction for the Year 1902*. In *Votes and Proceedings of the Legislative Assembly*. Vol. III, 1903. Sydney: Government Printer, 1903.

New South Wales. Department of Public Instruction. *Report of the Minister for Public Instruction for the Year 1909*. In *Joint Volumes of Papers Presented to the Legislative Council and Legislative Assembly*. Vol. I. Sydney: Government Printer, 1910.

New South Wales. Department of Railways and Tramways. *Annual Reports of the Railway Commissioners for 1890, 1911 and 1941*. In *Votes and Proceedings of the Legislative Assembly*. Vol. V, 1890; Vol. III, 1911–12. Sydney: Government Printer, 1941.

New South Wales. Division of Reconstruction and Development. *The Macquarie Region: A Preliminary Survey of Resources*. Sydney: Government Printer, 1950.

New South Wales. *Farmers' Relief Act*. No. 33 of 1932.

New South Wales. *Fortieth Report of the Department of Lands Being for the Year Ended 30 June 1919.* In *Joint Volumes of Papers Presented to the Legislative Council and Legislative Assembly.* Sydney: Government Printer, 1920.

New South Wales. *General Election for the Legislative Assembly, March 20 1920.* In *Joint Volumes of Papers Presented to the Legislative Council and Legislative Assembly, Second Session, 1920.* Vol. I. Sydney: Government Printer, 1921.

New South Wales. *General Election for the Legislative Assembly, 25 March 1922.* In *Joint Volumes of Papers Presented to the Legislative Council and Legislative Assembly, Second Session, 1922.* Vol. I. Sydney: Government Printer, 1922.

New South Wales. *General Election for the Legislative Assembly, 30 May 1925.* In *Joint Volumes of Papers Presented to the Legislative Council and Legislative Assembly, Second Session, 1925–26.* In Vol. I. Sydney: Government Printer, 1926.

New South Wales. *General Election for Legislative Assembly, 8 October 1927, Statistical Returns.* In *Joint Volumes of Papers Presented to the Legislative Council and Legislative Assembly, Second Session, 1928.* Vol. I. Sydney: Government Printer, 1928.

New South Wales. *General Election for Legislative Assembly, 25 October 1930.* In *Joint Volumes of Papers Presented to the Legislative Council and Legislative Assembly, Second Session, 1930–31–32.* Vol. I. Sydney: Government Printer, 1932.

New South Wales. *General Election for Legislative Assembly, 11 June 1932, Statistical Returns.* In *Joint Volumes of Papers Presented to the Legislative Council and Legislative Assembly, Second Session, 1932.* Vol. I. Sydney: Government Printer, 1933.

New South Wales. *General Election for Legislative Assembly, 11 May 1935, Statistical Returns.* In *Joint Volumes of Papers Presented to the Legislative Council and Legislative Assembly, Second Session, 1935–36.* Vol. I. Sydney: Government Printer, 1936.

New South Wales. *General Election for Legislative Assembly, 26 March 1938, Statistical Returns.* In *Joint Volumes of Papers Presented to the Legislative Council and Legislative Assembly, Second Session, 1938–39–40.* Vol. II. Sydney: Government Printer, 1940.

New South Wales. *General Election for Legislative Assembly, 10 May 1941.* In *Joint Volumes of Papers Presented to the Legislative Council and Legislative Assembly, Second Session, 1941–42.* Vol. I. Sydney: Government Printer, 1942.

New South Wales. *General Election for Legislative Assembly, 27 May 1944, Statistical Returns.* In *Joint Volumes of Papers Presented to the Legislative Council and Legislative Assembly, First Session, 1944–45.* Vol. I. Sydney: Government Printer, 1945.

New South Wales. *General Election for Legislative Assembly, Statistical Returns, 3 May, 1947.* In *Joint Volumes of Papers Presented to the Legislative Council and Legislative Assembly, Second Session, 1947–48.* Vol. I. Sydney: Government Printer, 1948.

New South Wales. *General Election for Legislative Assembly, 17 June 1950, Statistical Returns.* In *Joint Volumes of Papers Presented to the Legislative Council and Legislative Assembly, Second Session, 1950–51–52.* Vol. I. Sydney: Government Printer, 1952.

New South Wales. *General Election, 1894.* In *Votes and Proceedings of the Legislative Assembly.* Vol. I, 1894–95. Sydney: Government Printer, 1895.

New South Wales. *General Election, 1895.* In *Votes and Proceedings of the Legislative Assembly.* Vol. I, 1894–95. Sydney: Government Printer, 1895.

New South Wales. *General Election, 1904.* In *Joint Volumes of Papers, Presented to the Legislative Council and Legislative Assembly, Second Session of 1904.* Vol. I. Sydney: Government Printer, 1905.

New South Wales. *General Election, 1917.* In *Joint Volumes of Papers Presented to the Legislative Council and Legislative Assembly, Second Session of 1917–18.* Vol. III. Sydney: Government Printer, 1918.

New South Wales. Legislative Assembly. *Hansard.* Sydney: Government Printer, 1879.

New South Wales. Legislative Assembly. *Votes and Proceedings of the Legislative Assembly.* Vol. 4. Sydney: Government Printer, 1882.

New South Wales. Legislative Council. *Fourth Interim Report from the Select Committee on the Conditions and Prospects of the Agricultural Industry and Methods of Improving the Same, Dealing with Rural Credit and Finance; Together with the Appendices and Minutes of Evidence.* Sydney: Government Printer, 1920.

New South Wales. Legislative Council. *Parliamentary Debates.* Sydney: Government Printer, 1908.

New South Wales. New States Royal Commission. *Evidence of the Royal Commission Inquiry as to the Areas in New South Wales Suitable for Self-Government.* Vol. 5. Sydney: Government Printer, 1934.

New South Wales. New States Royal Commission. *Evidence of the Royal Commission of Inquiry into Proposals for the Establishment of a New State.* Vol. 4. Sydney: Government Printer, 1925.

New South Wales. *Parliamentary Debates.* First session 1899. Second session of the Eighteenth Parliament. Sydney: Government Printer, 1899.

New South Wales. *Parliamentary Debates*. Second series. Session 1915–16, Vol. LX and Vol. LXIII. Sydney: Government Printer, 1916.

New South Wales. *Public Instruction (Amendment) Act*. No. 51 of 1916.

New South Wales. *Report of Inquiry into the State of the Public Lands, and the Operation of the Land Laws*. In *Votes and Proceedings of the Legislative Assembly*. Vol. II, 1883. Sydney: Government Printer, 1883.

New South Wales. *Report of the Chief Inspector of Stock, 1884*. In *Votes and Proceedings of the Legislative Assembly*. Vol. III, 1885. Sydney, 1885.

New South Wales. *Report of the Department of Agriculture for the Year Ended 30 June 1919*. In *Joint Volume of Papers Presented to the Legislative Council and Legislative Assembly*. Vol. 1, Sydney: Government Printer, 1920.

New South Wales. *Report of the Department of Agriculture for the Year Ended 30 June 1920*. In *Joint Volume of Papers Presented to the Legislative Council and Legislative Assembly*. Vol. 1. Sydney: Government Printer, 1920.

New South Wales. *Results of a Census of New South Wales Taken for the Night of 5th April 1891*. Sydney: Government Printer, 1894.

New South Wales. *Results of a Census of New South Wales Taken for the Night of the 31st March 1901*. Sydney: Government Printer, 1904.

New South Wales. Royal Commission as to Decentralisation in Railway Transit. *Report of the Royal Commission as to Decentralisation in Railway Transit*. In *Joint Volume of Papers Presented to the Legislative Council and Legislative Assembly*. Vol. II. Sydney: Government Printer, 1911.

New South Wales. Royal Commission of Inquiry on Forestry. *Minutes of Proceedings, Minutes of Evidence, and Appendix, Part II*. In *Joint Volumes of Papers Presented to the Legislative Council and Legislative Assembly, 1908 (Second Session)*. Vol. I. Sydney: Government Printer, 1909.

New South Wales. Royal Commission of Inquiry on Rural, Pastoral, Agricultural and Dairying Interests. *Commissioner's Report on All Matters Other than Dairying Interests*. Sydney: Government Printer, 1917.

New South Wales. Royal Commission on Strikes. *Report of the Royal Commission on Strikes, Minutes of Evidence*. Sydney: Government Printer, 1891.

New South Wales. Standing Committee on Public Works. *Report Together with Minutes of Evidence, Appendix and Plan Relating to the Proposed Railway from Dubbo to Werris Creek*. In *Joint Volumes of Papers Presented to the Legislative Council and Legislative Assembly*. Vol. III. Sydney: Government Printer, 1913.

New South Wales. *Statistical Register for 1900 and Previous Years*. Sydney: Government Printer, 1902.

New South Wales. *Statistical Register for 1910 and Previous Years*. Sydney: Government Printer, 1912.

New South Wales. *Statistical Register for 1920–21*. Sydney: Government Printer, 1921.

New South Wales. *Statistical Register for 1930–31*. Sydney: Government Printer, 1932.

New South Wales. *Thirty-Seventh Report of the Department of Lands, 1916*. In *Joint Volumes of Papers Presented to the Legislative Council and Legislative Assembly*. Vol. I. Sydney: Government Printer, 1917.

New South Wales. *Twentieth Annual Report of the Department of Lands Being for the Year 1899*. In *Votes and Proceedings of the Legislative Assembly*. Vol. III, 1900. Sydney: Government Printer, 1901.

[New South Wales Government Railways]. *Working Timetable for Passenger and Goods Trains, Western Division, from 31st May, 1931*. [Sydney, 1931].

O'Farrell, Patrick. *The Catholic Church and Community: An Australian History*. Kensington: New South Wales University Press, 1985.

O'Shea, Helen. 'Country Halls'. In *The Oxford Companion to Australian Folklore*, edited by Gwenda Beed Davey and Graham Seal, 73–8. Melbourne: Oxford University Press, 1993.

O'Shea, Helen. 'The Golspie Hall'. *Meanjin* 47, no. 4 (1988): 701–8.

Oppenheimer, Jillian. 'Munro, Grace Emily (1879–1964)'. *Australian Dictionary of Biography*, National Centre of Biography, The Australian National University. Published first in hardcopy 1986. adb.anu.edu.au/biography/munro-grace-emily-7686/text13451.

Oppenheimer, Melanie, '"We All Did Voluntary Work of Some Kind": Voluntary Work and Labour History', *Labour History*, no. 81 (2001): 1–11.

Page, Sir Earle. *Truant Surgeon: The Inside Story of Forty Years of Australian Political Life*. Sydney: Angus & Robertson, 1963.

Patmore, Greg. 'Working Lives in Regional Australia: Labour History and Local History'. *Labour History*, no. 78 (2000): 1–6.

Peterson, Merrill D., ed. *Jefferson: Writings*. New York: Library of America, 1984.

Pike, [Justice]. *Report on the Losses Due to Soldier Settlement*. In *Papers Presented to Parliament*. Vol. II. Canberra: Government Printer, 1929.

Polanyi, Karl. *The Great Transformation: The Political and Economic Origins of Our Times*. Boston: Beacon Press, 2001. First published 1944.

Portes, Alejandro. 'Social Capital: Its Origins and Applications in Modern Sociology'. *Annual Review of Sociology* 24 (1998): 1–24. doi.org/10.1146/annurev.soc. 24.1.1.

Portes, Alejandro. *Economic Sociology: A Systematic Inquiry*. Princeton: Princeton University Press, 2010. doi.org/10.1515/9781400835171.

Read, Peter. *A Hundred Years War: The Wiradjuri People and the State*. Canberra: Australian National University Press, 1988.

Read, Peter. *Returning to Nothing: The Meaning of Lost Places*. Cambridge: Cambridge University Press, 1996. doi.org/10.1017/cbo9781139085069.

Readman, Paul. 'The Place of the Past in English Culture c. 1890–1914'. *Past and Present*, no. 186 (2005): 147–99. doi.org/10.1093/pastj/gti008.

Reynolds, Henry. *Nowhere People: How International Race Thinking Shaped Australia's Identity*. Camberwell: Viking, 2005.

Reynolds, Henry. *The Other Side of the Frontier: An Interpretation of the Aboriginal Response to the Invasion and Settlement of Australia*. Townsville: History Department of James Cook University, 1981.

Rickard, John. *Class and Politics: New South Wales, Victoria and the Early Commonwealth, 1890–1910*. Canberra: Australian National University Press, 1976.

Roberts, Stephen H. *History of Australian Land Settlement, 1788–1920*. Melbourne: Macmillan & Co., in association with Melbourne University Press, 1924.

Robinson, Geoffrey. '1930'. In *The People's Choice: Electoral Politics in 20th Century New South Wales, Vol. Two, 1930 to 1965*, edited by Michael Hogan and David Clune, 1–50. Sydney: Parliament of New South Wales and University of Sydney, 2001.

Robson, L. L. *The First AIF: A Study in Its Recruitment*. Carlton: Melbourne University Press, 1982.

Roe, Jill. 'Women and the Land'. *History Australia* 2, no. 1 (2005): 3-1–3-2. doi.org/ 10.2104/ha040003.

Rolls, Eric. *A Million Wild Acres: 20 Years of Man and an Australian Forest.* McMahons Point: Hale and Iremonger, 2011. First published by Thomas Nelson Australia, 1981.

Rosekelly, Muriel. '"Parkdale" (Wheeler Family)'. In *A Compiled History of Coboco District*, edited by Pat Fisher, Robyn Healey and Sandra Burns, 39. Narromine: Coboco CWA, 2002.

Rosenzweig, Roy. *Eight Hours for What We Will Do: Workers and Leisure in an Industrial City, 1870–1920.* Cambridge: Cambridge University Press, 1983.

Rozenzweig, Roy and David Thelen. 'The Presence of the Past: Popular Uses of History in American Life'. In *The Public History Reader*, edited by Hilda Kean and Paul Martin, 30–55. London and New York: Routledge, 2013.

Russell, Lynette. *Savage Imaginings: Historical and Contemporary Constructions of Australian Aboriginalities.* Melbourne: Australian Scholarly Publishing, 2001.

Rutherford, J. E. L. 'Rutherford, James (1827–1911)'. *Australian Dictionary of Biography*, National Centre of Biography, The Australian National University. Published first in hardcopy 1976. adb.anu.edu.au/biography/rutherford-james-886/text7415.

Rydon, Joan, R. N. Spann and Helen Nelson. *New South Wales Politics, 1901–1917: An Electoral and Political Chronicle.* [Sydney]: New South Wales Parliamentary Library and Department of Government, Sydney University, 1996.

Scates, Bruce and Melanie Oppenheimer. '"I Intend to Get Justice": The Moral Economy of Soldier Settlement'. *Labour History and the Great War, Labour History*, no. 106 (2014): 229–53. doi.org/10.5263/labourhistory.106.0229.

Scates, Bruce and Melanie Oppenheimer. *The Last Battle: Soldier Settlement in Australia, 1916–1939.* Cambridge: Cambridge University Press, 2016. doi.org/10.1017/cbo9781316408766.

Schedvin, C. B. *Australia and the Great Depression: A Study of Economic Development and Policy in the 1920s and 1930s.* Sydney: Sydney University Press, 1970.

Schivelbusch, Wolfgang. *The Railway Journey: The Industrialisation of Time and Space in the 19th Century.* Berkley: University of California Press, 1986.

Scott, J. K. 'Merinong'. In *A Compiled History of Coboco District*, edited by Pat Fisher, Robyn Healey and Sandra Burns, 68–80. Narromine: Coboco CWA, 2002.

Seddon, George. 'Prelude: Dual Allegiances'. In *Landprints: Reflections on Place and Landscape*, by George Seddon. Cambridge: Cambridge University Press, 1997.

Seixas, Peter. 'Introduction'. In *Theorizing Historical Consciousness*, edited by Peter Seixas, 3–20. Toronto: University of Toronto Press, 2004. doi.org/10.3138/9781442682610.

Sewell, William H (Jr). 'How Classes Are Made: Critical Reflections on E. P. Thompson's Theory of Working-Class Formation'. In *E. P. Thompson: Critical Perspectives*, edited Harvey J. Kaye and Keith McClelland, 50–77. Cambridge: Polity Press in association with Basil Blackwell, 1990.

Shearing, Gwenda. 'Mulwarree'. In *A Compiled History of Coboco District*, edited by Pat Fisher, Robyn Healey and Sandra Burns, 57–61. Narromine: Coboco CWA, 2002.

Simms, Marian. *From Hustings to Harbour Views: Electoral Institutions in New South Wales, 1856–2006*. Sydney: UNSW Press, 2006.

Sommerlad, E. C. 'What is Ahead of the Country Newspaper?' Address delivered to the 46th annual conference of the NSW Country Press Association, Sydney, 23 October 1945.

Sommerlad, Ernest C. *Mightier than the Sword: A Handbook on Journalism, Broadcasting, Propaganda, Public Relations and Advertising*. Sydney: Angus & Robertson, 1950.

Stedman Jones, Gareth. 'From Historical Sociology to Theoretical History'. In *History and Class: Essential Readings in Theory and Interpretation*, edited by R. S. Neale, 73–85. Oxford: Basil Blackwell, 1983.

Stedman Jones, Gareth. *Languages of Class: Studies in English Working Class History, 1832–1982*. Cambridge: Cambridge University Press, 1983. doi.org/10.1017/cbo9780511622151.

Stock, Jenny Tilby. 'Farmers and the Rural Vote in South Australia in World War I: The 1916 Conscription Referendum'. *Historical Studies* 21, no. 84 (1985): 391–411. doi.org/10.1080/10314618508595714.

Stoddart, Brian. *Saturday Afternoon Fever: Sport in the Australian Culture*. North Ryde: Angus & Robertson, 1986.

Stoddart, Brian. *Sport, Culture and History: Region, Nation and Globe*. Oxford: Routledge, 2008.

Sturt, Charles. *Two Expeditions into the Interior of Southern Australia, during the Years 1828, 1829, 1830, and 1831: With Observations on the Soil, Climate, and General Resources of the Colony of New South Wales*. Vol. I. London: Smith, Elder and Co., 1833. doi.org/10.5962/bhl.title.131080.

Taksa, Lucy. '"Defence Not Defiance": Social Protest and the NSW General Strike of 1917'. *Labour History*, no. 60 (1991): 16–33.

Taksa, Lucy. 'Like a Bicycle, Forever Teetering between Individualism and Collectivism: Considering Community in Relation to Labour History'. *Labour History*, no. 78 (2000): 7–32.

Taksa, Lucy. '"Pumping the Life-Blood into Politics and Place": Labour Culture and the Eveleigh Railway Workshops'. *Labour History*, no. 79 (2000): 11–34.

Talbragar Shire. *The Council of the Shire of Talbragar 1906–1966.* [Dubbo: 1966].

Teather, Elizabeth K. 'Remote Rural Women's Ideologies, Spaces and Networks: Country Women's Association of New South Wales, 1922–1992'. *Australian and New Zealand Journal of Sociology* 28, no. 3 (1992): 369–90. doi.org/10.1177/144078339202800304.

Teather, Elizabeth Kenworthy. 'The First Rural Women's Network in New South Wales: Seventy Years of the Country Women's Association'. *Australian Geographer* 23, no. 2 (1992): 164–76. doi.org/10.1080/00049189208703065.

Thomas, Alan. *Broadcast and Be Damned: The ABC's First Two Decades.* Carlton: Melbourne University Press, 1980.

Thompson, E. P. 'The Moral Economy of the English Crowd in the Eighteenth Century'. *Past and Present* 50, no. 1 (1971): 76–136. doi.org/10.1093/past/50.1.76.

Thompson, E. P. *The Making of the English Working Class.* Harmondsworth: Penguin Books, 1980. First published 1963.

Thompson, Roger C. *Religion in Australia: A History.* 2nd ed. South Melbourne: Oxford University Press, 2002. First published 1994.

Townsend, Helen. *Serving the Country: The History of the Country Women's Association of New South Wales.* Sydney: Doubleday, 1988.

Turner, Frederick Jackson. 'The Significance of the Frontier in American History'. In *Annual Report for the Year 1893*, American Historical Association, 199–227. Washington, 1894.

Turner, Ian. *Industrial Labour and Politics: The Labour Movement in Eastern Australia, 1900–1921.* Canberra: The Australian National University and Cambridge University Press, 1965.

Twigg, Karen. 'The Role of the "Local Dance" in Country Courtship of the Nineteen Thirties'. In *'But Nothing Interesting Ever Happened to Us ...': Memories of the Twenties and Thirties in Victoria*, by Department of History, University of Melbourne, 17–27. Victorian Branch of the Oral History Association of Australia, 1986.

Uhr, John. '1910: Fisher Leads Labor to Victory'. In *Elections Matter: Ten Federal Elections That Shaped Australia*, edited by Benjamin T. Jones, Frank Bongiorno and John Uhr, 26–44. Clayton: Monash University Publishing, 2018.

van Vree, Wilbert. *Meetings, Manners and Civilization: The Development of Modern Meeting Behaviour*, translated by Kathleen Bell. London: Leicester University Press, 1999.

Vanclay, Frank. 'Place Matters'. In *Making Sense of Place: Exploring Concepts and Expressions of Place through Different Senses and Lenses*, edited by Frank Vanclay, Matthew Higgins and Adam Blackshaw, 3–11. Canberra: National Museum of Australia, 2008.

Vernon, James. *Politics and the People: A Study in English Political Culture, c.1815–1867*. Cambridge: Cambridge University Press, 1993.

Ville, Simon. *The Rural Entrepreneurs: A History of the Stock and Station Agent Industry in Australia and New Zealand*. Cambridge: Cambridge University Press, 2000.

Wadham, Samuel. *Australian Farming 1788–1965*. Melbourne: F. W. Cheshire, 1967.

Wadham, Sir Samuel, R. Kent Wilson, Joyce Wood. *Land Utilisation in Australia*. 4th ed. Parkville: Melbourne University Press, 1964.

Walker, R. B. *The Newspaper in New South Wales, 1803–1920*. Sydney: Sydney University Press, 1976.

Ward, Russel. *The Australian Legend*. Melbourne: Oxford University Press, 1958.

Waterhouse, Richard. 'Locating the New Social History: Transnational Historiography and Australian Local History'. *Journal of the Royal Australian Historical Society* 95, part 1 (2009): 1–17.

Waterhouse, Richard. *The Vision Splendid: A Social and Cultural History of Rural Australia*. Fremantle: Curtin University Books, 2005.

Waterson, D. B. *Squatter, Selector and Storekeeper: A History of the Darling Downs, 1859–93*. Sydney: Sydney University Press, 1968.

Watson, Don. 'Once a Jolly Lifestyle'. In *Watsonia: A Writing Life*, by Don Watson, 107–12. Carlton: Black Inc., 2020. First published in *The Monthly*, May 2005.

Whitehead, Kay. 'The Spinster Teacher in Australia from the 1870s to the 1960s'. *History of Education Review* 36, no. 1 (2007): 1–17. doi.org/10.1108/0819869 1200700001.

Williams, M. 'More and Smaller Is Better: Australian Rural Settlement 1788–1914'. In *Australian Space, Australian Time: Geographical Perspectives*, edited by J. M. Powell and M. Williams, 61–103. Melbourne: Oxford University Press, 1975.

Williams, Michael. '"Vegetables Varied and Excellent, Chiefly from a Celestial Garden"'. *History: Magazine of the Royal Australian Historical Society*, no. 153 (2022): 9–11.

Wood, Marilyn. 'The "Breelong Blacks"'. In *Race Matters: Indigenous Australians and 'Our' Society*, edited by Gillian Cowlishaw and Barry Morris, 97–120. Canberra: Aboriginal Studies Press, 1997.

Worster, Donald. *Dust Bowl: The Southern Plains in the 1930s*. New York: Oxford University Press, 2004. First published 1979.

Zeitlin, Jonathan. 'From Labour History to the History of Industrial Relations'. *Economic History Review* 40, no. 2 (1987): 159–84. doi.org/10.2307/2596686.

Ziino, Bart. 'Enlistment and Non-Enlistment in Wartime Australia: Responses to the 1916 Call to Arms Appeal'. *Australian Historical Studies* 41, no. 2 (2010): 217–232. doi.org/10.1080/10314611003713603.

Unpublished

Australian War Memorial. AWM194, Item 719193, [Allotment of 1914–1918 War Trophies] Wongarbon, NSW.

Australian War Memorial. PROO716, Phyllis Lynch Letters [Wongarbon].

Baird, Dorothy. 'Macquarie Picnic Race Club'. Typescript. [Undated]. Dubbo and District Family History Society.

Braithwaite, Edgar Arthur. Untitled manuscript. [1990]. In possession of Colleen Braithwaite, Dubbo.

Carey, Hilary M. and David A. Roberts, eds. *The Wellington Valley Project. Letters and Journals Relating to the Church Missionary Society Mission to Wellington Valley, NSW, 1830–45*. A Critical Electronic Edition. 2002. downloads.newcastle.edu. au/library/cultural%20collections/the-wellington-valley-project/.

Dubbo and District Family History Society. Minute Books, Rule Books and Miscellaneous Correspondence of the Macquarie Picnic Race Club.

Evans, Pearl. Speech Delivered at the 80th Anniversary of Brocklehurst School. Manuscript. [1958]. Western Plains Cultural Centre, Dubbo.

Graham, Don (b. 1932). Interview by author. Wellington. 7 September 2017.

Holy Trinity Anglican Church, Dubbo. Minute Book of the Parochial Council of Holy Trinity Anglican Church, Dubbo, 1883–1911.

Jervis, James. 'History of Dubbo 1818 to 1949'. [1949]. Unpublished manuscript. Macquarie Regional Library, Dubbo.

Lavender, T. W. 'Young Bill's Happy Days'. [1969]. MS 8155. Unpublished manuscript. National Library of Australia.

Minute book of the Gollan branch of the FSA, 1907–15. In possession of Frank Rowe, Dubbo.

Minute books and financial statements of the Wongarbon branch of the CWA. In possession of the branch.

Narromine Library, Macquarie Regional Library. Burraway Letters, 1881–96.

Narromine Library, Macquarie Regional Library. Edward Cahill Diaries, 1913–41.

Narromine Library, Macquarie Regional Library. Edwin Phillip King Diaries, 1893–1959.

National Archives of Australia. B2455, First Australian Imperial Force Personnel Dossiers, 1914–1920.

National Archives of Australia. MP1170/1, Broadcasting Stations Files Ranging from (1925–69) Relating to Technical, Programming and Licence Aspects.

National Archives of Australia. SP32/1, Post Office Files.

National Film and Sound Archive of Australia. 'The Grand Parade, Episode 26, Dubbo'. No. 415949. Macquarie Broadcasting Services for the Rural Bank [1935].

National Library of Australia. MS 1006, Ulrich Ellis Papers.

National Library of Australia. MS 4744, CLA and Hilda Abbott Papers.

National Library of Australia. MS 6789, Gwen Meredith Papers.

New South Wales Nationals. Minute Books of the Central Council of the Progressive/ Country Party (NSW) 1919–2005.

Noel Butlin Archives Centre (ANU). E256, Graziers Association of New South Wales Deposit 1.

Noel Butlin Archives Centre (ANU). N385, McKillop and Sons Deposit.

Nott, Nancy. 'The Cobbora Hall 1915–1996'. Manuscript. [2011]. In possession of Penny Stevens and Rob Ingram, Cobbora.

Oxley Museum (Wellington, NSW). 'Teachers at Windora School', 1887–1954'. Manuscript.

Page Research Centre Library, Charles Sturt University Regional Archives (Wagga Wagga, NSW). PG2904, Minute Book of the United Western Movement and the United Country Party, Western Division (1931–38).

Registers of Admission to Wongarbon Public School, 1915–50. [Copy]. In possession of Colleen Braithwaite, Dubbo.

State Archives and Records NSW. NRS 3829, Department of Public Instruction/ Education, Correspondence Branch, School Administrative Files.

State Archives and Records NSW. NRS 4014, Returns and Enrolments for Subsidised Schools, 1924–46.

State Archives and Records NSW. NRS 8052, Soldier (Closer) Settlement Promotion Files, 1913–58.

State Archives and Records NSW. NRS 8054, Closer Settlement and Returned Soldiers Settlement Transfer Files, 1907–51.

State Archives and Records NSW. NRS 8058, Department of Lands, Returned Soldiers Branch, Returned Soldiers Settlement Loan Files.

State Archives and Records NSW. NRS 13188, Farmers' Relief Board, Supervisors' Files.

State Archives and Records NSW. NRS 13654, Supreme Court of New South Wales, Insolvency Files (to 1887).

State Archives and Records NSW. NRS 13655, Supreme Court of New South Wales, Bankruptcy Division, Bankruptcy Files (1888–1929).

State Archives and Records NSW. NRS 13736, Surveyor General, Letters Received from Surveyors, 1822–55.

State Archives and Records NSW. NRS 15318, Chief Secretary's Department, Theatres and Public Halls Branch, Files Relating to Licences for Theatres and Public Halls.

State Archives and Records NSW. NRS 19669, Farmers Relief Act Files.

State Library of New South Wales. B 1055–B 1057, Edward Josiah Garnsey Papers, 1942–47.

State Library of New South Wales. B 899–B 917, Papers of W. B. Simpson, Surveyor, 3 May 1861 to 1879.

State Library of New South Wales. ML MSS 6899, Cameron, Tom, Papers Concerning the Development of a Chain of Department Stores in Country NSW, 1889–1970.

State Library of New South Wales. MLMSS 301, W. B. Simpson Letterbooks, 1861–1879 and Cash Book, Day Book, Account Book.

Taylor, Simone. 'Kerosene and Calico: The History of Dubbo's Tin Town'. Paper presented at the Western Plains Cultural Centre, Dubbo, 16 August 2018.

Western Plains Cultural Centre, Dubbo. Minute Books of the Geurie Branch of the CWA, 1932–47.

Western Plains Cultural Centre, Dubbo. Minute Books of the Terramungamine Branch of the CWA, 1926–45.

Western Plains Cultural Centre, Dubbo. Minute Books of the Westella Hall Committee, 1934–79.

Western Plains Cultural Centre, Dubbo. Minute Books of the Westella Tennis Club, 1932–42.

Western Plains Cultural Centre, Dubbo. Minute Books of the Windora-Comobella Branch of the CWA, 1942–50.

Westpac Group Archive, Sydney. Branch Managers' Diaries. Series S01–0051, Dubbo Branch (Bank of New South Wales).

Woodley, Harold (b. 1931). Interview by author. Dubbo. 18, 19 June 2017, 28 December 2018, 16 April 2020, 16 November 2020.

Woodley, Jessie (b. 1907) Interview by author. Dubbo. 24 June 1981.

Woodley, Peter. 'Financial Institutions and Land Ownership in the Dubbo District: A Sample Survey, 1884–1931'. Unpublished paper, 2021.

Woodley, Robert (b. 1937). Interview by author. Isaacs (ACT). 20 December 2017.

Wye, Nancy. 'Family History of Frederick Stroud and Elizabeth Lawry Stroud'. Unpublished typescript. Dubbo: [2008].

Index

Note: Page numbers in italics indicate illustrations. Page numbers with 'n' indicate footnotes.

www.ingramcontent.com/pod-product-compliance
Lightning Source LLC
Chambersburg PA
CBHW071102280326
41928CB00051B/2613